MEN AND WORK
The autobiography of Lord Citrine

LORD CITRINE

★

Men and Work

an autobiography

HUTCHINSON OF LONDON

HUTCHINSON & CO. (*Publishers*) LTD
178–202 Great Portland Street, London, W.1

London Melbourne Sydney
Auckland Bombay Toronto
Johannesburg New York

★

First published 1964

*This book has been set in Times New Roman,
printed in Great Britain on Antique Wove paper
by The Anchor Press, Ltd., and bound by Wm.
Brendon & Son Ltd., both of Tiptree, Essex*

Contents

Illustrations

Introduction

THIS is not a history of the trade union movement. It is something of an autobiography; but, more than that, it is a collection of experiences in my trade union life up to the outbreak of the 1939–45 war. I have tried to keep the story in reasonable sequence, but it has been impossible to keep to a rigid chronological order.

I have drawn lavishly on my notes of events, have 'set down naught in malice', and have tried to make this book as objective and true as I can. Much of it is given here just as it was written at the time the events occurred, and I suppose it is bound to be self-revealing. It shows the state of my mind, my thoughts and aspirations as they developed. I have kept hind-sight to a minimum. What is the use of a man of seventy-seven writing as though his thoughts and actions had never varied or matured over fifty years or more? My character, like everybody else's, has developed in obedience to the laws of Nature. You must grow or you stagnate and decay. I hope I have grown.

For many years it has been my habit to keep copious shorthand notes of occurrences, interviews, conversations, meetings and what not, and to write these down the same evening, or very shortly after the event, from rough notes made at the time. Sometimes, as for example in the national strike, they were written while events were unfolding themselves. I have sometimes been credited with a remarkable memory: actually it has been little better than that of most people, but I made a real effort to remember everything when writing my notes. I have endeavoured throughout to produce the actual language used in conversation without any attempt to dramatize or embellish. I do not claim that in every case where I have used quotations I have always given the exact words of the speaker, but nowhere have I consciously altered them. Certainly I have written nothing here which distorts the sense. Long experience has taught me that by describing an interview or a conversation or an occurrence step by step as it actually took place I can recall language with greater accuracy than if I tried to compress or summarize my notes. I have always taken pleasure, since I learned shorthand fifty years ago, in writing down notes of events which interested me. Why did I take this trouble? Simply because I liked it. Besides, the notes were sometimes of great use to me in my work.

I had no intention of writing my life story, or I would have tackled it many years ago. It is only in response to the urging of many friends that I have at last ventured to do so. In this connection I should like to express my warmest thanks to Mrs. F. E. Timonen (née Macdonald) who helped me so much with the preparation of the book and to Hugh Chevins for his expert assistance in editing the manuscript. My principal difficulty has been to condense the mass of material into readable brevity. Like most authors, I have hated to cut: it has felt like mutilating the subject. I have had to leave out much that I think interesting, including chapters about my activities at the Ottawa Conference in 1932 and the Spanish Civil War in the later thirties; that has been inescapable. You will find here no attempt at a display of erudition. Mine is just a plain story of experience and people: I hope you will like it.

I have said little about my married life, mainly because I think there is something beautiful about the marital relationship which is best preserved by privacy. It is sufficient to say that I drew a prize in the lottery and have kept her as my sweetheart ever since. My two sons are also happily married and settled in their professions of solicitor and doctor respectively.

The Citrines

CHARLES DICKENS heads the first chapter of *David Copper-field* with the portentous announcement 'I am born'. Perhaps I shouldn't refer to my birth at all; perhaps it was a matter of no importance. Still, the same thing happened to me as to David, at a house in Eastbourne Street, Liverpool, some seventy-six years ago. My father was a seafarer and my mother a hospital nurse. At the time my father was at sea, and news had reached Mother that his vessel was wrecked and my father was presumed to be drowned: a sad time for Mother and not the most propitious start for me.

I knew nothing concerning the circumstances of my birth until one Saturday evening during my adolescence. I had gone to Birkenhead Market, the exterior of which in those days bore a resemblance to a fun-fair, with many stalls not directly concerned with the sale of goods. Amongst these was one occupied by a phrenologist. Out of curiosity I went inside. He was a man of about forty and seemed rather a cut above the types one met in such surroundings. He subjected my head to a careful examination before saying anything. Then a stream of words poured out concerning my character and qualities, but little predicting my future. I remember being told that I possessed a double temperament which enabled me to work either in or out of doors with equal facility. He surprised me by saying that at the time of my birth my mother was suffering from some great trouble, and that at times I was inclined to have bouts of depression. I must cultivate self-confidence, he said.

I disputed some of what I was told, and he earnestly besought me to speak to my mother about what he had said as he felt absolutely sure he was right. On the way home I recognized the truth of many of his observations, particularly that about my fits of depression. I lacked self-confidence and on almost every electrical job to which I was sent I had inner misgivings about my ability to do it efficiently and expeditiously. It was not that I was lacking in technical or even practical knowledge; it was just that I felt unsure of my capabilities.

On arriving home I told Mother of what had occurred and she fully confirmed what the phrenologist had said. Mother told me that when ship-wrecked Father eventually reached home from sea she couldn't recognize him, he was so thin and bedraggled. At first she thought he was a beggar. So I felt that the threepence I had paid the phrenologist was worth while; and because of this incident I developed an interest in palmistry and related subjects which has remained with me throughout my life.

It is not surprising that I was a delicate child and that Mother was assured by her kind neighbours and friends that she would never rear me. It certainly looked very much like it, as I had scarcely started to walk when I sustained a double rupture which remained with me until I was an adult. My mother, like the prudent Scot she was, insured my life with the Liverpool Victoria Legal Friendly Society. The premium was a penny a week and the benefit £2 10s 0d.

I was one of six children, four boys (one of whom was a step-brother) and two girls. Because I was a weakling there is no doubt that I was spoiled and became headstrong and self-willed. I always wanted to boss others and was fond of getting my own way, a habit I haven't entirely lost. My sister has recently confided in me that I was a little devil. Yet I was sensitive and easily hurt. I had to correct this in later life, particularly when I was a trade union official. The corners get knocked off one in that hard school.

Unfortunately on my father's side the origin of the family is obscure. I know that my great-grandfather was married in London, but whether he was born in England or not I have never been able to ascertain. My grandfather was born in London in 1816 and my father in Liverpool in 1852.

Many people have asked me about the origin of our name. My grandfather, although born in England, bore the name of Francisco Cirtini and my father was registered in that name. It is fairly apparent that the name originated in Italy. Some years afterwards the name must have been changed, since my father was married as Alfred Citrine. We cheerfully surrendered our right to those mysterious estates in Italy about which my grandfather occasionally dropped vague hints.

Mother, a kind soul if ever there was one, was born of Scottish parents at St. Vigeans, Arbroath, and was registered in 1847 as Isabella McLennan. Physically she was a little woman, as small as my father was big. She became a hospital nurse and was trained in the Royal Infirmary, Liverpool, and was frequently sent out to do private nursing: she was selected to nurse the young Duke of Westminster, at Eaton Hall, near Chester. She married my father, who was then a widower, in 1881, and had five children. She had to rear her family most of the time under conditions of poverty owing to my father's intermittent work. But we never went hungry and we were respectably housed and clothed. I never knew her to touch alcohol, and, though not a regular churchgoer, she was a staunch Presbyterian and a true Christian. She died at the age of sixty-five, when I was twenty-six, after a married life full of worry and anxiety except for a brief ten years before her passing. She carried with her to her grave our undying love and gratitude.

Life would have been still harder for her had it not been for her younger sister, Catherine McLennan, who lived with us from the time of my birth. She never married, and she made me her special care. Her self-denial and the love and devotion she bestowed on me are as fresh now in my memory at seventy-six as in the days of childhood. I loved her intensely in return and was wildly jealous of any male who proffered his attentions. One of my greatest regrets is that these two devoted women passed away before I was in a position to provide them with the security and comforts they had lacked for most of their lives. My only slight satisfaction is that I always gave my mother the whole of my earnings, without the deduction of a penny. She saw that I didn't go short, but anything in the nature of bargaining would have been hateful to us both.

I have said that my father was a seafarer: so were his father and all his brothers. The sea was in their blood and, despite the almost incredible hardships which most of them endured, they all lived to what father called the 'Citrine dying age', in the region of eighty-five or so. Father had a most eventful life. He went to sea in a sailing vessel at the age of eleven. My grandfather was in business in Liverpool as a master rigger, fitting ships out with their running gear. My father often accompanied him on such jobs, not to work but out of that insatiable curiosity and love of adventure which are characteristic of boys.

It was then a common practice for the captains of sailing ships to be accompanied by their wives on their voyages. As luck happened, Mrs. Speir, the wife of the captain of the *John O. Baker*, came across my father and took a liking to him. She had no children of her own, whereas my father belonged to a family of eight children. The outcome was that Captain Speir offered to adopt my father and take him to sea. My grandfather wouldn't agree to a formal adoption, but liked and trusted the captain and his wife, and soon it was all settled. Father once told me:

'I joined the American sailing ship *John O. Baker*, bound for Philadelphia. The captain had promised my father he would look after me and he and his wife helped me all they could. I couldn't read or write and the captain's wife taught me. I used to go every afternoon to her cabin to get my education.

'We had a bucko mate and he thought I was being spoiled. He used to whale hell out of me whenever I came near him. Every time he saw me on deck he would make a swipe at me with a rope's-end. I dodged him whenever I could, and once when we were at sea and pretty well becalmed I saw him making for me so I climbed on the rail and when he got close to me I jumped overboard. I could swim like a fish and I sometimes dived right under the ship. I had no fear of sharks, so I stayed in the water about a couple of hours. At last he put out a boat to bring me in.

'The commotion caused by getting the boat out brought the captain and his wife on deck. When I told him why I had jumped overboard Captain Speir decided to put a stop to this brutality. Things were much better for a time, but the mate's dislike of me was still there. He took it out of me in other ways—chasing me up aloft and keeping me from my regular sleep. One day it was blowing a gale, and seeing me standing about doing nothing, the mate came to me and asked, "Alfred, what sort of a knife have you got?" I took it out of its sheath and showed it to him. He told me to go and sharpen it. I went to the grindstone and put a good edge on it and returned. Then the mate said, "Alfred, you see that pole up there"—pointing to the main topgallant mast—"get up there and scrape it down." It would have been a pretty stiff climb in calm weather, but I had to go up in the teeth of a roaring gale and set to work.

'After I had been up about half an hour I glanced down at the deck and I could see that the captain and the mate were having words. They started calling me down, but I knew the mate would send me up again at the first opportunity, so I pretended not to hear and I went on and finished the job. When I scrambled down the captain's wife was calling the mate a "murderer" and the captain gave him a real dressing-down. He sent the mate to his cabin, and followed him there and went for him again.

'The mate stood this for a while. Then he took a piece of chalk out of his pocket and drew a line across the cabin entrance. He pulled out a revolver and shouted, "Captain Speir, if you step across that line you are a dead man." He had scarcely got the words out of his mouth when the captain had him by the throat and threw him on the deck. He gave him the licking of a dog, but the mate never forgave me.'

Father went on to tell how when the vessel got to Philadelphia he deserted her, but was brought back. He served in her for five years and was promoted to third mate. He remained for some years with the same captain, who transferred to the *George Schofield*, a well-found vessel.

Such was the account of my father's going to sea which I took down from him in shorthand a few years before his death. He served in American ships of various kinds, all of them sailing vessels, until he was twenty-six or so, but unfortunately that part of his life is obscure. From what he told me he was as much a 'bucko mate' as anyone else.

In those days such men were appointed not so much for their nautical skill as for their strength and ability to keep the crew in order during the long voyage they had to make. The crews were usually fed badly on 'salt horse' and hard biscuits infested with weevils. From the time of signing on, the officers were engaged in fighting the crew. The mate who couldn't keep discipline, using an iron belaying-pin and bullying the sailors into working, didn't last long. Father used to say that there was a regular system of 'hazing' in some ships. The mates drove the men almost to open mutiny and treated them so unmercifully that when they reached port, either foreign or home, many of them would desert without waiting for their pay.

Father was a big, powerful man of six feet or thereabouts and strong as a horse, always ready to fight—a word and a blow was his rule—with a clear intelligence and a masterful personality. He was a heavy drinker, but he had long spells of sobriety, and during those periods our home life was supremely happy. He wasn't cruel or really inconsiderate to us children—I never recall his thrashing me, although he often threatened to. He usually drank beer, but when he took spirits he went frantic: poor Mother had much to put up with on those occasions and we children were terrified. When we came home after play in the evening our first question when Mother opened the door would be 'Is Father drunk?' If he was sober we went in. If not we stayed out until he had gone to sleep. He was careless with money, and when flush, instead of turning his much-needed cash over to Mother, he would sometimes dissipate it on his drinking friends. His habits changed as he got older and he became steadier. The contrast I found in my father when he was in drink and when he was sober, and the worry and sorrow he caused my mother, had a profound effect on me. I resolved never to let drink get a hold over me. I have kept that resolution.

Whilst attending the Oakdale Mission, where I went to Sunday school and bible class, I signed the pledge not to take alcohol. Soon afterwards I joined the Anti-Cigarette League. It was a point of honour with members of the League never to smoke until they had reached the age of twenty-one. By that time the non-smoking habit had become so firmly rooted that I never at any time afterwards have had the desire to smoke. I never touched strong drink until I was thirty-eight. Temperance people may ask why I ever did start. The only reason was that, like so many others who succumb, I didn't want to appear unsociable.

I am certainly not unsociable, although I don't like cocktail parties with their incessant standing about aimlessly and with people rushing away from you in the middle of a sentence. Like Falstaff, I stick to sherry, but, unlike him, I confine myself to one glass as a rule. I am not here engaged in a tirade against those who do drink, most of whom (in my experience) are temperate, good-natured fellows. I know full well, as Jack London said, that men relax more over alcohol than anything else. Then one sometimes sees more of the real character of a man than at any other time. But I saw so much unnecessary sorrow in my childhood both in and out of our own home that I have never let drink get the better of me. I have never gone into a public house on my own to have a drink, nor have I made a practice of going amongst company where rounds of drinks were the order of the evening. Economy? No!—simply because I don't like it.

During his days as a master rigger my father would often take ships round to their last port of call before leaving England, accompanied by a few of his own men to test the standing and running rigging and ensure that everything was in working order. Sometimes he would take me with him.

I remember one stormy night going on deck while the crew were taking in sail with much shouting, My father noticed me and told me to 'Sit there', pointing to a coil of rope. After a time I got tired and went below. Subsequently there was a great commotion on board, with seamen searching everywhere for me. Finally it was concluded that somehow I had slipped overboard, and Father went down to inform the captain, only to find that I was safely tucked up in bed with the captain's wife. I should add that I was then about seven years old.

Big, burly, and courageous though my father was, he would bring all his troubles home. If he had quarrelled with someone at work he would tell us all about it. He would describe to us how in taking a mast out of a sailing ship in one of the Liverpool docks an accident had occurred and two men had been killed. He would inform us that next day he had to do a similar job. There we were, Mother and children, all gathered round the table drinking in every word he uttered and dreading what might happen on the morrow. We would go to bed with the fear that next day Father was going to be killed. This made me resolve that I would never worry my mother or wife with any of the difficulties and dangers that arose in my own work. Father's fears were not groundless by any means. He had met with several serious accidents which had left their mark on him. He had his left hand badly crushed when releasing a rope from the tug docking a vessel at Birkenhead, and he lost two fingers and much of the use of his left hand as a result. His right knee had been badly knocked about in another accident. He had wonderful stamina and survived hardships which would have killed many men: he was ship-wrecked three times and narrowly escaped with his life on more than one occasion.

For some years he served in the Liverpool Pilot Service, teaching the apprentices seamanship; afterwards he worked for John Gibney & Sons on marine salvage work; later he was employed by the Liverpool Salvage Association. My uncle, James Citrine, was the principal diver for this body and he had acquired a reputation for his work. He was a deeply religious man, steady and sober, quite different from my father, who was of the devil-may-care type.

I have said that the sea was in our blood. All my father's brothers were connected with the sea, except one, who emigrated to the United States when quite young. One was a diver, another a carpenter, and still another worked on the docks in Liverpool. My brother Arthur was a tinsmith employed by a Liverpool firm mainly on work for the galleys, sidelights, and other apparatus for ships until his death in action in Flanders in 1914. On leaving school I wandered from ship to ship in the Birkenhead docks seeking a job as cabin boy and was unsuccessful. My younger brother, Stanley, went to sea for some years, having served seven years as an apprentice sailmaker. He went at first in a sailing vessel. This life was not an easy one, and after a few years he secured work ashore. He had been a member of the National Union of Seamen for some years. He had served as a delegate on some of the vessels on which he worked and he had attracted the notice of the union. He was eventually appointed as an official in the Mersey area working under the district secretary.

Unfortunately, the scourge of the Citrines, tuberculosis, which carried off my mother and younger sister Violet, and my step-brother Alfred, attacked him also. So the family which was a united and happy one, and every member of which attained adult age, was shattered by war and illness within a few short years. Father survived the vicissitudes which assailed all the family save my eldest sister Emily and myself. He died at the age of eighty-five of heart failure,

B

while out walking. He had not achieved his foremost wish, which was to die and be buried at sea.

Our family moved from Liverpool when I was two years old and we lived for a few years in Seacombe, part of the township of Wallasey and a more ancient place than many people think. It is mentioned in the Domesday Book. We lived in a small house in Palatine Road, a neighbourhood mainly occupied by people of the artisan class. We had no gas or hot water. We used to heat water on the open fire. There was no bath; oil lamps and candles furnished illumination.

On Saturdays and Sundays there was a good deal of gambling in the fields nearby; I have watched men playing pitch and toss for hours, without any interference from the police, who couldn't get near enough to them because of their well-positioned look-outs. Naturally enough this sport spread to the children; the young ones gambled with buttons, the older boys with halfpennies.

I was too young to understand properly what was going on, although my mother had impressed upon me the wickedness of gambling. In any case I have never had any love for games of chance. Betting is a rare thing with me—possibly because I generally lose whenever I invest a modest bit on the Derby or the Grand National. Neither football pools nor bingo attract me in the least. I am not a spoilsport and I fully understand the thrill of a flutter, but I have never felt the need for it. I get my excitement in other ways.

One warm summer evening my father and mother and most of the family started out from the Liverpool landing stage on one of the vessels bound for the Bar Lightship. When we reached this spot the vessel stopped, and suddenly a man, fully dressed, jumped overboard. All the passengers rushed to the side to see what had happened, only to find that this was an exhibition of swimming and life-saving by a so-called 'professor'. I said 'all the passengers', but not quite all, as the clinking of glasses in the bar plainly indicated. The 'professor' had hardly touched the water when a man dashed out of the saloon, flung off his jacket, and also jumped overboard.

We all thought this was part of the show, but it wasn't. The next thing we knew was that the man was struggling with the 'professor' and evidently trying to rescue him. Apparently he had been drinking with friends and, feeling the boat list over with the rush of people to the side, the would-be rescuer had dashed out. He espied the 'drowning' man and without asking any questions he sprang overboard. He was my father! It took quite a time to console the 'professor', but eventually all ended happily with a prolonged visit to the bar.

I loved the Mersey and the ever-moving spectacle of the vessels, large and small, ploughing its surface, bound for all parts of the world. When in later life it was decreed that I must leave the area I missed it more than I can say.

Seacombe was considered to be a poorer district than the other parts of Wallasey, but as far as I can remember there were only a few real slums. I have seen a good deal worse both in England and overseas.

One evening when I was about eight we were playing football in the gathering dusk, with coats for goal-posts, when someone shouted, 'Look, there's a fire.' At first it appeared to be a reflection of the dying rays of the sun, but soon it became apparent that Buchanan's flour-mill on the Dock Road had caught fire. We raced towards it, and covered that half-mile more or less in record time. No fire-engines were visible and it was a considerable time before one arrived, accompanied by a mob of spectators. By this time the mill was ablaze, and when the fire hoses were eventually brought to bear they didn't appear to make any impression. It certainly was the biggest fire I had seen.

It was hours before the fire brigade were able to control the fire. The mill was connected by a bridge to a warehouse across the Dock Road, and vain attempts were made to direct the hoses on to this to prevent the fire spreading. Then we saw a man climb up the face of the warehouse by some means, and help to get the hoses in position. We all cheered lustily, but it was not until I reached home some hours later that I discovered that the man was my father! The mill was gutted when at last the flames died down, and it was unusable for some time. I did not know then that the fire which I was enjoying so much was destroying the mill at which I was later to become employed.

Swimming was a great pleasure to me. My first recollection of bathing was in a clay pit—Monks's Pit in Oakdale. It was shallow at one end and deep at the other. We had strict demarcation rules with the boys who occasionally came across from Birkenhead: they had to confine themselves to the shallow end. I was nearly drowned when one of the older boys pushed me out of my depth and then laughing stood and watched my struggles, not realizing the danger I was in.

Although in later years when I was an adult and we were living in Egremont I bathed frequently in the Mersey, in my childhood the docks were my favourite.

The West Float was about thirty feet deep; the water was comparatively clean, there was no tide, and there were flights of steps down to the water level every few hundred yards or so. To me this was an ideal swimming bath. The principal drawback was that bathing was prohibited—at least that was the common belief—although I never recall anyone being prosecuted. As to my clothes, I had little to attract a thief and I always hid them snugly in some of the nearby stacks of timber. The only occasion when anything was stolen from me was not at the docks, it was in a bathing tent at Egremont specially reserved for swimmers. I was then an adult and someone managed to rifle my pockets. What was worse, they stole the only medal I ever won for swimming.

The police winked at our bathing in the docks and as it was unusual for me to bathe in the company of others I was never molested. The vessels moored to the quay were an added attraction —it was exhilarating to dive underneath them. I could always tell their depth by the figures painted on the bow. Sometimes there was a little flotsam near the steps, carried there by the wind. One afternoon as I was skirting this to reach the steps after a swim I saw something which resembled a cabbage. Striking out with my arms I accidentally knocked it and nearly sank with fright. It was the head of a dead man. I left the water as quickly as I could, rushed over to my clothes, hurriedly dressed, wasting no time in drying myself, and in a high state of excitement dashed along the dock wall intending to report the matter to the first person I saw. It was a sunny afternoon, and soon I espied a policeman sitting on the deck of a schooner chatting with a sailor. I stammered out my news, to which the policeman asked calmly, 'Is he dead?'

'Yes,' I replied.

'Then don't hurry, it isn't a fire,' said the officer, and, walking in leisurely fashion, he accompanied me to where the body was floating. Then he sent me to one of the ships for a rope and when I had procured this he directed me to put it round the shoulders of the drowned man. He himself did nothing but give orders. I won't go into the details as to how we got the body ashore: they would be rather gruesome. It transpired that the dead man was a seaman who had been reported missing several months before. He had evidently walked into the dock on some dark night, and the inquest showed that the body must have been in the water nearly three months. Needless to say, I wasn't brought into the case. Believing that bathing in the docks was prohibited, I was quite satisfied.

I had as good an education as most other sons of working-class parents. It was only elementary; in later life I realized what I had missed. Little as my education amounted to, I consider myself fortunate when I compare the advantages I had with those of men like Will Thorne of the General Workers', or Ben Tillett of the Dockers' Union, neither of whom had any formal education at all. Such teaching as I did receive I liked, but the earliest stages of the processes of learning were distasteful. I felt much like the little boy whom Shakespeare had in mind when in *As You Like It* he wrote about the whining schoolboy with his satchel and shining morning face, creeping like snail, unwillingly to school. My first visit was something of the same order. I certainly had no desire to go to school. I was content to remain at home in the loving care of my mother and aunt, who always denied themselves for me.

I have heard of people who, long after their own schooldays are finished, speak of them as the happiest days of their life. Looking back on mine I cannot say that my schooldays were much different from any other period in my life in that respect. As a child I had my worries and anxieties, which were as real to me at the time as the greatest problems I had to face in later life. Trivial as they now seem, they were then overwhelming, particularly during the first few years at school. I worried about my ability to do my lessons to the satisfaction of my teachers, just as much as I did over the more serious issues of later years. Certainly had I been able to see things with the eyes of an adult instead of with those of a delicate and sensitive child I would have treated my little problems differently. But I was a child upon whom had been lavished at home love and kindness far beyond anything I could expect from others, no matter how considerate.

During the early days of my schooling it was common for parents to keep their children away whenever they felt inclined. The system of appointing school attendance officers was then in its infancy, and no one bothered much about them. Before I finished my schooling it was different: parents and scholars had to give a valid reason for absence. I say a valid reason, but on occasions some boys would play truant for weeks on end, unknown to their parents. Others would take a day off now and then. We called this 'sagging' and the younger boys were disposed to regard the 'saggers' as heroes. I never played truant, so I never became a hero. I tried to do my lessons as well as I could and when my homework became difficult I could always rely upon the willing but not always competent assistance of my aunt. If my arithmetic was too much of a puzzle for both of us we called in the appropriate expert—my elder brother —to pull us through.

The classes in our school were even larger than they commonly are today. The masters were as considerate as their duties would allow; in retrospect I do not envy them their task of trying to teach a mass of unruly boys the rudiments of arithmetic, grammar, geography, and history. One of the female teachers, a harassed but kind-hearted woman who taught the infants, used to scream out her instructions so loudly that passers-by outside would stop in wonderment and marvel at her lung-power. My favourite teacher was Mr. A. W. Heap, a tall, athletic man and an adept at cricket and rugby football, who in after life was generous in his tributes to me. Even the headmaster, who was looked upon as a bully by many boys and their complaining parents, treated me decently. I recall one morning when my elder brother and I were lined up with about twenty other boys waiting to be caned for lateness. The headmaster worked systematically down the line until he reached me. I put out my hand, but immediately my brother spoke up. 'Please, sir, can I take his punishment as my brother is delicate?' The headmaster stopped, rather astonished at this unusual request. The outcome was that he allowed both my brother and myself to go to our classes unpunished. I never was late again.

My favourite subjects were geography and history, and I was fascinated by the meaning of words. Sometimes a teacher would take each of us in turn as we sat in class and ask us the meaning of a particular word or passage from some literature he was reading to us. When most of the class were stumped he would ask any of us to volunteer the meaning. I had an uncanny faculty for knowing the approximate meaning of words I had never heard before, and I was often allowed to go home early because of distinguishing myself on such occasions. It is a puzzle where this knowledge came from, as I was by no means a voracious reader, and had not at that time come into contact with really good literature. My reading was confined to the *Union Jack* (where I made the acquaintance of Sexton Blake, the detective), *Pluck*, and a rather better-quality paper, the *Boys' Friend*, which was not so lurid as the others.

I could perhaps have elevated myself by reading the book prizes I won at school, but this occurred mostly at the end of my schooldays, and I found Sir Walter Scott rather too heavy for my youthful taste. No one had bothered to tell me that he had written a book called *Ivanhoe*. I had read Bunyan's *Pilgrim's Progress*, but it was certainly not because of any extensive reading that I was able to understand the meaning of words, and the conversation of my companions was not exactly of an erudite kind.

I was fond of poetry, and I fervently declaimed the lines of Shakespeare, Scott, Southey, and others in a manner which would have astonished them. Kipling didn't seem to have arrived at our school. I sang lustily Campbell's 'Ye Mariners of England', and the morning and evening hymns. We ended the day with the hymn 'The Day Thou Gavest, Lord, is Ended'. I never forgot it. In middle and later life this beautiful hymn always awakened in me a tinge of melancholy. Nor did I ever forget 'Ye Mariners'. In the gloomiest days of World War II Winston Churchill and I recited it together in the Cabinet Room in Downing Street, he taking one verse and I the next.

Before leaving school I developed the dictionary habit, and found pleasure in ascertaining the meanings of words and tracking them down to their source. Our family reference library didn't run to anything more comprehensive than a half-crown Nuttall's dictionary, but I found it an invaluable book which amply sufficed for my needs. When in after years I became associated with Ben Tillett, one of the outstanding orators of the trade union movement, he told me he used to go hunting through a dictionary as an antidote to insomnia. He would chase from word to word until at last he fell asleep.

I liked history, and as I had been fortunate enough to come across a rhyme which gave the dates of the reign of every monarch from William the Conqueror onwards, I had no difficulty in using this as a mental chart. Our history seemed to consist solely of the doings of kings and queens. It was long after I left school that I learned there was such a thing as economic history.

Geography was always an easy subject for me: I could memorize the names of capitals, rivers, and mountains as well as the next boy. I had a rather vivid imagination, and when I read of far-off cities and places my imagination clothed them in far finer garments than later life proved to be the reality. Arithmetic had no attractions for me. Algebra was a mystery which I encountered during my last year at school. Its symbols baffled me then as they do now.

We always had prayers before starting our daily lessons, and bible-reading was given from time to time, but such religious education as I received was mainly due to attendance at the Oakdale Presbyterian Mission. Here we were taught scripture with great patience by the lady teachers who voluntarily gave their services to instil into our minds the tenets of Christianity and generally to awaken any latent goodness in us young reprobates. It was a thankless task, but most of us behaved ourselves reasonably well, and tried in one way or another to reciprocate the kindness with which we were treated. It wasn't all moral instruction, for now and again we were invited to a school outing. These were most enjoyable, a trip on the Mersey always being my favourite.

I have always loved music and when I was old enough I joined the Oakdale Mission Band: thus began my musical education. We had a set of old brass instruments which must have been purchased from a scrap-metal merchant. At first I played the tenor horn, but later I went on to the cornet. My two brothers joined in on the baritone and trombone. We attended band practice twice a week and now and again we marched through the streets, greatly to the astonishment of passers-by and to the admiration of all those who had relatives in the band. The bandmaster, who must have suffered from deafness, would stride out proudly ahead of us. Almost every instrument was badly out of tune, but we enjoyed ourselves as much as though we were 'the Besses-of-the-Barn'. Somehow we were licked into shape, and even our dilapidated instruments were brought more nearly into tune, so that in time we pleased others as well as ourselves. This gave me a liking for brass bands, and when later on I was employed at New Brighton Tower I took lessons from one of the professional cornet players. I never attained top rank, but I played successively in the Seacombe Victoria, Birkenhead Borough, Moss Bank, and finally for a brief period in the Nutgrove Band at St. Helens. All those last three bands proudly included the word 'Prize' in their titles.

At Oakdale I won two prizes, one for a general knowledge of scripture, and another for regular attendance. They were both books, *John Halifax, Gentleman* by Mrs. Craik, and a bound volume of school stories from the *Captain*, a popular magazine. I read the first from a sense of duty, and the other with avidity. C. B. Fry, the famous footballer, cricketer, and all-round athlete, edited the Athletic Corner of the *Captain*, and P. G. Wodehouse, Frank Swainson, R. S. Warren Bell, and a host of others contributed to this excellent magazine. I realize that with the exception of Wodehouse, and possibly Fry, these names mean nothing to the present generation, but they were famous in their day and not only amongst schoolboys. Only a few years ago I came across some bound volumes of these magazines, and once again I relished reading them. 'What a juvenile mind this fellow must have,' says some highbrow who may have taken out this book from his local library by mistake. Well, let it be so. I am not ashamed to say that a re-reading of the works of Jules Verne has given me more pleasure than many more modern and sophisticated books. P. G. Wodehouse told me in a letter a year or so ago that he thought that 'Acton's Feud', by Swainson in the *Captain*, was the best school story he had ever read. His own stories were always a pleasure for me to read and showed the qualities which have made him one of the best modern writers in the English language. The lady who gave this prize had awakened in me a thirst for good literature which time has never quenched.

I recall that whilst at the Mission a series of addresses was given to us when I was about sixteen or seventeen by a most sincere and devout Christian who gave almost every moment of his leisure time to endeavouring to instruct us young heathens. They were based upon the Old Testament and I recall how earnestly our teacher insisted that the dimensions of the Ark had been proved to be sound to the satisfaction of naval architects. I cannot recollect his explaining to us how the multitude of animals of all kinds lived in amity and contentment on an inadequate diet during the period of the flood. This perhaps was an oversight.

There were a number of sincere teachers associated with the Oakdale Mission, and although in adult life I found some gaps in their theological reasoning, I became only too conscious of the depth of gratitude I and many others owed them.

I didn't know the difference between a Presbyterian, a Methodist, or a Congregationalist, nor in fact any of the other denominations. But I could recognize sincerity and devotion without bothering my brains about sectarianism. Oakdale and its congregation of worshippers were quite good enough for me.

2

I Join the Union

I LEFT school after passing what was called the Labour Examination. This was a test of one's educational fitness to leave school before reaching the age of fourteen. I was then twelve and a half, and was in Standard Seven. I could have gone no higher by remaining at school. Whilst still at school I had delivered newspapers both before and after school hours for 2s. 6d. a week. For another period I also worked at a butcher's on Friday evenings and all day Saturday. This was much harder work, and at times I was still taking out orders after midnight on a Saturday. I received 2s. 6d. for this.

After some casual jobs I secured work at a local flour-mill. The hours of work at the mill were long, from six o'clock in the morning to six at night, which, after deducting half an hour for breakfast and one hour for dinner, made up a ten-and-a-half-hour day. We finished at twelve o'clock on Saturday, so our working week was fifty-eight hours. My wages were 6s. a week. I was employed in the self-raising department along with half a dozen other boys of about my own age. My job at first was filling paper bags with flour from a bin which was fed periodically from a hopper. Other boys did weighing, wrapping, and pasting of labels. The work was heavy and the dust in the atmosphere was considerable. In those days little was known about dust extraction, and no one bothered much about our breathing flour-dust. It wasn't that the firm was callous. No one thought about the consequences. I was on this work for over nine months, doing each of the separate processes in turn.

The boys in our department were a cheerful lot and the men with whom I came into contact treated me decently. But I couldn't stand up to the work. We had no seats and at the end of the day I could walk only with considerable difficulty. Night after night I would go home with aching ankles, thoroughly worn out and scarcely able to eat my evening meal because of weariness and pain. I bear the consequences of this even today.

On top of this I developed inflammation of the lungs and kidneys. So ill did I become that I was confined to bed for three or four months. One morning after the doctor had examined me and was about to leave the room he turned to my mother and said something to her quietly. Not so quietly, however, that my sharp ears hadn't caught the words: 'I am afraid he cannot get better.' At first I wasn't sure that I had heard aright, as I had no idea I was so seriously ill. When a little later my mother came back into the room and I saw that she had been crying, I knew. I was dreadfully frightened and determined to get well. From that day onwards my health steadily improved and Mother, long afterwards, told me it was my spirit which kept me alive.

When I had fully recovered, my father secured me a post as an apprentice with a firm of electrical contractors in New Brighton. Those were days when it was common for the parents of an apprentice to have to pay a premium if they wanted their son to enter the electrical trade. My parents were too poor to do that, and so it was arranged that I would receive no wages for the first six months and afterwards 2s. 6d. a week. I didn't get much training; I spent the early months learning the intricacies of brushing out the shop, doing a bit of elementary book-keeping, and boiling the workmen's tea-cans in the various buildings in which they were installing electricity. But I liked the work and was disappointed when a couple of years later the firm went bankrupt. Whether it was my half-crown a week which broke the camel's back, I don't know! Fourteen years later, when I had become the district secretary of the Electrical Trades Union, I assisted my first electrical employer to join the union.

I had to look for another job. I was now styled an 'improver', which meant an apprentice who had already served part of his time. In the spring of 1903 I obtained employment with the New Brighton Tower Company on the electrical staff. Now I was in heaven! The Tower had been completed in 1900 and was a truly magnificent structure. To my eyes it was infinitely more graceful than the Blackpool Tower, and it was about fifty feet higher, standing 621 feet above sea level. It had a splendid ballroom and a theatre, both built between the wide steel legs of the tower.

We had our own generating station; and there were extensive grounds tastefully laid out, as well as a lake on which a couple of gondolas plied. Every evening the grounds were profusely lit by some 30,000 red, white, and green fairy-lights which were festooned along the numerous pathways. There were plenty of sideshows, and indeed everything the management could think of to amuse visitors. My work at first was out of doors, and the clean fresh breezes blowing straight across from the Irish Sea made me feel fitter than ever before in my life.

The hours were rather long (we started during the season at ten o'clock in the morning and finished at ten at night), but we had long breaks and I didn't feel we were overworked. In winter we worked from 8 a.m. to 5.30 p.m. I served in turn in the generating station, on the outside lighting, on the inter-communication telephones, and on the theatre switchboard. Here, under the guidance of a skilled electrician, I learned how to work 'to a plot'. By pulling out or pushing in switches and manipulating dimmers and a few other devices we could miraculously produce thunder and lightning, sunsets or moonlight scenes at will, while the men in the flies produced a snowstorm at a moment's notice.

It was at the Tower that I first saw the Gilbert and Sullivan operas *The Mikado* and *Princess Ida* performed. The company were amateurs of the New Brighton Operatic Society, with a professional orchestra. They had been thoroughly rehearsed and I saw the final dress rehearsals as well as the performances of both these operas.

It was at the Tower in 1903 that I saw Georges Hackenschmidt, the 'Russian Lion', then the reigning champion wrestler in the world. I never saw a finer-built man. The muscles used fairly to ripple along his bare back when he was exercising or wrestling. He was not a tall man, only about 5 ft. 8 in. or so, but his muscular development was something at which to marvel. On one occasion he gave me a postcard photograph of himself, and this, along with others that I bought, was carefully preserved for many years. Before I first saw Hackenschmidt he had been in England only a few years, and had created a sensation by defeating the Graeco-Roman champion Tom Cannon of Liverpool, breaking Cannon's arm in the process. Watching Hackenschmidt at close quarters, I became fired with the desire of emulation. I learned all the principal holds, and could soon beat any of the younger members of the staff.

I also learned to swing Indian clubs, and use dumb-bells— exercises which have remained a habit until today. I must have been a bit of a fanatic, because for a time I followed Eugene Sandow's system of dressing myself immediately after a cold bath without drying myself with a towel. Whilst walking along the street I practised deep breathing, taking as few breaths as possible between the lamp-posts.

In my early youth I was always a nervous chap and tried to conquer my fears by walking at night through the darkest and most forbidding places I could find. I would march along the dimly lighted quays of the Birkenhead docks, which were deserted at night save for an occasional Lascar, and go down the back entries of the most grim-looking streets.

I now had the opportunity to test my nerves in another direction. Why should I not try to climb to the top of the Tower? Others had done it, so why not me? I knew I would be prevented if I told anyone, so one evening in the gathering dusk I set about it, and did it.

By far the biggest fright I got occurred one Bank Holiday, when I had undertaken to relieve one of the regular attendants on the main Tower lifts. I had occasionally worked it previously, but it had always been lightly loaded. On this occasion I took up some passengers, only to find that about thirty or forty were waiting to descend. Once my lift was empty, they rushed in and refused to get out, despite my telling them that we were badly overloaded.

I foolishly decided to risk it. I switched on the electric motor and immediately I knew we were in trouble because we shot down far more rapidly than was normal. As quickly as I could I switched off the current, but the lift showed no sign of slackening speed.

I couldn't do anything more and I was fearful of saying anything which might alarm the passengers and cause a panic. So I just waited and hoped. It seems scarcely credible, but that lift ran down about 200 feet with the current switched off. Sixty-four years ago, when the building of the Tower was completed, lifts were not fitted with the many safety gadgets which are in common use today. It was later discovered that the brake blocks were defective and not capable of holding the overloaded lift.

The lift stopped, and there we were, suspended halfway down the Tower. I was scared to death and couldn't take the risk of restarting her, as I had visions of the same thing happening and our crashing into the ballroom immediately below us. I told the passengers as calmly as I could that the current had failed and that we would have to wait until it was switched on again: I emphasized that there was nothing to be afraid of.

After about five minutes my mates below saw our predicament and sent the neighbouring lift up empty. Between us the driver of the empty lift and I explained that it was necessary to transfer the passengers to lighten my load. After some demur this was done without difficulty, the passengers only having to step across a couple of short planks which had been brought up together with a rope handrail. When the other lift had gone down I started off again, but this time well within my authorized load, and arrived without further incident. I did no more relief work on those lifts. My hair turned grey comparatively early in life and no doubt this incident helped!

After I had been nearly three years at the Tower business became slack. The number of visitors declined seriously. Staff were laid off, and the work became seasonal. So I had to look elsewhere for a job.

So far I had always worked on the Cheshire side of the Mersey, but now I found a job with a firm in Liverpool. We worked the hours then usual in electrical contracting—from 7.30 in the morning to 5.30 p.m., finishing at one o'clock on Saturdays. I never lost touch with New Brighton Tower, and went back to work there in subsequent years when opportunity afforded.

My new firm had a good range of business and, like many small contracting firms, they did work of first-class quality. In only one firm was it made clear to me that I was expected to do work which was palpably shoddy and I quietly left that firm, although I had no other work to go to.

My first job was on a new building which was being erected for Elder Dempster and Company, the shipping firm. It was situated at the bottom of Water Street, Liverpool, and was called Colonial House. Here I came across an electrician named Tom Brett, and I was foisted on him as an improver for several months. Brett was a most disconsolate-looking individual and a skilful workman. He had to be or he wouldn't have lasted long with the Socialist views he was always expressing. A man of about thirty-five years, he was an active member of the Social Democratic Federation, a Marxist to his finger-tips, and one of the wittiest and politically best-informed workmen I ever met. He was cordially hated by most of the other workmen because of his sarcastic manner, and perhaps because he always defeated them in argument.

At dinner time we would assemble—a rather motley crew—for our food, sitting on a plank supported on a couple of trestles, with our tea-cans and sandwiches alongside us, warming ourselves at a fire fuelled with scrap pieces of timber. I said 'our tea-cans' but I never drank tea. Tom pumped Socialist doctrine into the other workmen, much to their dislike, and deluged me with pamphlets and arguments. Eventually I joined the Independent Labour Party. This disgusted Tom, who regarded the I.L.P. as 'reformist' and not 'Socialist' in any real sense. He felt that his advocacy had been wasted on me.

Brett and I worked together for some months on Colonial House. When the job was completed I was sent to work on my own, mostly on repairs, gaining experience all the time. Some of this work was on board fishing trawlers and other small crafts. Whilst I was so engaged I received a letter from a chap whom I will call Watson, with whom I had once worked. He had been appointed as a foreman in the electrical department at Pilkington's, the well-known glass-makers at

St. Helens, and he induced me to go there with a promise of regular employment.

This was my first job away from home, and as the working hours were from six o'clock in the morning until 5.30 p.m., with the usual breaks for meals, there was no possibility of my travelling to and from St. Helens daily from my home in Wallasey. I found lodgings in a collier's cottage only a few minutes' walk from the Cowley Hill Plate Glass works, so that I could 'lie in' until nearly half past five. I had to reach the time-lodge promptly at six o'clock or before, for if the hooter had finished its half-a-minute's moaning when I arrived I would be shut out until after breakfast. We called this loss of two hours' pay 'losing a quarter'. Moreover, if we had worked overtime that week the two hours were deducted at overtime rates. The loss of a quarter meant something to our pay-packets when wages were low.

Pilkington's indulged me by allowing me to go home to Wallasey whenever possible at weekends and to return after breakfast on the Monday morning. Of course, I lost my quarter. At the beginning of 1906 Pilkington's were easily the biggest employers in St. Helens. They bore the reputation of being a hard firm to work for. A strike had taken place some years before and trade unionism was in disfavour. The glass-bottle makers (who were not employed at Pilkington's but by other firms) were always well organized. I was not a member of a trade union, but I resented the way in which Pilkington's obtruded the doctrine that they were the bosses and that anyone who didn't like it could get out. They dominated St. Helens, and everyone knew that to be sacked from Pilkington's meant great difficulty in getting another job in the town.

On the whole I had little to complain of as to my treatment by the firm. Those of us in the electrical department were given a good deal more rope than other employees.

The long hours were my biggest hardship, as I still suffered from weak ankles. I hated the early-morning start. In industry generally hours were excessive by modern standards. When later I was employed at Cammell Laird's shipyard, Birkenhead, and had to get up before five o'clock and walk some three miles to work, I made up my mind that if there was anything I could do to prevent workpeople being dragged out of bed in the middle of the night I would cheerfully do it. I hope I have contributed something to that end.

I left Pilkington's at short notice. I was told by Watson, the foreman, just as I was going through the gate at noon one Saturday, that I would have to come back after dinner and work throughout the weekend. On inquiry I found that the job could easily have been done during the ordinary working week. I felt thoroughly fed up. I made up my mind then and there to get away from it all, and I brusquely declined to heed the kindly advice of the building manager, a religious man who was not in the least to blame for the incident, which was entirely Watson's fault. Watson was not a bit conciliatory or perhaps I might have acted differently. He got on his high horse. I told him what I thought of him. Within a few minutes I had drawn my back pay and left the works.

I secured another job in Liverpool. A week or two later I received a letter from the electrical engineer at Pilkington's referring to the recent incident and saying that they were very annoyed with Watson, the foreman, and that if I wished to return the job was open for me. To my shame I never answered the letter, not because I bore any grudge against the firm but through sheer carelessness. I wish they had told me that they had discharged Watson, as in fact they had done. I would willingly have gone back, as I liked the work and the experience was invaluable.

In the course of the next few years I put in a season or two at the New Brighton Tower, but most of my time was spent in wiring houses for electric light in the Wallasey district. Again I was fortunate in working for a firm which had deservedly earned a reputation for doing good work. It was pleasing employment.

There were many speculative builders engaged on Wallasey housing projects in 1908 and 1909 as the district was being rapidly built up. I got used to starting an electrical installation at one end of a road and working right through to the other, wiring each house in turn. Needless to say, the electricity service was confined almost exclusively to the better-class neighbourhoods, as its amenities were still beyond the reach of working-class people. I often told myself, 'Some day I and other workers will have electricity just like these people.' I was not infected with the class-war bug, but I meant it just the same.

In the early part of 1910 work slackened and, regretfully, the firm and I parted company. I was out of work for several weeks. Every morning I made the round of electrical firms in Liverpool seeking work. I began to understand how it is that an unemployed man can become demoralized. Time after time I had to pluck up courage even to ask for work. I was treated so cavalierly by clerks and others that I felt humiliated. One would have thought that I was asking a great favour in wanting to be employed. Refusal after refusal so depressed me that I began to think that no one wanted me. I was in danger of becoming afraid to ask for work.

It was no use visiting firms during the afternoon. The only chance of seeing a principal or manager was in the morning. I spent the afternoons in the Picton reading room, where I became more closely acquainted with the standard authors. I greatly enjoyed the works of Conan Doyle, Marryat, Mark Twain, Galsworthy, Dumas, and others. Bernard Shaw, whom I had read casually, and W. S. Gilbert, of the Gilbert and Sullivan operas, were a real joy to me. But not even this peep into the world of literature could compensate me for the absence of employment. Almost in desperation I went again to St. Helens and applied for work at Pilkington's. Naturally, the electrical engineer who had written me on the occasion of my last leaving the firm reminded me of his letter and reproached me for not answering. I knew that he liked me and I frankly admitted my delinquency. He forgave me and took me back into the firm's employment. The matter was never referred to again. I didn't know then what I learnt afterwards, that it was most unusual for Pilkington's ever to take back into their service any person who had left them without their consent.

This latter incident taught me a lesson which I have never forgotten. I never again made the mistake of not answering a letter. Although in the course of my work in the trade union movement and elsewhere there have been letters from cranks and lunatics (which, after an initial acknowledgement, I have left unanswered), I have always made a point of replying to letters on the same day that they were received.

Working in Pilkington's for the second time I found that the electrical staff had been considerably enlarged because of the extensive electrification which had gone on. Some were, of course, strangers to me. I resumed my lodgings in the little cottage in Seddon Street. By this time my former landlady had died, one of the daughters had married, the two sons had emigrated to Canada, and only the elder sister and her children remained. I and another lodger, who also worked at Pilkington's, were for some months the only other occupants, but we were joined by one of the electricians who had recently started at the firm. He and I slept in the same bed.

When I first thought of going to St. Helens I must confess I didn't relish it at all. It was only the prospect of regular work and the wider experience which attracted me. I found the work interesting and often stayed beyond my time to wrestle with some electrical problem, unknown to the management. The firm were installing some of the biggest direct-current electric motors in the country, and heavy traction work was all new to me. I was deeply interested in electrical theory and there was plenty here to occupy my attention.

I had many friends amongst the homely Lancashire folk. The

C

people I lived with were as good working-class types as one would find in a day's march. I tried to acclimatize myself to their ways, and I even tried to wear clogs at work, but they nearly broke my toes. I couldn't climb ladders in them with safety, so I abandoned the attempt. Living conditions were not of the best, but I grew accustomed to this. The cottage where I lodged was on the outskirts of the town and I paid only 10s. for board and lodgings from Monday to Saturday, and 14s. when I stayed the full week.

I was excellently fed. I had the use of a tiny parlour in which I could practise on my cornet or get on with my electrical studies. Our cottage had no hot water, of course, and the collier sons coming home from the pits, who always started and finished earlier than I did, had to wash themselves in the miniature scullery, standing in a zinc bath with a few inches of hot water heated on the kitchen fire. This, incidentally, was always blazing away. One would scrub the back of the other and occasionally I took a hand in this. As for myself, I washed under the scullery tap or in a bucket in the garden outside. Sometimes the sons would come home so tired that they would sit over the fire smoking and then eating their food without first washing themselves. But I never knew them to go to bed without thoroughly cleaning themselves. They read economics and philosophy and could argue intelligently. One was a strong Socialist and between the three of us we had animated discussions.

I never needed an alarm clock, as I could always hear the knocker-up shout at the top of his voice in the early hours, 'Nah then, Billy,' or, farther down the street, 'Come on, Tum.' Then would ensue a loud hammering at the doors of the neighbouring houses. I think his clients paid him sixpence a week for this service.

Looking back, I am glad I worked at St. Helens. It brought me into contact with aspects of life of which I had no experience. Conditions in the industrial world have been vastly improved since then. At Pilkington's a new generation of directors came on the scene and an infinitely broader-minded policy was pursued in the sphere of welfare and human relations. The trade unions are now fully recognized and wages and conditions are much better. The firm were noted pioneers in the shorter-hours movement, which cut the working week to forty-four hours.

I remained with Pilkington's until September 1911, when I returned to Merseyside.

I was fortunate in working for contracting firms who, although employing only a comparatively few electricians, carried out contracts and repairs in many different industries and services so that I was enabled constantly to broaden my experience. I spent eighteen months working on new installations at Lewis's, the Bon Marché, and other large shops, warehouses, hotels, and offices. I was also engaged on a new hostel connected with the Liverpool University, and one day a young, broad-shouldered chap came round accompanied by the architect. It was Frederick J. Marquis, the new warden, who afterwards became Lord Woolton. The architect and he examined my plans, made suggestions as to the positions of lights, plugs, switches, etc., and left me to carry on. I can see them now, the architect pointing with his foot at any electrical point under three feet from the floor. As Mark Twain might have said, he was economical in the use of his hands.

As a young man I was never a chap who spent his leisure loitering about with companions or playing organized games. I attended band practice regularly, but most of my evenings were spent studying electricity. I say studying, but I had little knowledge of mathematics and some of the textbooks seemed to have been written in language which only professors could understand. When I was engaged on repair work and came across some fault which puzzled me I wrote down an account of it in a notebook and stated all I could of the salient facts, reasoning out a solution as I went on. I filled several notebooks in this way and described in detail some of the curious faults I came across. As I had no companion to talk to, I would sometimes find myself travelling along the wrong track. Instead of crossing out what I had written when I discovered this, I would write a sentence or two describing what was puzzling me. Then I would return to the problem on the next evening after reading over what I had written.

At this time I was courting the girl who became my devoted wife and she would sit patiently whilst I was struggling with these problems evening after evening, knitting or sewing and never interjecting a disturbing remark. The habit of reasoning out my problems on paper stuck to me right through my working life. I don't mean only during the years I worked as an electrician. I applied exactly the same methods during my trade union days and right through my chairmanship of the British Electricity Authority. In these latter days, of course, it was much easier to reason out my problems by dictating memoranda, but I never abandoned my practice of quietly arguing out the subject in my notebook.

For many years I have adopted Napoleon's method and kept a scribbling pad by my bedside. If I awaken with an idea, a suggestion, or a thought which seems worth recording, I put it down at once and then return to untroubled sleep.

I don't wish anyone to think that I was always working. Far from it. In my young days I was as keen as most adolescents to enjoy life, and nothing suited me better than to walk along the promenade at New Brighton when the winter gales were smashing the seas against the wall, throwing up the spray twenty or thirty feet or more. It has always awakened something primitive in me to battle against the elements, whether wind, rain, or sea. I often used to walk along the shore beyond New Brighton during darkness, entirely alone, enjoying the buffeting against the wind as I rounded the Perch Rock Battery. The fiercer the breeze, the better I liked it. Occasionally I would find a vessel had gone ashore on one of the sandbanks which often proved most dangerous to vessels approaching Liverpool in fog or bad weather. Then there was great excitement and sometimes valuable salvage for the local people.

On my return to Liverpool from St. Helens I started work almost immediately for a firm of electrical contractors. I soon found that my fellow electricians were all strong trade unionists, and I was approached to join. I had no experience whatever of the work of the trade union movement, my interest in the Labour movement being centred almost entirely on political questions.

It was a period of considerable industrial upheaval on Merseyside. There was a great revival in trade unionism. In this environment I needed no inducement to join a trade union, and on 10th October, 1911, I became a member of the Liverpool branch of the Electrical Trades Union.

Almost from the date of my joining the union I began to take an active interest in its work. I studied the constitution of the union and carried a copy of the draft working rules around with me and attended the branch meetings every Monday evening. It wasn't long before I became responsible for submitting a report of the branch activities for printing in the national monthly journal of the union. When opportunity afforded I attended meetings of some of the other branches to familiarize myself with their procedure, and found that the general standard of discussion was good. There was little doubt that the meetings of the Liverpool branch were the best conducted. The chairman of the branch was a bull-headed fellow, stubborn but shrewd, who ruled the meetings with firmness and authority. He slapped down any interrupters and points of order were ruled out rigorously. He subsequently became an electrical contractor.

We established a system of shop delegates who acted as the union representatives, just as the shop stewards of today are supposed to act. A more active part was played by the rank-and-file members of the union than is customary today. Apathy is the enemy of sound

trade unionism, but it is not confined to workers' organizations. It is
met in every form of organization, particularly where the work is
carried out voluntarily.

I set about learning as much as I could about the theory and
practice of trade unionism. I had digested dozens of pamphlets on
Socialism, and the books of Robert Blatchford were well known to
me. But I felt that my knowledge of trade unionism was sketchy. So I
started hunting round the second-hand book shops for something
which would give me a closer insight into the theory and practice of
collective bargaining. I knew enough about economics from my
reading of Karl Marx and his disciples. I could quote whole sections
of *Value, Price, and Profit*. Experience had told me how helpless the
average man was to stand up against his employer. That was one of
my reasons for joining the E.T.U. Whilst an employer could usually
dispense with the services of one of his workers, he couldn't do
without the whole of them for long. There didn't seem to be much
theory about this. It was plain common sense to me.

My search through the book shops was eventually rewarded when
I came across the thing I was looking for. It was called *The Theory
and Practice of Trade Unionism* by J. H. Greenwood. I had read an
earlier book by the same author, who was a barrister, *The Law
Relating to Trade Unions*, and I felt I understood it pretty well. The
book he had now written was a most lucid summary of the larger
work by Beatrice and Sidney Webb, a remarkable volume entitled
Industrial Democracy. I had read the *History of Trade Unionism* by
the Webbs, rather casually, I am afraid, but it was some time before
I could obtain a copy of this book. When at last I secured one—
second-hand, as usual—I made notes in pencil on almost every page,
despite my disapproval of this obnoxious habit.

I felt now that I had a good grip on the subject of collective
bargaining. The principal object of any trade union is to combine
workpeople so that they will not sell their labour below the figure
which they themselves have agreed upon. This is what the union
aims at. It is not always successful. It finds itself faced with a trade
union of the employers. They don't often call it a trade union. It is
usually called an association or a federation, but it acts in just the
same way as the unions do. The principle running right through all
such bodies, whether of workpeople or employees, is the same. The
people forming them combine with one another to avoid cutting one
another's throats by unrestricted competition in the sphere of wages
or salaries. Many employers' associations have other objects as well,
and so have many trade unions, but here I am dealing with the
primary purpose of such organizations. Most skilled unions paid

benefits to their members for sickness, unemployment, or accident long before there was any State provision for any of these hazards. Nearly all unions paid their members benefits in trades disputes.

In 1911 many associations of employers had also the purpose of keeping up prices by rings or cartels or trusts, but usually that object was performed by a separate association. Unlike the employers, who were free to raise the price of goods or services which they sold, the trade unions couldn't just fix their rates of wages with the knowledge that these would automatically come into operation on a certain date. They had to bargain with the trade union of the employers, and by this process of negotiation or collective bargaining an agreement was usually reached. These agreements were not in any sense legally binding upon the parties. They were voluntary agreements, and the law gave them no recognition at all. If the parties could not reach the agreement they were usually free to act as they thought fit. The employers could lock the men out, or the union members could with-hold their labour, or, in other words, strike. Nowadays another course is usually preferred, and both sides agree to call in some person or persons as a conciliator or arbitrator. The difference between the two is that a conciliator can only make proposals to the parties, whereas an arbitrator can give a decision. Unless it is expressly stated beforehand that his decision will be accepted there is nothing more than a moral compulsion on the parties to apply his verdict. All this seems very elementary in 1964, but it was not so well understood in 1911.

There was no collective bargaining for electricians in the Mersey area when I joined the union. Our union, formed in 1889, was a young one as trade unions go: electricity was in its infancy, although its use was rapidly expanding. General organization amongst the electricians was on the upgrade, but, nevertheless, was not good. Throughout the whole country there were fewer than 3,500 members. Nor were the firms undertaking electrical contracting any better organized. An Electrical Contractors' Association had been formed in 1904, but under its constitution it was unable to negotiate conditions of labour with the trade unions. Some of the contractors joined the Master Builders' Association, but there were more who were in no organization at all. Electricians engaged in contracting work secured what wages they could by individual bargaining with the employers at the time of engagement. Generally speaking, except in cases of men with special skill, $8\frac{1}{2}d$. per hour was the general rate. Some firms paid only $8d$. an hour. The firm where I worked was one of the exceptions. The 'boss' himself had been an electrician, and as he favoured trade unionism and his men were well organized, he paid us all $9d$. per hour.

The E.T.U. members were principally employed in three sections of industry in the Mersey area: (1) shipbuilding, (2) shipping and ship-repairing, and (3) electrical contracting. There were no agreed wages or working rules in any of them. The firms paid what they considered fair, so we set about applying the principles of collective bargaining. Cammell Laird's were practically the only firm on Merseyside engaged in shipbuilding on a large scale. They were members of the Shipbuilding Employers' Federation, a very strong body, and consequently they were the hardest nut to crack. As Sir George Carter, the managing director, once said to me, 'I am in the big federation and you can't squeeze me.' But we tried to, just the same.

The workers on Merseyside were notoriously a militant lot, and the firm didn't have things all their own way. We had several branches of the E.T.U. in the Mersey area, the principal ones being in Liverpool, Birkenhead, and Bootle. They operated together through a district committee, on which each of them was represented. This committee drew up three codes of working rules, each of them adapted to suit a separate section and designed in such a way that the hourly wages in each would be approximately the same.

Our general secretary was Mr. James Rowan, a full-time official and one of the best negotiators in the movement. He sent these rules to the association of employers whose names and addresses we had given him, and also to those firms who were known not to be members of any association. Rowan expressed the readiness of the union to discuss these rules with the employers with the object of establishing an agreed code. The individual unorganized firms were asked to conform to them. Then the fun started. It was the duty of the members to do all they could to bring pressure on the different firms to induce them to come into line. Some firms did so without demur, but others contended that we should first negotiate our rules with the respective employers' associations. Then they would conform to whatever was agreed between us. Naturally we pressed them individually despite their objections, and were successful in getting many to accept. The most poorly organized section was, as I have said, electrical contracting, and there was much coming and going amongst electricians who moved from firm to firm chasing higher wages and better conditions. They were pretty successful, but nothing happened for months so far as the associations were concerned.

I was then a member of the district committee, which decided it was time to turn on the heat with the shipowners and the repairing firms. So it was that in December 1912 our first strike took place. It was unofficial and was run by a strike committee of members; we received no financial help whatever from the head office, nor did we expect it.

The effect of the strike was felt quickly, and promises were forthcoming from the shipping employers of an early conference provided the men resumed work in the meantime. This they refused to do, and finally a meeting of the Steamship Superintendent Engineers' Committee and the Mersey Ship Repairers' Federation and the Liverpool Master Builders united in offering a joint conference. On our advice the men accepted this. There was not much difficulty in getting appropriate codes of rules agreed, separate sets of rules being adopted to suit the different sections. The major difference was that the employers wanted a three-year agreement and the union twelve months. There was a real tug-of-war over this, and it was not until a strike of all sections of members had been threatened that the shorter period was agreed. Cammell Laird's had also assented to a code of rules, and advances raising wages to 9d. an hour were provided for In the contracting section there was to be a further increase of ½d. per hour within six months. The hours of work were to be fifty-three per week in shipbuilding and repairing and fifty in contracting. By July 1913 all three sets of rules were being operated.

When I was working for a firm of contractors in the spring of 1912 I was sent to wire a house in West Kirby. I was alone for most of the time and as the weather was mild and sunny I had my midday sandwich and lemonade on the top of a nearby hill overlooking the sea. There was a high obelisk at this spot erected where it could be seen easily from seawards. It was of sandstone and many visitors had carved their initials on its base. I had been courting my sweetheart Doris Slade for some years with a view to marriage in the following year. We were engaged formally and so I decided to commemorate this and cut out our full names on an unobtrusive spot with my screw-driver. I have inspected my handiwork several times in the intervening years and the inscription still stands out as clearly as it did when it was first cut. Vandalism? Well, perhaps. But I prefer to look upon it as a symbol of the way in which our lives were to be intertwined in an indissoluble bond of affection which has brought us fifty years of unbroken married happiness.

3
Learning the Job

I HAD several other jobs at my trade in Liverpool, Birkenhead, and the Isle of Man, until in October 1914 I was elected the first full-time district secretary of the E.T.U. Candidates had to be nominated by at least one branch, submit a written election address, speak to an aggregate meeting of members from all the branches, and answer questions as to their fitness to fill the position. I enjoyed the experience, and while there were other candidates whose trade union experience exceeded my own, I felt confident of the result. Nor was I disappointed, as the ballot showed a considerable majority for myself. I was familiar with the various agreements which had been reached in the district and I had a slight acquaintance with the officials of the different employer bodies through meeting them on delegations.

A levy to pay for the cost of a district secretary was insufficient to provide an office and a typist, or any other kind of clerical assistance, so I had to make do with a duplicate book supplied from head office to the branch secretaries. I was then living in Egremont and conducted my work from my home. I had no telephone. This was not my idea of efficiency and I was determined at the first opportunity to find some means of securing an office and a telephone. When my appointment started the district rates of pay to electricians in the respective sections of industry were: electrical contracting, 40s. 10d. for forty-nine hours; ship-repairing, 39s. 9d. for forty-seven hours; and shipbuilding, 44s. for fifty-three hours. Considerable overtime was being worked in all of these sections, particularly in ship-repairing and shipbuilding, which carried compound rates of pay. My salary was £2 10s. per week, plus travelling and incidental expenses, these amounting to only a few shillings a week.

After I had been in office for some months the executive council of the union were empowered to make a grant towards the maintenance of local full-time officials, another full-time district secretary having by that time been elected in the London area. This made things easier for me, and after working from my home for twelve

41

months I was authorized by the district committee to take a small office in Don Chambers, Paradise Street, Liverpool. The letter book was replaced by a typewriter—a second-hand one, of course—and a telephone was installed. Somehow or other I became sufficiently skilled to type my own letters, though I never got beyond the stage of using one finger on each hand. I started to learn shorthand as well; I soon grew fond of the Gregg system, with its shapely curves and absence of shading and positioning. I made rapid progress, having the good fortune to secure the interest of Ernest Crockett, one of the fastest shorthand-writers in the country. He took a special interest in me and he had the ability to read my notes upside down from the opposite side of the table from where I was sitting. He was then drilling me for speed-writing which I was eager to attain. I learned the outlines and phrases easily, my wife dictating them to me in the evenings, holding our little son on her knee and reading from the textbook in her other hand.

Why did I take this trouble? It was patent to me that when my colleagues saw that I was writing everything down verbatim they were almost certain to make me a member of various delegations to meet employers and others. I also had a sneaking ambition to show the employers that someone on the trade union side could take as accurate a record of meetings as any of their paid secretaries. My proficiency increased to the point when I was made a member of the Order of Gregg Artists, which was limited to those capable of writing artistic shorthand. Gregg shorthand has been my daily companion throughout fifty years.

When I was later able to engage a typist I selected one from the Gregg School, who was consequently able to read and transcribe my notes: I found this a great help. I was something of a pioneer amongst district trade union officials in taking an office and a typist for my trade union work: most of the secretaries and delegates of other unions had to work from their homes. This had the disadvantage not only of inadequate facilities but of making the secretary's family the victims of every disgruntled member who might come along at any hour to unload his troubles. Many district officials still have to suffer loss of their precious hours of leisure and the invasion of their home life owing to the absence of an office.

In my tiny office at Don Chambers I felt like a business magnate in comparison with them. I attended regularly the meetings of the Federation of Engineering and Shipbuilding Trades, to which the Electrical Trades Union was affiliated; and, as I expected, I found myself installed as a reporter to almost every delegation that was appointed. This gave me the sort of scope and experience I desired;

and after becoming a member of all the appropriate committees I was installed as president of the local federation in 1918. A year later I became the secretary, a purely voluntary office, and continued until 1920, when I left the Mersey district on being elected an assistant general secretary of the E.T.U. in Manchester.

I got on well with the employers. At first I used to slang them on the platform and sometimes to their faces, but as I became more experienced I realized there was little advantage in this. Most of them were people of the same clay as myself. I met all sorts of employers individually, as well as collectively—the amiable, the kindly, the aggressive, the suave, the evasive, the doleful, the dynamic, the procrastinators, the voluble, and the strong and silent. In short, I met most of the same types of humanity as the members of my own union. Usually they were better educated and more experienced in dealing with people, but I knew that in the same setting most of the trade unionists for whom I was working would act much the same as did employers. One of the employers used to make a final appeal to me 'as a man of the world'. I always knew when he brought out this phrase that he had exhausted his arguments. Some of them would pour out their troubles to me, exhorting me to believe that their only real object in life was to provide work for their employees. They would then go on graphically to describe the worries and cares of an employer's life. I didn't always believe them. I noticed that those who were full of their business misfortunes seemed somehow to be doing pretty well.

Meetings with the employers as a body were usually conducted in a friendly vein and seldom did they end in a row. They made full allowance for the strong language we sometimes used, feeling no doubt, as Sir George Carter of Cammell Laird's once said to me, 'I know you have got to do it: it is part of your job.' I am afraid I didn't so regard it. I really meant what I said, and I despised those who spoke with their tongue in their cheek.

The Electrical Trades Union members have throughout the union's history been a militant lot, and those of the Mersey district were amongst the most active. I made it my business to keep as closely in contact with them as I could. We were always having meetings: mass meetings we called them, although the numbers who attended were sometimes no more than a couple of hundred. Such meetings had to be held in the evenings when the men were able to attend, and what with visits to the branches in turn, attending district committee meetings and those of the Engineering and Shipbuilding Trades Federation, I had few evenings to myself.

I recall coming home very late one night from one of these

meetings. I ran into one of our members on the Wallasey ferryboat bound for Seacombe; we chatted for a while about generalities, and then he said to me suddenly, 'You don't mind if I tell you something?'

'Not at all,' I answered, thinking I was in for some secret concerning the union or its affairs.

To my surprise he said rather indignantly: 'You are going to kill yourself the way you are going on. It's all right thinking that when you are dead the workers will be going round saying, "Remember Citrine, remember Citrine." But you won't hear them because you will be dead. Don't be a fool.'

What astonished me was the air of genuine concern with which he uttered this. Perhaps he had heard that at a meeting earlier in the same week I had been compelled to stop in the middle of a speech because of a sudden pain at my heart. Fortunately I never had a recurrence of this suspected heart trouble.

I liked meeting the members and explaining things to them, particularly the shop stewards, who were the most active and the best informed. They were a valuable medium of communication between the union and the rank and file. There was a skeleton system of shop stewards in operation when I took over, and I developed this. Our district committee made a rule to the effect that wherever five or more men were employed one of them had to be appointed to represent the union as a shop steward. They were, of course, elected by their fellow workers.

I listed all the different firms in the various sections of the industry where our members were employed and gave each of these firms a number. The shop steward carried a credential card signed by me and also a numbered rubber stamp corresponding to the number I had given to his firm. I could tell at a glance on looking at any member's contribution card and seeing the stamp where he was working. If there was no stamp on his card I would interrogate him to find out the reason, as the shop steward (we called them shop delegates) was required to inspect the members' cards every month. It wasn't always easy to get men to serve as shop delegates. There was a feeling amongst them that they might make themselves marked men who would be discharged at the first opportunity because of their union activities. I met few instances of this actually happening. It was seldom that I had to complain of our shop stewards exceeding their duties by calling the men out, although this had happened under great provocation in isolated instances.

I have never wavered in my conviction that the shop stewards system should be an inherent part of the mechanism of trade unionism, and that those unions are wise who keep their shop stewards closely linked with the official machinery. Decidedly they were a great help to me in seeing that the electricians were well organized, that newcomers on a job were speedily brought into membership, and that the members' arrears of contributions were kept down to a minimum.

I loved to mix with the men on the ships, particularly the big Atlantic liners, and I had pretty well a free entry to all of them. It was not always so, as in the beginning I sometimes encountered opposition to my interviewing the shop steward or the members in their working time. I remember visiting a naval vessel on which a dozen or more electricians were working. It was my invariable practice to go to the foreman or chargehand and ask if I could see the shop steward. I did not like the method of stopping individual men and talking to them, as was the practice of some union officials. I was never refused permission to see anyone, but I always obtained it first. On this occasion, after I had gone through this routine, I was talking to one of the members when I was accosted by a petty officer. I told him who I was and a few minutes afterwards an officer arrived and demanded that I should go ashore. I refused to do this, and finally the commanding officer was brought. He had a telescope under his arm, although the ship was in dock. Possibly he wanted to see the correct time from the clock in the tower of the Royal Liver Building. He greeted me with, 'How dare you come on my ship?'

I retorted: 'Your ship? I thought this vessel belonged to the Government.'

With that retort the row started, and culminated in the officer calling a couple of the crew to escort me down the gangway to the quay. I made a hasty estimate of their combined strength and decided to go ashore. Soon afterwards the shop steward arrived on the quay; I explained to him what had happened. The outcome of this was that all the electricians on the ship were gathered round me on the quay in a protesting group. When this was observed by the commanding officer I could see that he was puzzled and rather worried. His anxiety increased when the chargehand told him who I was, and informed him that it was customary for union officials to be allowed access to their members. It was amusing when I was eventually allowed to return on board at the head of the electricians, led by the shop steward. I felt some sense of power which compensated me for the surliness with which I had been treated.

Tramping round the docks and on the ships was tiring. I hadn't the faintest knowledge of how to conserve my energy, and I was often puzzled why it was that I felt so tired at times when I had done apparently little physical work to account for it. I didn't realize the mental strain entailed by negotiations and meetings, interviews, making speeches, discussions, and the like. Nor did our members, who seemed to think that I had inexhaustible sources of energy to devote exclusively to their affairs.

Most of the local trade union officials were in the same boat as myself, but I seldom heard them complain. Like me, they were usually happy in their work. They had long ceased to expect any semblance of gratitude, no matter how valiantly they strove on behalf of their members. I was better off than most, both in salary and (I flatter myself) in the understanding which existed between the members and myself. Certainly I think that the methods I adopted in keeping in step with the rank and file were better than those employed by most unions. Our branch meetings were usually much better attended than those of the older unions, such as the boilermakers', carpenters', shipwrights', engineers', and others. Sometimes branch meetings of these organizations resolved themselves into some half a dozen members and were principally devoted to collecting contributions. Men would often send their wives with these. All this may have changed for the better, but it is still regrettable that so few trade unionists make use of the facilities they have for interesting themselves in the work of their organization.

Such leisure as I now had for reading was devoted almost entirely to newspapers and periodicals connected with my work. One day an electrician who sometimes worked as a bookmaker's clerk talked to me about literature and revealed a knowledge of books far beyond my own. He introduced me to Artemus Ward, Thackeray, and Charles Dickens. I became fond of them all and many other authors whose works are today regarded as classics. I read every book of Dickens, and some of them several times. When I moved from Merseyside nothing gave me greater pleasure than being presented by the members with a beautifully bound set of Dickens's works, which has remained one of my treasures ever since.

My liking for good literature didn't cause me to neglect the technical side of my work, but I think it broadened my outlook. I had not then discovered the joy of reading Shakespeare and Chaucer, which was later to bring me so much happiness. But I often visited the Liverpool Repertory Theatre to see the plays of Shaw, Galsworthy, Wilde, Barrie, and others. Whenever possible I was on the spot when the Gilbert and Sullivan London company visited Merseyside. I was slowly finding out that there were other good things in life besides trade unionism.

Throughout the whole of the time I was a district official I tried to learn everything which would help me improve my qualifications and broaden my experience. I was probably the youngest of the local officials, and I could not compare in maturity of judgement with the older men. I realized that more and more negotiations would turn upon questions of finance or economic considerations, and I set about getting to know something of commercial practice. I read various books on economics and accountancy, among them *The Accountant's Compendium* by a Wallasey man, Sydney Dawson, and a first-class book at that. I learned how to analyse a company balance sheet, and about such things as reserve funds, bonus shares, and depreciation.

I always had a hankering after legal knowledge and I came across a little book which I think was called Harris's *Hints on Advocacy*. I learned a lot from that. Eventually I felt competent to hold my own in the rough-and-tumble of discussion with the employers. I didn't neglect to read the financial columns of the Press and some of the trade journals, including the *Liverpool Journal of Commerce*, which dealt primarily with shipping. I did not do this with the idea of investing money in any concern, since I had none; and I have never held a share in a private company in my life. My purpose was to equip myself with knowledge which I felt was required to carry out my work efficiently. The *Industrial Democracy* of the Webbs became my bible, and I knew it from cover to cover. I began to realize that Karl Marx was not the fountain of wisdom in all he wrote, as I had previously supposed.

I learned a good deal from the employers: firstly, from their method of conducting a case. Instead of everyone feeling impelled to speak, as our chaps used to do, they usually had one spokesman only, their chairman almost invariably acting in that capacity. Secondly, whenever our delegations attended we found the employers already seated at the table with their backs to the light. They could watch our expressions much more clearly than we could watch theirs. A small thing, perhaps, but certainly not an accident. Usually their speakers were far more precise than we were, although their conversational style of speech struck me sometimes as a tactical method and lacking in sincerity. Most of us had not learned to get away from the platform style of delivery. We felt that the more emphasis we put into our statements, the stronger our case became. We frequently went into the room without any concerted preparation. It was assumed that our chairman and secretary would put the case, but no one felt that this implied any limitation on his own right to speak.

Apart altogether from individual employers, I had to correspond and negotiate with separate associations for electrical contractors, shipbuilders, and ship-repairers. All the leading shipping companies whose vessels sailed out of Liverpool were organized in the Port of Liverpool Employers' Association, which worked in conjunction with the Mersey Ship Repairers Federation.

My first important case to go to arbitration with this joint body of shipowners and ship-repairers was in November 1918. Strikes were prohibited by law in wartime and arbitration thus became compulsory, all the principal cases going before the Committee on Production, of which Sir George Askwith was the chairman. Incidentally, the secretary was Horace Wilson, who subsequently became the Permanent Secretary to the Ministry of Labour, and later still the trusted adviser of Baldwin and Neville Chamberlain. The Committee on Production orginally included Sir George Gibb, a former solicitor and ex-chairman of the Road Board, and Sir David Harrell, who at one time was Chief Commissioner of the Dublin Police. Askwith became noted for his method of settling disputes by attrition. A thin-faced man in his fifties, with a rather spare figure and a grey moustache, he would keep the parties in conference for hours at a stretch without any opportunity for food or refreshment. Sometimes they felt so hungry that they were glad to settle. Sometimes it worked the other way and made the participants so irritable that they were in no mood for compromise.

The volume of cases became so heavy that the Committee on Production had to be enlarged and split into panels. Both Gibb, nearing the seventies, and Harrell, a bearded man who was a few years younger, became chairman of these panels. Gibb, a gentle-looking soul with a smooth-shaven face, on one occasion said something to me which I have never forgotten. 'You don't prove a thing by asserting it, Mr. Citrine,' he said mildly. He beamed at me as he said it, but that did not diminish either its relevance or importance. Our case was a straightforward application for an advance in wages. I was at the time the secretary of the Federation of Engineering and Shipbuilding Trades in the Mersey district and it was my job to lead the case for the unions. I prepared thoroughly and went along to Old Palace Yard full of confidence.

After a preliminary opening by our chairman, Jim Smythe, I held forth for about twenty minutes. After slanging the employers in the approved fashion of the day I got within measurable distance of the merits of our case. Askwith and his colleagues listened patiently without batting an eyelid, although they must have known that some of my sources of information were not very reliable.

The reply from the employers' chairman, Mr. Charles Booth, was extremely fair and he was charitable in his references to the figures I had quoted. I was convinced we had established our case.

Afterwards we printed some thousands of copies of the shorthand notes and circulated them widely amongst the workers. Those were days when there was a good deal of mistrust of trade union officials among their members. I was satisfied that once the men knew what had been said in the proceedings some of this was bound to be removed. Later experience confirmed this, and as a district official I never had reason to complain of the relations between the members and myself. 'Keep your people fully informed', was my doctrine, and still is.

As I have said, strikes were prohibited by law during the war of 1914–18, but that didn't prevent their taking place. There was a crop of unofficial strikes on Merseyside. Some of them were caused by the autocratic way some naval officers treated the workmen. On one occasion at Birkenhead one of these gentlemen placed the shipwrights' and boilermakers' local officials under arrest because of a demarcation dispute. It didn't take the unions long to demonstrate the folly of this kind of conduct which, instead of settling disputes, merely provoked more of them. I remember one incident which occurred on the auxiliary cruiser *Teutonic*. She was one of the best-known vessels of the White Star Line and had been fitted out with guns earlier in the war. Late one afternoon I received a telephone message to the effect that two electricians had been placed under arrest by the ship's captain. He had remarked that they might be a couple of German spies. I at once went along to the *Teutonic* and found that all the electricians had walked off the ship. I discussed the matter shortly with the shop steward and was permitted to interview the two men. It appeared that the captain had come across them lounging on one of the lower decks and, according to them, he at once called upon a sentry who locked them up. What rankled most was that he had called them German spies.

After I had collected the men's story I saw the naval officer concerned, who at first took a high-handed attitude. While we were conversing, information came that the workmen of all trades on the *Teutonic*, some 500 of them, having learned what had taken place, were leaving the ship. The captain at once released the two men, and I hoped that the matter would be at an end. Not so. When I harangued the men, who were massed on the quay, I found they were demanding that the captain should be removed. I was told that some of the shop stewards had already departed for other vessels in port which were being repaired by the same firm, Harland and Wolff. The

D

probability was that they too would stop work. By this time it was after six o'clock, and I went to the office of the Port Admiral. He was not available, but after considerable telephoning it was arranged that an interview should take place on the following morning between the Port Admiral, the captain of the *Teutonic*, and myself.

Next morning, before the captain came, I explained fully to the admiral what had occurred, and stressed that trouble was spreading to other ships. My latest information was that nearly 5,000 men were now idle. The admiral was much perturbed at the precipitate conduct of the captain, but he was adamant against the demand for his removal. That could only be done by a court martial, he emphasized, and he didn't want the affair to go as far as that. Nor did I. I said that the men were particularly incensed by the captain calling the two electricians German spies. The admiral concurred, but said there were spies operating in the Liverpool docks.

After this the captain was brought in. I have seldom heard a man receive a more thorough dressing-down. 'What are your sentries at the gangways for?' demanded the admiral. The captain was subdued and repeatedly said that if he had done anything wrong he was ready to apologize. To which the admiral retorted: 'I haven't said you have done anything wrong. But you have acted like a bloody fool.' This was becoming embarrassing for me and I broke in to say that I felt sure that the men would readily accept the captain's apology for the mistake. But I was wrong. I went to the firm's yard to find a crowd of some thousands standing about and being addressed by the shop stewards from a lorry which had been drawn up as a platform. I climbed on it, and was introduced to the crowd who didn't know me from a crow. I could see several men in bowler hats, whom I recognized as foremen and managers, on the outskirts of the crowd listening to the speakers. I addressed the men, reporting faithfully the facts of the incident and concluding with the captain's readiness to apologize. There were loud shouts: 'Remove him. Clear the b——r out.' But I persisted, telling them that the captain would make his apology in front of the shop stewards of all the unions involved in the dispute. I asked them: 'How many of you would humble yourselves in such a public manner? Have you ever before heard of a senior naval officer doing so?' The shop stewards backed me up manfully and the men voted by show of hands to accept our recommendation.

We trooped along to the *Teutonic* and I went to the captain's cabin, the shop stewards having been marshalled in the gun room.

'The men are ready for you now, sir,' I said, feeling downright sorry for him. He was deathly pale and evidently suffering nervous strain.

We went along to face the dungaree-clad shop stewards who were standing in a half-circle. I simply announced, 'The captain has something to say to you.' He said, 'I have come here to apologize publicly for arresting two of your men.' He got no further, for at once there was a spontaneous shout of 'That's all right, sir. Everything's all right now.' The incident ended with the captain shaking hands with each of them. I admired both the captain and the shop stewards who were so sincerely desirous of sparing him the humiliation of a long explanation.

I came early on to understand that the process of collective bargaining between employers and trade unions must be based on good faith on both sides. I doubt whether many of the militant members of the Electrical Trades Union thought so, nor those of most other unions. The general impression was that both sides were 'at daggers drawn', and at times I was just as militant in trade union aims as were any of our members. But I knew that if our agreements were to be kept by both sides and interpreted fairly there must be reasonable confidence between all concerned. I have never wavered in that belief. Then, as now, I infinitely preferred voluntary agreements to State regulations in the relations between employers and workpeople. The operation of these would be impossible if both sides had the intention of wriggling out of their obligations at every opportunity. Most trade union officials of my acquaintance accepted that view but none of them was less vigilant for all that. I found that the men serving the employers' associations were chaps much like myself and they knew that continuous strife was of no ultimate benefit to either side. It was an advantage to them to know what the trade unions were thinking and how they were approaching any particular problem. Similarly, it was of value to me to have a clearer conception of what the employers were after than could be gained at the official meetings. So I set about cultivating the acquaintance of the employers' officials, and of being as frank with them as my duty to my members permitted. I tried to play straight with them and I found they did the same by me. We knew that ours was a continuing relationship, and that if one snatched a temporary advantage by sharp practice the other would be sure to get his own back some time or other. We fought each other in negotiations, but we never broke faith.

The wages of electricians in the contracting industry were settled by agreement with the newly formed National Federated Electrical

Association: this body had taken over the negotiations with the Electrical Trades Union formerly conducted by the Liverpool Master Builders' Association, whose secretary was the well-known Liverpool accountant B. B. Moss. He was a big cheery fellow of middle age and fresh complexion when I first met him, exact in his statements and scrupulously careful in all he did. On one occasion he asked me to call and see him. On my doing so he said that to recover the costs incurred by his members on Government and other contracts he would like me to agree in documentary form as to the actual wage advances which had been made to electricians during the war. We conferred together and agreed without difficulty, and I went away thinking the matter was settled. Soon afterwards negotiations took place in London between the executives of the N.F.E.A. and the Electrical Trades Union, the purpose of which was to secure a levelling-up of the overall advances which had been negotiated in the separate districts. By this agreement most of the districts received advances.

In the course of these negotiations the employers had produced the document signed by Moss and myself and had insisted that the national advance agreed upon must include the halfpenny per hour which had been granted at the beginning of the war in the Mersey district after a strike. This strike started in July 1914 and ended in August. It had always been looked upon as a pre-war advance and the effect of its inclusion in the national arrangements would have been to reduce the advance payable to the Mersey members. In other words, they would lose one halfpenny per hour. In 1964 this seems a small sum, but in 1914 the pound was worth more than four times its present value. Our executive felt compelled to agree with the employers' contention because of the document that I had signed.

Knowing that the Mersey members would kick up a row if they did not get the full national advance, plus the halfpenny per hour which they had obtained at the beginning of the war, the executive summoned me to a meeting in Manchester. It was plain that I was to be hauled over the coals. I went along and saw B. B. Moss, and told him the predicament I was in. He answered me frankly that he thought some of the employers were guilty of sharp practice. 'You don't think I would do a dirty trick like that,' he said indignantly. Turning to his secretary, he dictated a letter to me stressing that the halfpenny per hour must be kept distinct from the national advance and be in addition to it. I was grateful to him because there was nothing in writing to bear out my contention. At the executive meeting in Manchester I had to listen to severe reproaches of my carelessness. After enduring this for a while I produced the letter from Moss which completely vindicated my conduct. This staggered my critics and the case against me collapsed.

The longer I served as a district official the stronger grew the mutual confidence between the employers' officials and myself, so much so that individual firms would often ring me up and ask for my interpretation of any rule in our agreements which happened to be causing trouble. I always tried to consider these fairly, but, of course, if I could obtain a legitimate advantage for the electricians I did so. On the other hand, I don't think I ever lost the good opinion of the men by refusing to countenance extravagant claims for extra payment.

Generally speaking, our working rules were interpreted with fairness on both sides and I look back on a happy association with men of sterling character both on the side of the unions and of the employers. As I write, an array of people passes before my mind, the mere catalogue of whose names would occupy considerable space. Of the employers, I can mention three only. These were Charles Booth, who was the chairman of the Booth Steamship Company and also the chairman of the Employers' Association of the Port of Liverpool, Sir George Carter, who was managing director of Cammell Laird Ltd. at their shipyard in Birkenhead, and Lord Leverhulme, of Port Sunlight.

Charles Booth was about fifty when I first met him. He was a quietly spoken man of fresh complexion and medium height and build, always carefully dressed and affable in manner. I think he came from a Quaker family and that he was related to another Charles Booth who wrote of the Life and Labour of the People in London and on other social subjects. He was an excellent negotiator, patient and kindly, and never once that I recall did he lose his temper or show signs of irritability. We all felt he was a decent chap, and that counts for a great deal in industrial negotiations. I remember with pleasure that when on the occasion of his retirement a dinner was held in his honour, at which he was presented with a memento of his work in labour relations, I was chosen as spokesman on behalf of the trade unions who were represented.

Sir George Carter was a different type from Charles Booth. He was as rugged as they make them, powerfully built with a prominent jaw and strong and somewhat hard features. He was a shipbuilder to his finger-tips. He came to Cammell Laird's with a great reputation because of his experience in building warships. He was a few years older than Charles Booth, and a much harder nut to crack in nego-tiations. His approach on any subject was entirely informal, and, although I never heard him use bad language, I felt sure he could have rivalled most of his workpeople in a slanging match.

He became president of the powerful Shipbuilding Employers' Federation, and was quick to perceive and express himself forcibly on the controversial issues which so frequently arose with the trade unions. I well recall the scene in the Caxton Hall, London, shortly after the end of the 1914–18 war, when the unions were pressing for the reduction of the working week from fifty-three hours to forty-seven. Sir Allan Smith in his reply for the engineering employers had displayed the usual dilatory tactics he resorted to whenever a union demand was under consideration. The indignation which most of us felt was giving way to deep anger when Carter jumped up and in his outspoken manner completely repudiated the line taken by Smith, whose arguments he brushed aside peremptorily, greatly to the delight of all of us. It was the only occasion on which I have seen such open disagreement between the spokesmen of such influential employers' organizations. Its effect was decisive and made the result a foregone conclusion as was seen when the forty-seven-hour week was introduced in both shipbuilding and engineering shortly afterwards.

I infinitely prefer the outspoken, straight-from-the-shoulder type of man such as Carter to the subtle procrastinator who promises one thing and means to do something different.

I was not alone in possessing the confidence of the employers. Most of the local trade union officials would never have dreamt of breaking faith. Each of these men had their own strong individuality. They wouldn't have got far in the trade union movement without it. I can mention only three. There was Jack Clarke of the engineers, a speaker of great clarity, tenacious as a bulldog, and ready on the least provocation to have a row with his rivals in demarcation squabbles; Jim Smythe of the plumbers, whose Irish wit was added to a keen sense of humour and logical reasoning and who could put a detailed case with precision; and Tom Griffiths of the shipwrights, full of vim and a most persistent negotiator who hung on to a point long after most people would have given it up.

The third of the employers to whom I referred was Viscount Leverhulme. My earliest personal encounter with him was in October 1918. Earlier I had seen him on the election platform when he was contesting the Parliamentary Division of Wirral as a Liberal. I was only thirteen at the time but an enthusiastic politician. Not that I knew anything about politics, but that was no handicap, as my father was a staunch Conservative (he changed later to Labour) and what was good enough for my father was—by typical conservative reasoning—good enough for me.

Apart from politics, I had seen Leverhulme on a number of occasions long before he was elevated to the peerage, although I had never had any sustained conversation with him. He was a sprightly, fresh-complexioned fellow, small of stature but sturdy, and usually wore a grey suit and top hat and, on occasions, a fancy waistcoat. He had keen restless eyes and he would have attracted notice in most places. Few would have thought as they looked at his smooth clean-shaven face that at one time he had had a dark luxuriant beard.

Although I had transacted considerable business with Lever Brothers on behalf of the electricians, I had usually met the managing director, John Grey, a precise but reasonable man: but this time the issue was too serious for John Grey to settle on his own responsibility. In September 1918 there was a strike of electricians in the Mersey district over a non-union foreman employed at the Aintree munitions factory. The strike was settled by the foreman joining the union, and on its conclusion the Ministry of Munitions gave an undertaking that there was to be no victimization. Soon after the strike was finished the electricians complained to me that Levers were penalizing them by withholding or reducing co-partnership benefits. So, as John Grey did not feel he had the authority to settle the matter, it was arranged that I should meet Leverhulme at Port Sunlight. I marched up the stairs to the office in company with a few of my members and found myself faced with Leverhulme and half a dozen of his directors and officials. Leverhulme started not by asking me to put our case but by immediately taking up the running himself. I had written, of course, objecting to the firm's action and Leverhulme insisted that no one had any rights under the co-partnership scheme except those granted at the discretion of the founder (himself).

It is not the merits of his arguments with which I am here concerned: it is his method. He spoke in a conversational tone, and his discourse was so closely reasoned that he almost convinced me. When at length Leverhulme asked me whether I wished to say anything I started to controvert much of what he had said. I had scarcely begun before he butted in with an appropriate anecdote or an objection to counter my argument. It was all done courteously and indeed affably, but the result was that the interview finished with my feeling I had been completely defeated on every material point.

I left the room and I had reached the bottom of the staircase when I recalled that I had not asked for a copy of the shorthand notes. I returned upstairs and knocked at the door. There was no response. I could hear the sound of voices. So, thinking that possibly it was the secretary and the shorthand writer conversing, I turned the handle of the door and walked in. Standing in a line at the top of the room like a squad of recruits were the directors and officials. Leverhulme was walking across the front of them with his head down and his hands clasped behind his back. The directors could see me but Leverhulme couldn't until he reached the end of his traverse and turned to go the other way. Then he looked at me for a few seconds with a scowling face, flushed with anger. There was a silence whilst he struggled to regain control of himself. Then he said quietly, 'What is it, Mr. Citrine?'

I explained why I had returned and apologized for the intrusion, saying that if I had known he was still in conference I would have waited, but that I had knocked and there had been no reply.

Leverhulme at once accepted my explanation and gave instructions that I was to receive the shorthand notes immediately they were ready. What he had been saying to his directors I can only guess, but they certainly looked very chastened. He had the reputation for treating the directors and managers severely if they incurred his displeasure. He was credited with saying that 'no one is indispensable at Lever Brothers and anyone who thinks he is can quickly be paid off'.

After taking leave of my colleagues, who were waiting for me outside the building, I walked down the tree-lined avenues at Port Sunlight with its pleasant greens and neat Tudor-type houses, feeling very dejected. Up to that time I had been pretty confident of being able to hold my own with most of the people I had to meet. Leverhulme had shown how inexpert I was and (it seemed to me), how far I was below his intellectual level. It was this thought which troubled me most. Could I ever overcome the handicap of my elementary education and equip myself to face such men without a hopeless feeling of inferiority?

On reaching Birkenhead I crossed the River Mersey by the ferry-boat to the Liverpool landing stage and boarded a second boat for Seacombe. All the time the thought kept recurring to me, 'Will I ever be any good?' My confidence was shattered completely. Then a thought struck me. I recalled reading the libel action of Lever Brothers v. Associated Newspapers and Others, which had been heard at the Liverpool Assizes. Two separate actions had been taken by Levers, the first of which was heard in July 1907. Sir Edward Carson (later Lord Carson), then at the height of his fame, had led throughout for Lever Brothers, assisted by Mr. F. E. Smith (later Lord Birkenhead) and other distinguished counsel. Rufus Isaacs (later Lord Reading) appeared for the defendants. He, too, was at the zenith of his powers and it was a real enjoyment to me to read the speeches and questions of these two eminent men in the *Liverpool Echo*, my favourite evening newspaper.

The outcome of the first action was a settlement on Levers' own terms, £50,000 (an unprecedented amount) being paid by the defendants as damages and a public apology being made in court. In this action Lever had proved himself a dexterous and convincing witness. Not content with the heavy damages in this action, Lever Brothers sued other newspapers. But this time it was a different story. They had taken an action against the publishers of the *Leeds Mercury*. The case was heard on December 16th, 1908, when the brilliant powers of Rufus Isaacs as a cross-examiner were shown at their highest. The damages awarded were not £50,000 but £500 only, and when a few days later another action was heard against the Amalgamated Press and Associated Newspapers, Levers' counsel withdrew the case.

The first impression the cases made on me was the apparent mental superiority of Rufus Isaacs over Leverhulme when he was in the witness-box. Ruminating over this, I wondered to myself whether there was such a gulf between the intellectual capacity of Rufus Isaacs and Leverhulme as there appeared to be between Leverhulme and myself.

It came to me in a flash that such differences depended on method and environment. Leverhulme had had a great advantage over me in our interview. He knew his case thoroughly and, what was even more important, by his frequent interruptions, he never let me get my case out. It was his method as much as anything else which had nonplussed me. I resolved there and then that if I could manage it next time we met, I would hold the advantage.

It took much longer for the opportunity to arrive than I expected. Our next interview was very different and a completely informal one. The issue concerning the electricians and co-partnership had dragged on, and it was now becoming plain that the members of many other unions would be affected by whatever happened in the electricians' case. So I was invited to meet Leverhulme at the Liverpool offices of the firm, and I went there accompanied by the electricians' shop steward from Port Sunlight.

When we walked into the room it was to find Leverhulme seated at a little table on which were placed several instruments, the purpose of which was soon made known. This was long before the days of microphones and recorders. Leverhulme started off with: 'Mr. Citrine, Nature's been very kind to me. I went to the Congo and took too much quinine. It's made me very deaf, so I won't be able to hear the nasty things you are going to say about me, and if you put them in the newspapers I don't need to read them.'

'There is some philosophy in that,' I said, and I laughed. Leverhulme quickly responded and the interview proceeded smoothly. I told him frankly that the disqualifying of the electricians from co-partnership was his own personal decision and that his action went straight to the heart of trade unionism.

Our conversation went on in this vein and I think my shop steward friend, Fred Newton, made a good impression on Leverhulme, who agreed to re-examine the whole matter.

He then broached the much wider subject which had been raised by my criticism of co-partnership at Levers. Did this system provide any real remedy for the difficulties which arose in the relations between employers and workers? He remarked rather sadly: 'It took me twenty years to devise co-partnership in the form we have it at Levers, and now you tell me about all these defects. Perhaps my life's work has been all wrong. Perhaps I have misunderstood the minds of my workpeople.'

I felt rather touched by this, and remonstrated with him. 'Nobody could come to Port Sunlight,' I said, 'and see the great pioneering work you have done in housing as well as in the social sphere without realizing how far ahead you are of most other employers. I have never said that co-partnership was useless, nor that it was merely an employers' dodge to divorce workpeople from the trade unions, nor anything so silly. What I have said is that this scheme, good as it may be in its aims, is defective, and that these blemishes should be removed.'

Newton backed me up strenuously and Leverhulme seemed reassured by what we had said. We left Lever House with the promise that a thorough investigation would take place into co-partnership in which the trade unions would be invited to play a full part. The outcome was a full-scale inquiry at Port Sunlight which commenced on September 18th, 1919, and lasted several days under the chairmanship of Mr. W. A. Appleton, then the secretary of the General Federation of Trade Unions.

After the inquiry an interval of several weeks elapsed. Then I was invited to meet Leverhulme at the Liverpool office of the firm. I had not been warned by the firm, but I discovered that a number of co-partners, mainly electricians, had also been invited. I assumed from this that there was to be an attempt to show me up because of the leading part I had taken in the inquiry. But this time I knew the scheme backwards and was fully prepared for any emergency.

On arriving at the office I found assembled several directors and some thirty people in all. Leverhulme was in the chair and with the memory of our first meeting in mind I determined that this time the result would be different. I knew that Leverhulme had a fiery temper and I decided to rattle him at the outset. There was a strike of clerical workers in progress at Port Sunlight, so I inquired politely whether the person who was taking the shorthand notes was a member of the clerical staff at Levers. I was told that she was an employee of the company and I at once retorted that if she remained I could take no part in the proceedings. Leverhulme demanded angrily, 'Can't my own secretary take notes of this meeting?'

'Not whilst I am here,' I replied. After an animated discussion the proceedings were suspended until a shorthand writer was brought from Lee and Nightingales, a well-known Liverpool firm of reporters. By this time the atmosphere was far from peaceful, and Leverhulme turned to me and said rather peremptorily, 'What is it you want to see me about, Mr. Citrine?'

I replied, 'I am not aware that I wanted to see you.'

'Then why are we here?' he demanded.

'Because you invited me,' I said, pushing across to him a letter which he had evidently forgotten.

'That is not my letter,' he shouted, to which I retorted:

'It's your signature at the bottom but I don't know who dictated it.'

John Grey jumped up with the remark, 'There's a misunderstanding, sir.' He explained that he had dictated the letter after consultation with Leverhulme, who had signed it.

Leverhulme was taken aback, and figuring that I was on good ground I then read the letter aloud. It invited me to attend to consider the results of the inquiry into co-partnership.

I read the findings of the inquiry one by one, and when I came to the words that 'co-partnership and trade unionism at Lever Brothers are incompatible', Leverhulme broke out: 'That was Dr. Peck.' He turned and glared fiercely at one of the directors. 'I would never have admitted that.' Actually it was a unanimous conclusion of the whole inquiry, and Dr. Peck was no more responsible for it than anyone else.

When I received the shorthand notes of this meeting I found that all the acerbities had been removed. Whoever had edited the notes had striven manfully to give the substance of our exchanges without reporting the outspoken manner in which they had taken place. That suited me all right and I made no complaint.

In spite of everything I liked Leverhulme, martinet though I knew him to be. He was undoubtedly sincere in his efforts to make life better for his workpeople. He always disclaimed any element of sentimentality or philanthropy in his business affairs and asserted it was merely 'good business' which impelled his good actions. He was a pioneer far in advance of most employers of his generation. He was ready at one stage to introduce, entirely of his own free will, a six-hour day. This offer was made to the trade unions at a time when fifty-three hours a week, or even more, were common in many industries. I have no doubt whatever that he would have established this far-reaching reform but for the attitude of some of the trade unions who declined the proposal because it conflicted with their rules.

Many years later D'Arcy Cooper, who succeeded Leverhulme as chairman of the company, told me that the trouble with Leverhulme was that he wanted to be both chairman and office boy. One of his managerial colleagues who had had a lifetime's experience of working with Leverhulme said to me: 'He was a bit of a mixture. He firmly believed that whom the Lord loveth, he chasteneth. He felt that his young men should have their pants taken down now and again and be spanked.'

I have dealt with my Leverhulme experience at length because it was a decisive phase in my life. Had I not been able to recover my confidence I doubt whether I would ever have succeeded in my later work. As things turned out, I never again lost my self-confidence.

4

The Road to London

I BECAME interested in politics early in life from going canvassing with my father in blissful ignorance of what it was all about. I had attended election meetings with him and, like him, on election days I used to sport a blue rosette to show my staunch Conservatism. In my early days my workmate, Tom Brett, helped the process of political understanding with his daily diatribes against the capitalist system, but what I think first brought me into active politics was a quite different incident.

One Saturday evening I was strolling down Victoria Road, Seacombe (now Borough Road), when I saw a tall, slim-built man in a blue suit and wearing a soft black hat holding forth to a small but decidedly unfriendly group of onlookers. Curiosity caused me to cross the road to where he was standing at the top of one of the side streets. Whether it was that the rude interjections of his hecklers offended my sense of fair play, or whether it was the unruffled and easy manner with which the speaker dealt with the interrupters, I don't know, but I found myself listening intently to what he said. He would turn a jibe into a joke and set the crowd laughing at the interrupter. I was attracted by his self-possession and earnestness. I abandoned my intended walk and listened.

After the meeting I spoke to this man who had undertaken to speak entirely unsupported by any of his friends. It turned out that he was a commercial traveller named Jim Lunnon, and years later I met him at the Trades Union Congress. He was then an official of the National Union of Agricultural Workers. I resolved to follow his advice and go to the next meeting of the Independent Labour Party, which was to be held in an empty shop in Brighton Street. I was then about eighteen years of age. I had thought little about the basic questions of government or our communal life. When I arrived at the Sunday-evening meeting I found that about twenty men and women were present. There was a small stock of literature, chiefly paperbound books and pamphlets which could be bought for a few pence.

Amongst the books I bought were two, *Merry England* and *Britain for the British*. There was a visiting speaker who addressed the audience and subsequently answered questions for about half an hour.

When I reached home I started on *Britain for the British* by Robert Blatchford, of whom I had heard only faintly up to that time. My only source of Socialist propaganda had been Brett.

From its title I expected *Britain for the British* to be directed against foreigners in one way or another but to my surprise I found it a cogent and reasoned argument for Socialism. It was written with a clearness and bite which were unusual. I devoured the book and on the following Sunday I again attended the I.L.P. meeting. It wasn't long before I was enrolled as a member, and after having read *Merry England* I turned my attention to *Labour Leader* and a stream of Socialist pamphlets. It all seemed such common sense to me that I felt sure that once people had access to these founts of knowledge they couldn't avoid becoming Socialists. I didn't know so much about politics or human nature as I do today.

I was proud of my newly acquired knowledge, and got plenty of practice by starting an argument with my fellow electricians whenever I could, usually selecting a subject on which I had been doing some recent reading. By this process I gained confidence and eventually learned how to argue intelligently. Whenever I could I attended meetings addressed by prominent speakers and read everything I could lay my hands on.

The time arrived when I was asked whether I would give an address on some subject of my own choice to the members of the I.L.P. in Wallasey. I swotted up a subject which was of intense current interest. I borrowed a book by J. M. Robertson from the public library in Wallasey. It was on free trade and tariffs. The author was a highly competent writer and a strong free-trader. I memorized whole passages from this book, and, having carefully summarized Robertson's arguments, I went along to the meeting armed with copious notes to deliver my address. I created a favourable impression. As time went on I took the chair at other meetings both in and out of doors, gaining experience all the time. At length I was asked to be the speaker at one of the Sunday-morning meetings in Shiel Park, Liverpool. My chairman, an experienced old-timer, said as I climbed on to the little portable rostrum, 'Don't be afraid to bring in as much extraneous matter as you like, comrade.' What he really meant was, 'Don't hesitate to wander from your subject.' I didn't disappoint him.

I recall one question I was asked which is not unimportant in these days when dictatorships are challenging Parliamentary democracy as a system of government. It came from a regular attender who was probably an anarchist. He asked, 'Under Socialism, who will determine who are to be the controllers and who the controlled?' I disposed of this by blandly assuring my questioner that Socialism presupposed an intelligent democracy and I couldn't see such a democracy enslaving itself. Very convincing—in theory.

As the years passed, my enthusiasm was stimulated by hearing addresses from Ramsay MacDonald, with his organ-like voice and handsome presence, and Philip Snowden, then budding out as the financial expert—though not quite such an expert as he was reputed to be, as I discovered during my Trades Union Congress days. Snowden was always against strikes, and I don't think he cared much for trade unionism either. I rather agreed with Snowden at that time, as strikes seemed a clumsy and outmoded system of settling disputes. I was then barely twenty!

When I joined a trade union in 1911 and became immersed in its activities, politics receded more and more from my purview. I never weakened in my Socialist faith, but as I grew older I realized that political activity was not the only resource of the workers. I sought to attain some immediate benefits for working people by way of higher wages and shorter working hours, and I thought less about the ultimate advancement which I felt sure would accrue from politics. I didn't realize then as clearly as I do now that trade unionism and political activity, whether on the local or national plane, were not rivals but were complementary to each other and that each had its separate sphere, working in close co-operation with the other.

I had never shown any desire to become a Labour Party candidate for any sort of public office and I was surprised when in 1918 I was approached by a couple of politically active Wallaseyans to stand as parliamentary candidate in the forthcoming General Election. I was reluctant. I was fully engaged in trade union work, what with my duties in the Electrical Trades Union and my secretaryship of the local Federation of Engineering and Shipbuilding Trades. I wanted to concentrate on them. But I allowed myself to be persuaded, and on reaching home I announced to my astonished wife that, subject to the consent of my union, I was going to stand for Parliament. She, ever loyal and ready to subordinate her own immediate interests to my work, raised no objection, although she knew that if I was successful it would probably mean moving from the district in which she and I had been brought up. Consent was readily given by the Electrical Trades Union, and I started on my campaign: first by addressing the members of the Wallasey Labour Party and broadly outlining the sort of policy I would like to pursue in Parliament.

At the first public meeting at which I spoke I made a good impression, according to the *Wallasey News*, and wound up my peroration with the line of Robert Burns: 'A man's a man for a' that.' So carried away was I by my own eloquence—carefully prepared in advance—that I forgot to mention the programme on which the Labour Party would fight the election. It also seemed to have escaped the notice of the audience. No one seemed to mind.

I knew from the beginning that it would require a miracle for me to win such a notoriously Conservative seat as Wallasey, but I had heard that sometimes miracles do happen. The enthusiasm of my workers and supporters was infectious. My meetings went swimmingly, and the canvass was far from discouraging until the Prime Minister, Lloyd George, made his famous 'Land fit for heroes' speech. That dished the Labour Party. He promised almost everything, and he was the most powerful and perhaps the most popular man in British politics. There was little hope for us poor novices.

During the election the district office of the Electrical Trades Union was in The Arcade, Lord Street, Liverpool, and this gave me an occupier's vote in one of the city divisions. I received a communication to the effect that on a certain Saturday F. E. Smith (later Lord Birkenhead) would address the electors of this division. I turned up and to my surprise there were only about forty or fifty people present in the meeting room. When the great F.E. came along it was plain that he had lunched rather too well. There was no platform, the smallness of the room not requiring such a thing. F.E. placed his stick in front of him, leaned on it with both hands, and proceeded to deliver one of the clearest and most convincing speeches I have ever heard. He used no notes, yet each sentence was perfectly phrased and led in strict sequence to the next. I went away full of admiration for a man who could deliver a speech of such high quality under those conditions.

A few days before the votes were cast on 14th December, 1918, Lloyd George made a speech in which he said that the Bolshevists were running the Labour Party. What he meant was that the extreme elements in the party were deciding Labour's policy, which was as far from the truth as Winston Churchill's Gestapo election speech in 1945. The major difference was that Churchill's speech lost his party the General Election.

The Prime Minister carried the day, the voting being a landslide in favour of the coalition headed by him. The Labour Party secured 21 per cent of the total poll, their members in Parliament increasing from thirty-eight at the time of the Dissolution to sixty-five after the

General Election. The pacifists (alleged and real) in the Labour Party were all routed, Ramsay MacDonald and Philip Snowden amongst them. I came second out of four in the Wallasey election, but was still over 10,000 votes behind the successful candidate.

After this I determined to finish with politics, but some months afterwards I allowed myself to contest one of the wards in the Wallasey Municipal Election. This was a foolish decision. First, I didn't want to become a councillor; secondly, I had no time for municipal duties; and, thirdly, I could do no canvassing or organizing. Needless to say, here again I was defeated. I felt that such influence as I had attained during the General Election was utterly dissipated. To say that I had no political ambitions from a personal point of view would be to state the absolute truth, and from that time onwards I stuck to my trade union duties without any thought of entering Parliament. There was a time in 1940 when it would have been perfectly easy to attain Ministerial rank, but, far from tempting me, the opportunity merely consolidated my resolve to confine myself to trade unionism. Perhaps I felt I could wield more political influence out of Parliament than in it. Who knows?

My election as assistant general secretary of the union in the summer of 1920 entailed my working in the head office in Withy Grove, Manchester. (The head office is now on the outskirts of London.) I travelled daily from Wallasey by bus, ferryboat, and express train, the whole journey occupying roughly an hour and a half. The executive council of the union were considerate to me and provided me with a season ticket for the railway journey of roughly thirty-eight miles each way. I knew that this couldn't continue, and I prepared my mind for transferring my home from Wallasey to Manchester.

Curiosity prompted me to visit Mrs. Proctor, the widow of a well-known Liverpool phrenologist. Her son was a member of the Electrical Trades Union, and although his mother had ceased to practice, she readily received me. The note I made at the time shows that she gave me a thorough reading, mainly on character; and then came a curious prediction as to my future. She repeated several times that I was likely to live in London. I would be employed in some post in connection with the Government. It would not be a civil service post, but something like it. She was unable, however, to explain herself more fully. After all, how could she look forward to 1946 when I became a member of the National Coal Board, the first public corporation in British industry under complete national ownership and control? Many people besides Mrs. Proctor would

E

have been puzzled about the relationship between these bodies and the Government.

I looked forward eagerly to my work at the head office. True, there was not much inducement in the way of additional remuneration. At the time I left Merseyside I was the highest paid district official in the union. My salary was £6 7s. 6d. per week. My new weekly salary was £7 12s. 4d. The general secretary of the E.T.U. was paid £9 12s. 4d., but salary has never been, nor is it ever likely to be, the principal attraction which draws men and women to give their best service to the unions.

On my arrival in early August 1920 my main duties were connected with administration. The correspondence had fallen woefully in arrears, and letters from branches were continuously being received complaining bitterly of the absence of answers to their correspondence. But somehow I managed to work through a mass of back-log, keeping two typists busy for days. I took care to see that the incoming correspondence was answered promptly, making it a rule to reply on the date of arrival. The prompt receipt of replies was soon noticed by the branches, but in some instances it had the opposite effect to that which I expected. One branch secretary wrote from London indignantly protesting that his members didn't like Brother Citrine meeting the postman at the top of the stairs and handing him the reply.

As any trade union secretary must know, not all the letters were complimentary. They always started with 'Dear Sir and Brother' and ended with 'Yours fraternally', but the language in between was not always in conformity with these friendly statements. Many letters were abusive.

Our general secretary, Jim Rowan, took things philosophically. He could have papered the walls with the letters of censure he received during the many years of his secretaryship. The general secretaries of Rowan's generation were pretty hard-boiled. Jim used to say that if you left a letter long enough it would answer itself. So why bother too much?

As time went on I found that travelling daily was slowly sapping my energy by putting an extra three hours on my working day. One night a week I attended our sub-executive which had powers to deal with practically everything which didn't involve important issues of policy. It consisted of the president, the general secretary, and two assistant general secretaries, one of whom was myself, as well as the lay member living nearest the office. I rarely reached my home until midnight on these nights.

I felt, however, that I was now moving in the national sphere of trade union events; and had I lacked interest in the detailed work I was doing, I would have found full compensation in this. I had always been deeply interested in the wider aspects of the trade union movement, and while in Liverpool I had from time to time given lectures, particularly on the desirability of the trade unions being more closely linked together, nationally as well as locally. I had attended the annual meetings of the Trades Union Congress as a delegate of the Electrical Trades Union, and had thus been able to see the problems of the movement in a wider perspective than might otherwise have been possible. Yet I felt it lacked authority and that the movement needed a central executive body which could act decisively on behalf of trade unionism as a whole. I hadn't the slightest thought of superseding the T.U.C. by any new creation, but solely of widening its powers. I gave long consideration to this aspect of things and drew up what appeared to me to be a thoroughly practical scheme for endowing the T.U.C. with greater powers.

I thought that it must evolve into a general staff for labour, and by labour I mean the trade unions. I was certainly not thinking of the Labour Party. I could, of course, have sent this scheme to the head office of my union for the purpose of their putting down a resolution for discussion at the annual meeting of the T.U.C. I didn't do this because I was doubtful whether it would have been supported sufficiently (even by our own executive) for it to work. But I did send my proposals, in the form of an article, to the *Daily Herald*. It was never published, nor even mentioned in the *Herald*, nor was it returned to me with any editorial comment. I never saw it again; and I was staggered when, after some months, proposals not very different from my own were featured in the *Herald* over the name of Ernest Bevin. I don't mean to imply by this that Bevin ever saw my scheme.

He too was greatly interested in the subject, although I didn't know this at the time. We had met only once, at the Trade Union Congress at Glasgow in 1919. I had heard him speak there, but I had no direct contact with him until we bumped into each other at the temporary post office which is always provided at the Congress Hall for the convenience of the delegates. We met only a short while after I had spoken at the meeting on the police strike, when I had criticized the action of the Parliamentary Committee of the T.U.C. in not taking more vigorous action in support of the police and prison officers' union. While I was waiting at the counter of the post office a man swarthy of countenance and square of jaw, with the shoulders and chest of a heavy-weight all-in wrestler, greeted me with the words, 'You were up before me, weren't you?' He then introduced himself; but I knew already that it was Ernest Bevin. He went on to pay a generous tribute to my speech. I have reason to remember this, because it was the only occasion that I can remember in our long and intimate association of later years that Bevin paid me a direct compliment.

After about twelve months of constant journeying my wife and I decided to move to Crumpsall, one of the suburbs of Manchester. We found excellent accommodation for ourselves and our two little sons. I could be in the office in about twenty minutes after leaving home. I felt I was becoming a member of the leisured class.

But a disadvantage of being at head office was the absence of close contact with the members. I tried to remedy this by regular visits to branches, but it was a handicap, none the less. To be confined to an office induces the feeling, just the same as it does in the courts, that the whole of life revolves around that little area. But someone had to stay in the office and I was possibly the person best fitted for it by temperament. I was deeply immersed in the administrative work and soon instituted a new system of filing, with the full support of my colleagues. I installed various indices and recording methods which soon proved of value.

We had to economize: 1921 ushered in a period of trade depression, unemployment, and wage reductions which heavily drained our funds. Our membership, which at the end of 1920 had risen to over 57,000, fell to 31,000 by January 1923, and was to fall still lower. Our finances were drained. Yet the spirit of the members remained undaunted and, funds or no funds, they were alert despite adversity to resist any encroachments on working conditions.

So economies were the order of the day. Benefits had to be cut, and various levies were decided upon by ballot vote to keep the union going. Naturally, in these circumstances, some branches thought that my services were something of a luxury. It was well known that by instituting various reforms I had saved my salary many times over within a couple of years, but this was entirely disregarded by my critics. It may appear to be egotistical to claim credit for these economies, but it just happens to be true. It must be remembered that the principal reason for my appointment was to put the administrative system in better order. I say 'appointment', but I never forgot that I was *elected* by the whole of the members and not by the executive, which gave me a certain measure of independence. Further, I had the sustained support of my colleagues, including the general president and secretary. Such economies as I was able to effect were not the result of ingenuity on my part as much as careful study. I have never been afraid to copy good examples. I studied the methods of other unions and made myself familiar with business administration generally. I didn't believe in cutting down for the sake of saving. My object was to maintain the standard of service whilst spending less money. That is the only true economy.

On top of our other troubles the union suffered some defalcations by branch officers. Some of these were the result of sheer dishonesty. Others were the result of carelessness on the part of people not used to handling money. Other unions had their troubles, but ours seemed excessive. Eventually I hit upon a solution. Instead of allowing our branch officers to hold sums running into a few hundred pounds, why not require them to send these to head office? So it was decided that after every branch meeting the secretary or treasurer must send to head office all their takings over £5. If they required money to meet current branch expenses, they must apply for it to head office. We called this centralized finance, and it raised a wall of opposition and howls of resentment. Most of this was directed against me and my resignation was called for.

A ballot vote of the members put the scheme in operation and my fallen prestige began to rise again: so much so that on the expiration of my three-years term of office I was re-elected without the necessity of a second ballot. Many years after I had ceased to be an official of the E.T.U. I had the pleasure of hearing the president, Jack Ball, say publicly that 'the system of centralized finance which Citrine introduced saved the union'.

When our funds, like those of most trade unions, were at their lowest ebb and unemployment was rife, the engineering employers chose to lock out over a quarter of a million workers. Unemployment in shipbuilding was about 38 per cent and in engineering 30 per cent. A specious charge was made that the unions were interfering with managerial functions. The employers claimed that any changes which they thought fit to impose in workshop conditions must be operated without demur by the workers. If they didn't like the change they could raise the subject through the agreed machinery for settling disputes. The unions felt that this was a pretext to establish the employers' authority over the unions and their members at a time when they were least able to resist. The lock-out, which at first affected only the members of the Amalgamated Engineering Union, began towards the middle of March 1922, and ended in early May. The shipbuilding employers had earlier given notice to reduce wages by 16s. 6d. a week and after a stoppage the unions were forced to accept this in two stages.

During these negotiations I was sent to represent the union at a conference at Carlisle between the unions and the Shipbuilding

Employers' Federation. The employers were seeking severe reductions in wages of their employees on the ground that the cost of
living had fallen substantially from the level of 1914–18. They
asserted that labour costs were far too high to allow them to com-
pete in foreign markets. Great care had been taken to keep the Press
away from this private conference, but the journalistic sleuths
haunted the hotels in search of those scraps of information from
which they so often concoct a connected news story.

There were about 200 people present and the conference started
with the chairman, Sir James Lithgow, dolefully reciting the woes of
the shipbuilding firms, and with me taking down in shorthand all he
was saying. I was seated at the end of the front rows when I heard a
voice whispering something which I could not distinguish. As I was
anxious not to lose any part of what was being said, I waved the
intruder away. The next instant my notebook was snatched away
from me. I jumped up and protested loudly. Soon there were violent
objections being raised from different parts of the hall. The conference had to be adjourned for a time while the officials tried to sort
out what had happened. Eventually it transpired that one of the
officers of the employers' federation, observing that I was writing
shorthand, concluded that I was a journalist who had improperly
gained admission. When the row died down a full apology was made
to the conference, but I was still angry, and most of the delegates felt
similarly. It was a considerable time before the conference regained
its former composure.

The terms of settlement in the managerial functions dispute were
ambiguous, but the employers were required to give notice of any
change in practice to enable this to be discussed. The man who was
thought by unions to be the instigator of this lock-out was the professional chairman of the Engineering and National Employers'
Federation, Sir Allan Smith. I once heard him described as 'a cold-
blooded fish' who was loathed by most of the trade union officials with
whom he had to deal. His manner of dealing with union officials was
arrogant and his contempt for their intellectual capabilities was thinly
veiled. I believe he was a liability to the employers whatever his
superficial triumphs may have appeared to be. The unions have never
forgotten the managerial functions lock-out; the trouble it caused
bedevilled industrial relations for a decade. Smith became a Conservative M.P. but did not distinguish himself, and resigned because
of a difference with his local party.

The strife of the years following the 1914–18 war resulted in a
demand for closer co-operation amongst the unions. It was widely
felt that a greater concentration of power was needed. In 1921–2

amalgamations were proceeding with greater intensity than ever before. Ten unions joined to form the Amalgamated Engineering Union, which started with a membership of over 400,000. Under the inspiration of Ernest Bevin, the Transport and General Workers' Union was founded. It was far more original and flexible in form than any of its predecessors and its structure could, with advantage, have been copied by other unions. The Parliamentary Committee of the Trades Union Congress had been transformed into a General Council with an enlarged executive and with an industrial grouping system. A new standing order had been incorporated into the constitution of the T.U.C. which required the General Council to keep a watch on industrial movements and to co-ordinate industrial action where possible. It envisaged for the first time the T.U.C. as an agency for promoting common action on general issues such as wages and hours of labour.

Even the Electrical Trades Union, which—while fervently dedicated to the concentration of the forces of the workers—had declined to throw in its lot with the Amalgamated Engineering Union, felt impelled to seek an alliance with others. Negotiations were set on foot with the National Union of Enginemen, Firemen, and Electrical Workers, a strong little union of 30,000 members. A framework was soon formulated for the constitution of the proposed new union, and meetings were held in its support. I was sent out to address one of these in Birmingham in the autumn of 1923.

I arrived early and had some time to kill. I went to Warwick. A sort of fair was being erected and I noticed one booth with the name of Madame X, 'patronized by the Lord Mayor of Liverpool'. I peeped inside it; no one there. A neighbouring stallholder came across and inquired, 'Do you want to see Madame?' I replied in the affirmative and he rushed across to a public house, and was followed out in a few moments by a rather dowdy-looking, middle-aged woman. She gave an excellent description of the two colleagues with whom I worked in Manchester. One she called the 'sticker'. He was a 'come-today-go-today' type, she said, and would never move from his job. The other was a lighter-haired man, who occasionally wore glasses. She could see him passing things out with his left hand and this made her think he was left handed in some things. This was undoubtedly Jim Rowan, our general secretary. She passed to prediction. Some change was going to take place in my life within the next two months. She repeated this at different times during the interview. She could see me standing in front of several lines of windows. This made her think it was connected with a factory, but

she couldn't see things clearly. But whatever it was it would be good
for me.

On leaving her I wrote down in shorthand as quickly as I could
what she had said. I have it by me as I write. This was on the 12th of
October.

In early November the Trades Union Congress decided to appoint
an assistant general secretary. I was strongly advised by my colleagues to apply. I did so, and out of more than 200 applicants I was
selected for interview, together with four others. The interview was
to take place on 7th January, 1924, at the General Council office in
Eccleston Square. During the intervening weeks I studied diligently
the reports of the T.U.C. and every document I could lay my hands
on that was likely to be of assistance. In the late afternoon I walked
to Eccleston Square with Jim Smythe, an intimate friend of my
Merseyside days, who served with me as chairman of the Federation
of Engineering and Shipbuilding Trades. As we turned into the
square from Victoria Street I was suddenly struck by the array of
windows. They stretched in even lines of four storeys right round the
square. Then I thought of what the palmist had told me in Warwick—
'I can see you standing in front of lines of windows.' She had assured
me that the result was going to be good for me, but I am afraid my
faith was too slender for me to derive much comfort from that.

The interviews came at the end of a long meeting. I was the last of
the candidates to be called in, and on entering the room I could see
the Council members sitting rather listlessly in their chairs, no doubt
bored with the repetitive questions and replies which such interviews entail. Margaret Bondfield was in the chair, and when I had
sat down she turned to me and said sweetly: 'Well, we just wanted to
look at you, Mr. Citrine. We have the record of your trade union
activities in front of us. Every member has a copy. Would you like
to say anything in support of your application?' Like Falstaff, I had
much to say on behalf of that Citrine, but I could see that it would be
utterly unwise to say it. So I put my fortunes into a three-minute
speech, avoiding any attempt to extol my claims: I was content to
rely on the judgement of the experienced people who had my fate in
their hands.

I was then asked two questions. Was my health generally good?
Had I been in a decline I feel sure that I would have recovered
suitably for such an occasion. Secondly, did I write shorthand? Why,
of course I did! I had been drilling at verbatim speed on the mistaken
assumption that I might be tested. So it was that in an interview of not
more than ten minutes my future was decided. I went out of the room
feeling depressed. I felt that the General Council members had pretty

well made up their minds before I came in. But I was wrong and when later in the evening I was told by John Hill, a member of the General Council, that I had been elected by an overwhelming vote I could scarcely believe it. I was thrilled by the prospect of working at the headquarters of the trade union movement.

5

At the T.U.C.

I STARTED work at the Trades Union Congress on Monday,
20th January, 1924. When I reached Euston, contrary to my
usual practice, I took a taxi to the T.U.C. headquarters. As we
approached the office in Eccleston Square, the taxi-driver, an elderly
man, typical in appearance of those who used to drive the hansom
cabs, said, 'That is Winston Churchill's old house, isn't it?'

'No,' I replied. 'I believe it's the one next door where the Labour
Party now is.'

'I used to drive him from the House of Commons in the old days,'
he went on. 'We were always having arguments about the fare. He
said I was trying to charge him 3d. too much. It was the same every
time I took him home, but I always got my money'; and he chuckled
pleasantly as I gave him a 3d. tip on his fare.

I was shown round the premises by Fred Bramley, the secretary.
No. 32 Eccleston Square was an old-fashioned house of four storeys
and a basement, with large rooms but rather dark: not the sort of
house I would have chosen for an office.

I had only a few minutes with Bramley, as he was up to his eyes
in the railway strike of some 70,000 members of the Associated
Society of Locomotive Engineers and Firemen. This had been in
progress for a week: the railway service had continued to function
although with greatly restricted facilities. Drivers and firemen belonging to the National Union of Railwaymen had continued to
work, and the railway clerks and administrative grades were not
affected.

I plodded from room to room introducing myself to the occupants and wondering just what each of them was doing. There was no
plan of organization that I could readily consult, but I knew it
wouldn't take me long to grasp the scheme of things. I was, of course,
familiar with the general history and structure of the Congress and
its General Council.

Up to 1923 the secretaryship of the Congress was a part-time appointment, usually held by a prominent trade unionist who was also a Member of Parliament. The last holder of this office was the Rt. Hon. Charles Bowerman, M.P. He was a compositor by trade and held office from 1911 until 1923, when he retired at the age of seventy-two. Congress had decided that the next and subsequent secretaries must give their whole time to the work. In other words, the secretary of Congress could not in future be a Member of Parliament or hold any other paid office. The salary was to be £750 a year compared with £600 paid to his predecessor.

Fred Bramley had been assistant to C. W. Bowerman ('Courteous Charlie' he was called) for six years, but one would never have known it from the printed reports of Congress, his name never appearing on the title page. Fred was quite different from Bowerman. A rugged, stockily built, clean-shaven Yorkshireman, he had been elected by the unions at the Plymouth Congress in 1923 from six candidates. His general background was known to me. He was a good platform speaker who some years before he became an active trade unionist had toured the country on behalf of *The Clarion* addressing audiences of all kinds from a caravan on the theme of Socialism. By trade a cabinet-maker, he had been a national organizer for the Furnishing Trades' Association.

I saw the first flash of temper in him on the second morning of my service. The railway dispute was still on, and Bramley, with a small committee, had been trying desperately hard to reach a settlement. After an all-night session they had succeeded, but Fred came into the office at 9.30 a.m. looking jaded. Scarcely had he sat down at his desk and started to discuss the correspondence with me when a journalist came in and started to pop questions about the strike. Bramley answered him courteously for a few minutes, but the questions continued until Fred finally lost his wool with the remark: 'Damn it, man, I've been up all night. This is a private office. Will you please get out of here?' The journalist retired looking crestfallen and Bramley turned to me apologetically with the remark, 'You know these fellows have no consideration for anyone, but I am sorry I lost my temper.' I liked him for that.

We discovered that we had another interest in common besides trade unionism. We both had played a cornet in brass bands. Bramley, however, had taken lessons under one of the most famous cornetists of the day, John Paley, a Yorkshireman like himself. Paley toured the country playing at concerts. I had heard him only once and I was thrilled by his wonderful powers as an executant. His favourite encore was 'Drinking', in which Paley attained phenomenally low notes almost unknown on the cornet. Once, after he had played at a Sunday concert, a lady came to tell him that she thought it was inappropriate to play 'Drinking' on such an occasion. 'But, madam, I was trying to show how low a drunken man could fall,' replied Paley, and the lady went away mollified. Fred and I never tested out our respective ability as players, but I fear he would have won by a long way.

For the first few months after my arrival at the T.U.C. I lived in Balham with Jim Smythe, my Liverpool friend, who from being the district secretary had now become the assistant general secretary of the United Operative Plumbers' and Domestic Engineers' Association. He and his wife were kind to me and I was most comfortable. But I missed my wife and family dreadfully and I was very happy when after a month or so we secured accommodation for the whole family in Clapham.

The office staff were supposed to work from 9.30 a.m. to 5 p.m., but none of them was a stickler for rushing home. I found the work far too interesting to think about the time, and I never once recall looking at the clock with satisfaction that finishing time was approaching. The hours simply flashed by and it was often seven o'clock or later when I tore myself away. I had plenty to occupy my time and a generally well-educated staff with whom to share such problems as arose.

I started almost straight away speaking at weekend meetings and demonstrations; and Bramley encouraged me and gave me several useful platform hints. Just as when I became assistant secretary of the Electrical Trades Union I had concentrated on administration, so at the T.U.C. Bramley assigned this work to me. It wasn't long before I acquired a knowledge of the work of the departments and started to effect improvements with his full support. He was absent a good deal from the office on engagements, principally in the international sphere, so I was left to my own resources. I started to meet the principal officials regularly, including those in the joint departments —operated in conjunction with the Labour Party—such as Research, International, and Publicity. From the beginning I didn't much care for this joint arrangement, as it made the control and allocation of work somewhat difficult; nor did Bramley. I felt sure that direct control of our own staff was preferable. Bramley's absence gave me considerable scope in overhauling the filing system, which was a bit cumbersome, and generally improving the administration. The quality of the staff was surprisingly high and there was every evidence of their readiness to work in a spirit of co-operation with me.

One morning Fred Bramley came to me as I sat at my desk in a back room on the first floor, with a copy of the *Daily Herald* in

his hands. He looked at me over his pince-nez and with consternation in his face burst out: 'Have you seen who has been elected
secretary of the Miners' Federation? Cook, a raving, tearing Communist. Now the miners are in for a bad time.' I knew that Fred
and his wife were close friends of Frank Hodges, the ex-secretary
of the miners, and whilst I only knew of Cook from scrappy newspaper reports, I guessed that he would not be entirely beloved by
either of them. So I murmured a few noises intended to express the
surprise expected of me, then listened to Fred's candidly spoken
opinion of Cook's capacity and personality. I little knew how
prophetic Bramley's words were to prove.

Whilst Bramley was away on business a dockers' dispute loomed
up, and I was sent for by the Labour Government. I found a Committee of Ministers had been appointed to arrange for emergency
food supplies in case a strike materialized. I was asked to give advice
as to how best this could be done. I pointed out that I had been at
the T.U.C. only a little over a month and had no experience of such
a situation. I advised that nothing should be done by the Government behind the back of the transport unions. I knew how easy it
would be for a rumpus to occur if anything in the nature of black-
legging developed. Fortunately, before the matter got out of hand
Bramley returned, an emergency meeting of London members of
the General Council was called, and the full support of the General
Council was pledged to the unions. Within three days Ben Tillett
announced that a satisfactory settlement had been reached with the
employers.

A few days later A. A. Purcell was appointed chairman of the
General Council. He was a french-polisher by trade, a strong, forceful character, forthright in his opinions and incapable of finesse,
with wide trade union experience. Whenever Bramley was absent I
consulted Purcell on all-important matters of policy. He was the
M.P. for Coventry and was fifty-two years old. One day I called to
see him in the House of Commons and by arrangement went to the
Smoke Room. It was the first time I had been there. I waited patiently
for Purcell to come along. There were only two people present, both
of whom were strangers to me and both, by their evident familiarity
with their surroundings, M.P.s. I felt instinctively that they belonged
to the Labour Party. They were drinking what appeared to be milk
and I was admiring their abstemiousness when one of the waiters
came in. 'Two more disguises, Arthur,' said one of them, and a few
moments afterwards Arthur appeared with what I subsequently discovered was whisky and milk. From their occasional glances in my
direction I surmised that I was the momentary theme of their

conversation. 'Listeners never hear any good of themselves', runs the old adage, but I pricked up my ears, none the less.

'Who's his nibs?' asked one.

The other looked at me again before replying and then answered, 'Bramley's new assistant.'

'Any good?' queried the first speaker.

'No,' was the emphatic rejoinder. 'A dud.'

When Purcell at length arrived and introduced us I found the first solicitous inquiry came from Joe Toole, an alderman and later Lord Mayor of Manchester, one of the finest mimics I have ever heard off-stage. The other was Jim O'Grady, later Sir James O'Grady, K.C.M.G., the Governor of Tasmania. I wonder whether they ever changed their opinions of me.

My self-respect was a little restored a few days later when I received a telephone message from Bob Williams, the secretary of the National Transport Workers' Federation. After expressing good wishes Williams went on to say that when he first came to London from South Wales he felt a bit overwhelmed, and he thought maybe that his experience could reassure me. 'Don't be overawed by any of your colleagues,' he advised. 'From the provinces I used to look upon them as giants, but I soon found that they were pigmies like myself.' This was palpably well intentioned, but although I now and then noticed signs of exaggerated ego in a few of my new acquaintances, generally speaking they proved completely devoid of pomposity and arrogance. Most of them had come up the hard way, and they carried their directness of speech and tenacity of purpose with them.

Ernest Bevin was one of these. He was not at that time a member of the General Council, but, early on, Fred Bramley described him as Napoleon Bevin, and was surprised that I had never heard this cognomen before. Come to think of it, the description was not far out, whether it related to features or character. Bevin's approach to a subject was always constructive and yet, side by side with this, he was the finest drawer of 'red herrings' that I ever met. It was fascinating to listen to him in argument. When he felt he had a weak case he could divert a discussion so adroitly that no one could detect where the switch had taken place. I will have more to say about Bevin later on, as I regarded him from the first as one of the strongest, if not the strongest, personal forces in the trade union movement.

Fred Bramley was in indifferent health for much of my first two years at the T.U.C. During one of his absences I was invited to speak at a dinner of the Parliamentary Labour Party at the House of

Commons. I knew several of the party leaders fairly well, but none of them really intimately. I was seated a few places away from Ramsay MacDonald. As the meal proceeded I felt thirsty, and espying a large jug of orangeade on the table immediately in front of Philip Snowden, Labour's first Chancellor of the Exchequer, I reached over and helped myself to a glass. To my surprise Snowden glowered at me with resentment. Every line of his face showed his disapproval. I had no idea that the jug was set there for his exclusive use. But he seemed so irritated that I thought I would test his Socialist principles. 'To each according to his needs,' I thought, as I helped myself to a second glass. Snowden never uttered a word, but his looks showed me he didn't regard me with a very comradely affection.

When my turn came to speak I am afraid I widened the range of my unpopularity considerably. I took as my theme the necessity for a closer collaboration between the Labour Party and the T.U.C., compatible with the different functions of each and our different memberships. I had noticed that this was somewhat lacking in 1924 when the Labour Party was in office.

I reminded the audience that the workers didn't join the trade unions primarily for political reasons. They believed the unions could improve their wages and conditions of employment. Most of them were ready to pay the small political levy but it was only the comparatively active ones who were enthusiastic supporters of the party. The Labour Party was composed of people who believed deeply in Socialist principles and were ready to work for their attainment. The trade unions catered for all workers irrespective of their politics. Consequently at times the unions must have a different view on some questions from the Labour Party. This applied to economic and social subjects as well as politics. In other words, the party was politically homogeneous and the trade unions were not. The trade unions could not always be expected to see eye to eye with the party. This meant that the T.U.C., whilst affording every possible support to the party generally, must occasionally express a different view. It must retain the right of independent political opinion and expression. I hoped it would never surrender that right.

It was a difficult theme to develop before such an audience and I fear I must have shocked a good many. I am usually sensitive to the way in which an audience reacts to my remarks and I could feel the temperature going down steadily as I went on. I tried to be objective but I am afraid I did not succeed. When I spoke about the trade union movement several of the M.P.s who were themselves trade unionists called out aggressively, '*Our* movement,' as though to show me that I had no right to a monopoly when attempting to interpret

the views of trade unionists. At the conclusion my remarks were
not received with acclamation. I sat down not feeling elated. Yet I
felt it was desirable for the party leaders to realize that they could
not treat the T.U.C. as though it didn't count, and that the T.U.C.
could not accept as gospel truth all that the politicians thought fit
to say or do. I am afraid that I could not claim that my sense of
audience psychology was at its best.

In my first two years at the T.U.C. I came a good deal in contact
with George Hicks, who was a member of the General Council and
a close friend of Alf Purcell. I was then living in Clapham. Hicks,
who was the general secretary of the Amalgamated Union of Building
Trade Workers, had his offices nearby. One Sunday morning in
January 1925 the three of us went for a stroll over Clapham Common. As we were returning, Hicks suggested that we should call on
John Burns, whom he knew pretty well. I knew a good deal about
Burns, although I had never met him. He was president of the
Trades Union Congress when I was five years old. He was one of
the three outstanding men who led the dockers' strike in 1889. It was
a bitter struggle, the employers using every tactic they could to
starve the dockers into submission. The dockers' aim was to establish a rate of pay of 6d. per hour. Burns probably received more
publicity than either of his two colleagues, although from what Ben
Tillett later told me the spadework was done by himself and Tom
Mann.

Both Tom Mann and Burns had served apprenticeships as engineers and were members of the Amalgamated Society of Engineers
(now the A.E.U.). They were renowned as platform speakers, although their styles were different. Ben Tillett was probably the best
orator of the three and on occasions his language was superb. These
three had another characteristic in common, of which they were
probably unaware. I discovered this in 1928 when the T.U.C. published an illustrated history entitled *Sixty Years of Trade Unionism*.
I was responsible for this and thought it would be an interesting
memento to have my own copy signed by all the living personalities
whose photographs appeared in the book. I put the book in charge
of a secretary and invited, amongst others, Burns, Mann, and
Tillett to sign it at their convenience. They all came to our office on
different days. Each of them used his own pen with a broad nib
which left a strong and heavy signature. Each of them insisted that
his signature must be left to dry naturally and that no blotting paper
must be used.

Burns's house overlooked Clapham Common. On our ringing

the bell, the door was opened by John himself. 'Come right in, gentlemen,' he said, without the slightest question as to what was the nature of our business. We went into the library and sat down. I had heard of John Burns's library, with its rare collection of books, but I did not expect anything like the immense collection I saw. The room was a large one, and on every side except where the windows were there were large open bookcases extending from floor to ceiling. Later he told me that there were 5,000 books in this room alone. That was not the whole of his collection. After our interview he took us into the drawing-room, a tastefully furnished room. He said, 'This is where I keep my good books.' On looking round I saw several additional bookcases fitted in the Louis XIV style, all full of books. Then we had a glance into a small sitting-room: still more books.

Finally we passed up the staircase, on which, incidentally, I noticed a very fine painting of John as he must have looked thirty years previously.

Burns was sixty-six at the time of our interview, and his white hair and neatly trimmed beard and moustache, together with his double-breasted blue serge suit, made him look more like a ship's captain than a politician. He had the sprightliness of movement of a man half his age, and his sharp decisive manner of speech reflected a keen and alert mind.

On the first-floor landing there was another large bookcase. 'There is enough value in that bookcase to keep me in comfort for the rest of my life,' he said. 'That is one of the most famous collections in England. It is the whole of the works of Thomas Moore. You see that book?' (pulling out a thin volume from its shelf) 'I paid £600 for that alone.' It was a modest little thing of not more than about 150 pages. I do not remember the title.

Burns said to Purcell: 'You have been in Russia, haven't you? Well, tell me all about it. First let me say I am not a reporter, and Hicks will tell you I can keep confidences.'

'That's all right,' said Purcell, and described his impressions of his visit to the Soviet Union.

Burns expressed himself warmly in support of the Revolution. Then turning to me he said: 'I want to ask you something, Citrine. Why is the trade union movement moving over to the Left?'

I said, 'I think it is merely a reaction to the political situation generally.'

Burns continued: 'Do you think, Citrine, that the trade union movement has passed the stage at which it must continue to lose members?'

F

'Yes,' I replied, 'positively. The reports from the unions indicate a definite increase.'

Burns went on: 'Well, I am a trade unionist of forty years' standing, and I think I am in a position to speak. I think you are making a big mistake in the trade union world. You are devoting too much of your time to charts and plans and statistics. Good God! When I see the general secretary of the Glass Dolls' Clothing Weavers' Union going to a labour conference he carries a dossier with him. You are trying to turn out records and reports like Government Blue Books. You are neglecting getting out to the street corners. And the men are getting fed up with it too. You will be losing them. Look at Bevin. He goes to the dockers' inquiry, and he puts on a plate so many pennyworths of bread and potatoes and cabbages and God knows what else, and thinks he is winning his case. Why? I went to that inquiry. Practically every man on the court asked me to go and sit with them on this dais, as an old organizer of the '89 dock strike. But I said: "No, it is not my job. I am merely here to look on." And I told the employers who spoke to me that they were going to get it in the neck. Why? Because Lord Shaw—one of the most incapable of judges—was out to get his name down on the pages of history as the man who gave the Shaw Award. I told the employers that he would give the dockers £5 a day, never mind 16s. You don't know what men will do to get themselves into the picture. There are too many cinematograph leaders in the trade union movement—too many of you want to be in the picture.'

As neither Purcell nor Hicks showed any disposition to challenge this, I felt impelled to intervene. I said: 'I am not saying whether your criticism is correct or not, but it is a matter of policy which the trade union movement has been more or less forced to adopt. The balance of power in the trade union movement has shifted to its centre. That applies from both standpoints, internal government and negotiations with the employers. You have a powerful voice, Mr. Burns, and I have heard that you can reach an outdoor audience of 30,000. But even your voice couldn't be heard from Tower Hill to Liverpool, or Hull, or Glasgow. They were local strikes in your day, where the men could hear and see you. Now things are dealt with on a national level by officials whom many of the thousands of rank and file may never have seen. We have to hold conferences of delegates to ensure that the men are informed of what is going on, which means that the ordinary worker only learns about it second-hand. This requires a different kind of treatment from the methods of your days. We have accepted without question the policy of national agreements and large-scale organizations. Nowadays we cannot have a small strike in some obscure locality like Penistone without its involving the threat of a national lock-out.

'The effect of strikes today is much more serious than it was twenty years ago. Nowadays, a strike affects not a few hundreds of men on the docks of Liverpool or London but thousands at the docks throughout the whole country.'

'I know,' commented Burns. 'It is a matter of hundreds of thousands. I have all the figures here.'

'Well,' I said, 'we must try to settle our disputes by reason instead of by resorting to force. We now have negotiations and conciliation and arbitration to an enormously greater extent than we had in your days. What do we find when we meet the employers? They are armed with diagrams and charts, all of which are used to prove that the industry cannot pay what we are asking. Consequently we are driven back on research. We must prepare our cases. The alternative which you seem to be suggesting is that we should rely on force.'

'You are too dependent on the intelligentsia. You cannot do anything without statistics and records,' he retorted. 'If somebody throws a dirty floorcloth down on the floor you have Sidney Webb or a bunch of budding university students working out exactly what the component chemical parts of the charwoman's floorcloth are. Look at the Triple Alliance of 1921. Look at that tragic failure. If Jimmy Thomas had not met Frank Hodges going to the House of Commons, and if they had not got to talking, there would have been a strike. If instead of wasting time interviewing Lloyd George old Bob Smillie had clenched his teeth and the rest had followed him you would have had no wage reductions in 1921 and 1922. But now you must go to outside courts and bring in all sorts of bodies to do your business.'

'That is impartial arbitation,' I said.

'Impartial!' Burns retorted, with scorn. 'How can you have impartiality where labour is concerned? Better to have fought and lost than never to have fought at all.'

And so the conversation proceeded, with John giving his strong and emphatic opinions on what could be done in the trade union world. Hicks had told me that Burns was very interesting, and so he was—also that Burns would not give anyone else an opportunity of doing the talking. He would do it himself, and so he did; but the thing which surprised me was the amazing breadth of his knowledge, not merely on the affairs which people generally may read in the Press but on those intimate details which we in the trade union world think are our own special preserves. It could not come wholly from extensive reading. It meant that he must have met and talked with trade unionists who knew what they were talking about.

One other thing that Burns said was interesting. He was emphasizing the necessity for trade union leaders to keep faith with their principles—to stand by the demands put forward by their members in an uncompromising attitude. He said that they thought too much about their salaries; too often when a conference with the employers was taking place which might lead to a strike the trade union leader was thinking: 'What about the second instalment on my grand piano? What about my girl's education?' and asking himself a host of other domestic questions when he ought to be thinking solely of how he could strike and win.

Burns said that not only would it bring greater confidence from the rank and file but it would mean higher and better salaries for the officials themselves. I at once dissented from this. I said that no trade union official who stuck to his principles and was not out to achieve Press notoriety could hope to expect anything in the way of monetary recognition from the rank and file. I said that he would be deluding himself if he did. He must be strong enough to find recompense in his work.

Burns finally made this revelation. 'Do you know, the only big mistake I ever made was to take office in the Liberal Ministry. I took office principally to oblige C.B.' (Campbell-Bannerman) 'and for the sake of Ireland. When the war came I got out because I did not agree with them, but what happened? Within two hours of my resignation Arthur Henderson was round to see Lloyd George, and in a few days was saying that Mr. Asquith was an indispensable man, etc.' Hicks told me that this was the first time he had ever known Burns to admit that he made a mistake in joining the Liberals. Neither publicly nor privately had he been known to say it before.

We finished our conversation with mutual expressions of hope for a further meeting, with a promise from me to send him bound copies of the Trades Union Congress report which he had not got. He said: 'They used to send me copies for years, but Charlie Bowerman stopped it. I do not know why. He had a lot to thank me for. Do you know the reason we elected him secretary of the Trades Union Congress? Because the reports were in such a muddle and mess and we thought with his being a printer he could get them into a decent shape. It was not because we thought anything of his capacity. And now I don't get my reports.

'This is the best collection of Trades Union Congress reports in the country. Remember, you won't be giving them to me. This library at some time will belong to you.'

I resolved that I would speak with Burns again, but the T.U.C. never did receive his collection of reports or any other of his books.

Fred Bramley's indifferent health and his frequent absences on international business left me very much to myself. I can't say I felt weighed down with a sense of responsibility. I kept in close touch with the successive chairmen of the General Council and continued my method of regularly meeting our senior officers in informal conference. Whatever decisions I had to make were reached after full consultation with the people who ought to know.

The annual meeting of the T.U.C. was in the offing. This always starts on the first Monday in September and lasts roughly a week. These gatherings are usually referred to as the 'Congress', so that we heard people speak of the Hull Congress, the Scarborough Congress, and so on. I shall adopt the same practice here. I was resolved that the 1924 Hull Congress would be better organized than any of its predecessors and after an exploratory visit to Hull with Fred Bramley I set about ensuring that the documentary work would be adequately prepared and promptly circulated.

As the Congress approached, Bramley's health became worse and, despite his sturdy build, it broke down in early July, a couple of months before the Congress. It looked at one time as though he would not be able to attend, and this would have been a tremendous disappointment to him as it was to be his first Congress as secretary. By a strong effort of will he forced himself to continue at work and set about preparing the speeches he was to make in introducing the important aspects of the Council's report. Whenever he was available I always consulted him before acting, and invariably secured his support and encouragement.

Bramley and I worked on the principle that while policy was the function of the General Council, the executive action flowing from this and the office administration was our job. Occasionally some members of the General Council chafed at this and wanted to intervene in this sphere. Most of them, however, were general secretaries of their own unions, and they soon understood and approved of our arrangements. Indirectly this strengthened their own authority with their own executive councils, as they were able to cite the practice of the T.U.C. They had to deal with rank-and-file trade unionists, practically all of the union executives being composed in this way. Lay members could hardly be expected to understand problems of internal organization. At one time it was usual for them to feel that it was their privilege, and indeed their duty, to instruct their general secretary down to the last detail of his correspondence. We had no such trouble; once the General Council saw that we knew what we were about they left us to it.

A few days before the opening of the Congress the General Council met at Hull to go over the agenda and determine their policy on the more important issues. We had taken with us for the first time several senior members of the staff and delegated to them the duty of servicing one or more of the numerous committees which are indispensable to the smooth running of the Congress. I nearly wore myself out during the week moving from one committee to another to ensure that they had all the facilities we could provide. I took no part in the discussions at the Congress as this had always been the accepted procedure, and confined myself, as was expected, to supervising the organization. There was a heavy agenda, the principal matters from my point of view being the need to increase the powers of the General Council, the reconstruction of the trade union movement on the basis of organization by industry, and the visit of a delegation from Soviet Russia.

Fred Bramley's principal ambition was to make the T.U.C. a much more powerful body—to make it, in fact, the centralized leadership for the whole trade union movement in industrial matters. We talked about this at the office from time to time and he soon found that I had long been a convinced believer in this.

The establishment of the General Council itself was a step in the right direction, and Bramley had played his full part in effecting this. In addition he had helped in the formation of the National Joint Council which was composed of representatives of the executive of the Labour Party and of the General Council. This, unfortunately, was only a nominal form of association and met infrequently. To its credit, be it said, that largely through the initiative of Arthur Henderson, the secretary of the Labour Party, it had intervened in the engineering lock-out of 1922 and had assisted materially in securing the agreed terms of settlement. It was never intended to act as a general staff for the trade union movement but rather for the co-ordination of political policy. What was now required was an exclusively trade union body.

In my enthusiasm I was keen to go ahead at once and work out as complete a scheme as possible of a constructive character and put this to the General Council. But older and probably wiser heads than mine were convinced that this would be a mistake. The unions would never at that stage part with any of their autonomy and would reject outright anything which savoured of a considerable transfer of power to the General Council. A more gradual approach than mine was necessary. The outcome was that the General Council put down a

resolution to enlarge its duties and appointed George Hicks, an enthusiastic supporter of the idea, to move it at the Hull Congress.

The substance of this was that unions would have the obligation
of notifying the General Council whenever a dispute arose with the
employers of sufficient dimensions as to be likely to involve considerable numbers of other workpeople either directly or indirectly.
The General Council would not interfere so long as there was any
possibility of the difference being resolved, but if negotiations broke
down the Council could take the initiative in trying to promote a
settlement. If, despite this, the attitude of the employers caused a
stoppage, the General Council would be required to organize moral
and material support for the union or unions concerned.

When the resolution came before the Congress speakers stressed
that the employers were far ahead of the trade union movement in
endowing their central organizations with such powers. They cited
the Federation of British Industries and the Chambers of Commerce.
Curiously enough they never mentioned the one organization which
had really direct influence over the policy of the employer bodies in
the sphere of what was called labour relations. This body, the predecessor of the present British Employers' Confederation, was a
federation of employers' associations. Neither it nor the Federation of
British Industries had anything like the constitutional authority with
which they were credited by most trade unionists. The F.B.I. in
particular was regarded as a most sinister organization, always
working behind the scenes in some conspiratorial way to dictate the
policy of the employers. This was a distorted picture of the actual
part played by the F.B.I., but all of us believed implicitly that it
exercised much greater influence with its constituents in the sphere of
labour relations than did the T.U.C.

The resolution was easily carried and became part of the constitution of the T.U.C. I don't think anyone sensed that within two
years the whole trade union movement would be involved in the
greatest conflict in its history. None of us then envisaged the national
strike of 1926.

The second subject which seemed to me of outstanding importance was that of organization by industry, which had been put
forward by the Miners' Federation. In its original form it was bound
to invoke a clash of opinions between those unions which stood for
what they considered to be such a form of organization and the
craft unions, who believed that workpeople should be members of
their own skilled trade unions. Furthermore, there were the powerful
unions which enrolled workers in all kinds of industries and services,
such as the National Union of General and Municipal Workers and

the Transport and General Workers' Union. It seemed impossible to
reconcile this division of interests, but, as usual, consultations took
place at the Trades Union Congress between the movers of the
different motions on kindred subjects, and a composite motion was
put forward. This, after declaring that the number of unions should be
reduced—a sentiment which most union officials shared but few were
ready to apply—went on to instruct the General Council to draw up
such a scheme but also to draft an alternative which would secure
unanimity of action amongst the trade unions but which would not
necessitate the merging of the existing unions. This motion was
carried by a two-to-one majority, and although I was pretty sure
that the spadework in giving effect to it would fall most heavily upon
me, I welcomed the decision.

Important as these two earlier topics were, the one which excited
my imagination most of all was the forthcoming visit of the Russian
trade union delegation. I looked forward to it with eagerness, as ever
since the 1917 revolution I had closely followed events in the Soviet
Union. I had been enthused by Lenin's picture of an electric republic, organized on such lines as would ensure to every citizen,
however humble, the advantages of a planned economy and the
blessings of a modern civilization. I had read eagerly of the immense
strides in economic reconstruction which were rapidly enabling the
Soviet Union to recover from the effects of the Civil War. True, I had
read something of the reluctance of the peasantry to give up their
individualistic form of agriculture, but I had little doubt that this was
a transient difficulty which would be resolved in due course. I found
it rather baffling at times to obtain specific information, owing to the
tendency to express such progress in percentages or in roubles, the
true value of which it was nearly impossible to ascertain.

My enthusiasm brushed aside such considerations. I accepted
almost at its face value, without critical reservations, practically
everything which emanated from Russian official sources. I entirely
disbelieved the stories which appeared occasionally of the quarrels
between the Communist leaders, particularly Lenin and Trotsky,
and attributed these to the biassed capitalist Press. I was convinced
that our newspapers simply couldn't tell the truth about events in the
Soviet Union. I was resolved to do all I could to bring our two trade
union movements into closer relationship and to stimulate trade
between Russia and Britain. In conformity with the policy of the
T.U.C. I had taken part in delegations to the British Government for
that purpose armed with information—not always accurate I am
afraid—obtained directly from Russian sources.

The General Council had entertained a Russian trade delega-

tion during the summer and I had come into intimate contact with
their interpreter, Yarotsky, who described himself as a proletarian
professor.

The General Council had invited the All-Russian Central Council of Trade Unions to send a speaker to the Hull Congress, but it
was only two days before the Congress opened that we received a
telegram from Russia to the effect that five delegates (led by Mikhail
Tomsky, their chairman, and including Yarotsky) would attend.
Hurried arrangements were made for their accommodation, although we did not know definitely the date of their arrival. I was to
find in later years that this kind of uncertainty was for some strange
reason a characteristic of such missions. The Congress was well under
way when we were informed that the delegation had reached London
and was on its way to Hull. Joe Cotter, who was the secretary of the
Marine Workers' Union, and Lon Swales, of the Amalgamated
Engineering Union, undertook to meet the Russians and to escort
them to the hotel where we had our headquarters. Cotter afterwards
told me that he was rather taken aback when he saw how shabbily
the Russians were dressed. They all wore caps and seemed to be
in their working clothes, very different from the smartly dressed
officials we used to meet at the Soviet Embassy and on the trade
delegations. Cotter thought that this was a bit of stage management
to show how thoroughly working class they were. He plucked up
courage to advise Tomsky and his friends to have a wash and brush
up and to put on better clothes before coming to the Congress Hall.
This was taken in the right spirit and without any trace of resentment.

The Russians received a tumultuous welcome from the 700 or
more delegates as we climbed on to the platform. When it came to
Tomsky's turn, two days later, to speak everyone was on the tiptoe
of expectation. He was a little man with small twinkling eyes, large
protruding ears, and a rather sallow complexion. His voice was
harsh and metallic, with excellent carrying power. This was just as
well, as in those days we didn't use microphones at the T.U.C. His
speech showed that he had a sense of humour, and in subsequent
conversation he revealed a knowledge of English literature. He had
been a printer by trade and I should say was traditionally a good trade
unionist. His speech was divided into four sections and the delegates
were warned that there would be an interpretation at the end of each
section.

After conveying fraternal greetings Tomsky described the
structure of the Soviet trade unions with their 10,000,000 members
enrolled in twenty-five great unions. He showed how much more
concentrated the Soviet trade unions were as compared with those of

Britain with their 4,328,000 members organized in over 200 unions. He stressed the need for class solidarity and paid a tribute to the British unions for their resistance to attempts to draw Great Britain into war against the Soviet Union. He criticized the Versailles Treaty, the invasion of the Ruhr, and the Dawes Plan, and concluded with a strong appeal for international trade union unity. This latter part of his speech was closely in line with that of Fred Bramley, who had spoken on behalf of the T.U.C. at a conference of the International Federation of Trade Unions in Vienna only a couple of months earlier. The I.F.T.U. members as a whole were strongly against any alliance with the Red International of Trade Unions, of which the Russians were the principal members. I didn't know what difficulties stood in the way of achieving this unity, but it was an ideal which seemed to me well worth striving for. So felt the delegates, who accorded Tomsky warm and sustained applause.

Purcell's suggestion that without any formal resolution the delegates should empower the General Council, through the International Federation of Trade Unions, to give practical expression to the desire for unity, was unanimously accepted. I do not think anyone realized the long and arduous struggle upon which we were about to embark.

The International Federation of Trade Unions had its headquarters in Amsterdam; the Red International of Labour Unions was centred in Moscow. The national centres in practically all the countries where the trade union movement was well established were affiliated to the I.F.T.U. There were various dissident unions, some of them newly formed, and others breakaways from the older unions, who had become attached to the Red International. The Amsterdam and Moscow Internationals were not on speaking terms. They belaboured one another in public and private, the Russians being rather more adept at vilification than were their Amsterdam rivals.

It was the hope of the Trades Union Congress that these two bodies could be brought together into one united international. This proposal was coldly received by the executive of the I.F.T.U. who had a deep suspicion of the motives of the Russians, who they believed would carry on subversive work if any such scheme matured. The Hull Congress had empowered the General Council to continue its efforts to bring the parties together. The I.F.T.U. still insisted that the Russians should first become affiliated to their organization before any conference or discussions took place. This seemed to the T.U.C. to be unreasonable. The Russians went further and emphasized their view that any such organization should be founded on recognition of the principle of the class struggle. The T.U.C. had never tied itself to any such doctrine, which it felt was extraneous and irrelevant to day-to-day trade union activity. This was the state of things when a British delegation of seven members arrived in Moscow on the 11th November, 1924, in response to an invitation from the All-Russian Council of Trade Unions. They remained in Russia for approximately one month and travelled widely over the country. Generally the delegates were favourably impressed with the progress which Russia had made in both the economic and social spheres.

They agreed to support the Russians in their desire for a preliminary conference with the I.F.T.U., and this was endorsed by the General Council. Nothing resulted, and in April 1925 a meeting took place in London between the International Committee of the T.U.C. and the Russians. It was then decided that if the I.F.T.U. still declined to meet the Russians in a preliminary conference the T.U.C. would itself call one and would use its influence to secure a united international industrial organization. It was further recommended that to promote co-operation between the British and Russians a joint committee should be established. The delegates at the Scarborough Congress in September 1925, at which Tomsky attended as fraternal delegate, confirmed this. Fred Bramley, who made a moving speech, had taken a leading part in all that had occurred and had shattered his already precarious health in the process. The General Council sent him on a long voyage in the hope that this would restore him.

Immediately after the end of the Scarborough Congress the Anglo-Russian Joint Advisory Council met in London and issued a statement on the necessity for international trade union unity. In the same month Hicks and I went to the Soviet Union (more of this journey later). In December the I.F.T.U. carried by a two-to-one majority a resolution reaffirming its earlier decision. Another meeting of the Anglo-Russian Council was held, this time in Berlin, and a further meeting took place in Paris in July 1926. Tomsky was to have attended the 1926 Congress at Bournemouth but was refused a visa by the Government. No reason was given.

During the national strike—in May 1926—the Russians had offered a substantial sum of money (£26,000) to the General Council to help the strike. The General Council, already faced with the baseless charge of instituting a strike to overthrow the constitution, felt that however well intentioned the Russian offer was its acceptance would be misrepresented and politely declined to receive it. The Russians responded by a torrent of abuse. Not being able to send a delegate to the Congress, the Russians sent a 1,000-word telegram accusing the General Council of a 'bend the knee' attitude towards the Government and of 'unforgivable tactics' during the general strike. After battering us to their satisfaction, they wound up: 'We strongly believe Trades Union Congress will do all to further consolidate Anglo-Russian Committee.' The General Council circulated this to the delegates, with a strong protest at the Russian abuse of ordinary courtesies, and the Congress recorded its emphatic condemnation of the Russian action.

In January 1927 the *Daily Herald* sent me a pamphlet which they requested me to read and give them my views. The pamphlet was written by Lozovsky, the secretary of the Red International: it was a bitter attack upon the General Council. He called our former president, Arthur Pugh, a liar, and the General Council traitors. He impudently asserted that in no circumstances would the Russians agree to non-interference in the affairs of Great Britain, no matter how loudly the General Council might howl.

I felt strongly on this. I gave an interview to the *Daily Herald* in which I said that if this criticism was endorsed by the All-Russian Council of Trade Unions a serious crisis would be reached in the affairs of the Anglo-Russian Committee.

I said I believed that the limits of toleration had been reached, and that although we had been assured from time to time that Lozovsky did not represent Russian opinion, this sort of thing had to be stopped.

What irritated me most was the fact that just when we really were trying to preserve the Anglo-Russian Committee (subject to an undertaking from the Russians that there would be no interference in our affairs), this pamphlet quoted documents sent from us to the All-Russian Council of Trade Unions.

I was convinced that the Russians, while not officially replying to our communications, were, through Lozovsky, preparing the way for the reply which they would send later.

I asked in the *Herald* interview whether the pamphlet represented the views of the Russian trade union movement. Surely if it didn't there was no difficulty in their saying so. If, on the contrary, it did represent them I thought that our General Council could not possibly recede from the position they had taken up—they could not tolerate any interference in our affairs.

Some General Council members seemed to think that we should remain silent for ever under these venomous attacks. That would be one line of tactics. The other was to make our position perfectly plain. Subsequently the General Council backed me up.

Matters came to an end at the Edinburgh Congress in 1927 when

I moved a report on behalf of the General Council. This report was fully documented, and included a 3,000-word letter from the Russians, protesting their desire for international unity but including the usual tirade of abuse to which we were becoming inured. I pointed out in my speech that practically the same men who, two years before, had taken the initiative to establish the Anglo-Russian Joint Advisory Council, were now giving it as their considered opinion that no good purpose could be served by continuing the Council whilst the existing attitude of the Russians was maintained. I showed that there was a vast difference between the conception of the General Council and that of the Russians as to the purpose of the Anglo-Russian Joint Advisory Council. We looked upon it purely as a means of association between us in an effort to bridge the gap between the Russians and the Western unions as a whole. Our purpose was to see the Russians enrolled in the International Federation of Trade Unions. We had no intention of the Committee developing into a new International, or a rival of the I.F.T.U. Our purpose had been to exchange information and to consult together on the common problems of the British and Russian trade union movements. What we had found was that the Russians were constantly attempting to broaden the operations of the Committee, by making declarations of an international character on almost every conceivable subject, whether political or economic.

Our purpose was to smooth the way for the enrolment of the Russians in the I.F.T.U., and we had tried to keep the Committee's operations down to that essential task. We resented the use of such terms as 'traitor' and 'lick-spittle', although we had been told that these expressions were commonplace in the Russian movement and that nobody took any notice of them. Lenin had apparently said that the more intimate you were with the other fellow the greater was your entitlement to abuse him.

There was a sustained debate on the General Council's recommendation, but when the vote was taken it was carried by a four-to-one majority.

In the ensuing months nothing appeared on the horizon to indicate that the Russians had in the least changed their views, and so the General Council's efforts to achieve what we all considered a laudable purpose came to an end.

Did Tomsky really believe the nasty things he said about us in his telegrams? Did they express his true opinions?

I next saw Tomsky in Russia in 1935. He had in the meantime been removed from his position as chairman of the All-Russian

Council of Trade Unions and replaced by N. M. Shvernik. Tomsky had also ceased to be a member of the all-powerful Polit Bureau, the men who above all others control the country.

I had been visiting the Moscow-Volga Canal, which at that time was being built mainly by convict labour. I had had a heated argument about this and amongst other things had reproached the Russians who were with me at my not being allowed to see Tomsky. I wanted to renew our acquaintance on purely personal grounds. I said that when George Hicks was in Russia the previous year he had asked to see Tomsky but nothing resulted. Why couldn't I see him?

'Do you think we are keeping you from seeing him?' I was asked.

'It looks like it,' I replied.

'But he is on holiday in Tashkent and he may be there for some weeks,' they protested.

I let them see that I didn't believe this story. A few days later I was told that Tomsky had returned from his holiday earlier than was expected and would be glad to see me. So I went with a Russian interpreter to the State Publishing House, Tomsky now being head of that organization. He greeted me warmly and we had a long chat. I couldn't see any difference in him physically and he seemed just as full of vim as ever. He was elated at the achievements and successes of the Revolution. What his real opinions were I don't know, as I am sure he was very conscious of the presence of the Russian interpreter.

A year later he was publicly denounced and shot himself rather than face arrest. Twenty-six years later he was 'rehabilitated'.

My visit to Russia in 1935 was the last I saw of the leaders of their trade unions until 1941, when we set up another joint committee with them. Once again this was done on the initiative of the T.U.C.— my own, in fact. It was shortly after the Russians had been invaded by Germany and things looked desperate for them. We knew our purposes on most aspects of trade unionism were as far apart as the poles, but we did think we could collaborate together with them to defeat the Nazi aggressors. Again it was at Edinburgh that this important decision was made.

6

Off to Russia

DURING the Scarborough Congress in 1925 Tomsky had invited George Hicks and myself to accompany the Russian delegation to Moscow. He said he would be glad of our advice on the administrative problems with which the Russian unions were faced. We started from Liverpool Street on Saturday, 19th September.

En route from the frontier to Moscow, I had a long talk with Tomsky. He initiated the conversation and said he wanted to arrange a programme for us and was prepared to show us everything we desired to see. I told him that we had had no idea of making a comprehensive investigation when we had first decided to come, but now that we were there we would like to look at the trade union movement and its administrative methods. He said he thought I would be disappointed, because I would find their methods of administration much inferior to ours. They were young in the trade union movement and had a good deal to learn.

'You know, Comrade Citrine,' said Tomsky, 'you and Comrade Hicks are the first real trade union officials to come here to examine our administration. You will be the first delegates who have ever been in the Institute of Labour. Purcell and the rest when they were in Russia were so busy seeing other things that they had not time to examine the trade unions.'

I replied, 'Well, we are not expecting to be able to examine the whole structure of Russia in the time we are to be here, but neither Hicks nor myself are without trade union experience and we profess to know something concerning its methods.'

'All right,' returned Tomsky, 'I shall take you and introduce you to the members of the All-Russian Council of Trade Unions, and you will be able to examine things for yourself first-hand. You will have every opportunity. You will see the members of the

95

Polit Bureau as well—Kalinin, Stalin, Kaminieff, Rykov, and all the others.'

'Zinovieff also?' queried Hicks.

'Yes,' said Tomsky, 'you must not go back without seeing him.'

'What position does Kalinin occupy?' I asked.

'Oh, he is the President of the Republic,' replied Tomsky.

'What are his duties?' I asked. 'Are they administrative or are they actually concerned with the formulation of policy?'

Tomsky said something which I could not catch and smiled broadly. 'Oh, he is the King George of Russia,' said Yarotsky. It was quite evident to me that the intention was to convey that Kalinin's duties were of a social and ceremonial character.

After that we fell to talking about the relationship between the Communist Party and the trade union movement. Tomsky said in response to a question from me that he was a member of the Communist Party Polit Bureau, but that he had been out of Russia so frequently that he could only attend irregularly. The method adopted was to summon the next highest unsuccessful candidate on the list to attend while he was away.

'Does that mean,' I asked, 'that when you are away the trade union movement has no real direct voice in the counsels of the Polit Bureau?'

'No,' replied Tomsky. 'Dogadov is allowed to attend as a consultative member. He puts the trade union point of view.'

'Then you have no organic connection between the Communist Party and the trade union movement?' asked Hicks.

'Not as such,' said Tomsky. Dogadov, who was standing by, interjected something which I did not understand. Tomsky continued as if in reply to what Dogadov had said: 'Yes, that is so; we have hardly any real difference because we are the same people. It is all the same movement.'

'But do you think it is wise,' I said, 'to be too closely identified with the Communist Party? Would it not be better to retain your independence?'

'How can we have independence from the Communist Party?' said Tomsky. 'The Communist Party governs the country. Every one of the members of the All-Russian Council of the Trade Unions is a Communist. It is all one movement; there is no difference.'

I pointed out to Tomsky that this sounded very simple, but in practice it would not be found to work out that way. I said that our relationships with the Labour Party in England were close indeed. None the less, we retained our separate identity, and we had found during the period of the Labour Government's term of office in 1924 that it was necessary that our independence should be preserved. We had never surrendered our right to put forward views on political questions and I did not believe we ever should.

'But then you have not got a Socialist State, Comrade Citrine,' Tomsky smiled indulgently. 'The trade unions here are endowed with functions by the State that in other countries are carried on by State departments. We look after all the questions of social insurance, such as unemployment and health, which in your country are done by the Government itself.'

'It sounds very practical,' I said, 'in the way you put it, but I do not believe it is a good thing for the trade unions in any State to sacrifice their independence to the State. They are the protective instrument which the workers may require to use against the State.'

'But how can we use the instrument against ourselves? We are the State,' said Tomsky.

'What I'm afraid of,' I said, 'is that you will find your trade unions will be sacrificed to the political expediency of the Government and your members will tell you that you are not performing the job of looking after their interests where they may clash with the State.'

'But there is no difference between the interests of the State and the interests of the workers,' persisted Tomsky, 'they are the same.'

I said: 'That argument doesn't convince me. In other countries, too, it can be claimed that the people are the State.

'But we know there are occasions when the interests of the people and the interests of those at the head of the State may diverge. In those times it is necessary that the workers should have an instrument like the trade unions to put forward their point of view.'

Here Tomsky's young secretary, who evidently could follow something of the conversation, suddenly chimed in, with flashing eyes, 'But Lenin said that politics are concentrated economics.' I confess that I felt rather irritated at this interjection, as it seemed to me to be wide of the point that we were discussing, and I retorted rather warmly, 'Lenin wasn't Jesus Christ, and he said so many contradictory things that if you put them side by side they cancel out.'

The result of this statement was extraordinary. A silence

G

like a pall seemed to fall on everybody. Evidently I had out-
raged the deity. They sorrowfully bade me good night like good
comrades grieving over the apostasy of one whom they respected. We then went to our beds and my first insight into the
mentality of the Russian where Lenin was concerned had been
rather vividly obtained.

In Moscow we stayed at the National Hotel, which I suppose in
former days was regarded as one of the most luxurious.

Yarotsky, our interpreter, came round for us. I discussed with
him the question of the leadership of the Communist Party. 'Who
will you get to replace Lenin?' I said.

'Nobody can replace Lenin, Comrade Citrine,' he retorted
reverently. 'He was too great a man to be succeeded by anyone else
as good.'

'What about Trotsky?' I asked. 'Surely he was the closest friend
of Lenin. They worked together during the early stages of the
Revolution, and I should have thought that he was the outstanding
personality who would be chosen to succeed Lenin.'

'I don't think that Trotsky will be chosen,' Yarotsky said. 'He
wants to get his own friends in control of the party and that is too
dangerous. He never appreciated the significance of the position of
the peasantry in Russia. He always underestimated their influence.
I think that Stalin is the nearest approach to Lenin of any of our
present leaders.'

This was said while we were walking over to the Opera House,
where they were producing a play called *The Fair at Sarojinich*. We
were taken into a very private box: not the box formerly used by the
royal family, which is the centre of the theatre, but one much
nearer the stage on the opposite prompt side. There were several of
the Communist leaders present and I was introduced to them in
turn. Two of them I observed particularly. One was Voroshilov, the
People's Commissar for the Army and Navy, who suppressed the
Kronstadt revolt in 1921, and the other Joseph Stalin, who became
the secretary of the executive committee of the Communist Party.
He sat within two or three feet of me during the whole of the time
that I was there. We did not get into conversation.

He was a man about 5 ft. 7 in. in height, and well knit, but not
stoutly built. He was dressed in a khaki uniform and had dark, well-
brushed hair and a full dark moustache. He was rather pock-
marked about the face, and his dark eyes wore a somewhat dreamy
look, giving him a rather kindly expression. Yet Lenin had said to his
intimate comrades: 'I don't trust that Stalin. He is too ruthless.' He

seemed to me to be a rugged and rather simple sort of character. Certainly his face had not the intellectuality about it that betokened the thinker, but on the other hand there was a good deal of determination to be seen in it.

Thirty-one years later I sat in that same box with Malenkov. This was the sixth time I had been in Russia, but on this occasion I was heading a delegation from the British Electricity Authority, of which I was then chairman. Malenkov had been over to Britain to see what we were doing in the electricity supply industry. During the several weeks he was here I became well acquainted with him. The Russians had invited us to pay a return visit and our delegation of seventeen electrical experts had been busy learning all they could, not only about the way in which electricity was generated and distributed but about the Russian way of life also.

On 18th April, 1956, we had an early dinner at the Metropole Hotel and then went over to the Bolshoi Opera House to see the ballet *The Fountain of Bakhchisarai*. Malenkov accompanied us and we occupied the former royal box in the centre of the second tier. After the first act, while we were having refreshments in the spacious foyer, Malenkov asked me whether I would like to sit in a box nearer the stage. I welcomed this, and the two of us with Kuznetsov, Malenkov's special interpreter, proceeded through another room set apart for the giving of lectures on theatrical subjects and which, I should think, could hold about 200 people. We went down a narrow staircase, carpeted in red, and so to a box on the opposite prompt side. We were now only a few feet from the stage, and although I couldn't see everything which occurred on our side, the general view was full and intimate. Whilst we were going down the staircase I came across one of the five bodyguards who had accompanied Malenkov whilst he was in England. He took us into the anteroom adjoining the box, whilst two other guards remained on the staircase.

It was almost an exact repetition of what I had experienced in 1925, except that then there were a few more guards about. I recognized the box at once and I remarked to Malenkov, through the interpreter, that he was sitting in the same seat where Stalin had sat alongside me in 1925. Malenkov sat mute when this was interpreted to him. He didn't change expression or show the slightest sign that he had heard me. It didn't occur to me at the time that perhaps mine was not a tactful observation to remind him of Stalin, who was just then going through the debunking process initiated by Comrade Krushchev, who was Malenkov's rival.

But I have jumped far ahead of my story and I must return to 1925.

During the interval at the opera I took Melnichansky, who was one of the members of the All-Russian Council of Trade Unions, and who was about my own age, to one side. I wanted to talk to him about the leadership of the party. Lenin had died, leaving no immediate successor, and I knew that the principal Communist leaders were exercised in their minds as to who should be appointed. I was anxious to hear Melnichansky's opinion.

'Isn't Stalin one of the three men who is dominating the Communist Party?' I asked.

'There are no three men dominating the party,' said Melnichansky. 'There are seven, the Polit Bureau.'

'Yes, but surely he is one, isn't he?' I retorted. 'In any case, tell me what you think of him.'

Melnichansky reflected for a moment or two and said: 'I think he is rather a clever fellow, but he is also very simple. He is not like that other guy, Trotsky.'

'What do you mean?' I inquired.

'Well, I have known Trotsky since he was a boy,' Melnichansky explained. 'We were prisoners of war together in Canada. You know we were arrested when the Soviet Government made a separate peace with Germany. I slept in the same bed with Trotsky when we were prisoners. But you can't feel you can talk to him. Stalin is different. You can talk about anything to him and say what you like. He doesn't take offence.'

'Is he likely to replace Lenin?' I asked.

'Well, he is about the best we have got,' Melnichansky replied, 'but he will never be a Lenin.'

'Lenin was a genius, I suppose, and I can quite understand you can't replace him, but have you got anyone else in sight; any of the younger men?' I asked.

'No, I am afraid we have not,' Melnichansky said after a moment's pause. 'Stalin is the best of the bunch.'

After this conversation I had another good look at Stalin who seemed to be enjoying the fun on the stage. His nose was straight and he had fairly good teeth, although they were not very white. His expression was good-humoured.

The following day we had a long conversation with officials of the trade unions in which we were given a detailed description of their form of organization. The rate of contribution was usually 2 per cent of the earnings of the individual workers. The union collectors were supplied with earnings figures by the management so that they could soon calculate the amount of contribution due. I pointed out to Melnichansky that it would be impracticable to work such a system in England, as it would be impossible for the unions' officials to know the exact amount of earnings. Melnichansky agreed that it would not be worked out easily in the United Kingdom. It would, however, be quite feasible to base contributions on a percentage of the standard wages as distinct from earnings.

I reverted to the question of leadership of the Communist Party. Melnichansky, who spoke excellent English, repeated that he did not believe Trotsky would be successful. He said: 'You know, Mr. Citrine, I am a Jew. Well, Trotsky is a Jew also. I am sorry to say that there is still a strong feeling against Jews in Russia. You know that there used to be pogroms against the Jews in the days of the Tsar, and although these were fostered by the Government, none the less, the feeling was deep. I don't believe Trotsky will be elected because, apart from anything else, he is a Jew. He advertises himself and Stalin doesn't. Yet Stalin is the stronger man of the two. Trotsky is against the trade unions and is opposed to their policy. We won't support him.'

We spent the evening at our hotel and had a long discussion which ended rather acrimoniously. Melnichansky, Tomsky, Yarotsky, Hicks, and myself comprised the party, and after a time we were joined by a Mr. Peters, who, I was subsequently informed, was the head of the Cheka. He was a quiet, unobtrusive young man, of soft voice, medium height, and inoffensively mild in his appearance. I little knew that he was responsible for the execution of some hundreds, if not thousands, of people. I discovered this by accident because of a conversation which I heard between him and Yarotsky.

Yarotsky said something to the effect, 'You remember, I met you in Leningrad.' Peters then recalled the occasion, and in the subsequent discussion it was explained that Yarotsky had been arrested by the Leningrad Cheka—of which Peters was at that time, apparently, in charge. He was taken along by a party of soldiers and finally brought to a wall where he was to be summarily executed.

'Then I began singing the "Internationale",' said Yarotsky.

'Why did you do that?' I asked.

'Well, it was explained to me that I was going to be shot,' he said, 'and I thought I would die in my Socialist faith.'

Just at that moment it appeared there came along a party of sailors from the *Kronstadt*, who were very popular in Leningrad. They recognized Yarotsky as having lectured to them some time previously. They explained that they would vouch for his integrity, and Peters, apparently, liberated him.

I thought to myself, 'That is rather a good introduction.' But in the light of the subsequent conversation it might have seemed that Mr. Peters would have further work to do. Peters told us that he had lived in London, in the East End, for a considerable time. He said he was the man who was supposed to be Peter the Painter, of Sidney Street siege fame, but actually he had never had anything to do with the anarchist gang who were supposed to have been led by that legendary hero.

In the course of the evening's conversation Tomsky referred to the position of Harry Pollitt, of the Communist Party, in England. I said I did not think that Pollitt represented any considerable section of the working class. Tomsky turned to me and said, 'Which of the two, Pollitt or Jimmy Thomas, is the more representative?' I said that in my opinion neither of them was typically representative, but of the two I would say Jimmy Thomas. 'He is at least the head of a large trade union, and as far as I know is deservedly popular with them.'

'But isn't Thomas a traitor?' said Tomsky.

Now this remark might have been made in England, as in fact it has been made in my hearing many times, without provoking my resentment. But on this occasion it was made with such cocksureness that I felt bound to defend Jimmy. I did not know him well, except by his public reputation, but none the less I felt it incumbent upon me to dispute such an arrogant charge. I asked that his treachery should be proved, on any of three grounds. 'Prove first that Thomas has been false to any declared resolution of policy of his own union. Secondly, prove that Thomas has been false to any declaration of policy or principle, or anything of the kind, of the Trades Union Congress. Or, thirdly, prove that Thomas has been false to some of the principles commonly held by the working class.'

'That is easily done,' said Tomsky. 'Thomas doesn't believe in the class war.'

'Well, if that's all you have against him,' I said, 'you put me down as a traitor as well, for I don't believe in the class war. I believe in the class struggle, which is quite a different thing. But that apart, when has the trade union movement ever tied itself down to the class war?'

I continued: 'Let us get a bit nearer. When has Jimmy Thomas ever betrayed his own union or his own members?'

'What about Black Friday in 1921?' said Tomsky.

'Well, what about Black Friday?' I retorted. 'Has it ever been proved that Thomas was treacherous on that occasion?'

I could see at once that Tomsky didn't know the subject sufficiently well to argue, so we passed on. Tomsky admitted that Thomas had done well for his own union and had probably advanced the condition of his men. He also admitted that he could not prove that Thomas had been false to any declared principle or resolution of the T.U.C. All that he could do was to say that Thomas was in the pay of the capitalist class.

When I asked for some evidence of this he said Thomas wrote articles for the capitalist Press. I then asked if it was the act of writing for the Press which constituted the treachery or the nature of the matter written. Tomsky said the capitalists would not be foolish enough to pay unless the articles written were of the kind they approved. I said I thought I knew the British capitalist newspaper proprietors sufficiently well to believe that they would publish anything that would sell their newspapers.

I asked Tomsky if he meant that those who paid the piper called the tune. Did he mean that because Thomas wrote for the capitalist Press the capitalist newspaper proprietors dictated what he said?

Tomsky evidently saw where this was leading and said that was rather a vague question and what did I mean by it?

I said: 'I will be very plain with you. I know that you subsidize, through the Communist International, the Communist Press in England. Does that mean, therefore, that they are not free agents? That they write only what you allow them to write?'

The discussion was getting rather heated, and Hicks, who had perhaps been applying himself to the drinks a little too liberally, turned to me and said angrily: 'Walter, you have got a damned cheek. Here are these men who have gone through blood and fire, through a revolution, and you have the audacity to question them and criticize them.' I repudiated this warmly and said that the mere fact of people engaging in dramatic events might prevent them from seeing things in perspective. I had come to Russia to express my opinions, to say what I wanted to say. I was not going to say just what the Russians wanted me to say, and if my liberty to speak was to be circumscribed I would go back to England at once. Immediately Tomsky and the others jumped up to assure me that nothing of the kind was necessary and that I could say what I wanted to. George too, by this time, saw the difference was developing too far, and he assured me he would go away and I could remain. I said, 'We'll talk about that in the morning, George.' With this we went to bed.

Next morning George approached me and said he had a dim recollection of having said something disagreeable the night before. I explained to him what had happened, and he apologized and said we must not quarrel while we were away. We could discuss our differences on our return. He was an exceptionally good travelling companion and very adaptable and the last man in the world with whom I wanted to quarrel. I had a real affection for him, and our difference was soon patched up.

Later we went to the Kremlin, accompanied by an officer who remained with us throughout our visit. After passing through the new and old palaces which contained many historical exhibits, and the throne room resplendent in jewels and gold, we entered the hall of St. George, beautifully proportioned, with its floor worked in different inlaid woods, all grown in Russia. We came eventually to a training school where Red Army soldiers were being educated. Here there was an instrument operating on the principle of a roulette wheel, a revolving disc turned by a handle, bearing a series of numbers. Each of these numbers represented a question in the educational code. I thought I would experiment with this, and so I turned the handle and watched until the pointer stopped opposite one of the numbers. I referred to a card index and taking out the card marked with this number asked an officer whether he could give an answer to the question written on it. After a second's hesitation he did so. Yarotsky checked his answer with the wording on the card, on which the answer as well as the question was written. Of course, in this and subsequent questions Hicks and I had to depend entirely on Yarotsky for the interpretation of both questions and answers.

It occurred to me that the officer would naturally be better educated and more alert at answering questions than the men under him. So I said, 'Let us get one of the soldiers.'

By this time the news of the presence of English had got round, and the soldiers came crowding in, all trying to get a glance at us. I asked one of them, 'Why must a soldier of the Red Army study military art and technique?'

The answer came promptly: 'Because a soldier of the Red Army must defend the interests of the peasants and the working class, and he must struggle against capitalism and defend the Soviet Union. Consequently he must know how to fight in case of necessity.'

I put questions to several of the soldiers, who answered promptly and apparently accurately, and finally I asked one of them, 'What relations must there be between the Red Army soldiers and the public?'

He answered without a moment's hesitation: 'A Red Army soldier must behave himself in a way to be an example. But he must not lose the closest contact with the labour and peasant classes. He must try to take every possible opportunity to do educational work amongst the workers and peasants, and to give them all the political and other information he can.'

All these answers no doubt had been learnt by heart, and no doubt received some slight embellishment from Yarotsky while translating. Still it was interesting as showing the methods employed by the Government.

Later I asked the officer what were his impressions in regard to certain aspects of the army. Was the discipline as efficient as under Tsarism? Were the efficiency and equipment as good? He told me that he had been a clerk in private life and had been in the Tsarist army during the early part of the war. The discipline in the army now was as efficient as in the Tsar's time, but rested on a different basis. There was now no bullying allowed by the authorities. He was sure that the efficiency was higher and the equipment supplied was undoubtedly better.

Melnichansky then asked us if we would like to go on the Moscow river for a boating trip. We accepted and went in a motor-car some couple of miles until we came to the boat-house of the Moscow trade unions. There we saw tier after tier of light skiffs and racing craft, and many stalwart young fellows coming to and from the water's edge.

As we were pulling back to the landing stage I saw a fellow shoot by in an outrigger, rowing with wonderful precision which stamped him as an expert.

'Who is that chap?' I asked Melnichansky.

'Oh, he is one of the intellectuals,' he said. 'He was formerly a rowing champion, and now we make him teach the workers how to row.'

I watched this fellow row to the bank, pick up his long boat, and carry it into the boat-house. I followed him into the boat-house in which we were joined by Melnichansky and a number of others.

This man, who was about thirty years of age and who spoke English, exchanged a few words with us on Melnichansky's introduction, explaining that he had rowed several years on the Thames in the days before the Revolution. His only complaint was that he ought to have a new boat, as the boat he was then using was twelve years old.

The others went down towards the entrance of the boat-house and I remained for a brief conversation.

'How are things going here?' I said to the fellow. 'Don't be afraid, you can speak to me perfectly frankly, I am not a Communist nor have I been a Communist or associated with them. I am a trade union official in England and I only want to know the truth.'

'Things are not going too well,' he said, 'but we can't talk now.'

I could see him looking furtively towards the entrance through which Melnichansky had disappeared.

'Can you come to our hotel tonight?' I said.

He looked dubious for a few minutes and then said, 'Where is it?'

'The National Hotel,' I said.

'All right, I will come. What time?'

'Oh, about nine or half past,' I said, 'if that will suit you. It will be dark then.'

'All right,' he said, 'I will come.'

I regret to say, however, that we saw no more of him. Whether he was afraid to come, thinking it might excite suspicion to be seen talking to me, I don't know. But the fact is that he didn't come, although he evidently had something to say.

In the evening we went to the Opera House. Here I had a few minutes' conversation with Litvinoff, the Assistant Commissar for Foreign Affairs. He was with his wife, an Englishwoman. Litvinoff himself knew England well, having lived there for a good many years, and having been the first Russian plenipotentiary appointed by the Soviet Government to Britain. I remember his addressing the Labour Party Conference at Nottingham when he explained what the new Russian Government had already done in its first three months of life. Litvinoff told me that he thought the social revolution must come very soon in England. His wife, however, strongly dissented from this point of view. I thought to myself, 'I will trust the judgement of the Englishwoman, despite all the technical knowledge which Litvinoff may think he has.'

The next morning we were greeted at breakfast by an old waiter, looking sorrowful. We did not eat or drink enough for him. At every meal he placed on the table two bottles of wine, expecting that George and I would finish at least one each. At one time there must have been a dozen full bottles on the table. Finally we had to tell him to take them away as we couldn't drink so much wine.

Then there was a matter of eggs. For the first few mornings we had no eggs for breakfast. I said to George Hicks one morning, 'Surely, George, we can have eggs.'

He said, 'Certainly, let us ask for them.'

So we asked for eggs. In a few minutes our old waiter returned with twelve eggs each for us! 'Do they expect us to eat all these?' I said to George. We didn't do it, and the pained look upon the old man's face was pathetic.

On the morning of Tuesday, 29th September, we went along to see Bogdanoff, of the building trade workers, at his office. He told us that the earnings of the workers depended upon piece-work. This system was applied wherever possible. Everybody had a wage book and the works committee had to see this to assess the union contribution, which the individual paid on the basis of the 2 per cent of his earnings.

We left Bogdanoff and asked Yarotsky, the interpreter, if we could see Kalinin, the President. We could.

In a few minutes we were back in the motor-car and speeding through the streets in the direction of the presidential building.

I thought to myself, 'Now we shall get a glimpse of the way the Russian system of government works.' I visualized the precautions which would be taken to safeguard the person of the President, and fully expected to encounter a close mesh, through which the visitor would have to pass before he was ushered into the august presence.

We stopped opposite a dilapidated building, a considerable distance from the Kremlin, and after walking past the guard at the door, who looked at us apathetically, we found ourselves in a long narrow room.

There at the far end, standing behind a low counter dividing it from an inner room, was a perspiring and worried-looking little man, surrounded by dozens of jostling and insistent peasants and workers. His wrinkled brow and harassed expression looked something like that of a debtor trying to compound with his creditors, or a welshing bookmaker trying to explain matters to his deluded bankers.

This was the President of the Republic, Kalinin. We tried to get near him, but the effort was futile. No one showed the slightest disposition to give up an inch of vantage. There were many people sitting about on forms in the corridor through which we had passed. All of them were waiting hopefully in the firm conviction that sooner or later they would see Kalinin.

At Yarotsky's suggestion we doubled back on our tracks and knocked at the door of a small room, which was speedily opened. Inside were four or five people, apparently secretaries. Some of them were taking notes, while others stood waiting with sheaves of papers in their hands at the elbow of Kalinin. He was leaning over the counter which separated him from a row of peasants in the other room. The sight was extraordinary. People were pushing and shoving, all trying to get within speaking distance.

I walked up to Kalinin, whose attention was too busily engaged to take any notice of us. I asked Yarotsky to explain what was going on.

'Well, you know our system,' he said, 'is to bring our government as closely into touch with the people as we can. Kalinin insists upon dealing with cases first-hand. He was a peasant himself and he likes to see the people. Everyone who has a grievance in the Republic thinks that all that is necessary is to come to see Kalinin and it will be put right.'

It did not take Kalinin long to deal with these cases. Probably each one did not last longer than half a minute. Practically all the people, it was explained to me, were wanting some form of material help. One would require a room in a house; another had been sentenced by one of the courts to several days' preventive detention. He had appealed to the President to commute this to compulsory outdoor labour, and they had actually allowed him out of prison to come to see Kalinin.

Later the same day we went to a meeting of the Commissars. Melnichansky whispered to us that Hicks and myself were the first foreigners who had ever been present at a meeting of the Commissars. Whether this was true or not we had no means of judging. It was very interesting. They all sat at a long table. At the top end there was Rykov, while Litvinoff and Krassin were among others I recognized. We, of course, just sat quietly and said nothing. We were not introduced.

In the course of the discussion Melnichansky became interested and walked up and took the floor in the most natural way possible. He held forth for about ten minutes, and then came back and told us that they were discussing a question as to whether the children of the intelligentsia should be given facilities for education in the schools. He personally was strongly in favour of it and gave his reasons. When I remonstrated and said he had no right to intervene he said, 'Oh, they'll listen to us trade unionist, all right.'

Everywhere there were busts of Lenin and large pictures of him on the wall. Hicks remarked that the best service that Lenin rendered to the Russian people was to die. Certainly they had made him a god— he had taken the place in the minds of the people of the Deity they worshipped in the churches. In the chamber of the Commissars there remains, carefully preserved, the chair in which he used to sit. No one was allowed to use it, nor do I think anyone would wish to do so. It stands there as a reminder of the power and personal influence of this extraordinary man.

The next day we left for Leningrad by night train. We were awakened in the train about 6 a.m. by a band playing the 'Internationale'. This was becoming the rule. Grudgingly, as the strains of 'Arise ye starvelings from your slumbers' dawned on our consciousness, the starvelings crawled out of their beds and put their heads through the window. We were at a wayside station. Yarotsky and Bogdanoff also took a long time to get up. There was a large crowd on the station and evidently they wanted us to address them. We bawled out to Yarotsky, 'Go and tell them what is necessary.'

Yarotsky: 'I positively refuse.'

Myself: 'Look here, Yarotsky, it's your job; you go out and tell them what we said at the last station. You can make a speech, you know what to say.'

Yarotsky: 'I'm not going to say anything at all.'

In the middle of our argument the train started and Yarotsky howled triumphantly, 'That will settle that matter.'

We had a big reception in Leningrad. There were two bands this time to meet us and a crowd of about 1,500 people. It appeared that they got word late the previous evening that we were arriving and they had organized this gathering in the short interval. Hicks made a speech, as also did Bogdanoff, but I succeeded in escaping.

The next exciting part of this excursion from Moscow was the story told to Hicks and myself by Yarotsky. We had been discussing the revolutionary movement in Tsarist days. I remarked that it was strange to think of a man like Yarotsky being a member of the terrorist group, and I asked him to tell me his story. This he did, and I jotted down, verbatim, all he said.

'My father was a member of the old terrorist organization [Yarotsky started], and my cousin was one of seven who were hanged together in 1907, some of them being women. So from childhood I was imbued with the idea of fighting against Tsardom, and by methods which did not stop at killing his representatives. When I was sixteen I joined the Social Revolutionary organization.

'When the 1905 Revolution was defeated, and acts of reprisal were committed by various generals, the Social Revolutionary Party empowered various party organizations to kill certain generals. The party executive only had the right to pass a resolution of death sentence, and then empower the fighting organization to carry out the sentence. General Polkovnikov had been responsible for the deaths of many workers, and I got the news that he had requested to be transferred to some quiet place. He was appointed the head of the counter-revolutionary establishment at Poltava. He arrived there at almost the same time as myself. We got information from the Ukraine executive to say that he must be killed. Immediately the Fighting Body received instructions to take part in the hunt for him. I was not a member of the Fighting Body, but I offered my services, and was included in it.

'It was a difficult job to find the best opportunity of killing him. One had to verify all details of when and where he could be attacked. We spent three or four months following his foot-steps. I found that practically every evening the general left his home to go to a military club, but the time was always uncertain. Twice some of our people just missed him, so they asked me to find out the time when he would be most certain to be at home. I discovered that in a couple of months' time there would be the annual opening ceremony of the club, which would be the beginning of October, and that it would take place at eight o'clock. The general would be at the club at exactly 8 p.m. That meant that he would start from his home at about 7.40 p.m. I told this to the Fighting Body, and they appointed a man to execute the sentence. That man came from a different town, and had never met General Polkovnikov in his life. I, as one who had been following his movements and knew him by sight, had to show him the general. I asked this chap to come with me to the theatre one night and showed him by a glance of my eyes which was Polkovnikov. General Polkovnikov was killed on the date I selected. Only one shot was fired, and it was done easily, the chap who committed it escaping.

'At that time we got news that the Government was sending a railway van full of revolvers to a military establishment. The railwaymen decided to detach the van and send it to the Fighting Body. This would have made quite an addition to our fighting capacity. I was asked to inspect the revolvers and see whether they were good ones, because some of the revolvers used in the Japanese war were dummies. I was just over nineteen at that time and my name underground was Comrade Andrew. The police knew that someone called "Andrew" was making the trouble. Often I escaped by a hair's breadth from being arrested. It was only my youthful appearance and caution that prevented my arrest.

'A railway worker was bribed by detectives with 3,000 roubles to let them know who "Andrew" was. He met me when I was carrying two revolvers. He pretended he wanted my advice regarding a dispute in the trade union. I was explaining this when we came to a bridge leading to the town. He suddenly left me, making a hasty excuse. On walking over the bridge I was met by a strong body of police who arrested me.

'They took me to an hotel. They told me I was suspected of

carrying arms, and I at once said, "All right, search me." I un-
buttoned my coat and held it clear of my body. The officer
went over me carefully, searched my waistcoat, felt round my
body and legs, and said: "There must be some mistake. He has
got nothing on him." Another officer apologized to me and said
there had evidently been a mistake, and that I had escaped arrest
on a very serious charge. I at once assumed an air of injured
innocence and was just turning round to leave the room when
my coat caught against the hilt of the sword one of the officers
was wearing. They had not searched my coat and the revolvers were in my pockets. Immediately the officer heard the
click of the metal he knew what it was, and saw the mistake
they had made in searching my inner pockets only. They were
excited and began examining a revolver. I said, "Well, you might
as well have the other one," and I brought the other revolver
out of my opposite pocket. If that revolver had been loaded I
could have got away.

'They knew that I was Andrew, all right, but they could not
prove anything against me. They put me into prison for about
a couple of months. In the meantime the worker who had given
me away was killed by the Fighting Body. His 3,000 roubles did
not do him much good.

'By that time the futile attempt of the police to find the
person who had killed General Polkovnikov made the Central
Government very anxious. They collected all the evidence from
every source which pointed in any way to the people who were
connected with the killing of General Polkovnikov. A theatre
servant who saw me pointing out Polkovnikov in the theatre
recognized the photo of me which the authorities showed him.
I was brought before the military court in May 1907, the hearing
being transferred to Kiev.

'Here on the first trial the verdict of "Not guilty" was
returned. They could not prove that we took part. Then the
public prosecutor decided to appeal against this verdict. The
chief military court cancelled it, and ordered a new trial. The
new trial sentenced me to hard labour for seven years. The
others were sentenced to minor terms of imprisonment. We
appealed against this, as also did the public prosecutor. During
the third trial General Stolypin, the Prime Minister, sent a telegram suggesting that if we had not been sentenced according to
the military code we should be dealt with under the political
criminal law. They said that the maximum penalty was death;
and we were found guilty under that law.

'When I was in prison under the sentence of death the authorities got an official letter stating that I was to be liberated on bail of 2,300 roubles, and I was liberated immediately. This letter was a forgery, however, sent by my party organization. Inquiry was made, and they found that the signature was genuine The general could not remember having signed it, but nevertheless he had done so. One of his confidential clerks, who was inclined to be a revolutionary, had been approached by our people. He had written the letter and put it before the general, who had signed it without reading it. The clerk had stipulated that we must help him to escape, and we gave him 3,000 roubles, which enabled him to go to America. Immediately I was liberated I was met at the police court where I was given an identity book and taken at once to a train which started me on my way to the frontier. Eventually, I crossed the frontier successfully.'

7

Recalled to London

ON OUR return from Leningrad to Moscow during the 1925 trip Melnichansky took us to his flat. I noticed that in the large living-room there were several rifles stored in the corner. Melnichansky explained that these were remnants from the Revolution, but he always kept them by him.

I was struck by the appearance and mannerisms of Melnichansky's only child—a boy of six and a half years. He spoke as though he were an adult man. There were no symptoms of childish playfulness

Through his father, he asked me how long a little boy was at school in England. What did English boys do? What time did they go to bed? If there was a revolution would the little boys fight as well? Was there electricity in the houses in England? Had we got many books about the Revolution in England? Then, pointing to books, he said, 'Have you any books and stories like these?' He suddenly stopped and after a pause continued: 'Have you got any rich men? Have they got big houses?'

Hicks replied that we had many poor people in England. We had some rich men.

The child seriously pondered this question, and then asked: 'Have you as many electric lamps as we have on this table? Have you got any albums to put pictures in? How do the workers live in the villages in England?'

I was told that the little boy was a member of the Octobrists— the youth section of the Pioneers, something like the Wolf Cubs in our Boy Scout movement. So I said to him, 'How long have you been in the Octobrists?'

The child replied: 'I don't know whether I am in the Octobrists or not. Some say I am in the Octobrists and some say I am not.' Then he asked: 'What books do you read? Do you read children's books?' I said that I did sometimes. 'Why do you read children's books?' I said I thought children's books were written very simply and taught some grown-up people many things they did not know.

I thought this was an amazing battery of questions from a child of his age. He seemed so serious, so stolid, so reflective, that I don't think the youngster could have had much play in his life.

Mrs. Melnichansky said that she thought, with the social conditions in Russia being in a ferment, and with the child being born when they were right in the midst of the Revolution, he was affected by it. She thought it sometimes weakened the children's faculties.

We went to the premises of the Moscow Trades Council and had the administrative methods explained to us by the secretary, Mikhailoff. A glance at their methods of administration showed them to be a long way behind those of British trade union practice.

We had an interesting discussion with him regarding strikes. It appeared that strikes took place in private employment but not in any State organization. I reminded him that in the Co-operative movement in Great Britain we had had strikes, although the Co-operative societies were owned in some cases by the very people, amongst others, who came out on strike. I said that often the position of an individual as a producer and his position as a consumer were in conflict.

Mikhailoff, who was not more than thirty years of age, did not understand this point of view and we left him thinking, no doubt, that we British people were rather strange and illogical.

That night we left Moscow by train for the Crimea. We had a first-class carriage for our 750-mile journey. The slow journey was compensated for by the fact that the Russians had been thoughtful enough to secure for us the best berths they could on the train. The cars had belonged to the International Sleeping Car Company and were extremely comfortable. Still, confinement in a train has its irksomeness, no matter how good the conditions of travel may be. The train never seemed to exceed a speed of more than about twenty miles an hour, and the vast spaces through which we were travelling made it seem even slower.

At the station of Belgorod, which appeared to be a quiet little town, Hicks and I stretched our legs for a few minutes on the platform. There was little convenience for the passengers at these stations and the sanitary accommodation was lamentable.

While we were looking about we came across a gang of a dozen young boys, all of them begging. They were in a distressingly filthy state, and one of them was entirely naked, except for a pair of dilapidated trousers, which only partly concealed his loins. Most of them looked as though they had not used water for several months. It was pretty cold and I had my overcoat on. Yet all these kiddies were only partially clad. No one seemed to think it strange to see them, nor did they appear to excite the slightest interest in any of the passengers.

We were getting near Sebastopol, and sunshine brought buoyancy to our weary spirits. Hicks and I broke into song, to the consternation of Yarotsky. He at once informed us that penalties were posted up in the corridor for certain offences committed against the comfort of the other passengers. It seemed uncalled-for to describe my singing as an offence, but after hearing Hicks I could see the necessity for protecting the passengers!

We had a look at this list of offences, which was translated to us. It was as follows:

Swearing and immodest conduct	3 roubles
Getting out of the train while in motion	3 roubles
Improper use of the automatic brake	25 roubles
Card-playing for money	50 roubles
Singing, playing of musical instruments, and generally disturbing the quiet of the passengers	10 roubles
Improper use of lavatories at stations	3 roubles
Eating sunflowers and dropping the seeds about	3 roubles
Trading without special permission	50 roubles
Using small spirit stoves even though there may be no danger of fire	50 roubles

It appeared to us that life was scarcely worth living on a train journey in Russia!

Arriving at Sebastopol, we were met by a motor-car driven by an alert young fellow who was accompanied by the commissar for the district. We drove off with the usual cluster of curious boys gathered round the car, until we arrived at a building surmounted by a magnificent round dome. This was known as the Panorama and was erected to commemorate the Siege of Sebastopol during the Crimean War in 1855. It contained graphic records of that famous siege.

We climbed to the dome, and found ourselves in a circular chamber with a central platform. All round the walls were paintings of the siege in progress, designed to form one continuous and panoramic view 300 feet in circumference. The walls were some distance away from the central platform (probably about thirty feet) and the intervening space was occupied by life-sized effigies of combatants with all the accoutrements of war. It was a remarkable picture, showing, among other things, British men-of-war lying in the distance and shelling the town.

We went on to Balaclava over dusty roads and then to the famous Gate of Bidira. In passing the fields of Balaclava we saw the place where the Light Brigade made its desperate charge. Eventually we arrived at a rest home, which was evidently reserved for people in authority under the Soviet Government. One of them there was Yaroslavsky, the head of the Anti-God Society and secretary of the Control Commission of the Communist Party.

I had a long conversation with Yaroslavsky. On my remarking as I looked over the Black Sea how beautiful it all was, he answered, 'Yes, but it will soon be running in blood.'

'Why will it be running in blood?' I asked.

'Because the capitalists are determined to get hold of the oil that is down here,' he said, referring to the oil wells in the Caucasian peninsula.

'I see no reason why that should be the case,' I said.

'Oh yes, it will happen,' said he, 'it will happen almost certainly.'

He told us of the methods they had adopted in combating religion. He said they were doing this on scientific principles, both in illustrations and in pamphlets they were sending out to the villages. They now had a circulation of over 200,000 among regular subscribers. He considered it was essential to get rid of the idea of religion because this acted as a drug on the minds of the people.

After a few days of rest, free from the troubles and cares of the world and blessed with bright sunshine, a telegram arrived from the British Trades Union Congress asking me to return as quickly as possible. We hurried back to Sebastopol and caught a train the same evening for Moscow. I discussed with Yarotsky while we were on the train the question of why I was being recalled to England. All that he knew was that he had received a telegram from Tomsky to the effect that I was to return immediately. He had sent a reply telling him that we had started at once.

On the morning of Tuesday, October 13th, not feeling well, I stayed in bed in our compartment as long as possible. When the morning was well advanced I got up and found we had stopped at a small station called Lazovaia. On Hicks's advice I went for a breath of fresh air on to the platform. Then I noticed that Yarotsky was reading a newspaper he had just bought. He turned to me and blurted out, 'Look, Fred Bramley is dead.'

I was amazed at this and asked him to read it again. He read a message to the effect that Bramley had passed away on Saturday, 10th October, in Amsterdam. I asked, 'How could it be in Amsterdam, and what was he doing there?'

Yarotsky didn't know, and we presumed that he was attending

a meeting of the I.F.T.U., as that was the only reason we could find for his presence in Amsterdam. Tomsky had evidently got to know pretty early, because his General Council had sent a telegram of condolence to the T.U.C. Evidently he knew when he sent his wire to Yarotsky what had happened but didn't like to give us a shock.

We were ambling along at about ten to fifteen miles an hour in the train which seemed to crawl more slowly after we got the news.

We reached Moscow on the morning of 14th October and immediately went to the Hotel National, from where I telephoned to Melnichansky. Later I had an interview with Tomsky. Both strongly represented to me that it would be against the wishes not only of themselves but also of the Russian Government if I flew to Konigsberg *en route* for England. There had been so many deaths because of flights with inexperienced Russian pilots that the executive committee of the union had decided that none of their officers must fly except on the most urgent business. Hicks added his persuasions to these exhortations, and I could see that in the circumstances it was impossible for me to go against their wishes. They told me that they had arranged for an express train to leave the next evening.

We spent some time with Schmidt, the Commissar of Labour, and his wife, and a number of other friends. In the evening we went to the Kremlin for an interview with Zinovieff, who was the secretary of the Communist International or the Comintern. He was at a handsomely carved desk in a large room, lighted only by a table lamp. He was accompanied by the American, John Reed, who wrote *Ten Days That Shook the World*. I had a good look at Zinovieff. He was undoubtedly a Jew, dark, with a hooked nose and long, unruly hair. He had light blue eyes, and a high-pitched voice. He had a restless manner and when one was talking to him he could not keep still. He appeared to be a man who could quickly come to a decision. He was dressed plainly in a black blouse and breeches. All the furnishing in the room I could see during our conversation was the desk with a red leather top, a huge map on the adjacent wall, and a fine bookcase which matched the desk.

He was the man who was supposed to have written a letter of instruction to McManus, of the British Communist Party, instructing how to bring about revolution in England. This fell into the hands of the Conservatives and they accused the Labour Government of having the information and not publishing it. MacDonald had hesitated about his reply and the consequence was that the public got the impression that the letter was a genuine one, although in point of fact that was never established. At the best the Secret Service could not prove it was anything more than an extract from a speech which Zinovieff had made. The letter said that it was desirable that Communist cells should be formed in all units of the troops, amongst factories working on munitions, and at military store depots. The furore this alleged letter aroused was certainly one of the principal factors which brought about the defeat of the Labour Government at the General Election.

Zinovieff said that he had not thought much about MacDonald or his Government. He thought that MacDonald's policy would lead to a split with the trade union movement in England. What concerned him particularly was how we could reconcile the decision of the Liverpool conference of the Labour Party, at which they had decided to disaffiliate the Communists, with the decision of the T.U.C. at Scarborough held in September, at which a much warmer feeling was displayed.

I tried to explain to him that he must not overrate this, and that while on the whole we were not unfriendly to the Communists, at the same time we did not feel that they were an inherent part of our movement. I, personally, was not surprised at the decision of the Liverpool conference.

This seemed to disturb Zinovieff. I tried to impress him with the fact that there was a good deal of difference in the actions of the Russian Communists, faced with real problems, and the irresponsible advocacy of world revolution by the British Communists operating under the instructions of the Comintern.

Zinovieff thought that a world war was inevitable unless one inclusive Socialist and trade union international was established.

The conversation became desultory. I said suddenly to him: 'You have got pretty good surroundings here, at all events. I shouldn't think you feel very revolutionary when you look around. You have a magnificent desk but I see you offset that with a half-crown watch.'

This was translated to Zinovieff, who laughed, and we shook hands and left.

Later that evening Hicks and I were invited to a farewell function in the Kremlin which had been organized by Schmidt in our honour. We strolled across the square in front of the Bolshoi Theatre. I thought I saw a movement of a dog or something in a corner to my right.

I said to Yarotsky, 'What is that over there?' Whilst I was talking to him I looked closer. I could see there was a great heap of straw and that something was moving underneath. Out of curiosity Hicks and I went across. There we saw something which staggered us. In the straw we could dimly perceive there were about twenty people, some of them old men, some women, and some children. The children especially looked terrible. I remember seeing a lad of about fourteen years of age. All he had on was a cap and a pair of trousers. He had no boots or stockings. The upper part of his body was unclothed except for dirt. His hair was matted. Yarotsky advised me not to touch them as, he said, they were verminous.

'You know, comrade,' said Yarotsky, 'this is one of Russia's great problems. These children are some of the homeless. Their parents died during the years of famine and there are simply hundreds of thousands of them wandering about Russia.'

'But you can't leave them out here all night,' I said. 'Surely to goodness you can put them somewhere else.'

'Where can we put them?' Yarotsky demanded.

'I don't know where you can put them,' I said, 'but I am sure that there must be some café or building you could take them into and shelter them for tonight.'

I said this with some feeling, as the air was cold and we had our overcoats on. Tomsky, Melnichansky, and some of the others had walked on, apparently uninterested in what was taking place. Yarotsky simply shrugged his shoulders and said: 'Well, this is one of Russia's problems, comrade. We can do nothing about it.'

And so we went away.

Hicks and I were indignant and could scarcely get it out of our minds. However, once in the Kremlin, our attention was distracted by something else. Here we found ourselves in a long room, now being used as a dining-room for us. It seemed to have been converted on the spur of the moment. There was a little ante-room, where we were introduced to various Commissars. I remember one Commissar in charge of the railways, one in charge of the forests, another in charge of transport, and so on. I did not see Kalinin, Rykov, Stalin, or any of the principal Commissars. I should think that altogether we must have mustered some forty or fifty people.

We sat down at a long table covered with a white cloth. It groaned under the good things of life: there were fruits from the Caucasus and the Crimea, grapes and pears as large as any I have ever seen, and dozens of bottles of wine. We had gold knives and forks, and some of the other table equipment was picked out in silver and in gold. The dishes and the cut glass were exquisite. We were told that these were relics and were used by the Tsar and his family and had been 'inherited' by the Bolsheviks. It was certainly the grandest display of table cutlery I have ever seen.

After a time I heard a sort of chanting and, looking to the part of the room where it came, I saw a number of the Russians standing with their wineglasses full and raised. One of them held a very large champagne glass and was making his way towards us. He walked behind us, the whole of the company having risen to their feet in the meantime, and joined in the chant. Louder and louder the song swelled until they got behind my chair and proffered me the glass. They repeated the last line of the chorus, whatever it was, louder and louder and louder, until the row was enough to blow down the Kremlin itself.

I turned to George Hicks, with 'Pick me out from under the table afterwards, George.' I took the glass and drank the vodka as quickly as I could. The singing ceased. A little later the process was repeated for Hicks. I found myself getting merry, but certainly not inebriated.

I asked afterwards what this process was, and it appeared it was called the Charogaa. It is apparently a gypsy custom which they use at their festivities, and one is supposed to turn the glass upside down to show that none of the champagne or vodka, or whatever drink it might be, is left in it.

They put my own name into the song, and sang something about 'Walter, Walter'. The song is evidently intended to be a toast to the guest and they sing and sing until he drinks it down.

The next day Yarotsky asked, 'Would you like to see a political prison, a convict prison, or merely a short-term-detention establishment?' I said I would prefer to go to a convict prison. In accordance with our general plan we made up our minds that we would disclose our intentions as to where we would go at very short notice. We did this deliberately to avoid being shown only what the authorities might have desired us to see.

It was settled that we should visit the Sokolniky prison. We were given a description to make us familiar with the broad outlines of the system. They did not call these establishments 'prisons' but 'educational institutions for criminals'. The utmost length of detention of any person in this establishment was ten years.

The prisoners were paid the full trade union rates of wages, but one-half of this was retained by the authorities until the end of their term. The prisoners then received the balance in a lump sum, which was considered sufficient to give them a decent restart in life.

We toured the workshops, library, and dormitories, and interrogated a number of the inmates, who said they were well treated. We came to the prison co-operative stores, where we saw a plentiful supply of bread, butter, tobacco, cheese, soap, and other commodities on sale.

There were two men in this place, standing behind a low counter. One of them was doing some book-keeping in the corner, and I was surprised to find that both of them were prisoners.

The Commandant shook his head sadly when questioned about the book-keeper. He said it was a very unfortunate case, as this man had been a commissioner of a brigade in the Red Army and had attained the rank of general. He had, however, embezzled some of the funds under his charge, and had been sentenced to ten years' imprisonment.

Just as we were about to leave I noticed one of the men feeling in his waistcoat pocket. Finally he unearthed a cigarette, and after tapping it for a moment on the rack before him, as smokers do, he felt for a match. Discovering he was without one, he walked over to the commandant with the cigarette in his left hand. The commandant, who was smoking, in the most matter-of-fact way in the world held his own lighted cigarette so that the prisoner could get a light.

Hicks and I looked at each other, and it was as much as we could do to prevent ourselves from laughing.

'What sort of a place is this we have come to?' I said. 'Is it a Fred Karno gaol or a pantomime show?'

'I do not know,' said Hicks, 'but I cannot imagine anyone wanting to run away.'

We had a retinue to accompany us from the hotel to the station. Yarotsky accompanied us to the frontier at Zevash. Tomsky was quite affected at our departure, more by leaving Hicks than by leaving me, I am sure. He kissed George on both cheeks and turned rather hesitantly to me and did the same. I said to him, 'Well, don't stand waiting about in the cold on the station, you'd better get back to the Kremlin, it's snowing heavily.'

'Oh, we like snow,' he replied, and seemed really happy that the snow had at last arrived.

I thought of those people, and particularly the children, we had seen in the straw on the previous evening. I wondered to myself what would be their fate on a night like this. Would they have to stay out again in the snow?

I said nothing because I could see from the conversation the previous evening that our friends rather felt their position and were sensitive about our reproaches.

I tried to get a newspaper at the Moscow October Station, from which our train left, to see whether I could read anything for myself about Bramley's death, but the newspapers had not arrived. All I could be told was that he had died in Amsterdam. We were glad to get to bed, as it was late, and we had had a heavy day. Nothing eventful occurred on the return journey and we reached London, via Ostend, on 19th October 1925.

Perhaps it will be convenient if I deviate from a chronological narrative, and deal here briefly with my next visit to Russia. I was invited for the second time in 1935. My wife accompanied me and we spent several weeks there, travelling by the s.s. *Smolny* from London to Leningrad.

I had been for seven years president of the International Federation of Trade Unions, and the Russians were still pursuing determinedly their policy of closer unity with that body. What I have written in an earlier chapter indicates some of the difficulties, and these had not been lessened in the intervening years. Practically all the established trade unions on the continent of Europe were suspicious of the so-called United Front movement, and naturally as president of the I.F.T.U. I was quite sensitive to this. I knew that my activities while in Russia would be followed with some anxiety by the European unions. I also knew that the invitation had in all probability been extended to me in the hope that, in some way, my visit would facilitate the United Front. To do the leaders of the Russian trade union movement justice this matter was not at any time broached to me in a direct fashion, except upon the last day of my stay in Moscow. About this I shall have something to say later.

On my return from Russia I wrote some articles giving general impressions of what I had seen and heard, and subsequently my book *I Search for Truth in Russia* was published. This has long been out of print, and most of my readers may never even have heard of it, much less of the conclusions I reached.

I had made it clear before leaving for Russia that I wished to see things for myself. On arriving in Leningrad we were greeted by a delegation of trade union officials from Moscow and Leningrad. Soon I was conversing with Mr. Alexseyeff, the chairman of the Leningrad Trades Council, at the Palace of Labour. I thanked him for the facilities which were being placed at our disposal, to which he replied, 'Our instructions are that you are to go to where you like and see what you like.'

I replied that I did not want to see only the best. I wanted to see the worst as well. I did not want to be taken to the show places only.

'You shall see all you desire,' was the reassuring reply.

This was no empty promise, and during the subsequent weeks the facilities afforded us were exceptional. My wife and I travelled to Moscow, Gorki, Kharkov, Dnieproges, Kramatorsk, Gorlovka, Kislovodsk, and Baku; and throughout I was accompanied by a courteous and competent interpreter, who proved himself a pleasing personality.

I had to discard much of the information that I was given, not by my interpreter, but by others, particularly the guides provided by Intourist, the official travel agency of the Soviet Union. They were well trained and appeared to know all the answers. Sometimes, however, their information was not accurate. For example, while journeying by motor-car to the Stalin factory in Moscow I asked how many motor-cars there were in Moscow. I had been struck by the comparative absence of traffic, whether buses, private cars, lorries, or bicycles. Certainly there were more than I had seen in 1925, but nothing in comparison with the cities of the Western world. The guide immediately answered, 'About 200,000.'

'What,' I said, '200,000? They must be underground, then. Why, if you had said 20,000 I think it would have been a generous estimate.' Some days later I discussed the matter with the President of the Moscow Soviet and some of his officials. They laughingly told me, when I had recounted the incident, that the number in Moscow was about 16,000.

My Russian companion, Karchan, did not at any time, so far as I could judge, attempt to mislead me. He freely acknowledged the shortcomings of the Soviet Union in the economic sphere. When I came to political matters he was much more cagey. Never once did the slightest criticism of the Soviet regime or any of its principal officers escape his lips.

I knew it was the policy of the Soviet Government to spend an enormous proportion of the national budget on equipping the country to defend itself against any attack from without. It followed that the standard of life of the people could not rise as rapidly as it otherwise would have done. What I saw proved this. Clothing and shoes were shoddy. Housing was scarce and overcrowded. Food was crazily dear. Building work was atrocious.

I made strenuous efforts to find out how the standard of life compared with Western countries such as our own. This was no easy matter, as it was hopeless to try to make the comparison in monetary values. The Russian rouble was grossly overvalued. There was no real rate of exchange with other countries. The rates quoted by the Soviet authorities showed that we would receive five roubles and sixty copecks for every English pound note. This made each rouble nominally worth 3s. 7d. It is hardly to be wondered at that stories were brought back to the U.K. by British visitors of having to pay 4s. for an egg.

It was well known that there was a Black Exchange which,

although frowned upon by the Soviet authorities, was accessible to foreign visitors. I myself was accosted on several occasions. In the evenings a man would sidle up to me and ask in English whether I wished to exchange pound notes for roubles. The highest I was ever offered was 100 to the pound, but I had heard of cases where the rates had gone up to anything from 180 to 300 roubles to the pound. Needless to say, I had no traffic with such people, as I knew it was an offence under Soviet law. I had no intention of exposing myself to a charge.

I concluded that with the best will in the world it was impossible to credit the rouble as being worth more than 3d. in actual purchasing power.

It will be seen how difficult, with this artificial rate of exchange, it would be merely to compare the purchasing power of the average Russian worker with that of the British. I tried to make a comparison of a more realistic kind.

Once back home I was able to describe my Russian experiences in the February 1936 issue of *Labour*, the official organ of the T.U.C. and the Labour Party. By that time I had collected through the agency of the London Co-operative Society and other suppliers a list of comparable prices of the commodities which I had noted down in Moscow. At that time the average monthly earnings of the Russian workers were 250 roubles per month. I increased this figure by about one-third to allow for the socialized wage which covered all the advantages that the Russian workers were stated to have in the way of holidays with pay, low rents, free dental treatment, old age and disability pensions, and treatment in sanatoria and rest homes, etc. I took no account of any of these advantages which the British workers possessed. I took the latest figures issued by the Ministry of Labour of the earnings of men, women, youths, and girls, both skilled and unskilled, employed in Great Britain. Next I compared the prices of the commodities I had seen in Russia with those for the same British articles or foodstuffs, as near as I could judge. I then ascertained how many hours the Russian worker had to work to purchase these commodities and how long the British worker would have to be similarly employed to buy the comparable British commodities. I included only the cheaper class of British commodities, as these were more strictly comparable with those sold in the Russian shops, but it may be taken for certain that the quality of the British commodities was undoubtedly superior to the Russian.

The outcome of this comparison was to show that, taking the table of minimum prices as a whole, the Russian worker had to work at least four times as long as the British worker to purchase the same commodities. I have never claimed that the comparison is a strict guide to the whole standard of life, owing to the number of commodities quoted and because I could not give greater weight to some commodities quoted than to others in proportion as they figured in the standard of life. It did, however, give some insight into the problem which faced the Russian Government in raising the standards of its people to the level attained by the British workers.

My general conclusions were that the Communist Party was, beyond all doubt, the dominant power in Russia, and that the trade unions, like the Government, were subservient to its authority. Every union official whom I met was a member of the party and many wore the dark blue shirt and black trousers which seemed to be the distinguishing garb of the Communist officials.

The trade unions in Russia occupied a very different status from the unions in other parts of the world, being entrusted by the State with important social insurance functions. Striking changes were even then taking place in the U.S.S.R. Old methods and ideas were being ruthlessly scrapped to give place to modern ones.

I found no justification for the assumption, which I sometimes heard, that the Soviet Government rested on an unstable foundation. On the contrary, it seemed to me to be as firm as a rock. A new constitution was under consideration, but I knew sufficient of Russian affairs not to be deluded into the assumption that all that appeared in the constitution on paper necessarily represented what was being carried out in practice. It seemed to me that economically Russia was catching up with the Western world and I had little doubt that she would become, in time, one of the greatest industrial powers in the world. I thought I could detect the rise of classes in Russia, which seemed to me to follow inevitably from the vast difference in salaries between those in high managerial posts and the ordinary workers.

Russia was changing rapidly, I had no doubt of that, and I fervently hoped that it would be for the good of the people as a whole.

No attempt was made to approach me on the subject of the United Front, except on the last day I was in Moscow. An informal and private farewell party was given for my wife and myself on this night when I was introduced to a number of officials who I understood were members of the All-Russian Council of Trade Unions. We fell to discussing the impressions of my visit, and at one stage I became indignant—possibly because I was somewhat fatigued—at an attempt that had been made that afternoon to involve me in a discussion on the United Front. This had occurred at a meeting of alleged trade union workshop representatives. I had no means of telling who they were, and I regretted my lack of caution in engaging in this meeting without a fuller knowledge of my audience.

A young fellow had asked me why I was opposed to unity with the Russians. I answered that I believed in genuine unity, but that pretence would be worse than no contact at all; I recounted our experience of the Anglo-Russian Committee and the breach by the Russians of their pledge not to interfere with our internal affairs. They had appealed to our members over the heads of the T.U.C. General Council and had the temerity to claim the right to do this.

Another chap asked why we had interfered in the internal affairs of Russia by protesting against the shooting of White Guards after the murder of Serge Kirov, the leader of the Leningrad Communists and a close friend of Stalin. This was evidently a reference to a deputation headed by George Lansbury and myself to the Soviet Embassy in London when Ivan Maisky was the Ambassador. I retorted that it was the practice of the British trade union movement to protest to governments whenever we thought injustice was being done. We had protested to the German Ambassador when Dimitrov and other Communists were in danger of being shot because of their alleged participation in the burning of the German Reichstag. We had protested also against death sentences on workers in Spain, Austria, and other countries. All these were capitalist states and in some instances the accused men had taken up arms against the Government. How could we, then, remain silent when a so-called Socialist state shot, without any trial, over 100 people? I went on: 'You say these people were White Guards. How do I know that some of you are not White Guards? Over sixty of those shot were known to be Communists. If Hitler had known as much about the art of repression as Stalin the world might never had heard of Dimitrov. He would have been shot in a cellar.'

I listened carefully to see whether the rosy-cheeked and good-looking girl who was interpreting translated this. When she finished I turned to her and said sharply, 'Why didn't you translate what I said?'

She appeared to be taken aback, but I felt sure that she had not done so; so I insisted, and she haltingly stammered out a few sentences. An uncomfortable silence followed. No one seemed to know what to do or say next, so after a few moments I got up and left.

Now, how did I know that the girl had not properly translated my remarks? I couldn't speak more than a few words of Russian. But she didn't know that. No one really knew whether I had greater knowledge of Russian than I professed, but I was listening for the names of Dimitrov and Stalin, and she didn't mention either of them, so that I was pretty certain that she had not done so. I knew that many of the Russian interpreters were experts in avoiding awkward answers to questions and construing them in the way they thought most appropriate. So I took a chance and the frightened look that the girl gave me when I accused her was enough to convince me that she had not interpreted faithfully what I had said. The effect that my remarks produced clinched it. I don't know whether Shvernik (head of the Soviet trade unions) had received a full report of the incident. I felt they had tried to trick me into some kind of pronouncement on the desirability of having a united front with the Russian trade unions.

I had expressly stated before leaving England that I would not enter into any such discussions, and I repeated this to Shvernik on my arrival in Moscow. I was firmly under the impression that this meeting had taken place with his knowledge and that of his colleagues. I blamed the chairman of the afternoon meeting, Abolin, who was a member of the Central Council, for what I thought was a manœuvre to get me involved. I sensed that the questions put to me had been carefully arranged. My indignation soared to its heights when I said that I knew I had been talking to the puppets and parrots of the Communist Party. At this, one man, to whom I had not been introduced, speaking in English, said, 'You will not forget that these puppets and parrots are the people who made the Revolution.'

I replied as scornfully as I could: 'I should have thought that was rather difficult. The Revolution was eighteen years ago. The average age of the people I met this afternoon couldn't have been more than thirty at the utmost, and I didn't know that the Revolution was brought about by children.'

At this Shvernik quietly intervened with the remark, 'Let Lozovsky go on.'

I jumped up at this and demanded, 'Is this Lozovsky the secretary of the Red International?' On being informed that he was, I expressed myself in uncomradely language and declined to continue the interview. I had told Shvernik long before that I couldn't have any dealings with Lozovsky because of the misinterpretation that would be placed on my action. I had no particular feeling against him personally, but I knew that his organization was obnoxious to the trade unions of the West and that he was believed to be the instigator of most of the intrigues and subversive actions of which they complained.

After this acrimonious ending of our gathering at the Palace of Labour, we went along to the British Embassy and saw the official in charge, who was acting in the absence of the Ambassador. I told him exactly what had happened. He listened with a serious expression and when I had finished he said gravely, 'You are a brave man, Citrine'. 'No, I am not brave at all,' I replied, 'but I am a man who can calculate risks. Up to now I have been in no danger. Now I am not quite so sure.'

So it was arranged that my wife and I should be accompanied on the train journey to Leningrad by an official of the Embassy, who never left us until we had departed from Russia.

So ended my last night in Russia, until I returned some years later on more momentous visits.

8

The Mining Crisis

THE most dramatic event during my first few years at the T.U.C. was, of course, the General Strike of 1926, six months after I had returned from my 1925 visit to the Soviet Union and become the acting secretary. In a technical sense it was never a General Strike. We at the Trades Union Congress always called it the 'national strike'. We regarded it as a large-scale sympathetic strike. By no means all the members of the trade unions were called out; probably not more than 1,500,000 workers were engaged in addition to the miners. But it was the only strike of such dimensions in the long history of the trade union movement.

These memoirs would not be complete without some attempt by me to deal with the strike's human factors. At a distance of thirty-eight years from the actual events this may seem difficult. Fortunately I kept a full note in shorthand of all the more important developments. Much of what I have written here is quoted from my notes, written sometimes while meetings were in progress and other times on the evening of the same day, no matter how tired I may have been.

Let us see how the strike began. It was centred on the trouble in the coal-mining industry. Relations between the miners and the coal-owners had been a constant source of bitter strife for many years. Lock-outs and strikes were an almost daily occurrence. Often they were confined to a single colliery or a group in the same district. But there were occasions when they stretched over a county or even the whole of the nation's coal-fields.

When I joined the trade union movement in 1911 local agreements between the unions and the employers were the rule wherever the workers were properly organized. National agreements covering the whole country were few. This applied to coal-mines in particular. The predominant feature of organization of the mineworkers from its inception had been its local character. Rates of wages often differed from colliery to colliery, and were based upon ancient schedules which were a mystery to most people outside the mining industry.

Every colliery had its own union branch or lodge, and these were linked up into county federations called districts. They, in turn, were joined together in the Miners' Federation of Great Britain. The coal-owners were organized in similar fashion through a federal system consisting of district associations and a central body called the Mining Association.

The power to resolve differences lay almost entirely with the district federations. Even when an important issue of a national character was raised it usually had to be referred back to the districts. This became more noticeable on the side of the workers. There were ballots of the miners in the districts on practically every important issue. The results of these ballots were regarded as binding upon the Miners' Federation. There was a stubborn loyalty to the opinions of the rank and file, no matter how much circumstances might have merited a different course. Those who had any insight into the in-ternal affairs of the Miners' Federation were fully aware of the strong differences of opinion which arose from time to time.

Such conflicts occurred also within the owners' association, but they were not so noticeable. To the outside world both sides presented an appearance of unshakable solidarity. A continual underlying antagonism was felt on both sides, and nobody wanted to let his own side down. This antipathy was worse in some districts than others; South Wales in particular was something of a cockpit. Disputes were almost invariably fought with the gloves off, and no holds were barred. Furthermore, disputes in the coal-fields were usually far more protracted than in most other industries. Frank Hodges, secretary of the M.F.G.B. from 1918 to 1924, once said that he heard J. H. Thomas declare that he himself had led a strike of railwaymen for eleven days. Hodges observed:

> . . . he said it as though it were some wonderful and unique experience. It was—for him. But for the miners, whose strikes are very rarely less than three months, but which have been known to last, in certain instances, for six, nine, and twelve months, the strike or the lock-out is no exceptional thing.

It is important to remember this when considering the General Strike of 1926. The miners were accustomed to strikes: many other workers were not. The miners scarcely felt that they were really out until some months had elapsed. In some other industries and services, such as railways and road transport, there was a totally different psychology. Strikes had to be short and sharp if they were to be won. With the miners it was different. There was the lock-out in the Rhondda Valley in South Wales in 1910, and at one time or another 30,000 men were out: this struggle lasted over twelve months. Then there was the strike in 1912 for a national minimum wage of 5s. a day—not an excessive claim: this lasted for five weeks, over a million men being involved.

The war of 1914–18 saw a temporary improvement, but it didn't last. Dissension led to State control of mines in 1917. Two years later came a demand for shorter hours, an increase in wages, and nationalization of the mines. Conflict was only narrowly averted by the appointment of a Royal Commission under Mr. Justice Sankey.

Further trouble arose in 1920 over a claim for a wages advance and a reduction in the price of coal. The whole of the coal-fields were stopped for seventeen days. By miners' calculations this was a short strike, and it came to an end largely because of a threat by the railwaymen to strike in sympathy. The following year, in the midst of a trade depression, trouble arose because of the sudden decontrol of the mines. This threatened the miners with drastic wages reductions. As in the earlier year the Triple Alliance of miners, railwaymen, and transport workers was called in. They resolved to bring out their members on April 15th. This never took place because of dissensions within the Alliance. I knew about it not only from what I had read but also from what I was told by Ernest Bevin and Jimmy Thomas, both of whom took an active part. I shall say more about this later.

It is difficult here to disentangle the real reasons why the Alliance did not support the miners. But the essence of it was that the other unions resented the miners keeping them out of the negotiations and declining to meet the Prime Minister without any consultation with them. The other unions felt that had this meeting taken place a reasonable basis for a settlement could have been found. As it was the miners were left to fight alone, and the whole of the coal-fields were again stopped for thirteen weeks. The refusal of the other unions in the Alliance to back the miners by a strike caused tremendous indignation amongst those trade unionists who, like myself, had at that time no first-hand knowledge of the affair. Friday, April 15th, 1921, became known in the movement as 'Black Friday'. A day of shame. None of us wanted to see another such day.

I have avoided going into the merits of the various struggles in the coal-fields, my sole purpose being to show the atmosphere which prevailed. There was a lack of centralized leadership and of readiness to take responsibility. The federal system of organization was partly to blame for this, leaving as it did most of the power in the districts. The delegates who attended the numerous conferences of

the Miners' Federation regarded themselves as coming with a mandate. They were not disposed to exercise their own judgement. On
occasions they were not only tenacious but violent advocates of the
policies of their own districts. The system by which vital national
agreements could be terminated by a month's notice was altogether
wrong. It left far too little time for thorough review and adequate
consultation between the parties. This had the consequence of
importing an unhealthy air of crisis into their dealings. Nor must it
ever be forgotten that the miners usually lived in small communities
and villages. Few of them ever took part at that time in the general
affairs of the trade union movement in the same way as did most other
trade unionists. Their work clearly separated them from the general
run of workers. Mining was a traditional occupation, son following
father into the mines. No one else seemed especially keen to work
underground. They were good trade unionists, firmly attached to
their local associations and with a sense of solidarity that was remarkable. But they had little contact with the rest of the trade union movement except at national level. They looked upon strikes and lock-outs
as inevitable. They had come to believe that their salvation lay in the
mines being nationalized. They did not believe it possible that a
permanent cessation of strife could ever take place under private
ownership. This conviction deepened when the coal-owners gave one
month's notice in June 1925 to end the national agreement.

At the beginning of 1925 the situation in the industry was very
serious. Many collieries had closed down and about 300,000 miners
were out of work. The general trade depression was not the sole cause
of this. The growing use of oil and other fuels had made their contribution. Throughout Europe hydro-electric stations were developing in countries which formerly imported coal from Britain. The
British Navy and much of the Mercantile Marine were burning oil
instead of coal. Reparation coal from Germany, too, had played its
part. I couldn't see any means by which the coal industry would ever
again employ the same number of men as before; nor, I think, could
the miners themselves. Their attitude was that no matter how few
men were employed, no remedy was to be found in bringing down
wages.

In the spring of 1925 the Miners' Federation had joined the
owners' association, at the latter's invitation, in an investigation into
the conditions of the industry. The intention was first to elicit the
facts, next to find the causes, and then to see what remedies could be
put forward jointly. After several meetings this inquiry broke down.
The owners refused to submit information which the miners regarded
as essential. It was then that the coal-owners gave notice to terminate

the National Wages Agreement. They submitted new proposals which would have caused a lengthening of the working day and severe reductions in wages.

Three weeks before the notices were due to take effect the Miners' Federation met the General Council of the T.U.C. The miners reported to the General Council their determination to resist any reduction in wages or any extension of their hours of work. This was the first time I had met the miners' leaders at close quarters, though I had listened to the speeches of Bob Smillie and Frank Hodges, their then leaders, at various conferences of the T.U.C., and I had met the new secretary, Arthur Cook, a few times.

I thought I understood their attitude of mind. I knew a little about the conditions under which coal-mining was carried on: during the time I worked as an electrician at St. Helens I lived in a collier's cottage, where two of the sons worked in the pits at Haydock. Like myself, they were keenly interested in social and economic subjects. Often we would talk about the conditions of work in the mines as we sat in front of the blazing fire after our evening meal. I had been down a few of the local pits and what I saw below ground made me resolve never to work there. Apart from the hard work, I had no desire to be shut out from the daylight during the greater part of my working life.

I had, moreover, seen something of the misery caused by mining disasters. In August 1908 I had cycled from St. Helens to join the grief-stricken crowd of anxious-faced women and grim-looking men at the gates of the Maypole Colliery. An explosion had just killed over seventy men. I shall never forget those scenes. I had also mixed with the miners in the Labour Club at St. Helens, and I admired their sturdy independence and resourcefulness. A true collier had a curious liking for the struggle with Nature involved in his daily work. Now I had the opportunity of meeting their leaders first hand.

After hearing the miners the General Council passed a resolution backing them up and appointed a special Industrial Committee, with myself as secretary, to confer with them. We had several joint meetings and soon we were convinced that the attack upon the miners' wages was a prelude to a wider assault upon working-class standards generally.

At our first meeting Arthur Cook, excitable and fiery, hammered home his points vehemently, in contrast with Herbert Smith, the miners' president. I liked this old man. Smith was as straight as a die. I liked his calm way of looking at difficulties. Always cool and steady, he never got flustered. There he sat in his blue suit and soft collar, with his little moustache turning grey and his high balding forehead, with his spectacles resting on the end of his nose. Straight to the point, he told us that the coal-owners wanted to go back to district settlements instead of continuing the national agreement. What follows is taken from the notes I made at this time.

Smith said: 'They want to go back to the good districts so that they can make their wad of profits and not pass any to the poorer ones. They want district settlements so that they won't have to have anything like unification. We are out for nationalization, but if we cannot get that we will have some sort of unification. I am out to protect the poor fellow whose wages are down. I remember what the old pioneers said. Men like Ben Pickard said to me once, "Look here, Herbert, lad, look after the bottom wages—top 'uns will look after themselves." '

Herbert went on: 'Ah said to Bridgeman [the first Lord of the Admiralty, whom the Government had put on to try to get negotiations resumed]: "Well, we'll never accept these rates—they are a disgrace. They mean a reduction of 2s. a day on our rates and some of these are now down to 8s. and 9s. a day. We know what we are going into. We know we haven't much hope of coming out on top. But tha'll have a long job on it, my friend. Tha'll have to starve us into it." '

I could see the eyes of the other delegates gleam with intensity when Herbert said this. They were very quiet. Practically all of them, with the exception of Cook and Noah Ablett, and I think two others, were men past middle age. There was old Straker of Northumberland, neatly dressed—boots well polished, hair carefully parted at the side, and his little goatee white beard trimmed well, sitting quiet—more like a Sunday-school teacher than anything else, one of the most vigorous opponents of the new agreements. Then there was Tom Richards from South Wales, trembling of head and hand like a man with shell-shock. I don't know what is the matter with him, but he is always the same—old and evidently not in very good health, but with a perfectly clear mind —always to the point. Then old Finney of Staffordshire—brown eyes with a mild expression in them—more like a kindly grandfather than a vigorous, aggressive trade unionist. Yet these are the men who in a few weeks from now will be denounced as Bolshevists and extremists. I wonder whether out of all our research and careful training we will ever have the real human urge that these men have. One can feel it when one looks at them. The younger men, like Noah Ablett—who, strangely enough, does not have anything to say in these matters—do not seem a

very brilliant lot. Old and young are marked with the bluish
powder and coal-dust of shot-firing, which identifies the miner at
once.

We didn't see any more of the miners for a fortnight. They had
been attending a conference with their district delegates and came
back more determined than ever to stand up to the owners. One
morning during this interval I received a visit from A. P. Wadsworth,
the labour correspondent of the *Manchester Guardian*. He was one of
the few national journalists who at that time specialized in trades
union matters. Others were J. Vernon Radcliffe of *The Times*, V.
Brodzky of the *Herald*, Fred Peaker of the *Morning Post*, and Walter
Meakin of the *Daily News*. Such men were the pioneers of industrial
journalism in its modern form, and the predecessors of the generation
of capable specialists who serve all the principal national and
provincial newspapers. Men like Trevor Evans of the *Daily Express*,
George Thomas of the *Herald*, Hugh Chevins of the *Daily Telegraph*,
Fred Chant of the Press Association, Leslie Randall of the *Daily
Mail*, Ian Mackay and Margaret Stewart of the *News Chronicle* (the
latter the only woman labour correspondent of national status in
my days), and Eric Wigham of *The Times*—all owed much of their
success to the example of that small group I met in my early years at
the T.U.C. These men proved completely reliable, and whilst I did not
always agree with what they wrote, I found I could trust them with
background information which I wouldn't have dared to give to most
general reporters. They kept in close contact with our own Herbert
Tracey, himself a member of the National Union of Journalists, a
voracious reader, with a phenomenal memory, and endowed with a
creative imagination. Some regarded him as a word-spinner: I
know he could with ease make a column out of a wink. He was one
of my most trusted and valued colleagues throughout the whole of
my secretaryship of the T.U.C. In 1925 we had a joint Press Department with the Labour Party, with Will Henderson (later Lord
Henderson) at its head. Will was a chap with whom I always kept
close contact, and whose shrewd political and industrial judgement was
of immense service to me. I used regularly to talk over my more com-
plex problems of policy with them both. My secretary, Miss McDonald,
steered most press enquiries to them.

Wadsworth wanted the 'low-down' on the General Council's
attitude towards what was even then regarded as a coal crisis. I told
him frankly that the General Council would stand firmly behind the
miners. Wadsworth sniffed at this. He always appeared to me to have
a sceptical and rather cynical attitude of mind towards trade union

affairs. 'Well,' he said, complacently, as though he derived satisfaction from the thought, 'the Trades Union Congress can't do much about it.' Whether this was to draw me out or not, I do not know, and I contented myself with, 'Don't be too sure.' Subsequent happenings scarcely sustained his remark. Afterwards he became the editor of the *Manchester Guardian*, and a good one too. Possibly he had learned that what trade unions will do and what they won't do is not so easily predictable.

When we met the miners again Herbert Smith told us that they knew they couldn't fight alone. They had practically no money and in only one or two cases could their districts pay strike benefit for more than two or three weeks. But the men were embittered. They said, 'Whether our union has got money or not we are not going without snap.' They were going to get 'snap', which is the miners' expression for food, no matter what occurred. Herbert said, 'If anyone has got to go to prison I hope it will be people like me and not the people outside.'

After they had gone we decided to seek a meeting with the Prime Minister, Mr. Baldwin. We also communicated with the railway unions and the Transport Workers' Federation asking them to consider putting an embargo on 'black coal'. A few days later we met them in conference and they readily agreed to refrain from moving coal in the event of a dispute.

It was just about this time that some articles appeared in the London *Evening Standard* by J. M. Keynes, the eminent economist who afterwards became Lord Keynes. These were expanded into a pamphlet entitled *The Economic Consequences of Mr. Churchill*. Keynes gave the reasons why unemployment was so bad in England at a time when world trade was reasonably good. He stated that the prices of British exports in the international market were too high. He ascribed as the main reason for this that the value of sterling money abroad had been raised by 10 per cent whilst its purchasing power in Britain remained unchanged. Keynes insisted that the alteration in the external value of money was the deliberate act of the Government. Winston Churchill was the Chancellor of the Exchequer at the time and he got the full blast of Keynes's criticism.

I knew that a committee had been appointed by the Government some years earlier to consider the financial problems which were likely to arise after the 1914–18 war. This committee had as its chairman Lord Cunliffe, who was the Governor of the Bank of England. He died before the committee finished its work but he signed its interim report. The report was broadly to the effect that there should be a fixed fiduciary issue with the remainder of the note issue limited by the amount of gold reserve in the Bank of England. This had been the position when war broke out in 1914. So what the committee was really saying was: 'Base the amount of money available mainly on the value of the gold in the vaults of the Bank of England.' This is what is meant by the phrase 'return to the Gold Standard'.

Apparently the final report of the committee had lain in abeyance for five years until Winston Churchill became Chancellor of the Exchequer. Keynes went on to explain that whenever anything was sold abroad either the foreign buyer had to pay 10 per cent more in his money or the British exporter had to accept 10 per cent less in sterling. In practice this really meant that British exporters received 10 per cent less for their products. Yet they had to pay just as much in wages as before.

Keynes went on to criticize Winston Churchill, who he felt had been misled by the financiers and experts:

> In doing what he did in the actual circumstances of last spring, he was just asking for trouble. For he was committing himself to force down money-wages and all money values, without any idea how it was done.

Then Keynes made a grim prophecy. The Government's action would mean:

> Engaging in a struggle with each separate group in turn, with no prospect that the final result will be fair, and no guarantee that the stronger groups will not gain at the expense of the weaker. The working classes cannot be expected to understand, better than Cabinet Ministers, what is happening. Those who are attacked first are faced with a depreciation of their standard of life, because the cost of living will not fall until all of the others have been attacked too; and therefore they are justified in defending themselves. Nor can the classes first subjected to a reduction of money-wages be guaranteed that this will be compensated later by a corresponding fall in the cost of living. . . . Therefore they are bound to resist so long as they can; and it must be war, until those who are economically weakest are beaten to the ground.

This pamphlet made a deep impression on me, and it was simply uncanny to see how Keynes's prophecies worked out. Unfortunately, as he foresaw, most people never discerned the real causes which threw the coal-owners and the miners into conflict. Had I had any doubts it was now plain why the miners were the first to be attacked. Wages formed two-thirds of the cost of coal production. The miners had little choice about resisting any reduction in their standard of living.

The Mining Association, through its secretary Mr. Lee, soon confirmed Keynes as to the effect of raising the bank rate and restricting credit by an early return to the Gold Standard. He pointed out that the effect of this was to put practically 1s. extra on the price of coal. I noted in my diary after reading this:

> This makes one think. Is it possible to resist a fall in wages whilst the bankers pursue this policy? Eventually prices should fall and the cost of living will decline, but for the time being the monetary policy now being pursued is damaging in every way to us.

On the 27th July we again met the miners at a preliminary meeting just before seeing the Prime Minister. I argued as strongly as I could that we should ask for a postponement of the notices. But what was to happen during the period of postponement? I thought there must be a court of inquiry or something of that kind to find a way out of the difficulty. The miners were very evasive on this. I think they were fed up with the numerous inquiries to which their industry had been subjected. George Hicks said to me quietly afterwards in kindly fashion: 'Walter, you are too logical. Trade unions are never logical. You look too far ahead. Don't worry. Let the thing develop.'

When we met the Prime Minister, A. B. Swales of the engineering workers spoke first, and I was asked to support. I told Baldwin, frankly, that we could not allow the miners to be beaten on this issue, and I appealed to him to make a public statement asking the mine-owners to withdraw the notices. He said he would do everything he could to get a peaceful settlement. He was taking the matter in hand himself and he would see the mine-owners the next day.

I noticed, when Swales pointedly said, 'We are out to back the miners and we mean to support them,' that Baldwin looked suddenly and keenly at every member of the deputation in turn. It looked to me as though he was trying to see by their expressions whether they supported this or whether it was bluff. My diary says:

> Looking at the Government side, I could not see any sign of fear of anything we were going to do. They seemed to be perfectly calm about it. Of course, they can hide their feelings very well.

We adjourned to the offices of the Miners' Federation in Russell Square to report back to their executive. After this Cook told me privately that at the royal Garden Party on the previous Friday several members of our General Council had been present, Mary Quaile being one of them. She was so impressed by Cook's speech at the special Trades Union Congress which was held on the day before that she told the Queen about it. The Queen was very distressed. The outcome was that the King sent for Cook to go to Buckingham Palace. Cook refused. He said to me belligerently, 'Why the hell should I go to see the King?' I replied, 'Well, it shows how things are going.' Cook retorted, 'I'll show them that they have a different man from Frank Hodges to deal with now.'

I noticed in the morning papers that the King's Private Secretary, Lord Stamfordham, had visited the Prime Minister. This looked as though Cook's story about the King might be true. He says that Mary Quaile called on him first thing this morning. She couldn't sleep for the trouble.

Cook told me in the presence of Will Henderson [the head of our Joint Press Department] and Milne-Bailey [our Research Officer]: 'I am going to fight these people. I believe a fight is certain. There may be a postponement but a fight is certain. There is only one way of going it. That is to fight.'

I said, 'Yes, but make sure that you are fighting with discretion.'

Cook replied: 'Don't forget I have something to pay back. It is just six years ago since they not only handcuffed me but led me in chains from one end of the train, in Swansea station, to the other, in full view of the public. The same at Cardiff station.'

Time was now getting short before the notices expired, and there was much coming and going practically every day and a special conference of unions on July 30th. The conference decided unanimously to back the General Council in whatever form of financial support might be necessary. There was no talk of a General Strike. Some controversy arose in our committee deliberations as to whether the Labour Party should raise the subject in the House of Commons. I didn't disagree with this, but I soon found that there were strong views against it. Bevin was particularly opposed to it, while Thomas was just as strongly in favour. Also opposed was Bob Smillie, although he himself was a Member of Parliament. He reminded everyone that in 1921 the direct cause of the division in the miners' ranks was because Hodges and others had visited the House of Commons and had been closely examined there by astute politicians. Herbert Smith and Arthur Cook were also strongly against it.

Ramsay MacDonald phoned me soon afterwards and invited Swales and me to come to see him. He wanted to know how matters stood. I scraped together as quickly as I could the members of the Special Industrial Committee and we went along to the House of Commons, where we had dinner.

Afterwards we proceeded to the Leader of the Opposition's room.

It was a large, oblong-shaped room, and we first passed through an outer office, where MacDonald's secretary was sitting. At the desk in the inner room MacDonald was sitting, the only light coming from a desk lamp at his side. The walls of the room were panelled in dark oak and there was an air of restfulness which took one miles away from the realities of the outside world.

MacDonald sat with his dark face and rather dried-up complexion, reading a letter, which was on the table before him. Sitting on his left was Arthur Henderson, with Thomas reclining on a couch close by. Nearby there were Roberts, Snowden, and others, all anxiously looking at us.

MacDonald said that the Prime Minister was going to make a statement, and he, MacDonald, wanted to have the facts so that he could effectively reply. His idea was not to say anything very much but merely to focus things on the wages issue.

We explained to him the view of the miners so far as we knew it and advised him to say as little as he could. Tillett said that MacDonald ought to refer to Baldwin and say that we resented his autocratic and inefficient conduct. Swales and myself dissented strongly because Baldwin had been anything but autocratic. He had been very decent indeed.

Later we went upstairs, into the House of Commons to the Distinguished Strangers' Gallery, to hear the statement. It was a fluke, however, because we had hardly got there before it was announced that the Prime Minister would not make any statement as he was then meeting the parties again.

We immediately hurried out and I got on the telephone to Cook and found that the Prime Minister had asked the miners to meet him at ten o'clock that night.

While we were still at the House of Commons the news came through from Cook that negotiations were proceeding very well. The miners were getting practically everything they required, according to him.

I retired at midnight with the feeling that unless something very unexpected happened, the whole business was practically settled.

The next morning, Friday, July 31st, our committee went to the Ministry of Labour, where we found the miners already assembled. It seemed that the Prime Minister was having a busy time with the owners, and that the latter had now gone to consult privately at the office of the Mining Association. We had nothing to do but to wait, so we split up for lunch and later returned, spending the hours of waiting in telling stories and exchanging experiences.

Old Herbert Smith said to me quietly: 'I told Baldwin last night that when the T.U.C. passed that resolution yesterday it didn't make me happy. I'll bet there was no more miserable man among you than I was. When I get to thinking of all the suffering that will be caused to thousands of people who are now connected with this dispute—supposing a railway strike starts—well, it makes me very unhappy.'

At 3.50 p.m., when Herbert was right in the middle of one of his stories, the door opened and the Prime Minister walked in, accompanied by Winston Churchill and Lane-Fox and one or two departmental officials. The Prime Minister looked tired and worn. He had been up practically all the previous night, trying to make a settlement. He told us that the Government had arranged with the mine-owners that notices should be suspended for a fortnight and that the Government would give financial assistance to the industry until May 1st, 1926. A few questions were asked, after which Baldwin hurried away, as he had to speak in the House of Commons on the situation. We then had our own separate meeting and the miners heartily thanked us for what we had done. . . .

It was arranged that we should send out immediately a telegram to all the transport unions, telling them that the dispute was settled and that their members should remain at work. We were not sure of the the exact terms of the settlement, because there was no signed document concluding the negotiations which in my opinion, and that of several of my colleagues, was a little curious. I wrote out a telegram and at one part I said, 'Notices are suspended for a fortnight in order to allow the Government and the owners to discuss the matter in detail.'

Winston Churchill just came out of the room where the Ministers had been and I handed him the telegram, saying, 'Is this all right?' He did not express any surprise, although I don't know whether he remembered seeing me in the conference room.

He replied, 'Yes, that is splendid; that just hits it off.'

'I want to send it out to our people', I explained.

Just as I said this Arthur Cook came up and remarked, 'Well, sir, I am glad we have settled it.'

'Yes,' replied Churchill, 'it is a good job it is over, but you have done it over my blood-stained corpse. I have got to find the money for it now.'

Then Evan Williams, the chairman of the Mining Association, came up. He was a different style of individual from what I expected. I had imagined him to be keen, young, and alert-looking. Instead, he was well past middle age and not very neatly dressed or smart-looking. He said to Cook: 'Look here, Mr. Cook, now you should help us. You ought to tell some of these sheltered trades that they have got to make some sacrifice.' I could see Williams's game straight away, so I interjected, 'It is my business, Mr. Williams, to look after both the sheltered and unsheltered trades, so it is no use your asking for sacrifices there.' He looked at me for a second or so and didn't continue the conversation.

Churchill did not seem at all affected by the negotiations. He was fresh-faced and very much like the cartoons in the newspapers. He was smoking a long cigar all the time. I noticed that when he was in the room with Baldwin, during the negotiations, he put his tall silk hat on the table in front of him, with his gloves and walking stick alongside it. Possibly some of these actions were characteristics of his journalist days. Purcell told me that Churchill was a decent chap to speak to. Churchill had told Purcell that some of his friends should be in gaol, but they didn't matter.

9

Conflict Looms Again

M OST trade unionists were jubilant at what they thought was victory. I didn't feel that way at all. I knew that our forces had not been tested, and I said so publicly in speeches and articles. Everyone who thought at all must have realized that the subsidy would last only until May 1st, 1926, and could not possibly be enough to transform the finances of the industry. True, a Royal Commission had been set up headed by Sir Herbert Samuel (later Lord Samuel), a former Liberal Home Secretary. The real problem was not only how quickly they could get to work, but (more especially) how rapidly could any recommendations they made be put into operation. I couldn't see the coal-owners acting speedily on anything except issuing notices to miners. I felt convinced that the Government would have to subsidize the industry for another year at least and possibly continue to give financial support even beyond that until the reorganization of the mines was well under way. It was patent to me that trouble was to be apprehended in the spring of 1926.

I wrote several articles in which I said that trade unionists must not become inflated with any mistaken sense of victory but must try to appraise the results at their proper value. We must regard the events of 1925 as nothing more than a skirmish of outposts. It was certain that the Government would not allow a similar situation to arise without seeking to establish methods whereby the trade unions could be combated. I wrote that I thought next time the Government would show no inclination to evade the issue. It would be prepared to force matters to a conclusion on grounds of its own choosing. I stressed the need for (1) centralized authority and united leadership, (2) the development of proper administrative machinery, and (3) some form of co-ordinated dispute policy.

This was the kind of reasoning which animated me in drafting the report of our Special Industrial Committee, to be presented to the

Congress at Scarborough a month later. I kept the report as chronological and factual as I could, but added an addendum in the following terms:

The Committee consider it necessary to call attention to some
of the factors which have emerged from the Dispute.

The Mining Crisis is not an isolated incident; a similar
emergency may arise at any time. If the General Council is to
function effectively, it must prepare the broad lines of its organization to deal with such contingencies.

The Committee propose, therefore, that a Special Industrial
Committee should be permanently established to work out a
detailed plan for application in times of dispute.

The Mining Crisis has served to indicate the probable ob-
stacles which will have to be faced at such times, and it would
be, dangerous to wait until a crisis had actually occurred and
then to trust to hastily devised expedients.

It is certain that something must be done to enable the
organized trade union movement to act decisively. At present, if
the constitutional procedure was rigorously followed, considerable time would elapse before the Unions as a whole could
function effectively.

The Committee consider that the first step should be for each
Union to make such alterations as may be necessary in its rules
to vest in its own Executive Council the power to declare a strike
of its members in collaboration and consultation with the
General Council. Some unions already possess such powers
and if a general extension could be achieved, the decisive
authority of the trade union movement would be greatly
increased.

Ultimately, it may be possible for power to be vested in the
General Council, but the Committee are of the opinion that
attention should be concentrated at the present stage on each
Executive Council being given the requisite authority by its
members.

Much to my chagrin the Committee regarded this addendum as
going too far, and it never appeared in the printed report of the
General Council. I realized that my suggestions would be highly controversial and that was why I put them in the form of an addendum
on a separate stencilled sheet which could easily be detached. But
someone had evidently taken notice of the articles I had been writing,
and a motion had been put down on the Congress agenda by the

National Union of Vehicle Builders. This proposed that the General Council should have the power to levy the members, to call for a stoppage of work to assist any union defending a vital trade union principle, and to arrange with the Co-operative Wholesale Society for the distribution of food in the event of a strike making this necessary. The unions were to be called upon to make any necessary alterations in their rules to give effect to this. This motion went far beyond what was likely to be accepted. It was one thing to give powers to their own executives to levy their own members or even to call them out on strike. It was quite another to transfer that power to the General Council.

The fate of the motion was a foregone conclusion. It was not accepted by the Congress, but was referred to the General Council for consideration. They, in turn, passed it over to the Special Industrial Committee which had been reappointed, who decided that the existing powers of the General Council were sufficient. This was far from being my opinion, but I had several times felt that I was carrying my advocacy for greater powers to an extent which was irritating to most of my colleagues. Strangely enough the actual report on the events of 1925 passed without comment save for a passing reference, and a few words of appreciation from Arthur Cook.

At the end of 1925 I began to get more and more uneasy at the lack of preparation on our side for the trial of strength which I felt lay ahead. The Samuel Commission was hard at work. The Government were going ahead with recruitment for an organization for maintaining supplies, and there wasn't the slightest doubt that they would be far better equipped to face any emergency in 1926 than they were in 1925. On our side the only preparation that was being made was the speeches of Arthur Cook and a few others, including myself, which were intended to strengthen the determination of the rank and file to meet whatever trouble might arise.

I argued the matter out with myself in my notebook and prepared a memorandum dated January 28th, 1926, which I submitted to our Special Industrial Committee. After consideration by them I revised it a little and it was sent to the Miners' Federation and brought before a joint meeting with them on the 19th of February, 1926. The memorandum has never previously been published. In fact, the General Council as such never saw it, but only members of the S.I.C. and the miners' executive. I recognize now its many shortcomings, but at least it was an attempt to face the situation. In the interest of historical truth I give it here just as it was presented to the miners.

K

THE IMPENDING CRISIS
MEMORANDUM BY MR. W. M. CITRINE

As the period of May, 1926, approaches, and the Royal Commission inquiring into the coal industry is now nearing the completion of its report, I have, on the instruction of the Special Industrial Committee, set out in this memorandum certain questions of principle.

1. *General Summary*
The first point in the memorandum deals with the policy which should be adopted.

(a) The decisions of the Coal Commission cannot possibly materialize for a considerable time, and the Committee should consider as to whether it is going to insist on a continuance of financial assistance pending reorganization.

(b) The possibility of a dispute materializing is examined, and it is thought that while avoiding anything in the nature of creating a state of public tension, the Committee should take reasonable measures to prepare for probable eventualities.

(c) The first step is a decision as to what form of consultation is to take place with other bodies. The Special Industrial Committee must have control of policy and this might be laid down right at the commencement. Consultations may be necessary with the Labour Party, the Miners' Federation and the Co-operative Union, and it may be necessary to incorporate representatives of these bodies on the Special Committee.

(d) It is suggested that publicity should be proceeded with as soon as possible, and this need not be restricted to documentary form. A vigorous platform campaign may need to be undertaken.

2. *Interim Policy*
The first point is one as to an interim policy. Evidence has been presented to the Commission by the miners in agreement with the General Council, the Labour Party and the Parliamentary party providing for the nationalization of the coal mining industry and its association with a national electric supply. This policy could obviously not be applied for a considerable time, so that its effect on the immediate economic position would not be appreciable. The coal-owners have put up a purely negative policy

and while it must be a matter of speculation as to what the Commission will propose, it is probable that some system of unification and grouping of the mines will emanate. But whichever of these policies is adopted, it is certain that a considerable amount of time must elapse before it could materialize. The question is, therefore, definitely raised as to what is to be done in the interim.

When the subsidy was granted in July last, there was a tendency in some parts of the Labour Movement to disclaim responsibility for it. The Special Industrial Committee will recollect, however, that they very strongly urged the Prime Minister to give some financial assistance to the industry. The question arises as to whether a continuance of the subsidy is possible. The outbreak of political opposition which succeeded the granting of the subsidy in July last, makes one reflect on the possibility of the Government's being stimulated to decline further assistance at the end of the present subsidy period. So far as I know, no definite official policy has been enunciated on this point, and it appears to me that the Special Industrial Committee should give consideration and determine as to whether advocacy is to be given to a continuance of the subsidy pending the adoption of practical remedies to restore the industry.

3. *Possibilities of Dispute*
If financial assistance is not furnished, it would appear that another crisis in the industry is inevitable. I realize to the full the danger there is in concluding that a crisis must result. I appreciate that there is a good deal that is psychological in the present situation. If the feeling is encouraged by any act of the Special Industrial Committee that a dispute is inevitable this would possibly be interpreted as provoking a conflict. It is probable that the opposition has been stimulated into the preparations which they are making by some of the injudicious statements that have been made from Labour Platforms since July last.

After giving full weight to that factor, I am impelled to the view that a crisis on a very large scale is at least reasonably to be apprehended. I fervently hope no such crisis will arise, but it would be unsafe to count upon any such vague security.

4. *Preparation*
The next question to be faced is that if a crisis appears to be reasonably probable, can we delay making preparations to meet it? There are two broad lines of policy which should be considered here.

Dealing with the first, I know it is the opinion of several experienced leaders that there is a danger of over-anxiety in the matter of preparation. There is a feeling that when the moment of crisis comes, the British Labour movement will be aroused spontaneously to an attitude of determined resistance; that unless resistance is spontaneous it cannot be really effective. To ensure this, the issue with which the movement is faced must be felt by the mass of trade unionists to be one vitally affecting their interests. This condition was produced last year by the general impression, *confirmed by the Prime Minister's assertion* that wages in all industries would have to come down. [Note the passage was deleted as the Prime Minister had denied this.] It is argued that no amount of organization can be effective unless the determination is freely present to support the miners.

The other line of reasoning takes the form that preparation should be made of a kind which will ensure spontaneity of action and not leave preparations to the eleventh hour.

It may be regarded as premature to make up one's mind in respect of either of these two points of view. The Commission has not yet published its report and until its general proposals are known preparations which are made might be directed against contingencies which in fact may never arise. I am conscious of the difficulties of making a decision on matters which must be to a large extent in the region of conjecture. Nevertheless I consider there is a duty imposed upon the Special Industrial Committee to examine in the closest degree the situation and to determine upon some form of preparation.

This conclusion is reinforced by a number of considerations:
(a) The Government's Financial Position;
(b) The Political Situation;
(c) Government Preparation.

5. *The Government's Financial Position*
Let us see the potentialities of the Government's continuing to render financial assistance. Apart from the organized outbreak at the alleged 'surrender' in July, the strongest possible pressure is continually being brought to bear on the Government to make radical economies in every branch of public administration. The subsidy has been denounced practically universally by the Press which normally influences the Government's policy. The continuance of the subsidy may necessitate an increase of the income tax and certainly shatter any prospect of diminution in taxation and neutralize the efforts towards economy which are being made in

other directions. Furthermore there is a feeling amongst industrialists that the subvention in July has rendered it impossible for them to enforce reductions in other industries or to receive any appreciable relief in production costs. The evidence of the coal owners before the Commission in denouncing the subsidy savours more of the views of the bankers in whose hands many of the colliery companies are at present than of the convictions of the Mining Association. The desire to secure cheap coal by a lowering of wages in the coal mining industry is undoubtedly present, and this, together with the urge for decreased taxation, must have considerable influence on the Government's policy.

6. *The Political Situation*
The outbreak of political opposition which succeeded the granting of the subsidy by the Government in July and allegations of pitiful surrender to the forces of anarchy make one reflect on the possibilities of the Government's declining further assistance. There seems a steadily growing tendency among the more vocal Conservative politicians to regard a struggle with the Trade Union Movement as inevitable and imminent.

The resuscitation of the Political Levy Bill, the threat of action by the die-hards against the Trades Disputes Acts, the exploitation of the Communist bogey, may from a political point of view be used to create a state of public tension. The Trade Union Movement may be represented as a menace to society and ordered government. All these may create the determination to wage a decisive struggle with Labour. The Prime Minister declared in a speech on November 5th last, dealing with the possibility of an industrial conflict, that it would mean a challenge by a minority to the right of the majority to govern. He added that the Government would see that the will of the people prevailed. These points may be entirely disassociated and undoubtedly a good deal of nonsense has been talked, but they are all possible factors which act in a cumulative sense. It may be that a General Election would be forced in order to enable the Government to gain support for its policy and to place Labour at a disadvantage. There are considerable risks to the Government in this, but they may decide to take that course.

7. *Government Preparation*
The most tangible sign is the preparation that the Government is making. The circular 636 issued by the Minister of Health setting up a Civil Commissioner in each of ten divisions to deal

with transport, food, postal services, and coal is well known. The formation of the Organization for Maintaining Supplies and the extensive and informative correspondence in *The Times* immediately subsequent to the July crisis, shows that there will be no lack of determination to organize alternative services should a dispute occur. There has been unmistakable evidence of preparation for possible public disorder next year, and the swearing-in of Special Constables is proceeding steadily. The Fascisti Movement is drilling and organizing its forces, and while as an economic factor this body can be safely ignored, it is more in the realm of enforcement of law and order that the dangers lie. There is little reason to suppose that the Government would not welcome the assistance of such an ally. Preparations which have been made to meet previous Labour disputes, notably in 1919, have been perfected, and it is reasonable to suppose are very much more complete.

Can we afford, in view of these obvious preparations, to delay in making our preparations?

8. *Consultations With Other Bodies*

It appears to me that the first question to be faced in considering preparation is as to the extent to which consultations shall take place with other bodies. It is no doubt a disadvantage to spread the area of consultation too widely, but there would appear to be interests concerned in the matter which at some points would have to be taken into account. It is necessary to get an understanding as to which body is entrusted with the conduct of the dispute. There is at present no single authoritative body directing the policy which is to be pursued. Statements are being made with increasing frequency from the platform and to the Press, none of which can be taken as expressing any real co-ordinated policy. It appears to me that if responsibility is to be taken by the General Council through its Special Committee for organizing the Trade Union Movement in defence of the miners' standards, then the General Council must determine the policy to be pursued. It would not only be inadvisable but even dangerous to allow individuals, whether they be miners' officials or politicians, to create a state of tension and lay down lines of policy to which the General Council might feel itself unable to subscribe.

The mining situation has ceased to be exclusively a miners' question; it certainly is not a purely political question, and the imperative need is to get a recognition generally that whatever policy is laid down by the General Council shall be the policy for all concerned.

The point of practical importance here is as to whether the Special Industrial Committee considers itself able to lay down such a policy, or whether it would prefer to invite the co-operation of representatives of the political movement and the Miners' Federation.

9. *Form of Preparations*

I realize to the full the dangers of doing anything which will enable the Government to distort the issue into a political one. If, as is anticipated, financial assistance has to be given to the industry during the period of reorganization, and if the Government's hand has to be forced in this matter, they may attempt to represent that the Trade Union Movement, by endeavouring to enforce the continuance of the subsidy, were denying the rights of the Government to determine its own financial policy, in short, that industrial action was being used for political purposes. In view of the outburst in the Press in August last, this is extremely probable. It may be that the full pressure of the political side of the Labour Movement will be necessary to propagate throughout the country the necessary support to force the Government to a favourable decision. It is of great importance that a sound decision should be made upon this political point. Last year the Committee were able to avoid any political complications but some resentment was felt that the Parliamentary Labour Party had not been consulted until the final stages had been reached. The practical question to be considered is whether it is possible to keep the issue a purely industrial one while at the same time having the fullest consultation with the political wing of the Movement.

10. *Essential Services*

The issue is complicated somewhat by the resolution of the Liverpool Labour Party Conference on Essential Services during Time of Trade Disputes. This resolution is to be considered by the National Joint Council, and whatever expression of opinion is made there will undoubtedly influence policy in connection with the Mining Crisis. It may well be for the Special Industrial Committee to consider this issue separately and to lay down some general lines of guidance to our representatives on the National Joint Council which is to consider this matter. There are principles involved in this aspect of the question which reach right down to the roots of Trade Union policy. Our strategy is developing along such lines that this issue is raised in a more acute form as the magnitude of the disputes increases. Put bluntly, the question appears to be: 'Does the Trade Union Movement admit the right of any Government to erect essential services during the time of trade dispute?' A good deal depends on the form of a dispute, of course, but assuming that the conditions were repeated of July last, where a railway and transport stoppage was imminent, what would be the attitude of the Movement towards an attempt on the Government's part to continue supplies of foodstuffs and other essential commodities? On the one side it would be the function of the unions to make the stoppage as complete as possible, and if this was carried to an effective conclusion, it would mean that commodities would be withheld from even our own members. We do not appear to have faced this issue as a Movement previously. It may be that we could devise a strategy which would enable our own people to store commodities in anticipation of a dispute, but not only would this be difficult, but in a national crisis affecting all the unions it would probably be found impracticable. I am driven to the conclusion that someone would have to provide the emergency service. Who is that someone to be? Can the Trade Union Movement, operating through the Co-operative Societies, erect such a service? Are the resources of the Co-operative Movement great enough to allow that to be done? Would they require to be supplemented by arrangements with private traders agreed to beforehand by consent of the Trade Unions? Whichever way it was done it would involve some arrangement being made in advance with the Co-operative Societies. It would therefore mean that the Trade Union Movement would require to allow certain services to be carried on but that these services would be defined beforehand and agreed by the Movement. The alternative would be, assuming a service is necessary, to arrange with the Government as to what commodities should be transported.

11. *Publicity*

A separate memorandum has been drawn up dealing with publicity, and there is very little doubt that effective publicity would have considerable influence upon public opinion just at the present time. Publicity, however, is not confined merely to the documentary side, and it may be that the time has arrived when an organized platform campaign should be undertaken to educate the Trade Unionists and the public generally as to the attitude of the Labour Movement.

12. *Meetings of Special Industrial Committee*
The members of the Special Industrial Committee at their meeting on the 19th January, 1926, were unanimous in the view that more frequent contact is necessary, and the Special Industrial Committee will require to meet more frequently to marshal their ideas as to the policy to be adopted.

13. *Suggested Parley*
Since the above was completed, a statement has been made by Lord Londonderry, the effect of which is practically to repudiate the policy of the Mining Association. Several of the leading daily papers have emphasized the need for an early conference between the parties, and it may be that the Committee will consider it opportune to consult with the Miners' Federation as to what policy should be adopted in relation to this.

Certainly no opportunity should be lost for trying to arrive at a peaceful solution, while, at the same time, not neglecting to make adequate preparation for contingencies.

Our committee had engaged in only a modest amount of publicity. Cook had caused some concern in the Co-operative movement by his statement that they had agreed to act as the 'victualling movement for the fighting forces of labour'. They had done no such thing, and they resented this assertion. We had had some discussion with the Co-operative Union on the subject but we found that with their recollection of the heavy losses some of the Co-operative societies had suffered because of unpaid debts during the 1921 strike, they were not anxious to repeat the process. They asked that the whole resources of the trade union movement should be made available as a guarantee for any financial assistance rendered by them. They wanted the signatures not only of the chairman and secretary of the T.U.C., which I am afraid from a financial point of view would not have been worth much, but also those of the officers of every one of the individual trade unions. Whilst we realized the justification for this attitude, from the standpoint of business prudence, we knew there was no hope of their requirements ever being implemented.

At our next meeting with the miners Herbert Smith, after complimenting me on the memorandum, said he thought there was no need to rush things and we had better await the issue of the Coal Commission's report. Thomas, as usual, had a good deal to say, and immediately he spoke the miners were on the alert. They seemed to suspect that Thomas would try to trick them. Cook told me afterwards that Thomas was completely distrusted. It was clear to me that the meeting did not want to face the issues raised in my memorandum and would do anything to put off a decision. I could see that the miners were divided amongst themselves and terribly suspicious, even of one another. Frank Varley, M.P., who was one of the miners' executives, remarked to me after the meeting: 'There is too much jealousy on this committee. You may take it for granted that everything I say Herbert Smith will contradict, merely because I say it.'

Pugh and I had a chat with Ramsay MacDonald a few days later, as he was anxious to know what was going on. He had already seen Arthur Cook and told us that Cook had been very decent and agreed to co-operate with him.

We had frequent meetings with the miners and consulted them immediately the report of the Coal Commission was issued on March 10th. It was then resolved that adequate time should be given to all the parties to consider the report. But the miners wanted the committee to declare itself at once in favour of: (1) no reduction of wages; (2) no increase in hours; and (3) no departure from national agreements.

Our committee considered that matters had not reached the point when any final declarations of the General Council could be made as negotiations were at an early stage. We asked for detailed statements of the views of the miners on the various recommendations put forward by the Coal Commission.

Pugh repeated that our committee would do anything they possibly could to facilitate a settlement. Soon afterwards meetings took place between the miners and the coal-owners, at which the employers refused to agree to the principle of national agreements, which was felt by the miners and our committee to be fundamental.

On April 14th a resolution was passed reiterating the General Council's previous declarations of support for the miners in resisting any degradation in their standard of life. A copy of this was immediately sent to the Prime Minister. The committee was successful in persuading the Prime Minister to try to secure from the coal-owners a statement of their willingness to negotiate nationally. Baldwin, indeed, suggested that our committee should take part in any future negotiations between the miners and the owners. We were, of course, willing to do this and the miners immediately agreed. The coal-owners, however, declined, but at the same time they announced their readiness to conclude a national agreement. They were, however, opposed to any provision being made for a national minimum wage.

Trouble was now looming ominously. I could see that members of our committee, like myself, were suffering from the nervous tension under which we had been working. The General Council had appointed a Ways and Means Committee, and this committee had reported on the methods that should be taken in support of the miners if they were locked out. This provided for a national strike, with the General Council in full control. A conference of all the executive councils of the unions attached to the T.U.C. had been arranged and some 1,300 representatives of them attended at the Memorial Hall in Faringdon Street on Thursday, April 29th. The Council had decided to put forward an adjournment motion which would permit the conference to be resumed on the following day, and in the meantime negotiations would be proceeded with. In a way it was a remarkable conference. The demeanour of the delegates was serious and there was none of that buoyancy of spirit which was so often present at our national gatherings. The hall was packed to suffocation: I have many times noted that a crowded hall adds to the excitement.

Arthur Pugh gave a comprehensive review of the events which had taken place and Thomas moved the resolution. Just before he did, he turned to me and whispered: 'Baldwin has told me privately that he is going to put up to the coal-owners that they should pay the minimum of 1921 and possibly a somewhat lower minimum in the poorer exporting districts. Do you think the miners will accept that?'

I replied at once, 'No, I don't.'

'Neither do I,' said Thomas. He made a forceful speech, and I was interested to observe the attentiveness of the audience.

Pugh remarked to me, 'Don't you think this conference realizes its responsibility?'

'I am not surprised you should say that,' I replied, 'as I have just jotted down a note on the same point.'

Bevin seconded the resolution, and Thomas, who has a keen sense of the feelings of his audience, observed to me, 'There is not that wild enthusiasm, is there, do you think?'

I replied to him just as I had done to Pugh.

Bevin in one part of his speech observed that in a few days we might all be fighting together as one unit to break the power of the employers to use the big stick and the weapon of starvation. This sentiment was warmly applauded.

Cook, who followed, gave a long survey of the miners' case. He worked himself up into a state bordering on hysterics, his face was flushed, and tears were standing in his eyes while he was speaking. He apologized for coming so repeatedly to the trade union movement for support. It was not the fault of the miners, it was the fault of a derelict industry, ruined by private enterprise.

Pugh, in an aside, whispered, 'This is not Arthur's usual audience.'

'No,' I replied, 'it is much more critical.'

Even in the most intense moment in Cook's speech there was scarcely any applause. Watching the delegates, it was a bit difficult to judge what their impressions were.

Looking round the platform, I noticed Ramsay MacDonald, Leader of the Opposition, and Arthur Henderson, secretary of the Labour Party, both of whom were keeping in touch with us.

All this time Cook was going ahead with his perfervid oratory, but it appeared to me he was getting prolix.

Pugh said, 'He is missing his audience, he is going on too long.' It was perfectly plain that the audience was getting restive.

A little relief was afforded when he said: 'Who is robbing the community? Not us, we never had a chance.' The delegates welcomed this relief of the tension and laughed heartily. Cook, in conclusion, said, 'Nobody can charge us with not having warned the country that this position must come about.'

Thomas smiled sardonically, and said to me, 'That is just the damned mistake which has been made.'

We conveyed the resolution to the Prime Minister, asking for the non-enforcement of the lock-out, and our Industrial Committee went to the House of Commons at 5.45 p.m. The Prime Minister spoke gravely, and thanked us for the help we had been giving him. He said that even now he did not abandon hope, although matters were serious.

Later we met him in company with the miners. After Baldwin's opening speech there was absolute silence. It really was painful. Nobody moved. Baldwin put down his pencil, glanced inquiringly at Pugh and then at Herbert Smith.

Herbert, in his blunt Yorkshire fashion, said, 'Are you waiting for us to speak, Mr. Prime Minister?' Then in a dogged manner he retorted: 'Do you think our people are likely to go back to longer hours? Ah don't think you can expect us to do it, and we're not going to.'

We had a long wait because at 10.30 p.m. we expected the coal-owners to come along. It turned out that the Prime Minister had asked to meet their full committee and they were being summoned from the provinces.

It was all very wearying. We had been sticking it during the last few days—late hours, long periods of waiting—and although the committee were keeping cheerful, all things considered, still we were feeling the strain.

I looked around the room as I was writing my notes in the dim light of one of the House of Commons committee rooms, and the thought flashed through my mind that we were playing a part in working-class history, possibly in national history. Outside, one could see the gleam of the Thames reflected from the masthead lights of a ship lying at anchor. Round the table were the miners and our committee-men, waiting for a message from the Prime Minister. All were stolid, determined-looking men.

I fell to talking with Thomas concerning the possibilities of a lockout. He said: 'I am perfectly convinced, Walter, there is absolutely no hope. Stanley Baldwin talks to me just like a pal. There is going to be trouble and I can see no way out of it at all. Baldwin told me trouble is inevitable.'

'Do you think they will go to extremes?' I asked.

'Of course they will, they are bound to,' said Thomas emphatically. 'You must remember there is a lot of Russian money in this country. The Government are well informed. By God, you don't know! When I was in the Government the railway sectional strike was on—you know, Bromley's strike. Well, do you know that I had on my desk every morning full details, photographs of letters that had passed, speeches made at private meetings—oh my God! They have tested the feelings in different parts of the country, and they have made up their minds that there will be trouble. They are going to smash it.

'It won't last more than a few days,' Thomas continued. 'A few of these people will get shot, of course [indicating the General Council members and the miners], more of them will get arrested. The Government will arrest the remainder and say it is a case of putting them away for their own safety. Of course, the shooting won't be done by them direct, it will be done by those damned Fascists and those fellows. You see, Walter, they have come to the conclusion they must fight. Who is this strike against? It is not against the coal-owners, it must be against the State. The money is not in the industry, so the strike is against the State. Well, Baldwin says that the State must be supreme, and he is right. Churchill is the man who will play the big part in this.'

'It is singular you should say that,' I remarked. 'I was talking to John Burns the other day, and I asked him what he thought of the coal situation. He said that it would depend entirely upon three men: Lord Birkenhead, Winston Churchill, and Joynson-Hicks.'

Just then Ben Tillett and Swales and one or two of the others, who were getting a bit restive at the prolonged waiting, started singing 'John Brown's Body'. Some of the miners' delegates were shying balls of paper at each other. A couple of them were trying to wrestle in another part of the room.

Thomas shook his head despairingly. 'You can't get these fellows to realize it,' he said. 'They won't finish this business. Some of them will be shot for a certainty.'

Then something deflected his attention, and I turned to Swales. I said: 'Jimmy must like ghost stories. He reminds me of a man who likes to sit up till two in the morning in a house without any windows or light or fire, talking about murders. He likes to make your blood curdle.'

'Why, what has happened?' asked Swales.

I explained. I said, of course, I fully expected to be arrested.

'I hope they do arrest us,' said Swales. 'It will be just the thing to rouse our movement.'

Pugh turned to me and remarked: 'You know, Thomas is an enigma, I can't make him out. I know he doesn't manage his railwaymen without knowing something about psychology.'

We hung about for some time and were told that no further consultations could be held with us that night. So off we went, as we were all very fatigued.

On Friday, April 30th, we went to the House of Commons and hung about in the Foreign Secretary's room waiting for the Prime Minister to come over from Downing Street. Meanwhile the delegates were in conference at the Memorial Hall.

Baldwin had not yet met the coal-owners, who were late in putting in an appearance. Evidently they were deliberating very fully on the proposals they were going to send.

At 1.15 p.m. the Prime Minister sent by hand, after repeated telephone messages, the terms put forward by the mine-owners. They were broadly a uniform minimum of 20 per cent over the 1914 standard and an eight-hour day. This was to last till December 1929, when a Commission should decide whether a reversion to the seven-hour day was possible.

Meanwhile our conference at the Memorial Hall had adjourned till 2.30. We never left the room at the House of Commons except to have some light refreshments, and then returned and stayed with the miners' executive for a long time, while the Prime Minister was again meeting the owners.

Then our committee went to meet the Prime Minister by ourselves. He opened the proceedings by saying that we had received a communication from him and that he was not so much concerned with the actual letter as with the enclosure, in which the mine-owners' terms were set out.

Pugh responded that the previous day we had submitted a resolution, passed by the delegates at the Memorial Hall conference, indicating the position of the General Council so far as it concerned the participation of the General Council in any further negotiations. Their ability to take part in such negotiations depended on the proviso in the resolution: namely, that the lock-out notices must be suspended or withdrawn. The position was, therefore, that unless other instructions were given us by the conference we could not continue to perform any useful function in whatever discussions or negotiations might take place.

Thomas strongly supported this and informed the Prime Minister that some of the miners were already locked out. If the coal-onwers did not want to suspend the lock-out the Prime Minister must impose a suspension on them.

The Prime Minister then asked whether we had any contribution to offer, and Thomas responded that he thought we had a comprehensive scheme based on the Report of the Samuel Commission. The Prime Minister indicated that if there was a reasonable hope that we could get real negotiations going he felt sure that his committee would allow some latitude.

We retired, and after a long discussion amongst ourselves we returned to meet the Prime Minister at a few minutes before six o'clock. It was, however, some time before we were able to see him, and it was nearly seven o'clock by the time we got down to discussions.

Hardly had we done so when Thomas produced a poster, a copy of which had come into our possession from one of the printing unions. Apparently it had been prepared in proof by the Organization for Maintaining Supplies, who had approached Odhams Press to print it in quantity for them. As far as I could judge, while the firm were willing to do this, either the printers or the paper workers or both had announced their determination not to handle the poster, which was in effect announcing that the Government had proclaimed an emergency. It was evident from this that the poster had been prepared in advance against the possibility of negotiations breaking down, and it gave us all an insight into the Government's determination to face a national stoppage if it should occur.

Jimmy Thomas looked the Prime Minister straight in the eyes and asked him had this poster been ordered by the Government and did it represent the mind of the Government? Baldwin flushed and then after a few seconds' hesitation said that it was true that the Government had taken the necessary steps to prepare for the proclamation of a State of Emergency, but the poster had not yet been published.

The silence was ominous. Every one of us concluded that we had been badly tricked. We felt we could no longer trust either Baldwin or anyone else and that they were simply playing for time to complete the arrangements which the Government had in hand. I was outspoken about this and I told the Prime Minister that whereas we had been relying upon his assurance of good faith, yet actually at the time when we were still convinced he was trying to secure a settlement, the Conservative Party, his own party, had sent out a circular to certain selected newspapers, saying that the Government wished these newspapers to emphasize the necessity for increasing hours of work. Baldwin disclaimed all knowledge of this, but I said that our information was unchallengeable and it had come to us direct from people who had handled the circular.

The atmosphere was tense indeed, and Thomas followed me with the gravest warnings to the Government. It was evident to everyone that he was deeply moved.

He concluded: 'I picture it as a whirlpool, knowing I cannot help being dragged in, knowing that the State must win on an issue like this. I believe that nothing which my colleagues or myself can do will prevent that plunge with the consequences that I believe are inevitable. That is why I feel it is a desperate state, and if we are a bit over-anxious too, remember our knowledge of our people. Our love of our country and our anxiety for the future of our country, not our politics, is the driving force, the impelling motive, that makes us plead more than we otherwise would. That is the only excuse I can offer.'

It was a dramatic statement and was not without its effect on Baldwin.

The Government then put to us questions regarding the possibility of considering a wage reduction, but we refused to countenance this and we said we would retire to consult the miners.

We consulted the miners and returned again to meet the Prime Minister at 9.45 p.m. There were now present Baldwin, Steel-Maitland, Bridgeman, Lane-Fox, Neville Chamberlain, and Salisbury. Bridgeman and Salisbury were in dinner-jackets. No doubt they had been hastily called away from dinner.

Churchill met Thomas just outside the Prime Minister's room for a casual moment, and asked, 'Is it over?'

Thomas said, 'Yes.'

Churchill replied: 'Well, it is over as far as we are concerned. I have given you twenty-four millions, and that is all you are going to get. You can't have another bob.'

It was just on eleven o'clock when we finished, and after a few minutes' discussion with the miners in an adjoining room we at once went off to report to the conference of trade union executives who were waiting for us at the Memorial Hall. As we put on our coats Big Ben chimed out the hour of eleven o'clock. We were indeed at the eleventh hour—if we were not past it. It was the sound of battle which was booming out!

Alf Purcell had, as a past chairman of the T.U.C., from time to time announced to the conference, as well as he could, what was transpiring between our Special Committee and the Prime Minister, and at 11.25 p.m. our committee returned.

Pugh read the letter from Baldwin and the miners' reply, stating that negotiations had broken down on a mere phrase.

Thomas followed, and after giving a review of the situation announced that tomorrow the executives would be called upon to take the most momentous decision any body of trade unionists had ever been called upon to make. He asked them not to do this in passion or in heat, and concluded: 'We still want peace. The nation wants peace. Those who want war must take the responsibility.'

Immediately afterwards the chairman announced that the general secretaries could obtain in the library a copy of the instructions which the General Council's Ways and Means Committee had drawn up for conducting the national strike, if that course was decided upon.

10

The Government Breaks Off Negotiations

I T W A S now well after midnight, the early hours of Saturday, May
1st. Our General Council retired to a room below and had a brief
discussion, after which it was decided to meet the same day, for,
of course, we had actually started May Day. What a May Day! We
agreed to meet at 11.30 a.m.

In an adjoining room, the doors of which were carefully guarded,
the general secretaries of our affiliated unions were being addressed
by Purcell and Bevin, and the Memorandum of Instructions was being
explained to them. They were asked specially to take care of the
document, and, after consulting their executives, to come prepared to
announce whether their unions would accept the instructions. These
instructions were broadly to the effect that a stoppage of work should
take place in the productive industries such as iron and steel, printing
trades, transport, etc. Other sections were to hold themselves ready
to act at the General Council's discretion. Food services were being
maintained and other unions were to place their powers in the hands
of the General Council. I did not leave the hall until 1.30 a.m., and
the meeting of the secretaries was still in progress.

The same morning at 11.30 the Chairman gave a brief report,
when it was decided to make a roll-call of the unions at the conference upstairs, and ask each general secretary to report whether his
executive council was in favour of carrying out the General Council's
instructions.

The miners' officials were sent for, and they informed the General
Council that they were prepared to hand over the dispute entirely to
the General Council, provided that they were allowed to be present
at the negotiations.

We adjourned to the conference upstairs, and one could feel a
thrill of excitement running through the delegates. Some of the unions
had already sent in their replies in writing. The first letter I opened
was from the Asylum Workers' Union. They announced full support!
No one laughed. All were too deadly serious.

The first union called upon was the Scottish Colliery Enginemen and Boilermen's Association, and the firm 'Yes' that was returned by their spokesman was symptomatic of what followed.

Cheers greeted the reply of the railway unions and the Electrical Trades Union got its share of appreciation. When we came to the cotton group there was silence among the spinners, and it was reported they had gone to consult their executive at Manchester. It was the only disquieting note in the whole conference. The weavers reported that they were prepared to act on the Council's instructions, subject to confirmation by their full executive.

The conclusion of the roll-call was greeted with cheers, after which Bevin, and then Bromley, addressed the meeting. Herbert Smith was then called upon by the chairman.

As the old man advanced to the front of the platform the audience rose and applauded frantically. While he was speaking there came from the street outside the sound of cheering, and a few moments later the rumbling of the traffic gave way to the sounds of a drum-and-fife band. I thought that possibly this was subtle intimidation by the Government, who were perhaps sending the Guards band past the conference.

I noticed the same thing the previous day while we were debating with the Prime Minister. When we looked through the windows of the Prime Minister's room we saw a parade of Guards of inordinate length, and it occurred to me that it might have been staged for our special benefit. Today, however, I was in error. Somebody reminded me it was May Day, and probably this band was heading the procession to Hyde Park. This proved to be true, as subsequent events showed. Herbert Smith was followed by MacDonald, who made a glorious speech.

We adjourned at 2.45 p.m., and the General Council met again at 3.45 p.m. Arising from their decisions, I dictated letters at once and sent them by hand to the Prime Minister. The first announced that we were now empowered to conduct negotiations on behalf of the miners, and the other offered to co-operate in the distribution of essential foodstuffs.

Our Industrial Committee was reappointed as a Negotiating Committee to carry on any negotiations which might ensue. The Council set up a number of committees to deal respectively with:

Negotiations	Public Services
Food and Essential Services	Publicity
Powers and Orders	General Purposes.

I was given authority to engage a hall or suitable premises solely for the purpose of conducting the strike, if that was necessary. I had already made arrangements for our staff to stay at hotels adjacent to our offices.

Swales mentioned the advisability of the Council's arranging for a shadow Cabinet, as it were—people who could officiate in case the General Council members were arrested.

Thomas mentioned the 1919 incident, when for three hours the Cabinet discussed whether they should arrest him. He got the tip from a friend in the Cabinet. Bromley here interjected in an aggrieved tone, 'Christ, Jimmy, you didn't give me the tip!'

He said this in such a tone of expostulation that there was a howl of laughter from the Council. Thomas turned and consoled him with: 'It didn't matter, John. I don't think they considered you were important enough to arrest.'

Soon after our letter had been sent by hand the Prime Minister's secretary phoned and arranged a meeting for 8.45 the same evening. We met at Downing Street. Our full Negotiating Committee were present, and Baldwin was accompanied by Birkenhead, Steel-Maitland, Neville Chamberlain, Bridgeman, and Lane-Fox. Baldwin asked whether we were the responsible body to negotiate, and after receiving an assurance he raised the question as to whether Herbert Smith had accepted the Commission's report. Pugh pointed out that now the General Council were handling the negotiations we were really starting afresh, and there was no need to go over the ground again.

Thomas pressed for the withdrawal of the lock-out notices as a preliminary to discussions, but Birkenhead wanted to know whether we could give any assurance as to the advice we were going to give the miners. He denied that we were quarrelling on a phrase. He said we were concerned with a fundamental question of economics. There was no alternative to a subsidy except a reduction in wages or an increase in hours during the reconstruction period.

It was then suggested by the Prime Minister that it might be advisable to appoint a small committee from each side, say three, together with a permanent official. We had a long consultation in an ante-room amongst ourselves, and finally decided that we should do so.

I was dubious about the wisdom of this course, not that I did not recognize the much greater freedom which negotiations could take without shorthand notes and with a small body, but I was thinking about the damnable suspicion which had been aroused on every point. I found the others shared my view, but finally we agreed to appoint our small committee, provided that a full report was made to our Council and to the remaining members of the committee.

When we went back into the Cabinet room we found only Baldwin, Steel-Maitland, Birkenhead, and Wilson, and our negotiations at once took a much less formal turn.

Jimmy started talking to Birkenhead in the tone of an old college friend. It was a case of 'Fred' and 'Jimmy', and we certainly did get along much more cordially and less ceremoniously than we had done hitherto.

Birkenhead said: 'Look here, Jimmy, you know me personally. You know I am not out of sympathy with the miners. My great-grandfather worked as a miner in the Wakefield pit. He was champion prize-fighter of Yorkshire.'

'Oh,' said Swales, 'that must have been before Herbert Smith's time. Herbert held a championship.'

'Oh, but my great-grandfather would be nearly a hundred years old when Herbert Smith was in his prime,' said Birkenhead. 'You know they didn't fight with gloves in those days. It was a case of bare fists.'

The one question which was uppermost in the minds of the Cabinet representatives was whether we could give an assurance that negotiations would be conclusive, and that in some way a settlement could be arrived at.

We retired while they were considering a point, and after a while Horace Wilson came out to us. We were sitting round the fire in the hall just outside the Cabinet room—all of us nearly asleep, as we had had many late nights.

Wilson started to talk to us about the possibility of giving some assurance to the Cabinet. Thomas was rude in the extreme. He first read a lecture to Wilson on his position.

'Don't forget you are a civil servant, a permanent official. Your business is to advise the Minister. You are not responsible for policy, and you want to keep that in mind.'

'But what the Prime Minister wants,' said Wilson, 'is just something to satisfy his own mind that there will be a settlement. You know that I have a difficult team to handle inside, and Baldwin wants to feel sure of his position.'

After a time Wilson went into the Cabinet room and returned with a note containing the following words:

The Prime Minister has satisfied himself as a result of the conversations he has had with the representatives of the Trades Union Congress, that if negotiations are continued (it being understood that the notices cease to be operative) the representatives of the Trades Union Congress are confident that a settlement can be reached on the lines of the Report within a fortnight.

It was now early Sunday morning, May 2nd, and we went back into the Cabinet room. The note I have quoted was read to us by Baldwin, and it was agreed we should call the miners together and consult them during the morning.

After that we should see our General Council and let the Cabinet know the position some time during the afternoon.

Steel-Maitland offered to find me a bed for the rest of the night, but I preferred to go home. Pugh went along in Birkenhead's car, and they got a taxi for me.

I found that Cook had been on the telephone, and I at once rang him up and told him the position. I then found that the miners' executive had returned to their districts, and that they could not possibly meet in the morning. This was very unfortunate after what we had told the Cabinet Committee. I told Cook so. Cook undertook to wire them and to get them back as soon as possible. I went to bed and was soon sleeping like a log.

Our Negotiating Committee met at our offices at 10 a.m. We had a General Council meeting later.

Cook did not turn up or phone, so I got in touch with him and a wire was dictated by us to his executive. It was also agreed to ask Cook to come along to meet the General Council.

He met the Negotiating Committee a few minutes after one o'clock. The position was explained to him and the formula which Baldwin had proposed was read.

Cook then stated that the miners had never agreed to accept the report, and insisted that Herbert Smith had no right to make such a statement the previous day at the conference. We then went into the full General Council meeting, and at 4.25 Cook repeated his statement, saying that he had specially told Herbert to make a correction, which he alleged was given to the Press, but which none of us had actually seen in print.

Cook held firmly to his view that he could take no responsibility for any decision, and that the earliest we could get a reply from his executive would be late that night or on Monday morning.

Our Council recognized that the decision which we were to make upon this point was a crucial one. Both Pugh and myself emphasized that if we told the Prime Minister that we were confident a settlement could be achieved that would pledge us as men of honour. But the miners' position was dubious. It was true that Herbert had said at the conference that he would take the report from page to page, and accept their findings. But Cook had forced him to make a qualification, and when Herbert addressed the conference again he said that he had meant to say that he was prepared to examine the report from page 1 to the last page, and to stay by the results of the inquiry. We had none of us perceived the significance of this qualification, but we could now see the position we were going to be in if the miners refused to endorse Herbert's original acceptance.

We had visions of Black Friday, 1921, in our minds. On the present occasion the miners had expressly handed their powers over to the General Council, but it would not do to attempt to force a decision upon them.

If we accepted the withdrawal of the lock-out notices as a conclusion in itself there was a danger that we should lose our power. We might not be able again to generate amongst our members at large the strong determination to stand by the miners which then existed. We were at the crossroads.

The Council felt that the formula read to us at the Cabinet Committee could be accepted in substance, but were not at all clear as to what was meant by the latter part, which appeared to pledge us to a settlement definitely within a fortnight. The Council thought a fortnight was too brief a period, and it was decided we should aim at trying to get a month at least.

After the General Council adjourned at seven o'clock I rang the Prime Minister's secretary.

We had kept the Cabinet waiting practically the whole day, and it was plain to me that there was a changed tone in the conversations. They did not seem particularly anxious to see us. However, after some talk it was arranged that we should meet at Downing Street at 9 p.m.

When we got there Thomas, who had gone ahead of us, informed me that he had met Tom Jones, the Prime Minister's secretary, privately a few minutes before. He had said that the Cabinet were rather offended because we had not met the miners. They were under the impression that the miners were going to remain in town, and would see us on Sunday morning, so that we could have had our answer and been in a position to talk to the Cabinet earlier in the day. The Cabinet had waited over an hour and a half and had adjourned a second time, so that they were not in the frame of mind to arrive at a settlement.

It was decided by us that our best plan would be for our sub-committee (Pugh, Swales, Thomas, and myself) to meet Baldwin,

Birkenhead, Steel-Maitland, and Wilson, instead of attempting to meet the full Cabinet Committee. We met them. They looked rather resentful.

Birkenhead sat back in his chair with an injured air, and said that a painful impression had been left on their minds by the fact that we had not met the miners.

We explained the position. I said I realized I should have notified the Prime Minister's secretary earlier that morning that the miners' executive were not available. I pointed out that I had only received the information from Cook in the early hours of the morning, and in the stress of our meetings I had completely overlooked the possibility that the Cabinet would be meeting this morning. This statement seemed to reassure the Prime Minister and his colleagues, and they became intimate in explaining their own difficulties.

Birkenhead said they had been going through it with the Cabinet. They had been criticized for meeting us and making any new proposals in the form of the document which they had sent to us via Horace Wilson. This was the so-called formula which was to the effect that the Prime Minister had satisfied himself, after talking to us, that we were confident that if negotiations were continued a settlement could be reached within the lines of the report within a fortnight. Birkenhead went on to say that the members of the Cabinet felt this was ambiguous, and they had blamed the Prime Minister and him for it.

Birkenhead continued: 'Of course, I told them that it was not a document between you and us in any legal form. It was merely an understanding to make sure that the Prime Minister had got the right impression from you as to the possibility of a settlement.'

Baldwin here interjected with an aggrieved air, 'They hadn't been sitting and talking all day trying to settle a difficult dispute and drawing up a document at one o'clock in the morning.' He put down his pencil and took off his glasses with the air of a man who feels that his efforts have not been appreciated by his colleagues.

Birkenhead was frank. He said he did not see how we could secure any agreement unless it was pretty certain between us that the miners would, if the necessity arose, at the end of a fortnight accept some reduction. He was emphatic: 'I don't believe you can get this thing really organized in a couple of weeks. Every one of these damned colliery owners who owns a pit is going to play the devil. They will want every one of their paltry, individual pits considered separately.'

Birkenhead, supported by Baldwin, tried hard to persuade us that it was reasonable for the miners to contemplate the possibility of a reduction.

Birkenhead then read out some words he had jotted down in the course of the discussion. I had not got the Prime Minister's formula in front of me when he spoke, but, as far as I can recall, the words were identical, but he wished to add a most important sentence to the effect that negotiations would be carried on with the knowledge that these might involve some reduction in wages.

We said we could not possibly put this formula to our people, as they would be certain to reject it, and if we did so it might look as though we had some sympathy with it. We argued that the mere insertion of these words implied that the negotiations would begin on the assumption that they would end in a reduction of wages. In other words they completely prejudiced the negotiations.

Birkenhead seemed fed up, but he soon recovered his equanimity.

The discussions were continued, constantly revolving round this point. We could all see that we were not getting any further towards a solution.

The proceedings concluded with Birkenhead remarking: 'I feel we should face it. If we have got to have a break it might be as well to have it now as to have it in another fortnight. We, personally, can be good friends just the same, even after this sorrowful business is over.'

We separated, the Cabinet members going to consult their colleagues who were meeting in another part of the building, and we four—Pugh, Thomas, Swales, and myself—going upstairs and through an intercommunicating door into No. 11 Downing Street, where we found the members of our General Council waiting for us in the boardroom of the Chancellor of the Exchequer's residence. The miners' executive had not yet arrived, although it was after ten o'clock.

It was a big square room with a large electrolier in the centre, the bottom covered over with linen so that the lamps were not visible. The concentrated light shone down on the table, leaving the walls in semi-darkness. At the end farthest from the fireplace was the chair in which Queen Anne had sat. There was a huge fire burning away merrily in the big fireplace, which would hold about a hundredweight of coal. It was a very appropriate setting, and illustrated the connection between coal and comfort.

Pugh, Thomas, Swales, and I gave our reports of the discussion that evening in turn. There was dead silence while we were talking. Old Bob Smillie, who stood at some distance from the table, his face partially hidden, with quiet insistence asked pointedly of Pugh: 'Are you indicating, Mr. Chairman, that the miners must accept a reduction in wages? If so, they will never do it.'

Purcell asked, 'What is this about a formula?'

Pugh explained that the formula was merely a note which Baldwin had drafted to read to his Cabinet, showing the basis upon which the negotiations could proceed. Swales or someone else had mentioned that we had considered whether the formula should be destroyed. I am afraid that this innocent remark left a rather disquieting impression upon the Council. It looked as though we were concealing something from the General Council. I at once pointed out that so far as I was concerned I wished to take my full share of the responsibility. I said that we had gone into the negotiations as a small committee on the distinct understanding that what was said would be entirely without prejudice, and would not bind either side. We had agreed there would be no shorthand report, and that any records or rough notes that were taken by any of us would be destroyed. If we could not come to agreement the whole of the semi-private negotiations would be regarded as never having taken place. That was the only possible way to secure absolute frankness.

I said it was put to us as men of honour that we should all carry out this undertaking. It was on that distinct understanding that the four of us entered the negotiations. Both the full Negotiating Committee and the Council knew this, and I still stood by that position.

Soon afterwards the miners' executive arrived. Just as Pugh started to explain to them our position the clock on the mantelpiece chimed the hour of midnight.

It was now Monday, May 3rd. We were approaching the most fateful decision of the whole dispute. We knew any attempt to impose a decision on the miners would be resisted. They would say that they had been badly let down, and the movement would think that we had deserted them. It would be even worse than Black Friday of 1921. On the other hand every one of us knew that even if we started a General Strike we would have to face the economic position of the coal industry just the same in a few weeks' time.

Herbert Smith was sitting at the table, immediately opposite Pugh. He pointed out that the miners were now actually locked out. It was impossible to contemplate a settlement in a fortnight. If there had to be a reduction in wages it should be limited as to extent in time and the miners would insist upon the uneconomic pits going out of the industry.

There the old man sat in the centre, watchful and careful, looking over his glasses at Pugh. Behind him, in the shadow, with his hands in his pockets and with a troubled expression on his worn and wrinkled face, Bob Smillie stood. He felt his position. He was not in these negotiations as a member of the miners' executive, but as a member of the General Council. Yet, like Herbert, he lost sight of no point that could affect the miners' interests.

Herbert remarked pointedly: 'I think we are getting too near the sticks now, and some people are getting frightened. Well, we are not going to be afraid. We are going on. I would to God I could do without your assistance but we are absolutely dependent economically upon you now, owing to the position in which our societies are.'

While we were talking a message came to say that Baldwin wanted to see us. Pugh, Thomas, Swales, and myself went down. This time only Baldwin, Steel-Maitland, and Wilson were present. Baldwin looked very troubled, and before we sat down he said that the printers had refused to print an article in one of the London papers. That was a challenge to the Government, and no Government could go on negotiating in those circumstances.

'It is a direct challenge, a direct challenge, Mr. Pugh, and we cannot go on. I am grateful to you for all you have done, but these negotiations cannot continue.'

This was a bombshell to us, as we had no knowledge whatever of the incident to which he referred. We protested that we had had no chance to investigate the matter and knew nothing about it. It was evident that Baldwin's mind was made up. We concluded that this incident had deliberately been used as a means of terminating the negotiations. Our suspicions were confirmed when Baldwin handed me a letter which he said contained the Cabinet's views on the point.

We made for the door somewhat perplexed, and with a feeling that we had not been treated fairly. As we were shaking hands, Baldwin said to Pugh, 'Goodbye, Mr. Pugh, you have been a brick to me, and I hope when we meet together again we will meet with as friendly a spirit as we are leaving in now.'

As I passed him I said, 'It has been difficult for all of us, Mr. Baldwin.'

He replied, 'Well, I have been happy to meet you, and I believe if we live we shall meet again to settle it.' Then he added solemnly, 'If we live.'

With that we went out.

We returned once again to the room where our people were waiting. As soon as we took our seats at the table they came crowding round. They stood in a double row leaning over and listening intently to the reports we gave. They sensed that something was wrong. Thomas read the letter which Baldwin had handed to us, and which insisted that the General Strike must be withdrawn before negotiations could go on. Immediately he had finished that sentence there

was an ominous growl. Everyone drew back from the table as though
some invisible force commanded them.

'That settles it,' said Purcell, 'we will fight them.'

Bevin exhorted, 'Wait, wait, we must consider this.'

Thomas looked round belligerently.

'I have not been talking about this day coming,' he thundered.
'Some of those who have been talking have now got their will. They
must control this from now. We should inform the Government that
we regret any incidents that have happened and which have rendered
the task of the peacemakers more difficult, but we cannot accept
responsibility for them. You must control this thing, you who are on
top, or you will not be able to control it at all. You won't have the
opportunity to issue instructions very long, I know.'

Some of those present smiled, but Thomas turned viciously on
them, and replied: 'You won't have the power to issue instructions,
I know, I know. War has been declared.'

We then discussed for some moments whether we should draw
up a reply then and there to the letter. No one had any knowledge of
the newspaper incident, and it was suggested we should get into touch
with the printing trades at once. Others were against our leaving the
building, and demanded to see the Prime Minister forthwith. I went
downstairs, but I found that the Cabinet had gone. No one was left
on the premises but the caretaker and the detective who is always
there.

Just before we left Downing Street somebody shouted, 'Here it is,
on the tape!' Sure enough the whole incident was recorded! That
meant that Baldwin's letter must have been handed to the Press even
before we had received it. It told us something further—that the
Cabinet probably had been drafting that letter long before we had
retired from our first meeting with Baldwin earlier in the evening.

I felt we had been cruelly let down and that the other side had
been manœuvring for position. It was only later that I found that
Churchill had been to the *Daily Mail* office. The compositors had
refused to set an article which vindictively and viciously accused the
General Council of organizing a movement against the King and the
Constitution.

Pugh and I with a few others walked back to the office through
St. James's Park, arriving at Eccleston Square at 2.30 a.m. We
remained in session until about four o'clock and drafted a reply
which was despatched to the Government by hand. We dictated it to
the press representatives, who had been patiently waiting for our final
conclusions.

Broadly, the terms of the letter were to express our astonishment that, without any warning, the Government had abruptly terminated the negotiations. With regard to the statement that there had been gross interference with the freedom of the Press, we pointed out that the Government had given us no specific information on this and that we had no knowledge of any of these acts having occurred. The instructions we had sent out definitely forbade any such independent and unauthorized action for which we disclaimed responsibility.

We also said we were taking prompt measures to prevent acts of indiscipline, and that we regretted we were not given the opportunity to investigate and deal with the alleged incidents before the Government made these an excuse for breaking off the peace discussions which were then proceeding.

I was half asleep when I drafted this letter which, with the exception of a few small alterations, was approved by the Council before its despatch.

Pugh, Milne-Bailey, and I returned home by taxicab. I did not arrive until 5 a.m.

Six hours later the Negotiating Committee went to the House of Commons to meet the Parliamentary Labour Party executive. A subcommittee consisting of Pugh and Bevin, together with Herbert Smith and Cook, had had a meeting at 9.30 at the Transport Workers' offices. They made good progress towards drafting proposals for a settlement. I was a member of this committee but my other duties intervened and I took no part in its work. The Negotiating Committee (Hicks, Swales, Bromley, Tillett, and myself) waited in the House with the Parliamentary Party executive.

Eventually Pugh arrived with the draft proposals for a settlement from the sub-committee. These were of a constructive character, but provided for arbitration through a Mining Board on the question of any essential wages revision. This Board would be composed of an an equal number of representatives of the Government, owners, and miners.

Ramsay MacDonald said at the meeting of the executive that morning: 'My hair has gone greyer than when I started this morning. If this proposal is put forward it will complicate matters. It means that every constitution-monger will seize on the powers of the Board, and will destroy the whole thing at once on that. The Government will never accept it.'

Arthur Henderson also took the view that to put forward this document would be a tactical blunder. It might give the impression that our people were so disturbed that they had hastily got out a scheme in a frantic attempt to avoid trouble.

Later the Negotiating Committee met the miners' executive in another room. I had been called away for a few minutes. The document which the sub-committee had drafted was being considered by the meeting when I got in.

It was evident that there was a division among the miners' executive members. Both Richardson and Cook were against putting in anything which gave the impression that the national minimum could be attacked or revised. When it became clear that the miners were adhering to their decision, Bevin said: 'Well, if that is your decision the General Council must make its own decision. There are three and a half million men who must have their position considered.'

The miners then retired, and our General Council members came in. There was a good attendance. Purcell moved that the document of the sub-committee should be mentioned by MacDonald in the House of Commons, as suggested by Bevin.

Pugh made it clear to the Council that if negotiations restarted they would be on the basis of the sub-committee's document.

The General Council then agreed that the document, although rejected by the miners' executive, should be accepted in the same form as presented. This was carried unanimously.

Then the General Council went into another room to meet the full Parliamentary Party and the miners' executive at 2.35 p.m. In the presence of all, Bevin, who put the position on the document, said that the General Council was not committed to any slogan of any kind. 'On the discussions which have taken place the views of the General Council are that if the whole thing is examined on its merits the matters in the Samuel Report are then subjects for consideration.'

I went into the House at 3.45 with a ticket for a place under the gallery. I was squeezed alongside two chaps, one of whom I thought I had seen before, and who turned out to be Lee, the secretary of the Mining Association. Cook was on my left. The House was packed. Great attention was focussed on Baldwin when he rose to speak. He made a generally fair statement, and was followed by Thomas, who made an impassioned speech full of argument which seemed to me to be listened to with close attention and great interest. Then Lloyd George spoke strongly against the Government's attitude. He protested that it was foolish to talk about this being an attack on the Constitution. He argued that negotiations had taken place last year under the threat of what was practically a General Strike, and why were the Government now standing on their dignity?

The debate was continuing when I returned to the office and remained in my private room for some time attending to different matters before going in to the General Council meeting.

I went to have some food in the Pillar Hall at Victoria Station and while there I got news from one of the Labour Party staff that some of the Coal Commissioners were dead against the Government's interpretation of the report. Beveridge was alleged to have said that he was ready to give an interview to the Press to this effect.

I went at once to the House of Commons, as I thought this was a valuable point for Henderson to know in case he should be called on to speak, or alternatively to pass along to one of our other speakers.

While I was waiting in the lobby, having sent in a card for Henderson, Sir Horace Wilson and Tom Jones, one of the Prime Minister's advisers, came up to have a few words. They were both willing to talk and said that something might be done on the lines of the new scheme which, they understood, the Council had now drawn up. I thought it would be a good thing to let Pugh know this, so I phoned the office and asked for him or Bevin. Bevin came on the phone. I explained to him what had been said. It seemed to me from what Wilson had said that he was strongly in favour of the general outline of the scheme. I then said that I would come straight back to the General Council to see Pugh.

When I arrived Alec Firth, our acting assistant secretary, came to me in great concern and said the Council wanted to know where I had been. They had evidently got some wrong impressions as to what had been happening. I explained matters to them and told them that I had seen Wilson and just what had happened. The incident passed. It seemed to me that in the state of tension which now existed they were naturally somewhat suspicious of everyone. We sat in Council until well after midnight.

The E.T.U., it appeared, had sent out instructions that they were going to stop the power stations, as they could not discriminate between lighting and power. We sent Findlay with a letter from me to try to persuade them not to do this.

At midnight we got word that MacDonald and Henderson had met Baldwin and Churchill, but that no progress had been made. It appeared from what Henderson told me later that Churchill said he was going to prove that we could not dictate to the Government. 'You tried it in Italy and failed, and you are not going to be successful in Great Britain.'

Steel-Maitland had also got on his 'high horse' and had said to Henderson that 'it was about time we were put in our places'.

Henderson retorted, 'It seems to me, Winston, that you are trying to give us a dose of Sidney Street.'

Churchill replied, 'You will be better prepared to talk to us in two or three weeks.'

All this showed how high feeling was rising.

I had taken the precaution of engaging rooms close to the office at the Belgravia Hotel. I got to bed at one o'clock.

Diary of the General Strike

FROM this point to the end of the account of the General Strike, I describe the progress of events as I recorded it in my diary.

Tuesday, 4th May, 1926

Although the strike did not actually start until midnight, many of the workers had been coming out in anticipation. It appears that the article which should have appeared in the *Mail* denounced the General Council and the the trade union movement as enemies of the King. It alleged that we were out to smash the Constitution and starve the women and children. The men would not print it and it was sent round to the *Evening News*. The compositors there refused to set it and came out. In view of the fact that we had offered to co-operate with the Government for food supplies and had been ignored, this article was much resented. Then the *Daily Mail* tried to get the *Standard* printers to set it up and they struck work.

The movement spread, with the consequence that last evening, Monday, 3rd May, there was not a single evening newspaper in the city, although the strike was not timed to take place until midnight.

The Council yesterday had before them a telegram from the *Manchester Guardian* asking that *sane* newspapers should be allowed to continue. We were sorry to have to refuse, as the *Guardian* is generally very fair. But it would have been impossible to discriminate.

The strike is complete. The reports are simply marvellous. Everywhere the utmost solidarity and eagerness to respond to the Council's instructions. The Government themselves have admitted its wonderful effectiveness. The reports have come in by all sorts of means. The written reports are naturally somewhat sketchy because of the cessation of transport.

We have not allowed the Trades Councils to set up local committees. Although I was strongly in favour of that course, others, Bevin in particular, opposed it on the grounds that unions would not

M

hand over their functions to Trades Councils. My view is that it cannot be really effectively organized without the Trades Councils being made the nucleus of the strike organization. At present the initiative is left entirely to some union to form the local strike organization, and I do not think this is sound.

The Council remained in session during the whole day, and as a number of separate sub-committees were set up, it became difficult for the Council to be thoroughly informed as to what decisions were being made by these committees. I arranged for a member of the clerical staff to be attached to each committee and immediately a decision was made it was to be brought down to me, typed, and then stencilled and circulated to the General Council and each of the committees. This was a big job and threw a considerable strain on the staff.

Some of the Council members evidently do not realize there is a General Strike in progress, and they want all their documents from each committee put in folders for their examination. They have even set up a small committee with Elvin as chairman to see how this could best be done. I could not see any satisfactory way of carrying this out with the present committee system.

I got into the evening meeting of the Council a little late and found that Bevin had made a suggestion that he, personally, should be put in general charge of the Strike Organization. There was a storm as a consequence, and a good deal of straight speaking. Thomas and some of the others were very sarcastic at Bevin's offer. I pointed out that it was natural on the first day that there should be a good deal of confusion, and I advised the Council to wait a little until they saw how the organization worked.

The policeman who is on duty outside our offices reported this morning that the Fascists might get nasty, and he advised that I should get some plain-clothes men on duty inside the office. This officer made the significant remark that, so far as he knew, the men at his station were with us to a man.

I raised the matter with the Council, and I have made arrangements for a number of ex-policemen, who were members of the National Police and Prison Officers' Union, to remain on duty inside the house in relays.

No evening papers were out this evening, and just before midnight I had a visit from pickets from the printing unions. They say there has been an attempt to print *The Times* and that the police have drawn a cordon across the road to Printing House Square, and are constantly preventing the pickets getting near the place. I phoned the Superintendent in charge, and he agreed to allow six pickets to pass, so that two could picket at each of the three doors of the building.

Wednesday, 5th May
I spent the night at the Belgravia and got to the office at 9 a.m. I went into the Powers and Orders Committee of which Purcell is chairman.

The committee made recommendations, the practical effect of which would be to concentrate all decisions on strike policy in their hands. Reports would be made from the separate committees to them, and then twice each day, at twelve and seven respectively, reports would be presented by the Powers and Orders Committee to the General Council. This committee will now be called the General Strike Organization Committee.

The committee appointed practically every member of the General Council to a particular function; some of them of little use, I am afraid. Even the members of the Central Strike Committee, with the exception of Bevin and Purcell, were appointed to other duties, the net effect being to eliminate them from participation in most decisions, leaving only Purcell and Bevin to act. As Bevin remarked to me, 'We must not have too many generals in this business.'

According to Thomas, Baldwin admitted in the House that it was true that negotiations had been broken off while we were still conferring with the miners. Immediately there was a tremendous sensation in the House. Thomas said: 'You know, Baldwin is a damned honest fellow. He will never be a politician.' The Council howled at this, having regard to Jim's well-known proclivities as a politician. Thomas went on: 'I do not care whether you extend the strike or not. I am convinced that every hour we make it more inconvenient and show our strength, our position gets stronger.'

Bevin remarked that in transport strikes it had always been his policy not to throw the whole of the union's fighting strength into the first week. If they were all brought in at the same time it meant reaching the maximum of strength too quickly and the men would begin to drift away afterwards. On the other hand, by bringing up reserves and adding additional men after the first week, it always supported the strike and guaranteed the men being out a second week. It was something to look forward to.

Thomas intervened and pointed out that the longest railway strike, that of 1919, was of ten days. 'Our policy should be to balance our forces against the Government. If they made a move which seemed a successful one, we should counter it by another move withdrawing additional men.'

We fell to discussing the general position and Thomas recorded his view that the dispute would not be settled by an employer or a number of employers. It should be settled as the constitutional issue got more dangerous. The more danger to the constitution, the more those in authority would get afraid. 'Up to the evening of the strike the Government thought they knew our power, but the strike exceeded their greatest expectation. The position is that they are staggered. How does their mentality operate after the first shock? I can picture Winston—for he is dominating this—I can picture the Cabinet, I can hear him saying: " Wait until tomorrow, they will get tired. We will have our guns. We will have our volunteers. This cannot be a war of attrition. If it became that it would get out of hand in a week." '

It was strange to hear Jimmy advocating an extension of the strike, but I thought he was entirely right and I supported his argument. Bevin said, 'We must move as an army and bring our people in just at the right moment.'

I took the view that our people were not sufficiently disciplined to obey the instructions which were issued from headquarters. I said that our traditions were entirely against it, and while I appreciated the importance of enforcing discipline, that did not convince me that our people understood its necessity to the same degree that we did. Consequently, they were puzzled by some of the instructions we were sending out. How can the electricians differentiate between lighting and power? We had cut off power but allowed lighting to continue, with the consequence that men were accusing others who were left at work to run the lighting plant of being blacklegs.

I instanced further that the idea of a general strike was not clearly in the minds even of the executives of our unions; that the transport workers and the railwaymen took diametrically opposed views of policy about the transport of food. The railwaymen refused to run a service for one single commodity on the grounds that the running of trains meant that anything up to 75 per cent of the personnel of the railway staff would have to resume work. I regarded that estimate as a great exaggeration, but it serves to show the difference in points of view.

The transport workers on the other hand are prepared to move almost any food commodities. The result is practically open strife between them and the railwaymen on the Central Transport Committee.

I argued for a clean-cut instruction, bringing everyone out, although I recognized fully the wisdom of the other strategy of bringing out the members in battalions. I cannot feel that our people are sufficiently disciplined and trained to understand that.

At nine o'clock in the evening we were still deliberating when a telephone message came from Bob Williams, the general manager of the *Daily Herald*. He said, 'I am speaking from our office with three Inspectors alongside of me.'

'Are they with you now?' I asked.

'Yes, they can hear what I am saying. Three big burly fellows much bigger than I am. [Williams was a six-footer.] They have brought a warrant signed by Joynson-Hicks, holding Fyfe [the editor] and myself responsible for publishing the *Daily Herald* on Tuesday and containing powers to search our premises. If they find anything in the bulletin we are issuing today that is contrary to the Emergency Powers Act, they are going to confiscate the issue and proceed against us.'

I said, 'Wait a moment, and I will consult the General Council.' I did this, and immediately there was an indignant retort. 'Tell them to go on. Tell them to print and take the consequences.'

I went back to the telephone and spoke to Williams and he said he would go on printing, provided always that the police did not use *force majeure*. I said: 'There are three directors here, Bevin, Ben Turner, and myself. They can arrest us if they like.'

I returned to the Council room, and just as they were breaking up, Poulton came in with Tracey and Naylor, the night editor of the *Herald*. Poulton was labouring under a strong emotion and trembling with excitement. He gave a report to the effect that he had been to the *Herald* office to see about our strike bulletin and found the place surrounded by at least 100 police, many of them mounted. They had seized the telephone and were compelling staff to remain on the premises.

I volunteered to go down to the *Herald* offices, and Ben Turner and Bevin did the same. We dashed through the streets in one of the cars and found when we got there that the roadway was blocked with masses of people. There was a cordon of police drawn across the road, the mounted men being behind those on foot.

They would not let us through at first, but finally an Inspector was brought, to whom we explained our business. He went into the *Herald* office and brought out one of the editorial staff, who identified Ben Turner, and we all went in. When we got inside a strange sight greeted our eyes. The Despatch Room was packed with members of the staff. There seemed to be at least a couple of hundred of them there. Most of them were in their shirt sleeves and lustily singing the 'Red Flag'. Outside in the streets we could hear the refrain being taken up by the people.

We went upstairs to the manager's office and found a plain-clothes Inspector there. He was in telephone communication with the Police Commissioner and after we had waited for about half an hour he returned to say that the Commissioner said we could go on printing the paper.

Meanwhile, in the streets, we heard the people singing snatches of Socialist songs, and the *Herald* staff inside were shouting through the windows and encouraging them. I could not help reflecting on how easily a riot could be started. Here were these people, normally friendly and peace-loving, suddenly converted into militant, menacing elements by the precipitate action of the police and the authorities. Men who probably had never heard the 'Red Flag' sung before were joining in with gusto.

Then we heard a low rumble of the machines starting up in the basement, and the crowd outside responded with a tremendous cheer. After a few minutes there were brought to us some dozens of copies of our bulletin, the *British Worker*, which had been run off the machines. We hurried down to the waiting motor-car and got back to the council offices. I got to bed at half past twelve, feeling very tired and not a little concerned as to where it will all end.

Thursday, 6th May
First thing this morning I had a discussion with Thomas who came in early. He says the railway situation, from the standpoint of the completeness of the strike, is the best that they have ever known in their history. He seemed well satisfied, but undoubtedly he is anxious to get negotiations on foot as soon as possible and will seize the first opportunity. When the General Council meeting started it was evident that the miners had something on their minds. It turned out that Thomas was alleged to have said something in the House of Commons to the effect that the General Council had accepted the formula which Baldwin had put forward. Old Herbert Smith was very dour. 'I want Mr. Thomas to pull his weight, but I do not want him to be too anxious.' The incident passed without serious friction.

We are up against a Gilbertian position in regard to the *Herald* office. The electricians have been withdrawn from the station supplying the current to the printing plant, but the stations are being run by volunteers and naval ratings. Consequently we can only produce the *British Worker*, our strike paper, with the assistance of current supplied by them.

We gave consideration to alternative arrangements for carrying on the strike in the event of the General Council being arrested.

Thomas has now changed his point of view. He was confident before the strike started that we would all be arrested practically the first day. That some of us, if not all, would never live to see it through. Now he considers that the Government are not likely to arrest the Council.

He volunteered the information that Joynson-Hicks had said to him today—'I wish you had my job, J.T.,' to which Thomas replied —'No you don't; you are as happy as hell.'

'No, I'm not, it is a very worrying time,' replied Joynson-Hicks, and Thomas certainly judged from his appearance that he was really worried. However, Jimmy retorted—'Yes, and you see where your Mussolini is driving you.' This was a hint at Winston Churchill. Joynson-Hicks shook his head in doleful fashion, and it was evident to Thomas that he is carrying out his responsibilities with difficulty.

Friday, 7th May

At this morning's meeting Bevin, in a state of considerable perturbation, emphatically requested that no notes should be taken of the proceedings. Clearly his object was to prevent any evidence accumulating which could be used by the police in the event of their raiding our premises. This possibility has not been absent from the minds of the Council members, although it has never been discussed in open meeting. From the ready concurrence which was expressed at this suggestion it was evident that no one is anxious to furnish evidence against themselves. A wise precaution. [I continued to record my own notes which were secreted each night in a place where I knew the police would never find them.]

This morning the *British Gazette* (the Government paper) came out with a poisonous attempt to bias the public mind. They actually asserted that the General Council had accepted a formula stating that negotiations would proceed with the knowledge that they might involve a wages reduction. This is an absolute travesty and an illuminating example of the type of honourable men with whom we were supposed to negotiate.

Baldwin on the night of Saturday, 1st May, when he appealed to us to allow negotiations to be conducted without formality through the smaller sub-committee, expressly stated that any documents that emanated would be without prejudice to either party, and if we could not come to a mutual understanding at the end, they would be destroyed and no one would know they had ever existed. This so-called formula is nothing more than a note which Lord Birkenhead wrote down on Sunday evening and tried to get us to acquiesce in as an assurance which Baldwin could offer to the Cabinet. It was merely read over to us and at no time was in our possession. We never for a moment entertained the possibility of its acceptance, and plainly said so. Well, I suppose we must expect this sort of thing, but it does shake one's confidence in the integrity of the other side.

I sometimes wonder whether Baldwin is as honest, plain, and straight-forward as he appears, or whether he is a hypocrite and a humbug. When in personal contact with him he conveys the feeling of sincerity, but his subsequent actions can only be justified by the assumption that he is dominated by his Cabinet.

The report from the Strike Committee today showed the position throughout the country to be as solid as a rock. The arrangements for the issue of permits through our Strike Organization Committee have broken down because of the congestion. Eccleston Square this morning was crowded with huge vans and carts and motor vehicles of every description, all of them bearing the usual label 'Food Only'. Our committee could not possibly deal with so many applications for permits.

Then there was the difficulty of defining what food really consists of. I had a message from a firm of salt merchants and they convincingly demonstrated the hopelessness of continuing a food supply unless salt was liberated. They pointed out that the butchers would find their meat going bad on their hands without salt, while the bakers would be unable to bake bread. The Committee decided to leave the issue of permits to a Central Permits Committee, composed of the transport and railway unions.

This morning Bevin, who seems to recede in forcefulness as Thomas advances, raised the possibility of members of the General Council getting into conversation with influential business men who might be able to exert some power to achieve a settlement. The Council agreed that it was desirable that even though we are certain of the strength of our strategic situation, we should lose no opportunity of getting on to negotiations.

Thomas apprised us of a conversation he had had with Lord Londonderry, and produced a letter from him, written last night, in which he had stated that the Government had got the whole business in such a mess that something must be done. He also mentioned that he had seen Mansfield, the vice-president of the Federation of British Industries, and Dudley Docker. They had said that most business men realized that if the strike got out of control anything might happen. Mansfield had said: 'If Winston gets his way, we will have no country left. That is not going to go on. We must stop it.'

Thomas informed us this morning that he had had a telephone

message from Sir Herbert Samuel to the effect that he had returned from Italy and was willing to help in any way he could towards a settlement. Jimmy remarked that Samuel was willing to see our Industrial Committee at three o'clock this afternoon. We arranged to go along. We were to meet at the house of Sir Abe Bailey, reputed to be a South African millionaire.

We drove to Bailey's house in Bryanston Square and were at once admitted. We marched up the fine marble staircase and entered a long lounge or sitting-room. I noticed several pictures by Gainsborough, Reynolds, Lawrence, and other well-known painters. Waiting for us near the fireplace was Sir Herbert Samuel, standing with his hands behind his back and looking over his pince-nez. Thomas introduced each of us separately, and after we had sat down Samuel said: 'I was in Italy working away on a book I have been trying to write. After serving six months on the Coal Commission, I wanted a rest. I am interested in this book and I desired to get it finished.'

'Is it about Palestine?' Jimmy Thomas asked jokingly.

'No, it is about the effect of religion on morality. It is about what is wrong with the world. The world is out of joint and I am trying to get down to fundamentals. I want to make it a short book and it is much harder to write a short book than a long one.'

Then Samuel explained how he had telegraphed Baldwin saying that he was willing to give any assistance he could. Baldwin replied to the effect that as soon as he could utilize Samuel's services, he would do so. But no letter came. Consequently, Samuel returned of his own accord and arrived in London last evening. He said, firmly, that the attitude of the coal-owners was entirely opposed to the intention expressed by the Coal Commission.

'What we intended,' he said, 'was that there should definitely be National Agreements and a National Board, which should arrange what subjects could be dealt with in the districts. But that presupposed that both sides agree. It is not for the coal-owners alone to say what must be done by the districts. The miners must also agree.'

Then he read some notes he had written. Among other things, he suggested that any revision of wage rates should be for a period of one year only and that this should be regarded as the reorganization period, during which proposals relating to co-operative selling associations, amalgamation of mines, and other reforms should be put into effect.

Pugh, speaking for the members of our Industrial Committee, said we had suggested a National Wages Board analogous to the Railway Wages Board. Samuel at once remarked that this was easily the most constructive suggestion and far in advance of anything which had been put forward since the report of the Commission. He desired to have arrangements made between the chairmen of the different districts to avoid cut-throat competition. Further, he suggested international arrangements on the working hours of miners. He seemed to feel that the British miners should work the same length of time, approximately, as the German miners, but we at once pointed out that this was against the Commission's own report, and he agreed, after a few moments' consideration, that it would be disastrous to press this suggestion.

Finally, we arranged to meet Samuel tomorrow at the same place. On our return to headquarters we each entered the building separately so as not to arouse suspicion, as so many press sleuths are hanging about, although no newspapers are appearing.

Saturday 8th May

This morning we had a telegram from the All-Union Central Council of Trade Unions of Russia and a cheque from their bank for £26,000. We decided we could not accept this and to return the money.

Ramsay MacDonald said the Archbishop of Canterbury had seen Baldwin to get permission from him to broadcast a statement to the whole country. He had expressed himself very strongly that the Government were at fault in the present situation. Baldwin had refused to allow him to broadcast, although the Archbishop was representing a deputation of the Churches, including the Free Church leaders.

A heated discussion took place this morning at the General Council because of speeches by Cook and Herbert Smith, who insisted that the miners should be included in discussions that were taking place with Samuel. Bromley, of the locomotive men, was very emphatic. 'By God, we are all in this now and I want to say to the miners, in a brotherly, comradely spirit, but straight'—and he repeated: 'But straight—that this is not a miners' fight now. I am willing to fight right along with them and to suffer as a consequence, but I am not going to be strangled by my friends.' Herbert Smith seemed exasperated by this and he retorted: 'I am going to speak as straight as Bromley. If he wants to get out of this fight, well, I am not stopping him.' The incident ended with Herbert Smith saying that they didn't want to be in on conversations but only on definite negotiations.

At three o'clock in the afternoon, we again went to the house of Abe Bailey and met Samuel. He said he was sorry to say that his approach to Baldwin had not been met in a friendly spirit. The

Government were not discourteous to him, but it was plain that they were not prepared to negotiate, either privately or openly. He personally thought that the only remaining course was for him to make a public pronouncement, stating the terms on which he considered the dispute might be settled. 'Of course, I don't care to risk my public reputation as to what the outcome of this would be. I think it would be desirable to have the letter approved by you first. Just as we could agree on the draft of my letter, we could also agree on the wording of your probable reply. That would place the responsibility on the Government of saying whether they accepted my letter or not.' Thomas suggested that possibly a question could be asked in the House of Commons, but Samuel said that while this was a good suggestion, still he desired to be sure of the reply which would be given.

During later conversation, Samuel said: 'They [the Government] made an awful mess of it in taking three weeks over the report. The Commission never visualized any such thing; they always regarded national negotiations as imperative. I think you will have difficulty in getting the coal-owners to agree to anything, but they may have to be overruled. There is only one epithet I can apply to the present position. It is a *silly* business.'

We had a long conversation amongst ourselves with regard to the position of the miners. Should we tell them all about what was happening? It was risky because they might say that they must consult their full executive. They might even insist on calling their delegate conferences. Furthermore, if the word got out that Samuel was discussing matters with us, it would destroy his utility in any later negotiation. He could hardly pose as an impartial person when, in fact, he had been consulting with us. We came to the conclusion that it was extremely unlikely that the Government could approach us and we decided to tell the miners so. Samuel undertook to let us have a draft of his letter this evening and we would send for it to the Reform Club. Then we would send him an intimation as to whether we could meet him again tomorrow.

Later we had a meeting of the General Council, to whom we reported what had taken place. The full Negotiating Committee of the miners were brought in and I could not see any concern amongst them about the documents which members of the General Council were reading.

It was decided to adjourn until tomorrow, Sunday, morning.

Sunday, 9th May
This morning we started out to consider the suggestions which

Samuel had put forward yesterday. There was a good deal of concern amongst our people, and Thomas whispered to me: 'Unless the miners are prepared to accept a reduction in some form or other, it is no use going on. We will have to let our people know.'

Beard seemed to be thinking of what would follow any attempt to impose our will on the miners, or if they were left to fight alone, and said: 'Judas Iscariot played a dramatic part in history. There could have been no Jesus Christ without him.'

It was evident to me that the General Council were coming to the conclusion that it was simply hopeless to continue the strike if the intention was that in no circumstances and in no conditions would the miners accept any reductions. We cannot see any possibility of winning on this negative issue, yet we are all apprehensive of what will follow after the miners have been told that they cannot, in the view of the General Council, hope to secure an undertaking that there will be no reduction. It will be said that the General Council have deserted them, but the position the miners are taking up is that while the direction of matters is in the hands of the General Council, the miners must be the people to decide as to whether they will return to work or not with a prospective reduction facing them. It will be a repetition of Black Friday, with the difference that we will have had the General Strike, and we will have realized either our strength or our impotence.

Let me try to reason it out. Can we hope to force such a condition of things that the miners will be secure indefinitely against a reduction? I do not believe that any of us have thought in our innermost consciousness that we could secure such a definite guarantee. What we have thought is that we could make arrangements so that reorganization would be pressed so insistently that the reduction would be minimized, if not escaped altogether. But for a period there must quite evidently be some reduction, pending fructification of reorganization methods, unless we can, through the General Strike, force the Government to grant a subsidy during the reorganization interval. I do not think we are likely to succeed in this. We can hold out for three or four weeks at the longest. I do not think it possible to continue longer than that. Even the most ardent advocates of the General Strike have usually reasoned in terms of a few hours' or days' stoppage at the most.

The silent power of labour has always been visualized as being capable of enforcing a speedy decision. I have never heard anyone previous to this event who has contemplated a General Strike lasting even a fortnight; and this strike is complicated by a number of other considerations. Many of the men are running heavy risks. The railwaymen and electricians have struck in defiance of severe legal penalties. Certain of the railway grades are faced with the possibility of fines for breach of contract of between £10 and £50. These men have superannuation allowances, and I have heard Thomas say repeatedly in the last few days that his society has 500 railwaymen, all of whom are due to enter upon superannuation, and from whom those rights will disappear if the strike ends disastrously.

Can we afford to risk complete defeat? I do not mean defeat in the sense of our movement never being able to recover, but to risk the disintegration that may follow rapidly from a return to work in certain sections. The logical thing is to make the best conditions while our members are solid. We must retreat, if we have to retreat under compulsion, as an army and not as a rabble. At the same time we must not get too badly rattled merely because the Government is talking big.

We must not attach too much importance to the stress which the Government, though its broadcasting and publicity agencies, is placing on the so-called 'return to work' in different places. Services are reported to be becoming more normal. So many hundreds of trains are alleged to be running on each railway, but I cannot see any sign at all of activity on the Southern Railway, which is the only one within reach of our office.

The economic loss inflicted by the General Strike will not be affected by any spectacular displays such as the transport of food in diminutive quantities by gangs of troops accompanied by armoured cars. The principal danger is the effect such displays may have on the morale of our men. When some of them see their jobs being filled by scallywag volunteers they may get desperate and resort to forcible means.

That means disorder; and that in turn means an excuse for police and military intervention. Thank God it is good weather! The sun has been shining brilliantly and our cares lightened by its cheerful rays.

Today, Sunday, I was thinking how, amid all our distress, the strike really has its lighter side. Take the personalities of our General Council for instance. There is Bevin, brawny of chest and broad of brow, swarthy of countenance, afflicted with the most becoming modesty. On the Saturday when the General Strike was declared, he suggested that he should be added to the Industrial Committee. But Jimmy Thomas and his fellow conspirators had decreed that it should not be so.

Then, on the first day of the strike, Tuesday, May 4th, amid all our confusion and bustle and scurrying, with members of the

General Council—all gifted strike organizers—giving different instructions to members of our staff, with typists bordering on hysteria
through conflicting orders, and with everybody's nerves on edge,
with the Council sitting in session and expecting the office administration to be run with the orderliness of an automatic machine,
Bevin rose in the Council, with determination on his face, and offered
to sacrifice himself on the altar of duty. He was willing to undertake
the whole administration of the strike, and thus relieve the anxieties
of his colleagues. The lesser luminaries communed with themselves and were wroth at the proposed usurpation, whereat Bevin
was grieved.

Then we have Jimmy Thomas—always discovering new situa-
tions, with mysterious side glances and knowing looks—endowed
with facile entry into the innermost circles of Government. If we
only knew what he knew! He had seen a Cabinet Minister that
day in the House of Commons, looking very worried. 'By God, our
stock is up, but we must remember the serious consequences of any
hesitancy.' Or perhaps a well-known capitalist, whose name he withheld for reasons which we would all understand, had winked at him,
whereupon the said James requires an urgent meeting of the Industrial
Committee to debate the significance of the wink.

Alternatively the transport and the railway deities conduct a
psychic and sometimes verbal warfare. One moment the gloom of
depression settles on the one, and, strange to relate, the sunshine of
optimism radiates its glow on the other. Bevin rises in the morning to
make his reports, with lowering brow and serious mien. 'Martial
law has been declared in the East End. Serious clashes between the
police and the populace. People getting short of food. We must
have constructive proposals for a settlement.'

He had been talking to a prominent business man who exercised
great influence in the City, and who had emphatically asserted that
the Government had made a mess of the whole thing. 'But we must
not trust too much to that.'

Whereat Jimmy smiles sardonically and rises with pity in his
look. Did anybody think he had entered in this business without
recognizing what it would mean? Why, he knew from the beginning
the streets would be running in blood very soon. We were out of the
stage of talking now. There was no compromise. The Government
must fight until we are smashed. Of course, we all knew that we must
be smashed. How could anybody think anything different? Whereupon James sits down, leaving everybody in a state of gloom.

Next day Bevin comes forward with a report that the whole
movement is as solid as a rock; the dockers could not be persuaded

back to work for weeks. Anyone who suggested in the East End that the strike should be stopped would be in danger of his life. The Government food organization was *in extremis*. Their organization had broken down at the docks and troops were trying to distribute food. The strikers, on instructions of the union, were parading the streets in front of the troops in their war medals—and Bevin sits down, confident, determined to fight to the last transport worker and the last worker.

Then Jimmy slowly gains his equilibrium, looks round the Council, and with a drop in his voice says: 'My God, my God, if you only knew! I was talking last night to Lord Reading. He says Winston is out to smash the trade union movement. How can we win? We must find a bridge.'

This gives the necessary stimulus to Bevin, and he thunders in declamation that he had always recognized that the strike could not be settled for at least three or four weeks. And so the show goes on.

Arthur Pugh, our chairman, at the special request of the Negotiating Committee, undertakes to explain the position to the miners in a few terse sentences. He fixes his eyes upon the papers before him, and proceeds yard after yard, reeling it out, while his colleagues fidget in their seats, wondering when the torrent will stop.

Then Ben Tillett, who wants specially to avoid lecturing the Council [a friendly hint to me], gets up to make a contribution.

He is followed by John Bromley, who, as he assures everyone, would much sooner fight than talk. He confesses himself in a great state of bewilderment. 'Is this fight to be won by words or by deeds? Do the miners appreciate the sacrifice and crucifixion of others for them?' He is a plain, blunt fellow, but a straight one, as he assures the Council, and not likely to weaken.

Swales beams over his glasses, but looks doubtful about Jimmy. Poulton looks sad but resolute, and Maggie Bondfield calmly goes on with her knitting.

Then there is myself, the acting secretary, making copious notes, peeping from behind a pile of papers, and pouring a steady flow of advice into the unheeding ears of the chairman, bobbing up and down like a jack-in-the-box in a futile endeavour to get the floor to say nothing in particular. The rest of the members sit about looking tired, somewhat bored, worried but far from rattled, almost in a state of coma. Some improve the shining hour by reading the *British Worker*, unheeding the peroration of the orator holding the floor. Not much sign here of the alleged revolutionaries who are plotting to overthrow the Constitution and Government.

And so Labour's General Staff goes on, directing the fighting units, and, by a general mixture of sound sense and huggermugger, somehow and in some way guides the strike movement.

An extraordinary incident occurred today. At lunchtime, after the General Council had adjourned, I received an intimation that a man wanted to see me. I escorted him into my room and he sat down in a chair opposite me. He was a man of about fifty, small, with very little hair, a complexion which appeared to have been exposed to the sun, rather sharp hawk-like features, and a thin face.

He introduced himself roughly in the following terms: 'My name is Rivett Carnac, you can look up my family in *Debrett*. [We subsequently looked up the Rivett Carnacs in *Debrett* and sure enough the name was there.] I was a colonel in the war of 1914–18 and I had as my batman one of the best fellows I have met. He was devoted to me and he died in my arms. I swore to him that I would always do my best to help people like him. I have never had any contact with the Labour movement but I have always been interested in it. The other night at the Club I heard some fellow talking about this strike. He said, "Churchill is out to smash you, and one of the unions that are going to get it in the neck are the Alley Slopers." '

I was puzzled by this expression and I asked, 'Do you mean by any chance Natsopa?' [this being one of our printing unions— National Society of Operative Printers and Assistants].

'I don't know the name of the thing but it is something to do with printers. Anyhow, Churchill is going to smash you. They have got it all planned.'

I here interjected, 'It will take more than Churchill to smash the British trade union movement.'

'Oh, but you don't know what they are up to,' he retorted, and then went on with his story. 'I think you have got to do something yourselves, to take the offensive, and I have a proposal to put to you. All I want from you is £1,000 to carry it through.'

I said, 'Well, now, I do not know the nature of your proposal, but I think I should call down our chairman, Mr. Arthur Pugh, who I believe is upstairs.'

I went upstairs and told Arthur Pugh what our visitor had said, and Arthur joined me in the office.

'Can I speak in absolute confidence, in the assurance that what I say will never be repeated?' our visitor asked.

We gave him the assurance and he then came out with the most cold-blooded proposal to which I have ever listened. 'You are

Sir Walter Citrine (as he then was) addressing the Trades Union Congress at Bridlington after the outbreak of war in September 1939

At the time of the General Strike in 1926

With Ernest Bevin on the steps of Transport House

The author as a patient in Manor House Hospital, the trade unions' own hospital in Hampstead, in 1931. His visitor is A. J. Cook, the miners' leader

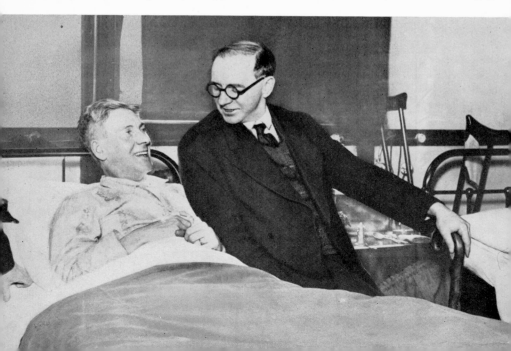

asking me for £1,000 to carry out some proposal,' I said, inviting him to continue.

'My proposal is very simple,' he said. 'I want 100 trusted men and if you cannot find them, I can. I will arm them, take them along to Downing Street, shoot the members of the Cabinet and hold Princess Mary's children as hostages.' He said this with such calm deliberation, without a trace of emotion, that we could hardly believe our ears.

Arthur Pugh broke in, smiling incredulously, 'But we don't do those things in the British trade union movement.'

'But you don't know what is up against you,' our visitor protested.

Both Pugh and I made it clear to him, in a very few words, that we would have nothing at all to do with his proposal. The interview then ended and he left us. We considered as to whether it was not our duty to inform the police of his visit, but in view of our promise not to repeat his statement, we took no further action.

[Some weeks after the national strike was ended I read in the newspapers of the arrest of a person for obtaining money under false pretences. I am sorry I did not preserve the newspaper account of this case, but it was to the effect that a man giving himself many bogus names, including Rivett Carnac, had for some time been imposing himself upon people and obtaining money by false pretences. According to the account, he had been particularly successful in getting money out of certain credulous women. A little later I read of a person calling himself Rivett-Carnac being charged under the Dangerous Drugs Act with obtaining morphia preparations unlawfully. He was a Eurasian, aged forty-four, and after being remanded he was eventually sentenced to four months' imprisonment. It was stated by the police that the defendant, under different names, had been convicted of fraud and housebreaking and he had been sentenced to three years' penal servitude in January 1923. He had been gassed during the war and was evidently a drug addict. He had no connection with the Rivett-Carnac family.]

Monday 10th May
We went once again to see Samuel this morning at 38 Bryanston Square. In the course of conversation, Samuel said: 'The Commission has never contemplated any such reductions as the mine-owners have imposed. The proposal is simply monstrous.'

After talking the matter over, we thought it advisable that Herbert Smith and the other miners' officials should accompany us

N

in the afternoon. At the afternoon meeting both Herbert Smith and Samuel spoke straightly to each other. Samuel, after being badgered by Herbert over certain parts of the report, burst out: 'I hate this business. I was content in Italy writing on philosophy, and I have come here not at anyone's invitation, but merely to try to do my best as a good citizen, and as chairman of the Coal Commission, to see whether I can put things straight. No one else is doing anything at all. The Government has closed the door and you have done the same. I am not at all happy. I was brought into this business of the Commission against my own inclinations and I had to record the facts. It is not that I want to see miners' wages reduced. I think they are too horribly low altogether.'

Grim old Herbert, not the slightest bit impressed by this, returned, 'If I could have gone to the same school as you, I would have had it up here,' tapping his forehead.

Samuel smiled approvingly. 'Oh, you need not be afraid of that,' he said, 'if everyone had the same capacity for argument as you, Herbert, no one would ever get anything done in this world. They would have too many arguments against it.'

Old Herbert lay back on the expensive couch, luxuriantly upholstered, and rocked with laughter. Then he said quizzically, 'Are you thinking of me and Markham?' This was a reference to one of the coal-owners who appeared before the Coal Commission, and said that miners spent 10s. a week on the cinemas. He received a pretty bad handling from Smith as a consequence.

Samuel shook his head, 'No, but when it is a case of Herbert against Herbert [reference to their first names], then there is bound to be a tug of war.'

Yesterday evening we met the full miners' executive. Herbert Smith was just as dour and as dogged as ever. Miner after miner got up and, speaking with intensity of feeling, affirmed that the miners could not go back to work on a reduction in wages. Was all this sacrifice to be in vain?

Cook, throwing out his hands imploringly, entreated the General Council: 'Gentlemen, I know the sacrifice you have made. You do not want to bring the miners down. Gentlemen, don't do it. You want your recommendation to be a common policy with us, but this is a hard thing to do.'

I glanced round at the hard-set faces of the miners, and I could not see the slightest sign of any compromise on any one of them. Thomas sat beside me at the table with his head resting on his hands. He tells me he cannot sleep at night, and has the exhausted look of a man completely worn out. Old Herbert sat unmoved, stolid, leaning over his papers with his glasses on the end of his nose, not in the least influenced.

Arthur Pugh, our chairman, had made what, I am sure, was one of the most intense statements he has ever made. He had put to the miners whether they were facing their responsibility to the movement in not putting forward any alternative proposals. This, it was true, had primarily been a miners' question, he said, but it had now ceased to be a matter exclusively for them, and every trade union representative in the room had to face up to his own responsibility. All of them would be required to give an account to their own members. If we were going forward on the assumption that the miners were to look at the matter entirely from their own standpoint: 'Then, gentlemen, we must close proceedings. It is no use talking. We must go on with this struggle until the process of attrition has brought the whole trade union movement to its knees.' Pugh emphasized that the Government could not come to the trade union movement and start negotiations while the General Strike was in progress. We on the other hand could not go to the Government and put forward our proposals until the lock-out of the miners had been withdrawn.

If the miners thought for one moment that we could get an indefinite application of the subsidy as it was paid before the stoppage, they were living in a fool's paradise. 'Speaking as the chairman of the General Council, I want to say that you must face your responsibility in this matter.'

Immediately Pugh had finished, old Herbert rose and said he could reply very soon. The miners were not going to accept a reduction in wages. 'It is no good Cook saying that he believes this and believes that. He does not believe it at all. Some of our people have a happy method of being away when they are wanted. I do not know why Smillie is away in Scotland. I do not know why Tom Richards is in South Wales. Our men in the coalfields have given us our instructions and we cannot depart from them.'

Shortly after 10 p.m. the miners retired to consider the proposals which we had discussed with Samuel, and our General Council took the opportunity of reviewing the situation separately. The trend of the discussion was clearly that while the position of our forces was strong, we could not count upon a continuance of the dispute without serious danger of breakaways. We must get a settlement as soon as we could. It might take days to arrange for complete reinstatement of the men who had come out. It was clear to me, if not to us all, we were heading straight towards a dangerous split. If the General Strike was called off by the General Council and the miners refused to accept the position, what would happen? How could we

possibly avoid the appearance of having deserted them in their hour
of need? On the other hand, even if the General Council made its
decision and the miners fell in with it, there was bound to be recrimination against us. Some would say we had sold the pass, we had
betrayed the movement.

Bevin, Purcell, Walkden, Hicks, and the others were all convinced that the miners would not accept, but they claimed that the
decision, if the General Council determined to call off the General
Strike, would not be an unpopular one.

Tuesday, 11th May
At our General Council meeting this morning a long discussion took
place about the position. It was reported that the districts situation
was satisfactory. There was no need for anxiety, but it was recognized that it was desirable that negotiations should be prepared for in
order to pave the way to a settlement before the strike reached its
apex. The principal point which perplexed some of our people was
whether we could be sure that Samuel could 'deliver the goods'. Grave
doubts were expressed as to whether the miners would really prove
as amenable to the General Council's decisions as they professed.

Bevin thought that the miners were doing just what they did in
1921. Once they had got the General Council to serve their requirements then they would hold us down ruthlessly.

As I am writing these notes with the meeting in progress, I try to
analyse my feelings, and find myself swinging first to one view and
then to another.

Half an hour ago, with Thomas delivering many doleful warnings
about the aftermath and the terrible risks which we were taking, I was
inclining to the view that the situation was getting hopeless. Then the
reports came in from the country and showed that the men are as
firm as a rock. What then can be the cause of apprehension? I think
it is because most of us know that no matter how determined our
men are now, once the strike has reached its highest point and the
maximum of members have been called out, a gradual decline in
economic power must ensue. Then we shall have dribblings back to
work here and there, and possibly large desertions. The Government,
through the *British Gazette* and *The Times* (which has now appeared
on the streets, although in a very reduced size), not to mention the
Daily Mail (which is being printed in Paris), are working propaganda for all they are worth. Reports of large resumptions of work,
huge increases in the numbers of trains, none of which has any
real foundation in fact, are all assiduously claimed for the purpose
of disheartening our members.

Thomas says that the railway companies are rather bitter, and he feels sure difficulties will arise over reinstatement. Jimmy is wearing down, and today there was none of that customary forceful driving manner.

Our Council have quickly come to the view that they must make their own decision in respect of policy.

Today Bevin said: 'I am not concerned what the miners may think about it. They can say what they like about me. My union came into this business on very definite terms, and I have told my men so. The dockers will stick out for weeks, and so will the miners, but I don't think it is right to go on asking men to make sacrifices if we can get justice any other way. The other side does not want to fight this matter out to a finish.'

Thomas readily assented. 'I don't think so either. Some of them do, but the business men don't.'

I am informed that there is a pretty powerful minority in the Miners' Federation in favour of the line along which we are working, but the strange thing is that the Federation rejects the simplification of wages, which is one of the proposals we have discussed with Samuel. Yet everyone knows their wages system is in a terrible mess.

Herbert Smith is immovable. Some of our Council members think he does not care who goes down. He will not give in.

In the afternoon we went once again to see Samuel and had a long talk with him. He mentioned that he had spoken to his colleagues on the Coal Commission. He did not think there would be any trouble about securing their assent to the proposals. It would be arranged that a letter should be sent to the General Council from Samuel, laying down the lines on which he thought the strike should be settled. Then the General Council would formally withdraw the General Strike and the Government would arrange for a withdrawal of the lock-outs. Samuel appeared to be speaking with knowledge of the Government's attitude, and from all information at our disposal it looks as though Baldwin has been having a pretty rough time with his Cabinet.

Arthur Henderson told me last evening that he had discovered the cause of Baldwin's changed attitude towards us on Sunday, 2nd May, when he gave us the ultimatum. It appears that five of his Cabinet threatened to resign: Bridgeman, Neville Chamberlain, Salisbury, Amery, and Churchill.

The General Council had another meeting at six o'clock today and it was arranged that Samuel would send his document to us by 8 p.m. The miners would meet us at the same time, and the General

Council would appeal to their executive to assist us by suggesting the termination of the General Strike.

It was clear that our people realize that the miners, suffering from a sense of grievance, will indulge in recriminations and say that we have forced acceptance upon them (I apprehend that very seriously myself). I am sure they are not really united on this subject, and I think some of them are looking to the General Council so that responsibility can be taken off them. I am writing this at 6.45 at the General Council meeting. My thoughts keep turning to the position of the miners. They are a stubborn lot.

Then we got a bit of a shock. Samuel told our messenger who called for the documents that he could not send them along; that a hitch had occurred, and that he wanted to see the Industrial Committee at once. We hurried in taxicabs to his brother's house at 12 Hill Street, and found that his fellow Commissioners did not agree with him in respect of the powers of the National Board. They thought that the title 'National Mining Board' created the impression that the management of the industry was being handed over to the composite body. They did not think it was constitutionally right for them as a Commission which had completed its work to have anything officially to do with it.

Samuel remarked a little dubiously: 'I don't know whether I shall be a hero tomorrow or not, but I am sure I shall be a villain in two or three weeks' time. I really would have liked time to consider the whole business, but I realize it must be done as soon as possible.'

Tillett shrugged his shoulders and replied: 'We are not thinking about being heroes. We shall be told we have betrayed the miners. We will get it in the neck, sure.' We sat round the oak-panelled room to copy out the terms.

Meanwhile the General Council were sitting in impatience waiting for us, and at half past eight we arrived. As soon as I got into the meeting I felt all my misgivings return. Pugh carefully and patiently went over the details of the negotiations and the consultations, and when he had finished Herbert Smith rose at once with a glint in his eye and said: 'I don't understand what has been going on in these conversations. I don't believe in these methods, and I protest against the miners not being consulted. Why should a decision be taken tonight? Have you committed us to anything?'

Pugh and Thomas replied that they felt sure that in the interest of the movement, and having regard to the duty, the obligation, and the responsibility of the General Council, it was imperative that a decision should be given that night.

Time after time Herbert Smith rose to say that it was no use the miners considering the proposals as they were being imposed upon them. 'I have just as much John Bull in me as anyone else, and I want to say this—it is this document we have to accept and nothing else [holding up the Samuel document], and it is in that spirit we are going to consider it.' With that, Herbert waved his colleagues out with him to the boardroom of the Labour Party next door to consider the matter.

Immediately they had left, indignant conversation broke out among the members of the General Council. Bevin expressed the feeling of most of us when he said that even if the document was accepted and we had not the opposition of the Miners' Federation, the Prime Minister might still refuse to accept it, and we would then be in a tragic situation. 'I don't know whether we can trust the Government at all. What about victimization?'

Some of us feel that we ought to get an assurance from the Government before we declare the strike off, but others say that the Government has no power to do anything like that. I do not feel that we should hand ourselves over, body and soul, to Baldwin.

Just before midnight, Herbert Smith and the miners returned. They declared that they could not accept the document, and the Council, if it accepted, must do so on its own responsibility. They handed this in as a typewritten document. This was significant: it is the first that has passed between us in these negotiations, and it left a nasty impression. It looks as though the miners are out to justify themselves in the eyes of their own people without any regard at all to the position of the Council, on whom the whole blame, if there is any, will be thrown. Everyone could see this.

Bevin counselled meeting the miners in the morning, and felt that even then it was possible to get them to accept it.

Hayday [father of Fred Hayday, the 1963 T.U.C. chairman] supported this, and pointed out that the miners were not aware of the general industrial situation. They were not trade unionists in the general sense. They were ignorant of the position. They lived in villages, and they thought in the mass. They did not realize that we could not keep people out much longer. They would never understand that all there would be left to sacrifice in a few days would be the broken-hearted best of our members.

Thomas followed and said that Hayday had put his hand right on the spot. The miners were not big enough. They were not trade unionists in a proper sense, and did not understand or very much care about what happened to the rest of the movement. He recalled that last evening the miners put forward an amendment to our document, the effect of which was practically to destroy it. 'I will carry my responsibility,' Thomas declared solemnly. 'I shall take my share of the blame, but when the time comes for me to explain, I will neither excuse nor apologize. I will justify my part. I will remember that 455,000 railwaymen are on the streets. I will say: "These men have trusted me so much. They told me to come here to Eccleston Square and stop and work with the General Council." I have scarcely seen my own people, but I am going back to them tomorrow.' Thomas sat down, leaving the Council in a disturbed state of mind. Then Beard rose and, in a tone of great indignation, commenced: 'I am told sometimes that I talk too much. I have not spoken much in this dispute.'

Tillett interjected: 'Well, lad, don't speak too much now. It is very late.'

Beard continued: 'Well, I want to say this. If Thomas goes out, I have not any further contribution to make. Those men have never readily put themselves into the hands of the General Council. That has never been the state of their minds. I am not prepared to put everything our unions have into the pawn shop and feel that it is not appreciated by those people. As far as I am concerned, I will not accept any longer the contributions of the poorest section of the workpeople, without the consent of the executive of the Workers' Union. I have trusted the Negotiating Committee, I believe they have worked like Trojans in this. But I pay my tribute especially to the work that Thomas has done. There is nobody who has been more maligned than he and nobody has done more for the miners.'

Just at that moment a message came in. 'The Prime Minister's secretary is on the phone and wants to speak to Mr. Citrine.' I at once went to my office. 'Is that you, Mr. Citrine? This is Gower speaking. The Prime Minister wants to know whether you have any news for him. He has been sitting up for you. Do you want to see him this evening?' I replied: 'Well, I cannot tell you. Will you wait until I have seen the Council? They are still in session.' 'Yes'.

I went upstairs to see the General Council, and they said, after a few minutes' consultation, that I should say we would see him tomorrow at twelve noon, and that was a firm decision. There would be no postponement. I went down and repeated this. 'The General Council instruct me to say that they will be ready to see the Prime Minister tomorrow at twelve o'clock noon, positively.'

'All right, Mr. Citrine, we may take that as fixed.'

Our fate was decided in those few seconds. Our decision to see the Prime Minister meant plainly to them the calling-off of the General Strike.

It was an eventful decision, and one cannot see how it will turn out. I hope we have decided rightly.

It was agreed later that the chairman of the Council and the members of the Strike Committee should go along to the Miners' Federation offices tomorrow and meet the executive to try to induce them to accept the Council's decision.

I got to bed about 2 a.m.

Wednesday, 12th May

I was at the office at 9.30 a.m. Samuel's letter had not arrived because of some little misunderstanding. I spoke to Samuel on the telephone and arranged for it to be sent to us by messenger. Meanwhile, our delegates with the Miners' Federation were having an unpleasant time. I phoned Purcell who was waiting for the miners to make their decision. He said he would wait until 11.45 at the latest, when he would positively come to Downing Street, whether a decision had been come to or not. I arranged to take a room at Downing Street where the Council could meet for a few minutes. It appears that the Cabinet were sitting up for us last night very late. It just shows how anxious they were! By the time we made our way from the office, crowds had gathered round. There was a feeling in the air that something was going to happen. The Press were very active, and we had to pass through a battery of photographers.

Thomas and I went to Downing Street in his car. On the road we passed Wellington Barracks, and saw troops drawn up on the parade ground. Some were practising with machine guns; others had gas masks on, while some were in full marching kit. A number of tanks were being overhauled, with their guns grinning ominously outwards on the public. On the way to Downing Street Thomas said to me: 'You know, Walter, this is a terrible business. We shall have awful recriminations now.'

Arrived at Downing Street, we walked along the corridor, and Pugh said to me, 'I wonder how long we are going to grovel on our hands and knees to the miners.' It was evident that he was fed up.

Bevin reported to us that the Strike Committee had met the miners and made the biggest appeal they possibly could. Feeling was bitter and mainly arose because Herbert Smith felt he had not been properly consulted. They called a conference for Friday next, and meanwhile no miners would resume work.

Bevin was afraid that we were likely to split the movement from top to bottom, and some of the unions would be badly affected.

We adjourned to the Cabinet room, which only a few days before we had left with all the anxieties of the strike before us. Now we were going to declare it at an end. Facing us, Baldwin, rather haggard and drawn, with Steel-Maitland, Worthington-Evans, Bridgeman, and Neville Chamberlain by him, welcomed us with obvious anxiety. He said, 'Mr. Pugh, would you be good enough to make any statement you desire?'

Then Pugh announced the calling-off of the strike, and said it had been dictated by considerations not of weakness, but of a genuine desire for peace and to allow negotiations to proceed. He was followed by Thomas, who made an eloquent appeal for better feelings.

Baldwin replied, 'I thank God for your decision,' and the relief that went through him and the others was very noticeable.

Then Bevin followed, and referred to victimization. He spoke in a confident, almost aggressive tone, and I could see at once all on the other side concentrated their attention upon him. It was no weak-kneed capitulation on his part.

Most of us were puzzled at the attitude of the Government. Baldwin said he would get the parties together as soon as possible to continue negotiations, but did not indicate anything about withdrawal of the lock-out.

We adjourned to the room reserved for us, with our uneasiness increased. We recognized that the position had been complicated by the miners' resolution and their refusal to resume work.

The net result of our efforts from a public point of view is the calling-off of the General Strike without any definite knowledge that the lock-out would be withdrawn.

Baldwin promised to make a statement in the House of Commons the same afternoon, and I was instructed to get telegrams to the unions at once to arrange for their members to resume work.

I had first to agree the press statement with Tom Jones, and I got an uncomfortable feeling that all they were out to do was to snatch the appearance of a victory. After we had provisionally agreed a short message, it was taken into the Cabinet: Worthington-Evans came out, wanting the word 'forthwith' added to our declaration to call off the General Strike.

I refused point blank to do this, and said that our members were being given instructions to return by arrangement with their unions, and we were not going to have a stampede back to work. Finally, we agreed to put in the word 'today', so that the notice would read:

'The General Council have terminated the General Strike today.'

While I was completing the wording, Eyres-Monsell, one of the Government Whips, came in, and I heard him say to Jones, 'Just give me the message will you, for my broadcast?' I appreciated the significance of this at once. They were going to broadcast a message, stating that the General Strike had been terminated, and our people would be left wondering what had happened. So I pressed him to allow a strike message to be broadcast, saying men must not resume work except on the instructions of their unions. I was very suspicious of them, and despite their assurances I waited while Davidson, one of the Downing Street staff, dictated my message over the telephone to the Broadcasting Corporation. Then I arranged for priority to be given for our telegrams to the head offices of the unions.

Pugh had the telegram and, on looking for him, I found him in the garden between No. 10 and No. 11. He was standing talking to the Prime Minister and Steel-Maitland. I approached them and got the telegram. Steel-Maitland looked like a petulant schoolboy, who was determined to vent his spleen on somebody, but I gave him no opportunity to enter into conversation.

After giving the telegrams to Miss McDonald, Pugh and I got talking to Sir Horace Wilson just outside the Cabinet room.

Pugh mentioned that he had told Baldwin that unless the lock-out notices were withdrawn at once, it meant that our people would think there had been a complete breach of faith.

While we were talking, Churchill, Baldwin, and Steel-Maitland were pacing rapidly up and down the garden, talking animatedly. There was no sign of jubilation amongst them, and Pugh muttered to me: 'I saw Churchill a few minutes ago, and he said, "Thank God it is over, Mr. Pugh." '

I returned to Eccleston Square and on the way met some members of the General Council. They were very disturbed. We had been absolutely led up the garden by these political people. 'Talk about Black Friday, it isn't in it,' said Bevin. 'What is the use of coming here with a doleful tale?' burst out Hicks. 'You cannot ignore the action of the miners. They have put us in the soup. They have no regard at all for the thousands of people who have sacrificed their jobs.'

All the evening telegrams were pouring in from districts wanting to know what were the terms of the settlement. The irony is that we could not tell them.

At best the Samuel proposals are an honourable understanding, and the Government have not yet given any real indication as to whether they accept them.

We issued a manifesto to our unions, explaining the position: then, weary and not a little despondent, I got to bed about midnight. Before I rested, I wrote the following:

Thoughts on the Termination of the General Strike
I have dignified these reflections by the title of thoughts, but I
wonder whether I am capable of doing any clear thinking at all. I
feel tired and somewhat disheartened although, in a sense, my com-
bativeness has been roused by the knowledge that the miners are
going to pillory the General Council.

It is too early to try to form a considered conclusion, but the one
thing that has stood out in all the negotiations we have had has been
the infernal, intolerable suspicion all through.

Probably this has contributed more than anything else to the
present position. The miners, although they declared at our conference on Saturday, May 1st, and indeed repeatedly through Herbert
Smith to our Negotiating Committee, that they were placing the
matter in the hands of the General Council, never in the real sense
did that. They always have had at the backs of their minds the idea
that the final right to make a decision was theirs.

Well, yesterday evening it came to a crisis. It was felt we could
not continue longer with the certainty of our members remaining
loyal. Reports had come in that men were trickling back, and we
knew that if that continued it would not be long before they were
streaming to work.

The distressing thing is that the General Council's action has
been rendered abortive by the decision of the Miners' Federation to
call a conference on Friday next, and not to resume work in the meantime. This means, in fact, that all the assurances Samuel gave to us
in our private conversations, about the lock-out being cancelled,
cannot materialize, and we are left in the position of appearing to
have been defeated. Had the miners risen to the appeal that Pugh
made to them last night, in one of the most earnest addresses I have
ever heard, they would have come along and said to us: 'We are disappointed with the result. It is not what we had hoped for, but we
realize that your men have made a sacrifice for us. We cannot expect
you to do more. We will go back to our members and tell them that,
on our own responsibility, having placed our case in your hands,
we had called the strike off.' But not they!

They had neither the loyalty to the Congress, nor to their colleagues, nor the appreciation of the sacrifices of the movement, to
enable them to rise above their restricted vision of their own coal-
fields.

Well, it is a hard business, but experience sometimes has to be
painful to furnish an example from which we can profit. The suspicion and lack of confidence that produced Black Friday of 1921
resulted in the call for 'all power to the General Council'.

We have had our General Strike. Imperfect as it has been, mechanically and in the evolution of policy, it has been the most magnificent effort of rank-and-file solidarity that the British movement has ever displayed. Never again will the Congress undertake the custodianship of any movement without the clear, specific, and unalterable understanding that the General Council, and the General Council alone, shall have the free untrammelled right to determine policy.

How can we, with the millions of interests and considerations to review, allow our policy to be dominated entirely by considerations of one union only?

Were we to continue the disruption and dismemberment of the railway and transport unions? To bleed white the organizations who had thrown their all into the melting pot? To sacrifice the individual members who, faced by heavy penalties for breach of contract, had responded with an unparalleled loyalty to the call of the movement?

The outstanding lesson of the General Strike of 1926 is that authority must be invested exclusively and entirely in the directing body.

Thursday, 13th May
We have had a stream of complaints about the way the settlement is being applied. Almost immediately after the strike was called off, Baldwin made a speech, the broad purport of which was to emphasize the duty of everyone to forget all recrimination and to look to the future. Employers were asked to act with generosity and workers to put their whole hearts loyally into their work. The Prime Minister made a strong appeal for a spirit of co-operation and goodwill, putting behind us all malice and vindictiveness. Not all the employers took the same view, and we had many reports of them trying to impose vindictive terms on the workers.

In a number of instances, attempts were made to induce the men to sign documents undertaking to accept reduced wages and never to strike again. In the railway world the companies asked the workers to sign a notice in the following terms:

> You are hereby re-engaged. Your reinstatement is on the understanding that the Company reserves any rights it possesses in consequence of your having broken your contract of service.

The railway unions decided to continue the strike, as they were resolutely determined to secure an organized return to work and to resist any attempt at victimization. They sent out telegrams to their members saying, 'In view of difficulties surrounding reinstatement,

Joint Executives call upon all railwaymen to continue strike until we secure satisfactory assurances.' The railway union officials, and Thomas in particular, were very perturbed at the attitude of the companies. Jimmy told me privately that he had never seen the general managers of the companies in such a resentful and belligerent mood.

We were also informed that 5,000 members of the A.E.U. had not resumed work at the Horwich locomotive works. This sort of thing can't continue, and I think the feeling is rising among the members of the General Council that desperate as the situation would be, there may be resumption, at least in part, of the strike if this kind of vindictiveness goes on. It is strange to find these employers disregarding the appeal of King George V. He made a most moving appeal along the lines of Baldwin's speech, and a summary of this was reproduced in the evening edition of the *British Worker* today.

The net result of it all is that millions of workers have not yet gone back, and the General Council decided to issue a statement, through the *British Worker*. Pugh and I had the job of drafting this and we made it brief and to the point. It read as follows:

STAND TOGETHER
Fellow Trade Unionists,

The General Strike has ended. It has not failed. It has made possible the resumption of negotiations in the coal industry, and the continuance, during negotiations, of the financial assistance given by the Government.

You came out together, in accordance with the instructions of the executives of your unions. Return together on their instructions, as and when they are given.

Some employers will approach you as individuals, with the demand that you should accept conditions different from those obtaining before the stoppage began.

Sign no individual agreement. Consult your union officials, and stand by their instructions. Your union will protect you, and will insist that all agreements previously in force shall be maintained intact.

The trade union movement has demonstrated its unity. That unity remains unimpaired. Stick to your unions.

GENERAL COUNCIL

TRADES UNION CONGRESS

We also decided to publish the salient parts of the correspondence that we had had with Sir Herbert Samuel, and this duly appeared in the same issue.

The *British Worker* published in full the manifesto of the General Council, signed by Pugh and myself, in the course of which we emphasized, as we have done in every issue of the *British Worker* since the strike began, that no attack was at any time contemplated upon the established political institutions of the country. We paid a tribute to the loyalty and discipline of the movement, and it is a remarkable fact that there has been practically no public disorder. One of the features has been the good spirit between police and the strikers, who have in places been playing football together.

There my diary notes on the General Strike itself end. The miners fought on.

12

The Inquest

As I hoped, the return to work straightened itself out. On the railways the companies agreed to take the men back as soon as work could be found for them. The principle to be followed in reinstatement would be seniority. The railway unions had to admit that in calling the strike they had acted wrongly and to agree that the companies did not surrender their legal rights to claim damages arising from the strike. This was rather humiliating but, as we were satisfied that there was no chance of the railway companies recovering damages as the dispute was protected by the Trade Disputes and Trade Unions Act of 1906, we advised the railwaymen to sign the agreement.

Thomas made a statement afterwards, as well as Bromley and Walkden, thanking the men for the solidarity they had shown and asking them to accept the agreement in the same spirit in which the companies and the railwaymen's leaders had done.

The speech that Baldwin made in the House of Commons also helped reinstatement. He said he had received a telephone message from Thomas, who hoped that by the time the Prime Minister had made his statement, a satisfactory settlement would have been signed.

The *British Worker* came out with an article headed: 'Reopening of the Negotiations'. It gave a brief history of why the strike started, and why the General Council had accepted the proposals of Sir Herbert Samuel as a basis for settlement of the dispute in the mining industry. It stressed the fact that having declared the General Strike to be an attack on the Constitution, the Government could hardly take up negotiations with the General Council. As a consequence of this, the mediation of Sir Herbert Samuel had saved the Government from the 'fruits of its own reckless folly, and although formally and publicly he appeared on the scene in quite an unofficial capacity, it was well understood on both sides that the terms he had mentioned

The author played a major part in the massive demonstration by working and unemployed members of the trade union, Co-operative and Labour movements against wage cuts, the economy campaign, and unemployment in 1933.

(*Above*) Taking part in the march on Hyde Park (without a hat and wearing scarf), with George Lansbury, bowler-hatted, next but one.

(*Below*) Addressing the rally from a cart. Standing beside him is Stafford Cripps

A Labour delegation in Downing Street in September 1938 (*see page 361*): Sir Walter Cit
Mr. Herbert Morrison and Dr. Hugh Dalton (as they were)

represented the views of well-informed public opinion as to the basis on which a settlement of the mining problem might be effected'.

Thomas made a fine speech in the House of Commons repudiating the charge that the object of the strike was to hold up the community: I was glad to find that he had said they were not going to crawl back and they insisted upon being treated as human beings.

The *British Worker* had been an excellent means of disseminating information on behalf of the General Council and the trade unions, and without it we would have been in queer street, as the B.B.C. was practically monopolized by the Government. The first issue appeared on Wednesday, May 5th. It was reported to us that Winston Churchill had tried to confiscate the supply of newsprint destined for it, but he didn't succeed. The only day upon which the paper did not appear was Friday, May 14th, and this was due to the general assumption that reinstatement would have been completed and that there was no longer any need for the paper to be published. This, however, did not prove to be the case. With the cessation of the *British Worker* news on behalf of the trade unions was published in the *Daily Herald*.

After the end of the strike I urged the General Council to call a conference of union executives as soon as they could. This was decided upon and we accordingly prepared a report for submission to a conference to be held on July 25th, 1926. On June 22nd, however, it was represented to the General Council that the holding of a conference would damage the miners in the carrying-on of the dispute. The Council decided to consult the officials of the Miners' Federation; they would not ask for a postponement of the conference, but said the holding of it would be detrimental to the miners' interests. The General Council thereupon decided to postpone the conference until the dispute had ended.

We saw nothing of the miners' executive for several weeks after the General Strike was called off. Relations between them and the General Council were rather strained, but my friendship with Herbert Smith and Arthur Cook remained unimpaired. Herbert kept quiet and would make no comment on what had happened. He said, 'My motto is to say nowt,' but with Arthur Cook it was a different matter. He made wild assertions and accusations against almost everyone. No doubt he was exploited by the Communists, and I had a shrewd idea that some of the nasty things in his pamphlets had been written by others. One day he called to see me, and as we were chatting a typist brought in a memorandum I had been dictating. As it lay on the desk, Cook's eyes caught his name.

O

'What was that you have been saying about me?' he asked, half smiling.

'Would you like to know?' I returned.

I then read a few pages to him. The document was composed of extracts from his speeches classified under headings such as: 'Mr. Cook on himself', 'Mr. Cook on his opponents', 'Mr. Cook on the T.U.C.', etc.

'But what do you want that for?' he asked wonderingly.

'Well, some time ago I thought to myself, "Cook has been going for everyone in the movement, some time or other he will go for me." So I got this prepared, and when you do attack me this will be waiting for you.'

Cook was frankly amazed at this. 'What, me attack you?' he exclaimed, as though the thought was something beyond the possible. He started a long avowal of his respect and friendship for me, which, I believe, was entirely genuine. But I knew how unstable he was and that at times he was incapable of controlling himself on the platform. So I didn't relax my vigilance. Cook was a remarkable chap. In speaking, whether in private or public, he never seemed to finish his sentences. His brain raced ahead of his words. He would start out to demonstrate something or other in a logical order and say: 'Now let us take what Thomas has said. No. 1. . . .' but almost immediately some thought came into his mind and he completely forgot all about No. 1 and never returned to it. He was extremely emotional and even in private conversation I have seen tears in his eyes. Lord Sankey once told me that he had gone casually into one of Cook's crowded meetings and stood at the back. Cook had been speaking for not more than a quarter of an hour, according to Sankey, when half the audience were in tears. Sankey himself, when he heard Cook describing the miner's life, said he had the greatest difficulty in restraining himself from weeping. Sankey was a judge and well able to control his emotions.

Yet somehow at our conferences Cook never made a deep impression—at all events, nothing like Bob Smillie would. The delegates regarded Cook as a demagogue. Poor Arthur! I came to be really fond of him, and I was with him in the days just before his death from sarcoma in 1931. Whilst he was lying in the Manor House Hospital I called to see him one morning. At his bedside were Sir Oswald Mosley, who had been expelled from the Labour Party, and Arthur Horner, the South Wales Communist, who was regarded as being principally responsible for securing Cook's election as the secretary of the Miners' Federation. Rather an odd group: an embryo Fascist, a Communist—and Citrine.

On July 14th, 1926, after the miners had been locked out for nearly eleven weeks, their executive met the General Council at our invitation. All of us felt uneasy. We had a vague hope that there was still some way in which we could help the miners. Much as I wanted to do something practical, for the life of me I couldn't see any means of assisting them any more than we were doing.

I warned the Council of the dangers of a futile meeting, and of how we would be represented as inducing the miners once again to consider a compromise; how we had been traduced as working from the beginning to persuade the miners to accept a reduction. I contended that the miners, although this was the eleventh week of the lock-out, were no more amenable to the Council's influence than they were at the beginning. If anything the resistance and determination were greater. They themselves had made clear the form of assistance they required. They wanted financial help and an embargo on coal.

With regard to the first, what more could we do? They had appealed to the unions over our heads and we had sent them £45,000 from our own limited strike funds.

With regard to the coal embargo, the miners had approached the unions but had no success. What hope was there that we could enforce a coal embargo? The transport unions had told us plainly that with their forces crippled and debilitated in consequence of the strike they could not possibly enforce an embargo.

Well, the Council decided to meet them, and the meeting took place. It was a hopeless business from the beginning. Pugh, who was chairman, was completely fed up, but his opening address was as reasonable as could be. He asked in what direction the General Council could help them. While he was speaking I looked round at the miners. Old Herbert Smith sat at the top of the table with his glasses on the extreme edge of his nose, looking rather sunburned but as dour and as dogged as ever. Cook had now shaved off his moustache and sat with his eyes gleaming attentively through his horn-rimmed glasses. The rest of them were as obdurate as ever I saw them. Suspicion of the Council seemed to walk in the room at the same moment as the miners. Noah Ablett, of South Wales, with fishy eyes and in a state of torpor, looked contemptuously around him. Richardson, of Durham, was reading an evening paper and taking not the slightest notice of the chairman's remarks.

I saw at once that there was going to be no response from them. Immediately Herbert Smith rose he posed the question of the coal embargo. That was the way to help the miners, he said. They did not

want lip service. While he had no intention of indulging in recrimination, they could not forget what had passed. He made it pretty plain
that the miners' executive intended to settle the dispute themselves
and not through the General Council. They didn't want the General
Council to try to get negotiations started. All they wanted was an
embargo on coal imports. They did not tell us what we learned later
from the Press—that they had been discussing the basis of a settlement with representatives of the Churches. The so-called terms they
arranged were printed in the evening papers as the 'Bishops' Memorandum'. They had also appealed to our affiliated unions for financial
help without consulting the General Council.

The miners seemed oblivious to the sacrifices that other unions
had made. They were told plainly by members of the Council that
it was impossible for the unions to impose a coal embargo and that
it was a matter for the individual unions who would have to operate
such an embargo. Altogether a very unpleasant meeting, although
Cook and Herbert Smith were nice to me personally.

In the fifteenth week of the lock-out, the miners' executive held
a conference on August 10th, 1926, to consider the proposals of the
bishops. These had been referred to the districts for discussion, in
pursuance of a previous decision of the executive. They were not
submitted to a ballot vote, and the practice in the districts varied
considerably. In some districts they had conferences of delegates;
in others, mass meetings, which Cook was remarkably active in
addressing. He advocated acceptance of the proposals, as he and the
other officials were signatories.

The net result of it all was that the reports from the districts
showed a majority against acceptance. The figures were not known,
but Yorkshire appeared to have turned the balance. The Federation officials had to accept the decision, and they so informed the
bishops.

After this the miners' situation became steadily worse. There was
no sign of any desire on the part of the employers or the Government
to make any concessions. But the miners fought on doggedly with
their organization becoming more and more attenuated until, after
being out for six months, they were driven back to work on terms
far worse than those in the Samuel Memorandum.

The General Council had been much criticized because they had
no assurance that the Samuel Memorandum would be accepted by
the Government. There was substance in this, but I had no doubt
that, had the miners agreed with the General Council that it did
form a basis for a settlement, it was extremely unlikely that the
Government would have rejected it. Baldwin as good as said so in

Parliament on June 1st, and we quoted this in our report to the union executives. After stating that he had said earlier that once the General Strike was out of the way, the position would be clear for a resumption of negotiations, he told how he had asked the miners for their view of the Samuel Memorandum:

> I understood that they had rejected it when discussing it with the Trade Union Council, and they made no attempt after that to press its adoption on the Government. I say that in order to clear away certain criticisms which have been made against the Government for not having adopted that memorandum as it stood. The miners' executive had publicly rejected that memorandum and they adhered to that view when they saw me. . . . I had no alternative at that moment but to put forward to both sides proposals which appeared to me to offer a reasonable basis of negotiations and settlement. . . . The suggestions which I put forward were almost exactly those—though expressed differently—which were contained in what was called the Samuel Memorandum.

It seems clear enough from this that had the miners acted differently the Government would have approved the proposals.

In Samuel's first draft of the memorandum he made the point that it was indispensable that the trade union representatives should not refuse acceptance of the general proposals in the Commission's report which dealt with wages, subject to any modifications which might be approved by the National Wages Board which it was recommended should be set up. Once this point was disposed of the deadlock might be ended as follows:

1. The General Strike to be terminated by the General Council of the T.U.C.

2. The Government then to bring the parties together and negotiations to be resumed. The subsidy was to be renewed until June 1926, the notices of reduced wages to be withdrawn, and the mines restarted on the conditions operating prior to April 30th. If it was necessary in the interest of a prospective settlement, the subsidy to be further extended to June 12th.

The miners rejected this as they did a final memorandum which included a simplified wages agreement which would not adversely affect the lowest-paid man, fixing reasonable figures below which the wages of no workers should be reduced in any circumstances, and arrangements for any new adjustments to be revised by the proposed National Wages Board. I often wondered in later years whether the miners realized how much they had needlessly thrown aside.

Once the dispute was ended, immediate arrangements were put in hand for a special conference of union executives. It opened on January 20th, 1927. The newspapers called it an 'inquest'.

As soon as the decision was taken, I called the whole of the staff of the T.U.C.—at that time about thirty-five all told—to explain the grave responsibility which rested on all of us to ensure that the General Council would be ready to meet any criticism. I delegated to some dozen or more members of the staff a group of files with the instruction that each of them must make themselves thoroughly familiar with every letter, or document, or newspaper cutting within their stock of files. They must be ready to produce it instantly, if required. I myself read every letter of importance and every one of the 654 decisions which had been made in regard to the strike. These were all properly indexed and filed in a convenient form. I had several rehearsals with the staff concerned, testing their knowledge and speed of response.

Senior officers were in charge, Herbert Tracey, the head of our Press Department, being responsible for the public relations aspects and the press cuttings. I took care to ensure that he and my assiduous secretary, Miss F. E. McDonald, who knew the subject as well as I did myself, were seated next to me on the platform on the fateful days of January 20th and 21st.

On the night before the conference opened—indeed it was in the early hours of that morning—I went to bed feeling thoroughly jaded. I had tried to anticipate every contingency which might arise and I had mapped out my course of action. I felt sure I would have to speak some time or other and I prepared my notes for ready reference. I even sketched out a few sentences which I thought I could memorize ready for use. In the stillness of the night they seemed most appropriate but next morning they sounded utterly artificial and lifeless. So I discarded my written phrases and resolved to rely upon such inspiration as the moment might provide.

An hour before the opening I was at the Central Hall, Westminster, checking over all the arrangements to ensure that no hitch occurred. Behind the platform our staff were unostentatiously distributed, with Vincent Tewson at the temporary intercommunication telephone we had rigged up from there to the platform.

The hall was crowded and I could feel the suppressed excitement amongst the delegates. No press men were admitted. The fact of the conference being private only increased their keenness to get a story. After the conference there were complaints of press leaks, and it took me some time to discover how the newspapers had obtained their information. I know that one journalist arranged with a couple of his fellows in turn to shut themselves in one of the cubicles in the lavatory in order to pick up any scraps of conversation uttered by delegates.

George Hicks was in the chair, he having succeeded Arthur Pugh. After a short opening speech he called upon Pugh to present the General Council report on the strike. Pugh, a deeply religious and level-headed man, with a strong sense of fair play, read from end to end the printed report although it had been circulated to the executives some days earlier. Attached to the report there was a chart which I had prepared showing in different columns a full summary of the joint proposals of the General Council and the Miners' Federation prior to the strike, the Samuel Memorandum, and finally the proposals put forward by the Prime Minister, Mr. Baldwin, two days after the national strike had ended. This facilitated a rapid comparison of the merits of each. Those present had also a printed report prepared by the Miners' Federation giving fully and critically their view of the strike and its aftermath.

After the reading of the report by Pugh, the remainder of the morning session was devoted to questions. In the afternoon session the attack on the General Council was opened by Herbert Smith, who criticized severely but fairly the General Council's actions, to which J. H. Thomas replied. Thomas asserted that Arthur Cook had been sent a letter by me asking him to desist from making statements concerning an alleged undertaking by the Co-operative societies to provide food for the workers should a strike materialize. Cook jumped up and vehemently denied this, to which Thomas calmly replied, 'Then we will have the letter.' I shivered at this as I knew no such letter had been written to Cook. What had happened was that the secretary of the Co-operative Union, which is the central body of the Co-operative movement, had written a letter to me in which he said, 'It is a great pity that Cook cannot be muzzled.' He then went on to protest against Cook's statement 'that the Co-operative movement would be the victualling movement for the fighting forces of labour'. No such arrangement had been made and consequently trouble was caused in the Co-operative movement because of Cook's unwarranted statement. So although Thomas was wrong in detail, he was right in substance. I think Cook must have known this, because he didn't follow up the charge by demanding the production of the alleged letter. Jimmy went on serenely with his speech.

That was Jimmy all over. I have seen him come in late to a General

Council meeting and, without glancing at his documents, embark on a disquisition quite contrary to their contents. Then someone would get up and exclaim, 'But the memo says so and so!' Thomas would look pityingly at the interrupter for a second or so and then observe, 'Isn't that exactly what I am telling you?' Everyone would fall into a stupefied silence, with Thomas immediately changing his line of argument.

Cook followed Thomas and, choking with excitement, made an almost incoherent speech. I followed him with a statement as factual as I could make it. I knew this was the effective moment for my intervention. I could feel then the air of expectancy amongst the delegates. I started quietly, striving to suppress the emotion I felt.

Cook contradicted me and I at once turned to find Herbert Tracey or Miss McDonald ready with the necessary report, or letter, or quotation. When Cook had jumped up and down half a dozen times like a jack-in-the-box and had always been instantly confuted, the delegates began to call out, 'Sit down, sit down.' The careful preparation we had made was now proving worth while, and although I was the recipient of the congratulations of the delegates it was really the product of good organization plus willing and efficient team-work.

The conference went on for two days and at the end the acceptance of the General Council's report was carried by 2,840,000 to 1,095,000. The miners naturally voted against the acceptance and as they cast a vote of 800,000, this really meant that, apart from the miners, the report was carried by a nine-to-one majority.

I basked in the reflected glory of press headlines for some days. I found myself described as Labour's Sir John Simon, which, although intended as a compliment, didn't exactly thrill me.

After the conference I didn't feel triumphant at all. It would be hypocritical to say I didn't experience a certain elation in having acquitted myself creditably in such a test, coming as it did within a few months of my being elected secretary. But I was rather chastened when I thought of the suffering which had been caused by the events of 1926, particularly amongst the miners and their families. But that didn't make me feel that our efforts had been altogether in vain. I did not regard the General Strike as a failure. Nor do I today. It is true it was ill-prepared and that it had been called off without any consultation with the unions who took part in it. Those indeed were the main criticisms levelled against the General Council. The fact is that the theory of the General Strike had never been thought out. The machinery of the trade unions was unfortunately not adapted to it. Their rules had to be broken for the executives to give power to the General Council to declare the strike. However illogical it may seem for me to say so, it was never aimed against the State as a challenge to the Constitution. It was a protest against the degradation of the standards of life of millions of good trade unionists. It was a sympathetic strike on a national scale. It was full of imperfections in concept and method. The miners and others criticized the General Council because they didn't prepare for the strike.

I have given my part in this, but I have long realized that had there been any protracted attempt to organize the strike it would have given rise to divisions amongst the unions and possibly a flood of injunctions against those wishing to participate. The General Strike was an abnormality outside the provision of trade union rules or even British trade union conceptions. It has been used on the continent of Europe before and since, but always with a limited objective, albeit sometimes an entirely political one. No General Strike could ever function without adequate local organization, and the trade unions were not ready to devolve such necessary powers on the only local agents which the Trades Union Congress has—the trades councils.

But was the strike the failure which so many have asserted? Let us never forget the fact, brutal though it is, that strikes have as their purpose the infliction of loss on their opponents in order to induce the employer to concede better wages or conditions. Similarly the lock-out is used by the employer to inflict loss of wages on the workpeople. It used to be employed to the point of starving workers into submission, but we are not faced with that extreme nowadays. It was publicly stated that the trade of the country had lost £400,000,000 and the Government about £80,000,000. Would any Government gleefully contemplate a repetition in an effort to teach labour its proper place as evidently as some members of the Baldwin Government wished to do?

A couple of years after the national strike I sat next to Winston Churchill at lunch in Lord Wimborne's house in Arlington Street. George Lansbury, Snowden, and others were present. He and I fell to talking quietly about the strike and I chaffed Winston on the Government's raising the constitutional issue. I said, 'You didn't believe all that stuff about our making an attack on the Constitution?' 'Oh yes, I did,' he replied. 'I was in the country at the time and I saw red. Don't forget that when there was a threatened mutiny in the Curragh I was one of the few members of the Asquith Cabinet who was ready to face it.'

I asked him: 'What did the Government gain from it? The trade of the country lost £400,000,000 and you, as Chancellor of the Exchequer, were poorer by about £80,000,000.'

Winston's reply left me with the impression that if the Government had known what it was going to cost, we could have had the £20,000,000. I would not tie Winston down to the exact language in the earlier part of what I have written, but I will swear I have given the gist of it. I told Ernie Bevin about this conversation and shortly afterwards the *Manchester Guardian* reported:

Mr. Ernest Bevin, general secretary of the Transport and General Workers' Union, speaking at a conference of tinplaters at Swansea this afternoon, disclosed for the first time, he said, a secret connected with the General Strike.

'If Mr. Churchill,' he declared, 'had not gone into the Cabinet Room on that Sunday night [the eve of the strike] with "the *Daily Mail* business", within ten minutes of that ultimatum to us the peace terms would have been in the hands of the Prime Minister, and there would never have been a General Strike. We were in a room in Downing Street, getting almost to the last clause for handing to the Prime Minister, when Mr. Churchill saw red, walked in and upset the Cabinet, and we had that ultimatum. That was the man who has since admitted in private that had he known what the General Strike was going to cost the country he would never have taken the line he did.'

Whether Bevin realized that the Press were present when he made this statement I do not know.

Winston promptly issued a denial. Probably he had forgotten the incident. I imagine there were plenty of people amongst the Government and its supporters who wouldn't have liked to see a recurrence of the 1926 strike and would strive to avoid it. How? By legislation. They certainly believed this in 1927, when the Government brought in the Trade Disputes and Trade Unions Act, 1927. It seemed to be watertight, but it was never tested.

I am certain that without the will to avoid such a strike on the part of the trade unionist, no legislation can prove an effective deterrent. The best guarantee for industrial peace is to be sought not in repression but in the inculcation of a sense of responsibility amongst trade unionists and employers alike, and a better understanding by all concerned of the need for ordered progress and stability. Workpeople demand security and a steady improvement in their conditions of work and standard of life. They are organized in their millions to try to obtain it. How? By force? Is that the only method? Can goodwill and co-operation in the service of the community make no contribution? Thoughtful people, public men, employers and trade unionists, were asking themselves these questions after the national strike of 1926.

13

Trade Union Structure

THE foregoing chapters on the General Strike, dealing as they
do with the complexities and the niceties of inter-union
relations, have a direct bearing on the long-debated problem
of trade union structure. Here is perhaps an appropriate point for
offering some views on this thorny subject.

Almost from the moment of its formation the Trades Union
Congress has been faced with demands for an inquiry into the
structure of the trade union movement. The first of these demands
was in 1874 when the Parliamentary Committee was requested to
draw up a report on forming a federation of the various unions.
By 1879 the Congress had committed itself to making an effort to
bring together all the unions in a single federated union. By 1910 uneasiness as to the effectiveness of the existing unions found expression in a resolution calling for the amalgamation of all unions,
industry by industry. The amalgamated body was to have one
central executive elected by the combined unions. None of these
proposals materialized. The demands were in themselves healthy;
they revealed a desire, gradually becoming more widespread, for a
better form of organization. But expressions of opinion, however
sincere, are one thing; their translation into practical effect is
another. That the demands had some effect in bringing analogous
unions closer by amalgamation, federation, or some looser form
of association, cannot be doubted. But the process was comparatively
slow and many active trade unionists were impatient and wanted
more speed.

The impatience had not abated in 1962, despite the not inconsiderable progress which had been made earlier. At the Blackpool
Congress in that year a resolution was carried insisting that it was
time the trade union movement adapted its structure to modern
conditions. It instructed the General Council to examine and report
on the possibilities of reorganizing the movement. For days before

the Congress opened a number of national newspapers were speculating hopefully on the outcome of this motion.

Articles appeared emphasizing the shortcomings of trade unionism and giving pungent advice to trade unionists on how to put their house in order. I listened carefully to the debate at Blackpool, as I thought it would possibly shed some new light on the movement's problems. But the supporters of reconstruction were far too wise to attempt to put forward any specific proposals. Had they done so, their scheme would have been shot at from many different quarters. It was enough for them to insist on the need for a prompt and expeditious inquiry. But how expeditious? And how thorough? Two years?

George Woodcock, the capable and outspoken general secretary, remembering what had been the result of earlier inquiries, was cautious. Whilst fully accepting the need for an inquiry, he estimated it would take a couple of years at least to complete it. He commented: 'It is not wholly a matter of structure. Structure, particularly in the trade union movement, is a function of purpose.' I pricked up my ears at this. It was almost identical with a phrase I had used thirty-seven years before in a memorandum I wrote at the request of the T.U.C. Organization Committee for consideration by the 1925 Scarborough Congress. A resolution had been passed the previous year at Hull calling for an inquiry into the structure of the trade union movement. This was almost exactly what the General Council was instructed in 1962 to embark upon. In pursuance of the Hull resolution the General Council was required to produce a scheme for the organization of the workers industry by industry, the aim being one union for each. But that was only half of the problem. They were also to draft proposals which, whilst securing unity of action, would not involve the merging of the existing unions. I knew this was going to be a long job and in fact it took three years. After a preliminary survey the T.U.C. Organization Committee left it to me to draft a memorandum which could be presented to the Congress in 1926 as a sort of interim report.

In my memorandum of fourteen closely printed pages I pointed out that the Trade Union Congress was itself a federal organization. I emphasized that it could not lay down any plan of reorganization which its affiliated unions could be compelled to accept. No matter what the T.U.C. said, the individual unions always had the last word. What I said then remains true today. I had learned enough to realize that without the willing co-operation of the unions no decision of Congress could be made effective. Many modern critics of trade unionism seem to overlook this.

I set out to examine the objects of trade unionism as stated in their rule books, but whilst the majority of the unions had been established with the primary purpose of dealing with improvements in wages and working conditions, in only a small number of cases was there a clear recognition that the trade union movement had any wider purpose. 'Function must determine structure,' I wrote, 'and that type of organization which will suit the minimum needs of a union's own members will not necessarily be best for the attainment of all the broader objects.' I defined these objects as (1) improvement of wages and working conditions, (2) a measure of control of industry, and (3) the ability to defend the workers against any onslaught by capitalism.

At that time it was doubtful whether there was complete agreement on the theory and objects of trade unionism. This may seem heretical to some, but whatever the *implied* objects of trade unionism may be its *declared* objects in 1962 were not much more clearly expressed than in 1925. About the first object—the improvement of wages and working conditions—there cannot be any doubt. Nor is there likely to be any substantial division amongst active trade unionists on the need for the unions exercising a measure of control in industry. There is not the least doubt in my mind that the necessity for securing this forms a definite part of the policy of the unions, whether it is stated in their rules or not. Some people may wonder at my including the third object—the ability to defend the workers against any onslaught by capitalism. This last object was always obscure, but there was a strong feeling—which I shared—that some time or other a collision would take place between the unions and the employers as a whole. I wanted the movement to be strong enough to meet that challenge if it ever came. Although I was never an adherent of the class-war theory of Karl Marx, I had imbibed enough of his doctrines to make me regard this as a possible contingency. Many trade unionists thought it was a certainty that such a struggle would come. A year or so later, in 1926, it looked as though the onslaught had begun when the miners were locked out to enforce wage reductions and the General Strike took place in their defence.

As to the defects in trade union structure, they had long been apparent. I set them out as (1) sectionalism, (2) competition for members, (3) unions offering different rates of contributions and benefits for apparently the same services, (4) demarcation of work, and (5) lack of a co-ordinated policy. I examined each of these in turn.

Sectionalism is of itself the main cause of the existence of most of the other defects. It must be remembered that the creation of a trade union is possible only where the workers have a common interest. That is the basis of all combination and the closer the realization of this identity of interests amongst the workers of any particular group, or trade, or calling, the more likelihood there is that any trade union they form will be permanent and durable. Practically all the British unions started as small local bodies covering the workers in a particular section of a trade or occupation. In that sense they differed materially from many of the trade unions on the continent of Europe.

Trade unionism in the United Kingdom is often criticized for its lack of an overall plan of organization and comparisons are made with other countries such as Germany where the unions are big national bodies covering the whole of an industry irrespective of locality. This is not a completely true picture of the whole of the European trade unions. In France, for example, the unions are even more local in character than those of the United Kingdom, with the exception of the textile industry. But of Germany, Sweden, and Holland it is true that the unions are fewer and more national in character. The principal reason is that in many of the continental countries the unions were formed much later than the British unions. They were planned by the Social Democratic parties who saw in them a source of economic power. They reflected in the industrial world more or less the social and economic conceptions of their founders. Over the years they have shaken themselves free of political domination to a great extent. But it is still a simple truism that no movement can be divorced from its history and, unlike their counterparts in most continental countries, trade unions were in operation in the United Kingdom a hundred years before the Labour Party came into existence. So the major difference between the planned continental trade unions and the British is that our unions grew naturally out of the industrial condition of the time.

I did not see when I wrote the memo as clearly as I do now that trade union structure in this country has a history that closely resembles that of British industry generally. Just as there are nowadays huge business combinations brought about by mergers, take-over bids, and amalgamations, so in the trade union sphere there are unions numbering their members in hundreds of thousands. One—the Transport and General Workers' Union—possesses nearly one and a third million members. The Amalgamated Engineering Union has about a million members, and the National Union of General and Municipal Workers over three-quarters of a million. Despite the giant corporations, there are still hundreds of thousands of small firms making a single product or only a part of it and carrying

out the work in one locality or district. So also there are trade unions
who count their tiny membership in hundreds or even less. Somehow
the little fellows manage to survive whether as firms or unions, despite
the competition of their more powerful neighbours. Most of the
small ones are linked up in labour matters through associations or
federations with the big firms or unions, and whether they are trade
unions or companies they strongly resist any attempt by central
bodies to interfere in their internal affairs.

There is an innate conservatism and individualism in the trade
union movement, just as there is in other sections of British life.
The central bodies of employers, just like the T.U.C., while always
ready to guide and influence the affairs of their constituent bodies,
carefully avoid bringing too much pressure and studiously refrain
from interference in their members' domestic affairs. I remembered
all this when writing my memorandum on union organization, where
I said:

Sectionalism cannot lightly be dismissed, and it will continue
vigorously so long as the small unions seem to fulfil more
effectively the most immediate interests of their members. Its
removal is only possible by a clearer recognition of the mass
interests of the working class. It is no use fulminating against
sectionalism. It exists, and may continue to exist for a long
time. Modern industrial developments break down the barriers
of craft interests only to erect other sectional divisions. The
tasks for those entrusted to form the new organization are not
merely to deplore sectionalism but to provide for its adjustment,
first by adequate representation for craft and sectional interests
in any new structure and, secondly, by intensive and educative
trade union propaganda.

Competition amongst the unions for members was much stronger, and allegations of poaching on one another's preserves far more
frequent, when I wrote my memorandum in 1925 than they are
today. They were materially reduced by the adoption at Bridlington
in 1939 of certain principles. The main feature of the Bridlington
principles was that no member or ex-member of a trade union
should be accepted by another union without an inquiry to his
former union. The former union was required to reply within
fourteen days stating whether the applicant had resigned, whether
he was free of arrears, whether he had been fined or penalized by the
union under its rules, and finally whether there was any reason why
his application should not be accepted.

Disputes between unions on the interpretation of the Bridlington principles, and of any other matters which may arise amongst them, have been regularly dealt with and usually settled by the T.U.C. Disputes Committee. I acted as secretary of this committee until our staff had expanded sufficiently to permit of an official making it one of his special duties. By such methods, whilst sectionalism has not been got rid of, some of its worst features have been removed.

Despite the existence of sectionalism, British trade unionism is far more concentrated than most people seem to realize. In January 1963 more than half of the 8,315,332, trade unionists affiliated to the T.U.C. were enrolled in six trade unions. Seventy-five per cent of the total T.U.C. membership was in twenty unions out of 176. Varied rates of contributions are still a bugbear, despite the efforts of the T.U.C. to straighten this out. Furthermore, most trade union contributions are far too low to permit of funds being sufficiently adequate to cover really efficient administration and to pay the overworked full-time officials satisfactory salaries. I know of few trade union officials whose salaries are comparable with those paid by the employers' organizations, Government departments, or the nationalized industries. I am not here talking about their clerical employees who are usually reasonably remunerated. I have in mind trade union secretaries, organizers, divisional or area officials, who devote practically the whole of their waking time to trade unionism. If only the British unions had adopted the method of basing contributions on a percentage of the rates of pay of their members the situation would have been easier. By this method contributions would have increased every time there was a general increase in the wages of union members. The average rate of contribution per member is about one shilling and fourpence per week.

As it is, the Trades Union Congress had to report in 1960 that many of the unions were in deficit on the year's working because they had not increased their contributions sufficiently. Some unions have since remedied this in some degree, but most have very small margins on which to work. As to the salaries of the officials, I can speak as one who has been through the mill. I was always one of the fortunate ones. My salary, when I was with the E.T.U. and as secretary of the Trades Union Congress, never troubled me—not that it was adequate by the standards I have mentioned, but I was usually better off than most of my overworked brethren. Most union officials do not regard themselves as employees in any real sense. They are part of the movement itself. They ardently believe in its principles. They know trade unionism to be a powerful force which, intelligently applied, has been, and can be, of immense benefit to the

P

millions of workers, and not only to them, but ultimately to the country as a whole. It is this deep-rooted conviction that makes them put up with abuse and harsh criticism even from their own members, and with conditions of employment which those same members would not tolerate if imposed upon them by any private employer. They know, too, that their unions, no matter how apparently wealthy, cannot afford in existing circumstances to pay them salaries comparable with those of officials performing not dissimilar duties in industry. The stark truth is that trade unionism is too cheap for the work it performs on behalf of its members.

Demarcation disputes between unions reveal a deplorable defect in trades unionism. This has proved a most intractable problem. Every trade union official I have ever met has regretted these unfortunate internecine squabbles. Although more frequent amongst the craft unions, demarcation disputes are by no means confined to them. Often enough, these struggles are started by a few men employed by a particular firm on some job or other, and the unions learn about it only after the row has started. The basic cause of these disputes is the fear of unemployment. One set of workers see unemployment staring them in the face because another set of men (though as good trade unionists as they consider themselves to be) are doing jobs which the strikers claim are theirs by custom of tradition. If neither of these claims can be substantiated then the strikers assert that by training they are more fitted to do the job. The employers usually feel helpless to redress this situation. If they decide in favour of the claims then the other fellows will cease work. It sometimes becomes a war of attrition and all the newspaper strictures in the world do not seem to affect the attitude of the men concerned.

It is of little use to tell these men that with a full-employment policy in operation nationally their fears are groundless. They do not believe it. They know that although full employment may exist, taking industry as a whole there are at the same time areas where thousands of men are out of work.

I am not here defending demarcation: I am trying to explain it. Eventually such disputes have to be settled round the table, and the formation of federations and agreements setting out the work which the members of each union should do, have all contributed materially towards reducing the frequency and the impact of these disputes. The T.U.C., through its Disputes Committee, has also done much to take the edge off this regrettable warfare. The amalgamation of unions (such as, for example, the shipwrights' and the boilermakers') is clearly the most certain means of eliminating such disputes. Another weakness lies in the lack of a co-ordinated policy. This is less obvious than it was in my day as a trade union official, but no one can be satisfied with the present arrangements, particularly in the sphere of wages.

I am happy to think that there are now signs that the unions, through the T.U.C., realize the necessity for co-ordination of effort in this sphere as in others. It is sufficient for me to say here that I firmly believe that the most effective road to that co-operation lies in strengthening the powers of the T.U.C. I believe this as firmly today as I did in 1925, when I pointed out that the Trades Union Congress had, in itself, the nucleus of the one big union, organized as it is in trades groups, and supervised by the General Council. It could be endowed with sufficient power to enable it to function effectively on all major issues, on behalf of the whole trade union movement. Its area counter part would be the trades councils which exist in every important industrial locality. These could be developed into active functioning bodies, their relationship to the General Council being much the same as that of the district or management committees to certain of the trade unions. Each trades council, in turn, would be divided into industrial groups corresponding in form to the grouping on the General Council. The groupings would have to be modified, no doubt, to suit local requirements. Responsible to them would be the shop stewards. I remain convinced that the shop stewards should be accepted as an integral part of trade union organization. There is no reason that I can see why the individual shop steward should not be regarded as the accredited agent of the *union* itself and not merely as the spokesman of a group of workers. The workshop committees, too, could be linked up through the trades councils. Their functions would be restricted to the consideration of domestic matters, strictly limited to the factory, workshop, or undertaking to which they were attached.

This is how I saw the problem in 1925, but I knew then that there would have to be a revolution in thinking before the executives of the trade unions would follow the course I have outlined. They were intensely jealous of their autonomy and afraid of their authority being usurped.

Ernest Bevin, constructively minded as he was, firmly adhered to this view: he believed that the trades councils would eventually seek to exercise functions that rightly belonged to the executives of the unions. As to linking up the shop stewards in any way with the trades councils, he strongly objected to any such proposition. Plainly it was hopeless for me to persist against such opposition in the then state of mind of the members of the General Council. The most I could do was to persuade the Council to a measure of association with the trades councils by the establishment of a Trades Council Consultative Committee, the representatives to be elected at an annual meeting of the various councils at a conference under the auspices of the T.U.C.

The final report of the Organizing Committee, published in 1927, extended to over fifty pages. Evidence was given before the Committee from all the principal unions both in memoranda and verbally. Many of the witnesses were utterly vague when it came to defining the kind of organization which would make for greater efficiency. Under cross-examination the advocates of organization by industry and closer unity put forward different and contradictory conceptions and interpretations of the resolution. Sincerely desirous as they were for a better form of organization, they hadn't a glimmer of insight as to how this could best be brought about. As the Committee observed: 'The ramifications of trade union organization and the differences in conception as to the best form of structure, as indicated by the witnesses and by the information collected, are such that no body of trade unionists could have fully appreciated without such an investigation.'

The Committee found that the varying structure and methods of working of the unions, the different circumstances in the various trades and industries, and the impossibility of defining boundaries, made the general application of any particular scheme impracticable. The General Council endorsed the report. They were just as much convinced as the most advanced trade unionists that greater co-ordination was imperative, and they felt that the most effective way of attaining this was by unions with closely related trade interests to seek amalgamation.

It seemed to me that the major problem was not only that of structure but of *power*—power to act on policy issues in a cohesive manner. This could be done only by a central body representing all the unions. People who thought like myself had for years been talking about a general staff for labour. 'All power to the General Council,' they declared. Such slogans seemed not only eminently desirable but just plain common sense. Alas! We didn't realize how conservative a force the trade union movement could be in relation to its own affairs. Our unions could draft plans in the course of a few sessions to put the whole world right. But the General Council had to be extremely careful not to try to press them into making internal changes they didn't care for. We had to carry our unions with us and retain their goodwill. They would not respond quickly to demands for changes in structure but they might approve of greater powers being exercised on behalf of the General Council. So I concentrated my attention on this feature, instancing the authority possessed by the central bodies of employers, mentioning in particular the Confederation of Employers' Organizations (now the British Employers' Confederation). This body acted for its federated organizations on all so-called labour questions. They were believed to control the general policy of the employers as a whole.

While later experience showed that we had an exaggerated conception of the extent of this power, we knew that their influence was considerable. It was assumed that the Confederation would be able to carry on centralized negotiations with the T.U.C. and I wanted the General Council to have at least that much authority. So, although somewhat chastened in my early enthusiasm for a sweeping reform in the trade union movement, I was greatly encouraged when the General Council, after pointing to the necessity for such centralized negotiations to deal with general questions, recommended that this necessary co-ordination should be in the hands of the T.U.C. through its General Council. In the debate which took place on the report, nothing whatever was said on this point, yet it was far more important, in my opinion, than the academic discussion on organization by industry which ensued.

In subsequent years I never lost sight of this objective; and, without ever bringing the subject to a sharp and controversial issue, I tried steadily to take the initiative in all those questions of general policy which were of common interest. Even then I realized it would be suicidal to try to extend the Council's powers by actively intervening in wages negotiations. This was something which I hoped would come later.

The 1962 Blackpool Congress resolution on structure raises an interesting speculation as to how the General Council will set to work to carry it out. Perhaps I may be forgiven for making a few suggestions. The first requisite, as I see it, is for the executive councils of the unions to obtain from their members powers enabling *them* to act in conjunction with the T.U.C. on all matters of policy. I cannot see how the unions can endow the T.U.C. with such powers by any other means. To secure these powers a vigorous propaganda campaign will be needed. Active trade unionists require no convincing, but the average apathetic member will have to be wakened up to the understanding of the need for such a step. Success is far more likely to be achieved if the unions are approached collectively to do this rather than to leave them to take the initiative with their own members.

Once the General Council possesses full powers it would be necessary for a regular system of consultation to be established between the Council and the Unions. I have in mind something in the nature of a half yearly Conference, at which every union would be represented. It would be much smaller than the Annual Congress, and would not need to be constituted on a strictly membership basis. An enlarged General Council would of itself furnish a wider area of consultation than is possible today. I can foresee the possibility of even quarterly conferences coming along eventually. Such conferences would afford the Council adequate opportunities for reporting on its work, and enable it to secure guidance from the Unions in the use of its extended powers. I am thinking here of matters of general policy, and not of the special subjects relating to the trades groups. On any serious issue of policy, which might subsequently arise once the Council possesses full powers, it would be essential for the Council to consult its unions by conference if time allowed. Such conferences would be in the nature of consultative gatherings to guide the General Council in the use of its extended powers. I know my colleagues of the T.U.C. sufficiently well to be sure that they would exercise their powers with prudence. They know the importance of retaining and increasing the confidence and loyalty of the unions and their members.

The necessity for a national wages policy has been so drummed into the ears of trade unionists that this difficult problem may well be one of the first upon which the General Council will require to obtain the power from its unions to act with decisiveness. There are bound to be many subjects which arise in the economic sphere and on the National Economic Development Council which will exercise the courage and statesmanship of the unions and tax the understanding of their members. Every important issue as it arises should strengthen the authority of the T.U.C., always provided it is handled with the courage, discretion, and breadth of outlook which the leaders of the movement undoubtedly possess.

It seems to me that most broad issues which are likely to arise in the next few years can be dealt with without any substantial change of union structure. Any signs which can be discerned towards amalgamation of unions will be warmly encouraged by the T.U.C. Experience shows that this is a rather dilatory process. The General Council have been at this for years. In the new spirit of the modern movement there may be better prospects of this being accomplished on a far more comprehensive scale than ever before.

In the absence of any extensive move towards amalgamation, what is left? Federation? 'What!' says the militant trade unionist, restraining his impatience with difficulty. 'That discredited bogey?' But it isn't a bogey at all. On the contrary it has been demonstrated to be a most practical device in bringing unions to act together as a single body on wages negotiations and related subjects. It has serious defects without any doubt. But so have the individual unions. It is far too easy for unions to secede or disregard federation decisions, although in practice this rarely takes place. Everything depends on the powers with which the participating unions have endowed their federation. Federation of itself has proved on many occasions to be the principal agency which has caused trade unions to amalgamate.

Federation has the supreme advantage that none of its constituent unions loses its identity. Most unions treasure this. In my later years at the T.U.C. I strove hard to bring the existing federations into closer association with us. I wanted them to become an inherent part of the T.U.C. This, too, met with strenuous opposition. The eighteen trade groups of the Congress were originally intended to be actively functioning bodies to help the unions in the different industries. They did little in this direction during my twenty-two years. I wanted to transform these groups so that they could carry out the duties for which they were originally designed. But whilst the federations remained outside this was an impossibility, and it would have led to serious overlapping and friction. The only logical and consistent course was to bring the federations in as part of the T.U.C. machinery. This could have been done without involving them in serious financial obligations. I hoped that in time close association in day-to-day working would lead to the federations being merged into the groups, with the federation officials eventually becoming responsible officers of the T.U.C. I never got within sight of this achievement. But we were successful in establishing a loose liaison with several of the federations.

The need for a concerted policy on wages and other industrial matters was not so closely perceived in my day as it appears to be now. Some of the members of the General Council I talked to had their doubts about the wisdom of such a move. Even Alec Walkden (later Lord Walkden), a fine type of trade unionist and the chairman of our Organizing Committee, was unconvinced. 'But that would stamp the T.U.C. as a trade union,' he argued.

'Why not?' I replied.

'Well, no one knows just what we are,' Walkden said reflectively, 'and I think there is some advantage in our constitutional position remaining ambiguous.' I couldn't see the force of this as I felt that sooner or later this issue might have to be tested in the law courts. I thought that far from weakening the status of the T.U.C., its certification as a trade union would give it more security and not less.

When a year or two later I persuaded the General Council that it was desirable to redraft our constitution I deliberately inserted among the objects the regulation of relations between employers and workpeople and between workpeople and workpeople. These are substantially the definitions in the Trade Union Acts. But there were strong arguments raised against the advisability of doing this, and I had to drop the subject. Today there is little doubt that the T.U.C. is not a trade union in the eyes of lawyers. So that it is fairly clear that if the existing trade groups were enlarged and given the authority to negotiate with the employers on wages and conditions of employment, and called this into effect, this alone would transform the status of the T.U.C. It could hardly be argued that the body which was determining policy on such matters, and whose unions were actually taking part in such negotiations, was not of itself a trade union. It is still my view that nothing could be lost by this. At all events the subject is worth while exploring. If there is anything in the idea of a link-up of the federations with the T.U.C. groups and the conversion of these into active participants in the sphere of industrial relations, the grouping system would have to be carefully revised and the numbers of groups considerably increased.

A corresponding increase in the number of members of the General Council would be necessary, but that would be all to the good. The Council membership was fixed at a total of thirty, including two women members, as far back as 1920. In 1963 it was thirty-five in all. If the General Council is to be endowed with considerably greater powers, I think it would be desirable to increase the number of its members to at least forty or even fifty in addition to two or three specially elected women. At some stage a small full time executive will be needed, within the larger council. It was always my view that whether or not the federations became part of the structure of the T.U.C., close joint working between them and the T.U.C. was imperative.

I was surprised to find there was objection to this from Council members. It was suggested that this would be an encroachment on the authority of the unions generally. Why, I could never find out.

What I have said so far concerns only the top structure of the trade union movement. But there is plenty of room for improvement lower down in the organization. In particular, vastly improved communication will be needed between headquarters, with its officers, and the rank and file. The ordinary branch machinery will not be sufficient to achieve this. Communication in all modern, large-scale business, right through the line of management to the individual employee, is flimsy, and usually quite inadequate. This is a subject of growing importance in the business world, and the trade unions would do well to think a little more about applying the best modern techniques to their own officials and members.

I hope I shall not be accused of pontificating to the unions. I know sufficient about the difficulties of implementing the 1962 Blackpool decision not to envy the General Council its job.

14

Secretary of the T.U.C.

THE dissertation on trades union structure in the last chapter has led me away from the sequence of my narrative.

After the death of Fred Bramley the T.U.C. General Council appointed me as acting secretary. This was in October 1925, and I held that position until September 1926, when the new secretary was to be appointed. He has always been elected by the delegates attending the annual meeting of Congress and not by the General Council. Every affiliated union is entitled to send in a nomination for the position, and I naturally anticipated that there would be keen competition for a post which was steadily becoming recognized as the most influential in the trade union movement. I did not rate my own chances high. First, because I was much younger than any of those who had occupied the secretaryship, and, secondly, I was far less well known than some of those who were likely to be nominated. I had in fact spoken only once in the annual Congress. Thirdly, during the national strike I had run the risk of blotting my copybook with the leaders of two of the most powerful unions in the Congress —the Miners' Federation and the Transport and General Workers' Union.

During the strike I had been outspoken on the policy and tactics of the miners, and while I had never criticized them publicly, on the inside both during and after the strike the views I had expressed could not have been palatable to them. Bob Smillie, Tom Richards, and Arthur Cook, the miners' officials who served on the General Council, had time and time again found me running contrary to the policy the Federation was pursuing. At the very moment when I did this the unions were being asked for nominations for the vacant secretaryship. I felt I had antagonized the miners and I could expect no support from them. As for the transport workers, it had been reported to me by one of our officers that Ernest Bevin had been so influenced by my attitude during these discussions that he had remarked: 'Citrine has courage. That has decided where our vote for the secretaryship will go.'

Alas, later events changed all this. Bevin brutally attacked the head of the T.U.C. Research Department, Milne-Bailey, for having written on the General Strike in an American publication. Carried away by the intensity of his feelings, Bevin had passionately asserted: 'They are all journalists. You can't trust any of them.' This was said in the presence of the full Council, and, what was worse, in the hearing of several of our principal officers, some of whom, like Milne-Bailey, were university graduates.

This incident occurred just before lunch. I hadn't time to go out for my food and I was sitting in my office eating a sandwich when three of our officers who had been in the Council chamber came in. Milne-Bailey was livid. The sum and substance of what they said to me was that they would not resume their duties unless and until Bevin withdrew his charge. I told them I could not discuss the matter with them and if they had anything to say to the Council they must put it into writing. Thereupon they wrote out a short note protesting vehemently against Bevin's conduct and announcing their determination not to resume their duties until there was an apology.

On the resumption of the meeting I read the note to the Council. I went on to say that I wished to be associated with the protest. I repudiated Bevin's allegations and told him flatly that he wouldn't have dared to treat any of his own officials in such a manner. Bevin was furious. He jumped to his feet, told the Council that 'I always knew the secretary had his knife in for me', and immediately stormed out of the room, to the accompaniment of rude noises from Jimmy Thomas. Bevin's charge against me was ridiculous. Not only did I admire him as one of the outstandingly constructive minds in the movement, but I was hardly likely to incur his enmity at a time when my future depended so much upon the big vote of his union. Truly I had never truckled to him or to any other member of the Council and had often spoken my mind without stooping to flattery of anyone. My protest was conditioned solely by the fact that I knew his charge against Milne-Bailey, who was a most capable and diligent officer, was unjust; and as he and the others to whom Bevin had referred were not in a position to defend themselves, I felt it was my duty to stand behind them. What made Bevin's statement more absurd was that the article which incurred his wrath was printed in an American trade union journal and was quite innocuous. I never once had reason to suspect any of our officers, either then or at any time, of breach of confidence or of divulging the Council's private business.

So here I was, with my prospect of becoming secretary seemingly ruined by loss of the support of two of the biggest unions. But it didn't work out that way. Soon afterwards Cook told me that the miners had decided to support me.

Events proved that I needn't have worried about the outcome of my candidature. I was nominated by several of the principal unions and at the Congress in 1926 I was declared elected without opposition. I think this was the first time this had occurred, and at thirty-nine I was the youngest secretary the Congress had ever had. I tried to conceal my feeling when the decision was taken, but I was deeply moved. The strain through which I had passed in recent months had worked me up to a state of nervous tension.

The 1926 Congress at Bournemouth witnessed an unseemly row. John Bromley, of the locomotive engineers and firemen, had been saying nasty things about the conduct of the miners. Most of them were true, which caused all the more resentment. His union had been nearly bankrupted by the national strike. Moreover, its members (like the rest of the railwaymen) had the utmost difficulty in obtaining reinstatement in employment.

The General Council, who had been abused and vilified almost beyond endurance because of the outcome of the national strike, had decided rather magnanimously to start a fund in aid of the miners. They appointed Bromley to move the resolution authorizing this and he had the moral courage to accept. None of the miners' officials on the General Council raised the least demur to this, but immediately Bromley rose in the Congress to move the resolution he was greeted with howls of protest, and the president, Arthur Pugh, was unable to restore order.

Visitors who have attended the annual meetings of the T.U.C. have often remarked about the orderly and disciplined manner in which the proceedings are conducted. Obedience to the president's rule is one of the strongest characteristics of the delegates. Now all was tumult. I was taken aback, like everyone else on the platform, but Pugh, with remarkable coolness and dignity, announced an adjournment for half an hour. This gave time for the more responsible delegates to use their influence with their colleagues. During the adjournment the Council met and there was complete unanimity to stand by the President and Bromley. Soon along came two or three of the most level-headed of the miners' leaders to apologize unreservedly and sincerely for the occurrence. Not that the responsibility was wholly borne by the miners: it transpired afterwards that the Communists had exploited the situation with their usual dexterity and had inflamed the passions of certain delegates, who thought, no doubt, that the choice of Bromley was deeply provocative.

On the resumption, a statement was made by W. P. Richardson, a tactful miners' official from Durham. This appeased the malcontents. The debate then opened, and Bromley's speech was restrained and unexceptionable. It was at this Congress that our stewards found evidence of Communist intrigue. A typed set of instructions to so-called 'Communist delegates' was discovered on one of the seats giving explicit orders as to who was to intervene in the debates and the line they were to take.

When I returned to London Arthur Henderson greeted me with the smiling query, 'Well, Walter, now that you have been elected secretary, we are wondering what you are going to do?'

I had already thought to myself: 'What am I going to do? Have I any ideas about the future of the T.U.C. Are there any clear thoughts in my mind?' At first I thought there were not. All that I had really done during my years as a trade union official was to do the work in hand as efficiently and promptly as I could. My mind had been devoted mostly to the finding of expedients to overcome specific difficulties rather than to the working out of any long-term policy. But that remark by Arthur Henderson set me thinking. I realized that people, both inside and outside the movement, would look forward —some sympathetically, some sceptically, some perhaps enviously, but all of them critically—to see what changes would take place during my years of office. Not that anyone could justifiably expect to see sweeping changes in the near future: the secretary of the T.U.C. is not a dictator; he has to work with and through other people; he has to persuade others and convert them to his ideas.

As time went on I felt my influence should become greater as I gained the confidence of the General Council, but I must try not to obtrude my views too much in the early stages. I couldn't compel anyone except my immediate staff to do anything. Even there I knew the big stick was no weapon for me to wield. My job was to secure the goodwill of both the General Council and the staff. Many times during my period as acting secretary I had said to our officials, 'Wait until I get power.' There were several changes I wanted to bring about, but they were practically all of them of an administrative or executive character. Policy was a matter for the Council and not for the staff. But I could work through and with the staff to influence policy, and I knew that, as time went on, I could do much to initiate it.

I felt competent to tackle our administrative problems, such as they were likely to be, and did so. But what was the policy I should

aim at? I had written articles by the dozen on administrative subjects
and I had extolled the virtues of large-scale organization. I had no
belief that the process of amalgamation in the trade union world
would produce the same quick results that one saw in the business
world.

The farthest I got in my reasoning was that I must try to make
the T.U.C. indispensable to the affiliated unions; to establish a
leadership which they would be willing to follow; to demonstrate
the capacity of the General Council really to act as the general staff
that most progressive trade unionists wanted.

The principal lesson I had learned was that the trade union movement must exert its influence in an ever-widening sphere and not be
contained within the traditional walls of trade union policy. Events
were moving fast and the widely held belief in the impending collapse
of capitalism would not suffice. We must try to expand the activities
of the T.U.C. until we could establish an efficient system whereby
the T.U.C. would be regularly and naturally consulted by whatever
Government was in power on any subject of direct concern to the
unions. I reasoned that this was a policy to be advocated whenever
I got the chance. So, almost without realizing it, I found myself
evolving a twofold policy, the parts of which were inter-dependent.
The first led towards more power to the T.U.C., and the second was
a demand for consultation in the widest area of economic and industrial policy.

I didn't want to arouse controversy by proclaiming these things
from the housetops. To do so would only be to invite opposition. The
thing to do was to act on the assumption that these were already
features of the accepted policy of the T.U.C. and to prosecute them
steadfastly but not noisily. Inside the office we discussed the subjects
threadbare, and every individual knew it was his duty to raise administrative efficiency to a higher degree than any of the affiliated unions
could reach. By that means the T.U.C. would be approached automatically by the unions to act on their behalf within the ever-widening sphere of national affairs.

It was here that the remarkable relationship of Ernest Bevin and
I had scope for development. Our ideas were so closely related, our
thinking so closely parallel, that without any formal collaboration we
reached similar conclusions. We were different in many ways. Bevin
read practically nothing about trade union theory or economics. He
didn't need to. His native intelligence and flair taught him many
things that were not to be found in textbooks or in the dogma of
economic theorists. He had great drive and a measure of ruthlessness
which I did not possess. He was subjective in practically all he did:

he personalized almost everything. When I once asked him what was his approach to a subject he replied, 'I don't reason things out—I depend a good deal on flair.' This was not entirely true. He had a good reasoning mind but he also had flashes of insight which bordered on inspiration.

We were both more inclined to look upon the constructive or positive sides of trade unionism rather than on the traditionally defensive and somewhat negative aspects. Bevin had plenty of courage, initiative, and energy. He also possessed something I lacked completely. He controlled, through his union, a trade union vote which could be decisive on occasions at the T.U.C., and which was destined to grow to over a million and a quarter in the years ahead. There was a power behind such voting strength which, whether brought to bear on the determination of policy or on the election of individuals, was not to be sneered at. Bevin was a power in the trade union movement. He also exercised a similar authority in the Labour Party conference, which was completely outside my scope.

In these circumstances, it might be thought that I would naturally have cultivated Bevin's support for those measures I wished to see achieved. But I didn't. Why not? Principally because of the certain knowledge that by playing up to Bevin I would undermine my influence with the rest of the Council who, naturally, would resent what they would regard as domination by the big fellows. Secondly, I had an independent streak in my nature which had long shaped my actions, so that I refused to be like 'that poor man who hangs on princes' favours'. Looking at it in a cold-blooded way, there was no need for me to play up to anyone. My strength lay in my independence and I was determined to preserve it.

Arthur Henderson, giving me advice in my early days as secretary, said: 'Walter, never fight your Council. Always wait until you have heard their opinions before you give your own.' I never took this wise advice. Many times I was in a minority of one. It was my practice in my later years always to declare myself at the beginning of a debate and not to sit on the fence until I knew which way the wind was blowing. Not good psychology, perhaps, but it worked. I wouldn't have dared to do this immediately after I was appointed: I had a lot to learn, and I knew it. I had been pretty outspoken during the mining dispute, and had risked something in the process, but as secretary I felt I must gain the confidence of the General Council as a first step to acquiring greater power.

The occasions on which Bevin and I discussed policy outside the Council chamber might be counted on one hand, certainly on two. Yet the occasions on which we differed on essentials could, I believe, have been counted within a still smaller compass. Sometimes Bevin would turn up late for a Council meeting. Meantime I had been expounding a certain line of action to the General Council in his absence. Bevin would come in and, without the slightest knowledge of what I had said, would traverse and support the views I had expressed with an uncanny similarity of reasoning. I sometimes wondered whether the rest of the Council members would think he and I had framed the whole policy together in private discussion. I can say with truth, after mature reflection, that I cannot now recall a single issue of first-class importance on which we seriously differed. On tactics, yes, but not on basic policy. So, without external collaboration, we worked together to increase the influence of the T.U.C., to establish its right to consultation in the national sphere, and to make it a centre with power to evolve policy and take decisions on general principles affecting the trade union movement as a whole.

Not long afterwards our policy began to bear fruit. A committee, under the chairmanship of Lord Macmillan, a distinguished lawyer, was appointed to inquire into the working of the finance and credit system. They were not to confine themselves only to the national aspects of the problem, but to several international operations also. Bevin was nominated by the T.U.C., and worthily did he acquit himself. Another member was J. M. Keynes, whom I regarded as Britain's foremost economist. It is true that he was apt to change his mind, but Keynes had courage, knowledge, and insight. Both he and Bevin kept me in touch separately with what was going on. Keynes told me that when the Governor of the Bank of England came to be examined he put up a pitiful exhibition. He didn't seem to know anything about economics or even the principles of banking. When asked how he came to particular decisions he answered, according to Keynes, 'Just nous.' Perhaps he was foxing; and, of course, 'nous' does play quite an important part in the decisions most of us have to make.

One consequence of this inquiry was that since that date few prominent public men ever advocated the cutting of wages as a remedy for a trade depression. Our policy was proved worth while. Our right to be heard on intricate financial questions was fully admitted. I served for years on the National Economic Council, set up by the Government, and later as a member of the Consultative Committee of the Treasury. The war of 1939-45 saw a rapid extension of this policy. The T.U.C. had established its right to consultation. Joint consultation in the individual industries came more slowly. But after the war, with the advent of the nationalized industries, it became an established system.

Shortly after the General Strike I called an informal meeting of our principal officials. I always found it an advantage to confer with them upon any problem, as some of them—particularly Herbert Tracey—were fertile in ideas.

What was to be the policy of the trade union movement? Were we to try to organize the movement so that if the necessity arose we could engage in still bigger and better organized strikes? Where would this lead us to? I did not share the belief that the trade union movement had been defeated. It had made a protest against the circumstances which had brought about the conflict, although this was only dimly perceived by those who took part in it. I did not believe that any government would wish to see a recurrence, nor did I believe that any really effective legislation could be devised which would prevent such serious conflicts. I felt we had to rely upon the common sense of all the parties—Government, employers, and trade unionists—and their sense of right and wrong. When I came to look back and recall what Keynes had prophesied I could see that little reason as the miners had to love the coal-owners, the employers had little choice. If they were to remain in business they must get costs down. It was easy to look to wages as the first step in lowering costs.

I had not changed my conviction in the least that there was little or no disposition on the part of the coal-owners generally to engage in effective reorganization of the collieries. However valuable the recommendations in the Samuel Report, there was little likelihood of their being implemented voluntarily by the employers. There were a few companies who were more progressive than the remainder, but they were the exception. There was little hope, it seemed to me, of the mining industry ever again attaining a state of prosperity under private ownership.

I was saddened at the thought of the human suffering which had been caused by the General Strike and the protraction of the mining lock-out. Industrial conflict, like war, has its casualties; and there could be no doubt that victimization of active trade unionists had taken place and would continue to take place. We must find some means of building up the trade union movement, increasing not merely its membership but also its efficiency of organization.

Here I came across the question of how the confidence of trade unionists could be regained by their organizations. The doctrine that the standard of life of all workers must steadily worsen under capitalism had been sedulously preached not only by Communists but by thousands of other adherents to the theories of Karl Marx. The Theory of Increasing Misery, as it was called, was nothing new. I was never a believer in this doctrine. It seemed to me utter folly for any

Q

trade unionist to insist that working-class standards under capitalism must become worse and worse. The whole purpose of the trade union movement was to improve such standards. It had succeeded in convincing millions of working-class people not only that their wages and conditions of employment could be improved but that this had in fact taken place as a result of trade union action. What folly it was to proclaim in one sentence that trade unionism was the only instrument at the workers' hand to improve their lot, and in the next sentence to tell them that under capitalism their standards must get worse.

The logic of the Theory of Increasing Misery was that the trade unions were embarking upon a hopeless task. If it was preordained by some undefined power that all their efforts must fail, what was the use of going on? It was a poor answer to argue that without trade unions the rate of decline in the standard of life would be accelerated and would reach abysmal depths. It certainly didn't seem worth while on the part of working people to pay contributions into a trade union which in fact could do little for them. I asked myself what was the power under the capitalist system which had pre-ordained that standards of life must decline? Was it any natural law which prescribed this? I had no belief that employers were in business for the purpose of improving the lot of their workpeople. I knew that all except a comparatively small number of progressive employers believed that by reducing wages greater prosperity could be achieved in some mysterious way because of the economies effected. It was not as clearly seen then as it is today that by reducing wages the employers were destroying the mass markets upon which their success in business depended. The purchasing power of working people must, in the nature of things, provide the greatest outlet for the goods and services which industry and commerce provided. It seemed absurd to think that such matters as the standard of living were in modern communities determined by purely natural laws.

It followed, therefore, that if the standard of life declined it must be the result of man-made decisions. If some men described as financiers or capitalists or employers could decree that wages must fall, so other men calling themselves employees or workers could use the force of their organization to improve their standards.

The decision to go back to the Gold Standard had been made by a group of men on a committee, and later in the Cabinet room. If they could make such a decision, other men could resolve to change it. It all boiled down to a matter of power. If the trade unionists were more effectively organized and stronger in every respect they could use their power industrially and politically to influence the development of events. I feel almost ashamed to describe this state of reasoning that I passed through. It all seems so elementary in 1964. It was less so in 1926. So it was that I did my best to convince working people that they, too, had great power and that this power was not limited to causing industrial dislocation.

The conversations I had had with people before and after the General Strike had shown me that there were many in influential positions who deprecated the events which had led to the stoppage. Why should we not do something to capitalize the goodwill which undoubtedly existed among such people? At first I felt it was hopeless to approach the two main employer organizations. The F.B.I. on one side was regarded by us all as a body dwelling on lofty industrial heights and dictating policy to their member employers. I know now how exaggerated an assumption this was. The National Confederation of Employers' Organizations (now the British Employers' Confederation) on the other hand, struck me as being as belligerent and uncompromising as any of our trade unions. I saw little hope of a constructive result accruing from any approach to them. Yet something must be done to develop contacts whereby the problems facing industry, not only in the sphere of labour relations but in the much wider economic sense, could be discussed.

Slender as the prospects seemed of achieving any material progress by discussion with the central employers' organizations I felt convinced that an attempt must somehow be made. For us to remain in separate camps without communication between us was utterly wrong. Surely there must be some subject of common interest on which we could agree. How could we regard a system of industrial relations as complete without providing in it any means of discussion on those matters which were of concern to the whole of industry? I took soundings, only to find that suspicion and pessimism, and even hostility, were too strongly entrenched to be easily dislodged.

It was just about this time that George Hicks came along to consult me about the address he was to present, as our president, to the forthcoming September 1927 meeting of the T.U.C. at Edinburgh. As in most organizations, I suppose, the theme of a presidential address is always discussed with the officials. At least it was so at the T.U.C., and within my recollection there was no president during my years of office who did not avail himself of the help of myself and other officials in the construction of his speech. George possessed a resilient mind, and we were intimately acquainted with one another's outlook.

So it was natural that I should tell him of my desire to see the establishment of joint central discussions with the F.B.I. and the employers' confederation. George was quick to seize on this and, in conjunction with Tracey and myself, an appropriate section of his address was drafted. After observing that much fuller use could be made of the machinery of joint consultation between employers and employed, he went on to say:

Practically nothing has yet been done to establish effective machinery of joint consultation between the representative organizations entitled to speak for industry as a whole. . . . Such a direct exchange of practical views between representatives of the great organized bodies who have responsibility for the conduct of industry and know its problems at first hand would be of far greater significance than the suggestion which has been made in certain quarters for a spectacular national conference under Government or other auspices to discuss a vague aspiration towards 'industrial peace'. Discussion on these lines would bring both sides face to face with the hard realities of the present economic situation, and might yield useful results in showing how far and upon what terms co-operation is possible in a common endeavour to improve the efficiency of industry and to raise the workers' standard of life.

I fully expected that there would be some response to this proposal from the F.B.I., but nothing was forthcoming until, in October, a statement was issued by the employers' confederation. In this the view was expressed that the problems of industry could best be discussed in the individual industries themselves. Those who drafted this must have known that this was no answer at all to Hicks's address, which referred not to the discussion of wage rates, hours, working conditions, and other matters which were peculiar to individual industries, but to other and broader questions of industrial organization, finance, technique, and management which are common to all industries. I was not slow to expose this statement of the employers as a thinly veiled rejection of the constructive suggestion of the T.U.C.

A similar statement was issued shortly afterwards by the Engineering Employers' Federation. This body was notoriously opposed to the claims of the trade unions in the field of management and policy and was, at the time, probably the most important of the constituents of the employers' confederation. But something was stirring nevertheless.

I had several approaches from people of influence in the industrial world strongly supporting the idea, and I was not surprised when I received a letter, on November 23rd, signed by Alfred Mond and twenty other influential industrialists—four names were added later

—inviting the General Council to a conference to discuss questions related to the entire field of industrial reorganization and industrial relations. I knew most of these people either by direct contact or by repute.

A copy of the letter was circulated to every member of the General Council, and it was decided to accept the invitation. There was considerable opposition in the trade union world, but the General Council members were, with few exceptions, united about entering the discussions. The Communists whipped up all the opposition they could, engaging in their usual stock vituperation. The criticism took the line principally that the Mond Group was not representative, that its personnel was objectionable, that there should be no meetings between the T.U.C. centrally and the employers, that the workers were being committed to policies without being consulted, and that the real objects of the meetings were against the interest of the workers. Cook took an active part and published a pamphlet called *Mond Moonshine*.

At the first conference, which took place at Burlington House, London, on January 12th, Mond gave us examples of what the employers would like to discuss:

> Rationalization and Amalgamation;
> Security and Status of the Workers;
> Housing, Health and Unemployment Insurance;
> Education and Industry;
> Effects of Taxation and Rates;
> Works Councils;
> Financial Participation by the Workers;
> Investigation into the Causes of Disputes; and
> Creation of a Permanent Standing Committee.

Ben Turner, of the wool textile workers, was our chairman. So it was that the meetings were described in the Press as the 'Mond-Turner Conferences', and it is by this name they became widely known. Turner, like Mond, emphasized that we would not trespass on the functions of existing organizations.

Cook made a violent attack on the whole purpose of the project. The employers had evidently been expecting this, and no one moved: there were no interjections from any quarter. He was completely ignored and it was plain that this disconcerted him far more than any reply.

It was decided to continue the conference, and a standing committee was appointed by the General Council, on which I served. It

was not long after this that George Hicks dropped a bombshell on us
by renouncing his support for the conference and allying himself
actively with the opposition. His early Marxian concepts, coupled
with his natural militancy, got the better of his judgement. His
opposition was, however, always genial, moderate, and devoid of the
personal antagonism which characterized so many of the utterances
of others.

An interim joint report was adopted by the full conference in
July 1928, and this was to come up two months later for consideration at the Swansea Congress of the T.U.C. Cook had excelled himself in the meantime by the publication of another pamphlet, *Mond's
Manacles*, published by Workers' Publications Ltd., the publishers
of the *Sunday Worker* and other Communist journals.

Much work was put into the drafting of various documents which
were finally approved by the full Industrial Conference. The secretaries, Milne-Bailey and Conway Davies (for the employers), were
most assiduous, and I thought the documents which emerged were
of high quality.

First a full syllabus was prepared of the various subjects and this,
after consideration, was expanded into a series of resolutions. Agreement was early reached on the subject of recognition of trade unions.
It was recognized that the Trades Union Congress, through its
General Council, was the proper authority to represent all the trade
unions on questions relating to the entire field of reorganization. In
the separate industries the most effective co-operation could best be
obtained through unions recognized by the T.U.C. It was emphasized
that it was most undesirable that any workman should be victimized
on account of legitimate trade union activities. This was especially
important because of the continued discrimination against some trade
unionists for their part in the 1926 stoppage. A valuable recommendation was the establishment of a National Industrial Council representing the T.U.C., the F.B.I., and the employers' confederation.
Its function would be to hold quarterly meetings for general
consultation on the widest questions concerning industry. The
prevention of disputes was thought to be facilitated by the establishment of Joint Conciliation Boards composed of representative
employers and trade unions.

The most debated issue was that concerning rationalization, a
resolution on which had been passed by the World Economic Conference in 1927. The tendency towards a rational organization of
industry and trade, including the grouping of individual units within
an industry into larger ones, was recommended and encouraged. It
was recognized that safeguards would have to be provided against

the displacement of labour. A resolution on the Gold Standard stressed that financial policy was of immense importance to all engaged in industry. With the recollection of 1926 in mind, I had no hesitation in supporting this. It was felt that a full inquiry into the best form of credit policy should be undertaken. This is all too brief a summary of the main work of the conference as expressed in the interim report presented to our conference at Swansea.

As the meeting approached, the howls of protest generated by the Communist Party reached their zenith. Their leaders bawled accusations of treachery against any trade union officers who dared to engage in discussions with the capitalist enemy. Distortion and abuse, their characteristic weapons, were given full play. That many sincere trade unionists were puzzled was evident. Indeed, there were few in the higher ranks of trade unionism who did not share a measure of scepticism as to whether anything really constructive could emanate from these conferences. Despite this, not once in the many meetings addressed did I ever encounter a really hostile audience.

There was doubt in other quarters too. One day Sir Horace Wilson accosted me in his quiet way with the inquiry as to how the conferences were going. 'Very well,' I replied. 'Up to now there has been no serious difficulty.'

Wilson looked thoughtful and remarked, 'I am wondering what will happen when the things get lower down amongst the employers' organizations.'

So was I, but I didn't say so. Wilson knew how adroitly the officers of the employers' bodies could side track any recommendations we had jointly made. Travelling back in his car with Mond from one of the conferences, I had said something to the same effect. I had in mind Sir Allan Smith, the chairman of the Engineering Employers' Federation, an expert in procrastination, whose icy-cold speeches were enough to freeze to death any warm impulses towards progress which his members might feel. And so we had the curious sight of the Communists lined up alongside the die-hard employers in opposition to the proposals for joint discussions between our central organizations.

I was given the job at Swansea of introducing the report. I recalled the history of the developments since the presidential address at Edinburgh and I showed how warily the General Council had acted in entering the conference with Mond and his colleagues, and how it was felt desirable that the talks should be exploratory without binding anyone. I thought it was an achievement to have convinced so important a body of industrialists of the justice of the trade union claim to have a voice in the control and administration of industry. Many of the Council's principal critics had complained in the past at the absence of leadership, but presumably that leadership was only good when it was in the direction the critics favoured. We had decided to enter the discussions, although we knew certainly that the employers did not represent their associations, and could commit nobody. It was illogical, therefore, to accuse the General Council of making pacts with the employers. How could binding pacts be made with people who themselves were unable to bind anyone? The discussions had been friendly and no one entered them as delegates with a limited authority. Finally I cited the normal previous experience of industrial negotiations—how, when trade unions were formed, they found no association of employers with whom they could negotiate. The unions had to meet some groups of employers and negotiate with them until they had banded themselves into an association. Here we had been told that there was no association which could act for the employers as a whole. I thought that the proposal for a National Industrial Council was a justification for believing that a similar development could take place in the sphere of centralized discussions.

The opposition concentrated on the assertion that the General Council had no right to take part in the discussions, that the employers were unrepresentative, and that the proposals which emerged were bad in themselves. Little evidence was presented to support any of these claims, and after a full debate, during which Cook's opposition was disowned by Herbert Smith on behalf of the miners, Ernie Bevin wound up in a forceful speech which clinched matters. The report was adopted by an overwhelming majority.

It was at the Swansea 1928 conference that we first used a rostrum. The normal practice was for a delegate to rise and speak from his place on the floor. Many of them had very powerful voices, but, more often than not, the speaker's back was turned on a considerable portion of his audience. I had only recently been engaged in conferences with the unions on the continent of Europe. I noticed that in all the large gatherings speakers had to address the delegates from a rostrum placed slightly below the level of the platform and inclining to one side of the hall. I thought we would try this, and I got a Swansea joiner to build one. In accordance with the usual practice, members of the General Council visited the hall on the Saturday morning prior to the Monday's opening. I can see Ben Turner, with his beard, pot hat, double-breasted serge coat, and large bow tie, entering the hall side by side with me. As soon as he spotted the rostrum his eyes flashed. Pointing his umbrella at the rostrum he said loudly, 'I am against that, lad, I am against that.' He spoke with such eagerness as to convince me that he wanted to go on record as the first person to object; he seemed to think that this might confer some distinction. Most of the members of the General Council were good-humouredly tolerant of this new freak of their secretary. But, alas, when the conference opened on the Monday morning and the presidential address and the formal reports had been completed, no one came to the rostrum. Speakers seemed to think it was a reflection on their capacity to project their voices.

After the conference had proceeded for some time John Clynes, the president of the National Union of General and Municipal Workers, got up to speak. I whispered to Ben Turner, 'Ask him to come to the rostrum.' Ben gallantly responded, and Clynes, like the good fellow he was, readily assented. When he had finished his speech the next speaker, determined not to follow a bad example, spoke from his place. As luck happened, his seat was not very far from the platform, so that his back was turned to the majority of the delegates. Almost instantly shouts were heard all over the hall, 'Rostrum, rostrum,' and the delegate grudgingly gave way. After this there was little or no hesitation on the part of the others, since when the T.U.C. always used a rostrum. The Labour Party followed suit.

After the Swansea Congress the General Council proceeded with the discussions whilst awaiting the decision of the F.B.I. and the employers' confederation regarding the proposal to establish a National Industrial Council. An interim report was issued on unemployment, which dealt with the long-range proposals as well as with the palliatives which could be applied immediately. It was not until February 1929 that a joint letter from the Confederation and the F.B.I. was received, explaining the limitations of their constitutions and that they were unable to support the proposed National Industrial Council. They suggested that a joint conference should be held with the T.U.C. in the hope that the discussion would help forward a better mutual understanding in industry. This took place in April.

I had a feeling that the F.B.I. were likely to be more forthcoming than the Confederation. The F.B.I. president said they wanted to establish co-operation and consultation between the parties but they had no power to deal with labour questions which had always been the business of the Confederation. This limitation prevented them from becoming part of a National Industrial Council. The Confederation, on the other hand, said they couldn't deal with anything except labour questions, and only those of a general character. So that they too could not join a National Industrial Council. Both bodies declared that they were ready for such consultation with the T.U.C. as their constitutions allowed. Nobody wanted a breakdown, and a joint committee to examine the best methods of consultation and co-operation between the three organizations was suggested. This was accepted by the General Council, and in anticipation that progress would be made, the meetings of the Mond-Turner Conference were suspended.

After meetings later in the year a scheme was evolved whereby the F.B.I. and the Confederation set up an Allocation Committee whose function was to decide whether any particular subject proposed for consideration came within the responsibility of the Confederation or the F.B.I. Meetings would then follow between the parties directly concerned. In view of this arrangement it became unnecessary to continue the Mond-Turner discussions, all three organizations joining in expressing appreciation of the valuable influence of the conference and thanking Lord Melchett's group for contributing to the new scheme. By the early part of 1930 the Allocation Committee was actively in operation. This arrangement was seen to be clumsy and an abortive attempt was made to amalgamate the F.B.I. and the Confederation. I am glad another proposal is on foot to achieve the same end. So at long last joint consultation between the central employers' bodies and the T.U.C. had been established. During the years of my secretaryship of the T.U.C. this association grew into a friendly intimacy and a confident relationship without any sacrifice of principle by any of the parties or any interference with the autonomy of the respective constituents. It also helped to broaden the outlook and sense of perspective of my colleagues and myself and, I hope, of the employers who took part.

I became very friendly with Sir Hugo Hirst (afterwards Lord Hirst) when he was president of the F.B.I.

Hirst was head of the General Electric Company, which he founded. He was extremely shrewd and a great driving force. I remember his telling me one day of the struggle he had with his managerial people to get them to realize the importance of making the initials G.E.C. universally known. I pricked up my ears at this and determined I would do the same for the Trades Union Congress. The heading to our notepaper in those days was quite a mouthful: 'Trades Union Congress General Council'. Gradually I cut this down to 'Trades Union Congress', although, of course, it was quite illogical to talk of the General Council as being the Trades Union Congress. I had the letters 'T.U.C.' displayed on all our literature and envelopes, and wherever we could put it under people's noses.

Forbes Watson (later Sir John Forbes Watson), the director of the employers' confederation, was a dour Scot, tenacious in argument and often unyielding and incapable of compromise. Yet he and I became friendly and we exchanged visits as a matter of course.

At first when he came to see me he was metaphorically looking over his shoulder with a nervous dread that some of his members might spy him. Usually he would, on these occasions, preface his remarks with the words, 'I have come here on my own responsibility, ma office bearers don't know anything about this.' I was rather amused at this, because exactly the same sort of suspicion was incurred at that time by any trade union official, who dared to become intimate with the officials of an employers' organization. All that, I am glad to say, appears to have passed.

Forbes Watson usually had a grumble against the Government. He felt that they were keeping his organization too much at arm's length. He envied the ease with which the T.U.C. was received in Whitehall. I thought to myself: 'This is all wrong. Why should the employers not have the same facilities for making direct representations to the Government?' What is more, I did my best to help this along. I sensed that there would be many occasions upon which it would be as well if the Government knew there was an identity of view between our organizations, although our representations might be made separately. I remember on one occasion when Forbes and I were going to the Ministry of Labour, just as we entered the building he turned to me and said, 'We owe this to you,' referring to the fact that we were both received with such facility.

Trade unionists generally believed that the Government of the day were the henchmen of the employers and that Government officials were invariably more partial to them than to the unions. At one General Council meeting the Ministry of Labour reported the setting up of a committee on some aspect of unemployment insurance. They suggested that the General Council should nominate to this committee Arthur Shaw, a wool textile representative, who was well versed in the subject. At this the Council waxed indignant. 'What right have the Government to tell the Council whom they should nominate? They wouldn't treat the employers this way,' said one member, amidst loud murmurs of assent. I knew how scrupulously careful Government departments were in such matters and how it was their practice to send almost identical letters to the employers' associations and the T.U.C. Much to the astonishment of the Council members, I said, 'I will go and find out.' With that I went to the telephone, spoke to Forbes Watson, found that his Council was

then in session, and that they were objecting just as strongly, with
his full support, to the impudence of the Ministry. 'Who are they to
tell us who we should send?' stormed Forbes. I reported this to the
Council and, amidst a burst of laughter, got them to agree that we
should submit three names to the Ministry. I reported our action to
Forbes Watson and the Confederation took a similar line.

15

Some Communist (and other) Libels

IN MY early days at the T.U.C. I was so imbued with the desire to
see the success of the Revolution in Russia that I was blind to the
disruptive tactics of the Communists in Great Britain. It seemed
to me that there was little difference between the views of the average
Communist and those of the militant trade unionist, such as I still
felt myself to be. Harry Pollitt, the then secretary of the Communist
Party, who proved himself ready to suffer for his principles, once said
to me in the T.U.C. office in Eccleston Square after a discussion on
the possibility of workers' advancement in the economic sphere,
'That sort of reasoning will carry you into the Communist Party.'
I scoffed at this, as I was never at any time tempted to join that
Party.

I did not at first think that the influence of the Communists
inside the trade unions was worth bothering about. It was a nuisance
but not really dangerous. But as time passed, and I saw more clearly
the objects of the Communist Party, I realized that it was a menace
which must be faced. I did not want to discourage militant trade
unionism, but this was different.

Here was a body which was determined to use every available
means to undermine the faith of trade unionists in their elected
officers, and to convert the trade union movement into a revolutionary force no matter what distress this might bring to the average
worker. I knew that their disruptive tactics had split the trade union
movement in several European countries, leaving it weak and its
members confused and disillusioned. They were not concerned primarily with improving the lot of the worker: they scoffed at any such
possibility. Under capitalism, according to them, workers' conditions
must become worse. Standards would fall progressively until, finally,
the whole economic and social system would be destroyed by internal
dissension. Capitalism was tottering to a fall, and anything which
could hurry the progress was all to the good. Any attempt to create
stability represented diabolical treachery against the workers. Good

relations between the unions and the employers were therefore detestable; and the more frequent strikes were, the better for the morale of the worker and the worse for the capitalist system.

Towards the latter part of 1927 I embarked on a series of articles in the *Labour Magazine*. I knew what the response from the Communists would be. Utterly unscrupulous methods, gross misrepresentation and vilification of whatever I attempted to do, were bound to follow my exposure of their activities. The laws of slander and libel were powerless against the subtle and malicious insinuations, accusations, and innuendoes which were the stock-in-trade of the Communist Press and officials. I expected to be attacked by any and every means that could be used to destroy my influence in the trade union movement. I wrote: 'After two years of careful thought, observation, and mature deliberation, I am convinced that it is the duty of all who have a sincere concern for the welfare of the trade union and Labour movement to abandon a negative attitude towards this problem of Communist propaganda, and to make up their minds positively on the question of whether the cancer of Communist influence is to be allowed to grow.' I called these articles 'Democracy or Disruption', and they were embodied and expanded in a pamphlet published by the T.U.C. after the series was completed.

Scarcely had the first article appeared than the hounds were in full cry and I was assailed with all the standardized abuse which the Communists were able to organize. At that time there was in existence a body called the National Minority movement. It was a Communist creation, but it passed for a 'ginger group' within the unions. It was, from its beginning in August 1924, under the auspices of the Red International of Labour Unions, a Russian-dominated organization aiming at the disruption of the free trade unions of all countries. Ostensibly it was out for unity. But it soon shed the disguise and in a manifesto addressed to trade unionists boasted that 'for the first time in the history of the Congress, a definite and organized opposition within the unions faces the existing leadership, and raises unreservedly the banner of revolutionary workers democracy in British trade unionism'. The firm belief that the end always justifies the means made possible strenuous denials that the Minority movement was the Communist Party under another name. Unfortunately R. W. Postgate, then assistant editor of *Lansbury's Weekly*, shattered this virtuous disclaimer with the retort: 'I was still a member of the Communist Party when the launching of the Minority Movement was considered, and I knew perfectly well, as everyone else did, that it was intended as a subsidiary to the Communist Party and had no other purpose whatever.'

The formation of subsidiary bodies to conceal the activities of the Communist Party had become a feature of Communist tactics. Many of these bodies began with laudable objects. They soon departed from them in practice. I followed a good rule: 'Look for the Communist nucleus.' Often it was hard to locate. But surrounded by well-meaning innocents, there it was, plain enough to the eyes of experienced observers.

In my concluding article in the *Labour Magazine* I said, without equivocation, that the Minority movement was affiliated to and financed by the Red International of Labour Unions, which existed for promoting the revolutionary overthrow of the democratic social system by violence. The Minority movement must carry out the orders of the International, which were to capture all the responsible posts in the trade union movement for the Communists.

My *Labour Magazine* articles were written entirely on my own responsibility, but as a result of a resolution moved by the Railway Clerks' Association at the Swansea 1928 meeting of the T.U.C. an official inquiry took place into disruption, the outcome of which was to confirm and strengthen the conclusions I had reached.

In the T.U.C. report, which was published in the following year, it was stated that 'investigation has been made into the activities of the Communist International, the Red International of Labour Unions, the Communist Party of Great Britain, and the National Minority Movement, and leaves no doubt that these organizations deliberately exercise a disruptive influence inside the trade union movement'. It was shown in this inquiry that for years the Communist International and the Red International of Labour Unions had discussed the tactics to be used in relation to the activities of the trade unions, and instructions had been issued to the various organizations in the different countries. The following quotation from the report is of vital importance and provides the key to the fomentation of the industrial unrest from which British industry has suffered so much.

The factory nucleus has been one of the favourite devices for bringing direct Communist influence to bear. The minutes of the meeting of the Commission of the Organization Bureau of the Comintern on the question of the Communist Party of Great Britain contain a very illuminating passage which was printed in *Inprecorr* 5th February, 1925 [Inprecorr—International Press Correspondence, an official Communist publication]:

'The nucleus in the factory should influence all the bodies and organizations in the factory, such as the factory committee, co-operative society, trade union, etc. . . . The nucleus should draw up the agenda and put forward candidates for the official posts in these organizations . . . Experience shows that if we make our plans beforehand, then it is usually easier to get our points carried . . . *The nucleus as such works privately, not officially* . . . The experience of the Russian workers shows that *it would be very useful if the nucleus could make use of an influential non-Party skilled worker who would act in the spirit of the decisions of the nucleus. By this means the source of the ideas could be kept a secret* . . . Leaflets attract the masses to the nucleus. *Of course, here too, care must be taken that the source of the ideas could be kept a secret* . . . We must emphasize that every Communist, no matter where he may be, must carry out the instructions of the Party. He must regard himself as the agent of the Party in the given position.'

The italics are mine and they help to explain how it is that shop stewards and others are used as unwitting instruments by the Communist Party. Such men would indignantly deny that they had any connection with the Communists.

The T.U.C. report finally summarized the position in the following words:

To sum up this survey of the general investigation, it may be said that by evidence taken from Communist reports, speeches, articles, and other documents, we can state confidently that the policy of disruption has been deliberately framed and applied by Communist organizations ever since the establishment of the Third International and the R.I.L.U. Directly and through subsidiary organizations they have set themselves to destroy the trades union movement as it existed in different countries. They have adopted deliberate tactics by which to split the unions, in the hope that the leadership being destroyed they could step in and seize it, in order to use it for their own ends. With this in view the Communist parties and Minority Movements, as well as other organizations, have acted under instructions from Moscow and have worked together, placing this aim above all others.

As I expected, my articles were followed by a campaign of calumny in which everything I did was distorted into some sinister conspiracy against the workers. Whenever I met this sort of thing in the course of a meeting I had no difficulty in disposing of the charges. Generally speaking, the Communists were a poor lot in discussion, their hackneyed phrases and stereotyped vituperation being easily anticipated almost with precision.

At annual meetings of the T.U.C., their language was, of course, much more restrained. Harry Pollitt and Arthur Horner were easily the best of the bunch. They both had good reasoning faculties except when Communist dogma bemused them, and they were inherently decent fellows. Neither of them ever seemed to bear any resentment towards me personally, although I gave their arguments some hard knocks. I could never reconcile this decency with their readiness to condone the savage atrocities which were committed under the Stalinist regime in Russia. Both were 'disciplined' by the Communist Party for deviation from the strict party line. But with the Communist Press it was an entirely different matter. No innuendo, no aspersion, no abuse was too scurrilous to be hurled at me. I stood this for a long time. I had no wish to risk being misunderstood and charged with trying to interfere with the right to free expression by suing them in the courts.

They knew well that it was due largely to my efforts that the trade union movement had awakened to the danger of Communists gaining control of the unions. I was the subject of repeated attacks in the Communist papers, *Worker*, *Worker's Life*, and the *Sunday Worker*, all of which were, I was convinced, subsidized by Russian money. Certainly none of them could subsist on their sales. Advertisement revenue was negligible. The document *Communist Papers* published by the British Government in 1926 had shown that £4,000 was contributed by Moscow to the *Sunday Worker*.

The *Sunday Worker* and the *Worker's Life* were published by Workers' Publications Ltd., and printed by separate companies, the Caledonian Press Ltd. and the Utopia Press respectively, both reputable firms. In late February or early March 1928 articles appeared in the *Sunday Worker* alleging that I was demoralizing the Labour movement by making overtures for peace in industry to the Federation of British Industries, receiving money from the capitalist Press, and that my articles on the Minority movement were written with the assistance of documents collected by Scotland Yard and supplied by Government spies.

The implications in these charges could be so damaging to me that, fantastic as they were, I felt, after consultation with others, that I must do something about them. I first gave the editors of each paper the opportunity to apologize, which they spiritedly refused to do, saying that I was at liberty to send them a denial of anything in their papers which I deemed to be derogatory. They would print the denial. I had no intention of engaging in a controversy on these lines, which

R

I knew would mean that the editors would have the last word. So I decided to take action against Workers' Publications Ltd. and the editors. The printers of both papers publicly apologized, dissociating themselves from any attacks on my honesty or integrity, either personally or in my official capacity. I was not out to make money and I accepted the apologies, although I knew full well that the printers were the only people of substance in a legal sense from whom I could recover damages.

Writs were issued on my behalf, and after the defendants had tried to get the action set aside and had failed, a special general meeting of the shareholders of Workers' Publications Ltd. was held, at which figures were given about the financial position. I received a report of the meeting, from which it appeared that the assets amounted to £7,630 of which goodwill accounted for £5,000, other assets £300, the balance being accounted for by proprietary rights. Liabilities amounted to £9,800. The balance sheet to December 31st, 1927, showed a loss on trade in that year of £3,965 and an accumulated loss of £8,510. A resolution was passed transferring the assets of the company to certain 'friends of the movement' and after struggling along for some time both *Worker's Life* and the *Sunday Worker* eventually ceased publication.

My legal advisers recommended me not to pursue the action further as I would find no substantial person against whom to obtain a judgement. This gave me an insight into the tactics which were likely to be followed in any subsequent attempt I might make to secure legal redress. No doubt those responsible for this skilful manœuvre chortled at the ease with which my efforts had been rendered ineffective.

The attacks on me did not ease off, and although I engaged in a little comradely retaliation now and then, I never attained the expertise in invective which distinguished my Communist critics. On the platform I was able to hold my own, except at one meeting in Hyde Park in June 1936. It was shortly after I had written my book *I Search for Truth in Russia*. In it I made a sincere attempt to depict the conditions there, free from bias or fear. It had been an immediate success, was widely read in this country, and was published in several other countries. It caused some concern to active members of the Labour movement who were prone blindly to regard Russia as the Mecca of civilization.

So it happened that for the only time in my life I was refused a hearing. When I was addressing a Labour demonstration in Hyde Park a small section of the crowd engaged in incessant interruption. Without a microphone I was unable to make any effective retort. So on the advice of the police I had the humiliating experience of having to leave the platform. There was the chanting of slogans in the approved Communist fashion, accompanied by howls of execration, so characteristic of their friendly methods of argument. A few days later it was officially denied on behalf of the Communist Party that they were in any way responsible, and that they regretted the shouting down which had taken place. This disavowal might have been a tactical device, but I was inclined to think it was really meant. Not that I believed the Communists had been converted to a sense of fair play, but they may have deprecated the enthusiasm of their followers on this occasion.

In 1930 the *Daily Worker* was started as the official organ of the Communist Party of Great Britain, as was shown boldly on its title page. Later these words were discreetly dropped, and there was no indication, except from its contents, that the paper had anything to do with the Communist Party. In 1930 Bevin took action for libel against the paper, which was published by the Workers' Press, and was awarded £7,000 damages. I do not think he received any money at all. In fact it was openly boasted in a Communist pamphlet that he had failed to recover the damages, the impression being created that the *Daily Worker* was immune from such worry as a libel action. So it seemed that the Communist Party could with impunity attack anyone without fear of legal consequences. Encouraged by this assumption, they never ceased to indulge their capacity for malicious invention against people who incurred their displeasure.

They suffered a slight reverse in 1937 when I took action against the *Daily Worker*. In May of that year they made statements the purport of which was that I was using my official position in the trade union movement to betray the interests of those who had trusted me, and that I was in league with an organization for spying upon trade unionists and hounding them out of work. There was a body called the Economic League, described by the *Daily Worker* as an enemy of the workers, with which I was accused of being in close co-operation. There was not a vestige of truth in the allegations, and no real attempt at defence was made by the *Daily Worker*.

They agreed to pay me £500 as damages, together with my costs and a full apology in court. The Lord Chief Justice, Lord Hewart, said on July 22nd, 'In my opinion Sir Walter has had the generosity to let these defendants off very lightly.' He commented: 'These were disgraceful libels. I will only add that those who write and publish libels are apt to forget that in this country libels may be a crime and people who perpetuate them may cool their heels sometimes in gaol.' This was a clear indication that it had been open to me to prosecute the defendants for criminal libel. This would have been repugnant to me; I never took that action, although I had plenty of provocation.

I was not yet at the end of my actions against the *Daily Worker*. In September 1939 the British Communist Party had supported the war, as a defence against an attack by the Nazis. Soon afterwards they changed their tune and discovered that it was an 'Imperialist War'. This was the line taken by Russia, which had concluded a treaty with Hitler in August 1939.

Soon after the outbreak of war I took the initiative in the formation of a joint committee between the T.U.C. and the French trade unions (the Confédération Générale du Travail). The purpose was to secure close co-operation between our two trade union movements in order to protect our respective conditions of labour and to strengthen our resolve to prosecute the war against Hitlerism in defence of our democratic way of life.

Early in December 1939 the *Daily Worker* said that seven members of the T.U.C. were going to France on a plane or warship chartered from the Government to confer with trade union leaders there. The real purpose of the meeting, they alleged, was to bring millions of trade unionists behind the war machine of British and French imperialism, and to erect a barrier against the Russian trade unionists. The union leaders were plotting to bring martial law into the British factories, and to introduce the sixty-hour week, compulsory deductions from wages, and the abolition of shop stewards. This theme was developed in subsequent articles, and it was further stated that at a secret session of the Anglo-French Trade Union Committee in Paris we were discussing the transfer of half a million British trade unionists to work in French factories under wage-cutting and speed-up arrangements. It was asserted that the stage was being set for a general introduction of conscription of labour at home and overseas. There was, of course, not the slightest truth in any of the *Daily Worker* assertions. They were malicious inventions intended to discredit all my six colleagues of the General Council and myself and to destroy our influence with British trade unionists.

The seven of us resented these calumnies and unanimously decided to take legal action against Mr. E. R. Pountney, the supposed owner and printer of the *Daily Worker*. Pountney was an official of the Shop Assistants' Union from 1927 to 1928, when he was discharged because of allegations that he was using his position as an official to further the propaganda of the Communist Party.

We knew we would get no money out of our action, but we wanted our accusers to be brought face to face with us in court, where their baseless charges would be fully exposed.

The case was opened on April 29th, 1940, before Mr. Justice Stable. We were represented by Sir William Jowitt (later Earl Jowitt) and Valentine Holmes (later Sir Valentine Holmes) as leading counsel, the defendants relying on D. N. Pritt, K.C. The case lasted six days, and my own evidence and cross-examination, as principal witness for the plaintiffs, occupied many hours. The defendants put forward two witnesses, one of whom, the industrial correspondent of the paper, swore that on the day he was giving evidence he did not know who was the chief sub-editor that day, nor who was the secretary of the Communist Party, nor who was the British representative on the Communist International (the Comintern), nor any of the members of the executive. This patent evasion was underlined by the refusal of Mr. Pountney to go into the witness-box.

Sir William Jowitt, in his concluding address, stated: 'I have never, I think, in my life had a case before in which the defendant Press have published a brochure indicating as plainly as can be that people who get damages against them have to whistle for their money. We have no illusions at all about this case. We realize to the full that in all probability we shall be whistling for our money.'

On this point the judge in his summing up remarked, 'I do not think that any one of the plaintiffs in this case, so far as money is concerned, cares a row of pins how much money I award them or whether they recover the money or whether they do not.' He went on to say that all we were concerned with was to vindicate the honesty of our views and our personal integrity and 'their sense of duty to the constituents who have placed them where they are and have trusted them. In that they have succeeded.' Earlier he had said, 'If I were reflecting in terms of pounds, shillings, and pence what I think of Mr. Pountney in this matter, the damages would be very large indeed.'

Mr. Justice Stable summed up the campaign against us when he said, 'This libel was, in my judgement, inspired in its origin, it was protracted and persistent, it was unscrupulous in its method, it was inspired from abroad, and when brought to the bar of justice, the defendant has not had the courage to go into the witness-box and tell me the truth.'

I was awarded what the judge called nominal damages of £300 and costs and the other plaintiffs from £150 to £200, all with costs. An injunction was also granted restraining the defendant from publishing or distributing any similar libel reflecting on the probity or integrity of any of the plaintiffs.

But we had to whistle for our damages, as was foreseen. Two days after judgement was given it was announced that the *Daily Worker* was now published by the Keable (Press) Ltd., which was registered on March 5th, 1940, a few weeks before our court proceedings commenced, with a nominal capital of £100. W. G. Keable was described as a clerk, from whom it was apparent the damages and costs could not be recovered. Thus, once again, the Communists demonstrated how easy it was to evade the law.

The Communists were not the only source of libels about me. Over ten years before the action I have just described, on a Sunday morning in January 1929, I was relaxing in the comfort of my bed when the telephone rang. A journalist of my acquaintance was inquiring rather excitedly as to whether I had seen the *Sunday Express*.

'No,' I replied.

'Well it has a story about you and Mussolini which I think you ought to know about.'

He then read a startling headline and gave me the salient features of the story.

What I heard was: 'Mussolini Whips Mr. Citrine. T.U.C. Chief fails to "save" Italy. "Audacity".' *The Sunday Express* is able to disclose today an amazing and amusing story of how Mr. Walter M. Citrine, secretary of the Trades Union Congress, and Mr. J. Sassenbach, secretary of the International Federation of Trade Unions, were severely whipped by Mussolini after they had bearded the lion in his den in Rome.'

This sounded so ludicrous that I laughed, but the journalist had not read much further when I realized it was no laughing matter. When the full text was before me I felt I could not let it pass without taking action.

The report was to the effect that Sassenbach and I had gone to Rome to try to persuade Mussolini to allow the Italian trade unionists to join our International Federation. Our task had been to win over Mussolini and return in triumph as the saviours of the trade union movement, since (apart from Russia) Italy was one of the few nations outside the I.F.T.U. We had gone secretly, not even my closest friends being told. We had been granted an interview with Mussolini, but we had found ourselves tongue-tied, presumably by the impressive and rich furnishings of the magnificent room. Sassenbach, according to the story, had spoken for twenty minutes, explaining how the Italian workers would benefit by being allowed to join the international movement.

'Mr. Citrine', said the story, 'was even more eloquent. He spoke for forty-five minutes while the Duce remained strangely silent. And then, when this strange deputation had exhausted all its arguments,

Mussolini rose and said: "Gentlemen, I will tell you a story." '
Apparently it was an even longer one than ours. 'For exactly an hour
and forty minutes Mussolini painted a picture of his career.' Quite a
speech, and an exhausting one when you remember that he was
standing the whole time and, as we did not understand Italian, the
translation must have taken probably another hour and forty minutes.
Poor Mussolini must have felt fatigued, but he had still enough
energy left to finish with: 'I am the dictator of fifty million Italians.
My word is law. I am Prime Minister of this country. I am Minister
of five of the Government departments. And you have the audacity
to come here and ask me delegate the rule of my workpeople to a
handful of political fanatics in Amsterdam? You have wasted your
own time, gentlemen; I don't know whose money. Your visit here
today only emphasizes the incompetence and lack of vision of the
Socialist Party. I AM MUSSOLINI.' The whole of this long passage was
printed in heavy black type.

The story went on: 'There was a dramatic pause. A bell rang, and
the door opened. "Good-day gentlemen!" and two great Socialist
leaders made a rather undignified exit from the Palazzo Chigi.' It
seems that Mussolini, although very emphatic, preserved his good
manners to the end. I secretly admired the vivid imagination of the
writer who could so faithfully report the precise words used in a
private interview. But there was one thing wrong with it: no such
interview had ever taken place.

The following day I issued a press statement to this effect: 'Mr.
Citrine desires to say that the story is absolutely fantastic and is a
malicious invention. He has been to Italy, but for different reasons
from those described in the newspaper. He states that at no time in
his life has he ever seen Mussolini nor any officer or official of the
Fascist Government, and he has had no communication with
them, either written or oral, direct or indirect.' I then issued a writ
for libel against the *Sunday Express*.

The next day the Italian Foreign Office denied the report that
Mussolini had administered a severe rebuke to me. The incident was
stated to have been an invention. The I.F.T.U. also issued a complete
denial from their headquarters in Amsterdam. These denials blew the
story sky-high, but it had been widely published, both at home and
abroad, without reference to the denials. I am sure that if Lord
Beaverbrook had seen the story before publication he would have
jumped on it and on the author as well. At no time did he ever behave
unfairly towards me, and he would never have allowed me to be
traduced in this way.

After the writ had been issued it became evident that a settlement would be reached. The outcome was that I received £500 in damages, the payment of my costs in the action, and a full apology made before Mr. Justice Horridge in the High Court of Justice.

What were the facts of my visit to Italy? For a considerable time the Italian situation had been occupying the attention of the International Federation of Trade Unions. Ever since the institution of the Mussolini regime it had become increasingly difficult for trade unionists and Socialists to exercise any liberty of opinion in Italy. The persecution and the oppression of their opponents by the Fascists became so acute after the murder of Matteotti in 1925 that many of them fled the country and established an office in Paris. From this office an attempt was made to carry on propaganda both inside and outside Italy, the object of which was to give the comrades who remained in Italy the assurance that they were not deserted or forgotten by their Socialist friends abroad, and to disseminate amongst the trade unionists and Socialists of the world at large reliable information concerning the situation in Italy.

A rigid censorship had been established by the Mussolini Government, the effect of which was to all practical intents and purposes to prevent any news passing through the customary journalistic channels, if such news was felt to be in any way detrimental to the interests of the Government. The maintenance of the Paris office was made possible only by the financial assistance given jointly by the Labour and Socialist International and the International Federation of Trade Unions. Both these bodies consistently supported the office, although doubts were entertained by the I.F.T.U. about its utility from a trade union standpoint.

As far back as February 1928 discussion took place at the General Council of the I.F.T.U. as to the advisability of continuing to support the Paris office. The principal reason advanced for withdrawing support was that it was impossible to carry on any useful trade union propaganda within Italy itself.

The matter was further discussed at subsequent meetings of the I.F.T.U. when both the General Council and the executive committee came to the conclusion that some attempt should be made to investigate the truth of the assertions that trade union propaganda was being carried on in Italy by the Paris office.

I advanced the view that, although we had often heard predictions about the early collapse of the Fascist regime, it seemed to me no more likely to collapse than the Communist regime in Russia. I furthermore said that so long as that Fascist regime lasted it seemed to be absurd to suggest that independent trade union work could be continued. I asked the meeting to consider what trade union work really meant. It meant the carrying on of negotiations with employers: it meant some means of improving the conditions of the working people, some method of representing their views and acting for them, whether in negotiations with the employers or with the Government. But in the case of Italy free trade unions could no longer exist. The establishment of the Fascist Syndicate, or trade union, had resulted in the liquidation of the former Italian Confederation of Labour. I recognized that what could be carried on in a subterranean fashion was a sort of propaganda which must necessarily be of a limited character. Propaganda could be utilized in such a way, possibly, as to keep the Italian comrades in touch with the international movement generally, so that if the occasion did arise when the Fascist regime was overthrown or came to an end by any other means, there would be a nucleus to constitute the leadership of a free trade union movement. I said, however, this was a separate question altogether from that of carrying on trade union work as we understood the term.

At another meeting in November 1928 Sassenbach was appointed to visit Italy in the near future and on his return to present a report to the next meeting of the executive. I thought Sassenbach did not feel elated over the task assigned to him. While we were having dinner one of the other representatives suggested that Sassenbach should not go alone. Leipart (Germany) asked me whether I would go. I said I thought I could make it possible. And the others immediately seized upon the suggestion, which was duly adopted the following day.

Sassenbach and I travelled to Milan on December 6th.

We clandestinely met many old trade union officials and rank-and-file members as well as ordinary folk in Milan, Rome, Genoa, and elsewhere. Most of them were living in poverty and danger. We had to arrange our meetings with extreme care and secrecy, for the sake of the physical safety of our friends. We were appalled at the economic and moral conditions we found. We came to the conclusion that there were formidable risks in communication to and from the Paris office.

It was not until late in our visit that we saw signs that our movements were being watched by the police. By that time we had obtained much valuable information and what I think were adequate impressions. In short, our view that Fascism was no good for the workers or for few others was confirmed; but we saw no hope that the Fascist system would collapse except in a disastrous war.

There is no need for me to go into the details of our conversations, which I summarized afterwards in agreement with some of our informants. Our conclusions were:

1. That the Fascist regime was stable and was not likely to be overthrown by revolutionary working-class means.

2. That any change would be gradual, and would be a relaxation in the direction of more freedom.

3. That the working class had no real voice inside the Fascist confederations, and that consequently they could not accept the Fascist corporations as being permanent.

4. That the Paris office was not of much value in the present circumstances.

This is the true story of my visit to Italy.

16

The Webbs

ON JULY 28th, 1927, at the invitation of the Webbs, my wife
and I went to their cottage at Liphook. We talked about the
national strike of May 1926; and at first Sidney Webb was
inclined to agree that such a strike could be immensely helpful,
particularly in securing negotiations. I am not so sure that he
preserved this point of view through the discussion which followed.

I said that for several years I had been working on the assumption
that what was necessary was a highly centralized organization
capable of acting decisively in times of national crisis and mobilizing
the forces of the unions. I realized that strikes would get larger but
fewer; there would be a greater recourse to conciliation and arbitration, and everyone would naturally desire to avoid great conflicts,
and would strain every effort to do so. I believed that this programme
called for more in the way of efficient research departments, publicity,
and negotiating skill.

They agreed with me to a certain extent, but Mrs. Webb said that
she saw no future for the trade union movement in a series of strikes.
She said: 'What you ought to do is to try to conceive the position of
the trade unions in the State and in industrial life. Respect for law
and for the power of the Government will develop so enormously,
what with broadcasting and other new instruments of power, that
your trade unions will simply not be allowed to hold up the life of
the community.' This was said in such a cocksure fashion that it
irritated me, but I suppressed my desire to dissent strongly.

'If the issue is fought out to a conclusion, the Government must
win,' Mrs. Webb continued. 'No Government could possibly allow
its authority to be usurped by the trade unions. Whether you have a
State founded upon democracy, or a "creed" autocracy like they
have in the Soviet system or in Fascism, whatever form of government you may have, I don't believe the people will allow their life to
be interrupted by strikes. You may have small strikes here and there,
but I am satisfied that these big issues will be determined by wages

boards, upon which the trade unions will be represented. You will simply not be allowed the right to strike.'

'Can you show me a single democratic country in the world where repressive legislation has been successful in preventing strikes?' I asked.

'Take Germany, for example,' she replied. 'The railwaymen there are not allowed to strike. The same is true in France.'

'That is a different matter,' I said. 'I was discussing trade union legislation. In Germany, where it has been attempted, it has simply been broken through, and, as you are aware, there is no special law regarding trade unions. They come under the common law. Moreover, you know the policy of the German unions has been not to use the weapon of the big national strike. So that is a bad example.'

Mrs. Webb retorted, 'But my point, Mr. Citrine, is that the State will simply not allow you to do it; and the trade unionists are, after all, only a minority.'

I said: 'This thing you call the State is not a magic body, endowed with unlimited power, as you seem to think. The State is powerful only in so far as it commands the goodwill of the people, and is able to use its forces to enforce its authority. You say that the State will not allow interference with communal life, and you say this irrespective of the justice of that interference or the type of government. Well, I think you are entirely wrong. Presuppose a Socialist State—the education of the masses, the development of a public conscience, with a sense of right and a desire to act fairly; in those circumstances, then, I appreciate that the relinquishing of the right to strike might be an entirely voluntary act. You know that action begets reaction; and if a Government (a Fascist Government for example) prevents the legitimate use of the strike it will cause a degree of resentment which may undermine its own authority. It is easy to say that the State must win if things are fought out; but remember that the State would be very foolish to raise an issue, the determination of which, if it went against the State, might result in a break-up of the ruling class of society. It is all very well to talk about "no negotiation" while a strike is on, but you know perfectly well that negotiations are going on all the time.'

Webb broke in: 'Yes, that is perfectly true, but the State, if things *are* fought out, must win. The whole must be stronger than any part.'

I replied: 'That is a generalization which is only partly true. It is true that the whole is stronger than any part, so long as all the parts are contributing to the one end, but it may be that the stronger part may not contribute to the same end as the State. It is one thing to say that there are only four and a half million trade unionists, but they are organized. If they are determined, and if their cause is just, it by no means follows that only four and a half million people would be found opposing the will of the State.'

Mrs. Webb, with her back to the fire, proclaimed her views to me somewhat in the manner of a schoolmistress dealing with a slow-witted pupil. She repeated that she did not believe in any great future for the trade unions. She could not see any really progressive young men or women rising in the movement, and, although I concurred, I said I did not think that the Trades Union Congress was necessarily the best place to find them.

She was satisfied that the place of trade unions in the State would be to act as the skilled advocates for the workpeople, not only on questions concerning wages and working hours but in almost every aspect of the workers' social activities. She thought the Miners' Federation had not cast up the best types; she believed the consumers' Co-operatives had a better type, probably because of the administrative requirements of the movement. The consumers' Co-operative movement would play a larger part in the State of the future, but the trade unions' part would be limited. Trade unions would require to develop research and publicity; she thought broadcasting should be watched closely, as biassed news was dangerous to the trade union movement. She thought Mrs. Snowden unsuitable to represent the workers on the British Broadcasting Corporation.

I pointed out to her that we were never consulted with regard to Mrs. Snowden's appointment to the B.B.C. board, and she maintained that we should have insisted upon the right of nomination.

'Oh, it would be no use our doing that,' I said, 'and, in any case, the bias of the wireless is only a replica of that of the public Press, which we have experienced for years.'

'Broadcasting is a public service now,' she contended, 'and you should insist upon your right to put the trade union point of view. What you get are the employers' views, thinly disguised; the trade unions should have the right to put their point of view as well.'

'The Government have never admitted our right to nominate for such appointments,' I said.

'But that does not matter,' broke in Sidney Webb, rather testily, 'that is not the point. The point is that you should claim the right.'

'Well, that is about the limit,' I retorted. 'When you were in the Labour Government you appointed the Balfour Committee on Industry and Trade with extensive terms of reference concerning piece-work, collective agreements, and goodness knows what, and you never even consulted us.'

'But we could not consult you any more than we could the employers,' he replied.

'But that is just it!' I said. 'The Conservative Government *had* consulted us on such matters, and they have done so since, in the case of the Electricity Commission. They do not always accept our view, but at least they consult us. You did not even do that.'

'What I did do was to make sure that Labour was adequately and capably represented,' he explained.

'The principle is just the same,' I answered. 'You, as a member of the Labour Government, claimed the right to decide what was proper Labour representation; so does the present Government in regard to Mrs. Snowden.'

'I do not know what we are discussing,' said Webb, and Mrs. Webb proceeded to explain her views with regard to the functions of the unions.

She said: 'It would all be a matter of publicity and research. If the unions' skilled advocacy, based on this, was not so effective as the employers', the unions would lose. There would be no big strikes.'

I was impatient at all this, but I controlled myself as best I could, and went to bed in a none too equable frame of mind.

Just as we were retiring Mrs. Webb turned to me and said, 'Well, we have had a long talk, Mr. Citrine, and although I cannot agree with all you say, I will say this, that the young people are right more often than the old ones.'

The following morning, Sunday, I had scarcely got downstairs before Mrs. Webb tackled me. She said, 'You know, Mr. Citrine, you are the first intellectual who has held such a responsible position in the trade union movement.'

'I have not a very high opinion of the intellectuals,' I said, 'so it is not much of a compliment to me.'

'Oh, I don't mean it in that sense,' she said.

During the day Webb told me in considerable detail, at my request, the story of his boyhood and education. He never went to a university, and his parents had a hard struggle to give him an education. He first went to the City as a very junior clerk; later he sat for the civil service examination and secured third place, being appointed to a position at £100 or so a year. He sat successfully for two subsequent examinations, and was finally appointed to a first-class clerkship in the Colonial Office at a salary of £250 a year. Then he drifted into journalism and lecturing, and left the civil service after ten years.

'Then I met my wife and she had some money; I had saved a

little, and almost as soon as we were married we started on our researches.'

Webb described to me the manner in which he and Mrs. Webb went about collecting data for their books. They started on the historical work, collecting the facts; then, from the facts, they divided their material into subject headings. They took six years to write *The History of Trade Unionism*.

It might be useful to give my personal impressions of the Webbs. At first I was suspicious: I was on the look-out for patronage, but I felt that they tried their best to avoid giving any such impression.

They were a unique couple. They always said 'we'. 'But *we* do not say that,' Webb would retort to me in the course of argument, and after I had heard this once or twice I was compelled to say, 'I don't know what *you* say, but I know what Mrs. Webb was saying,' and sought to draw a distinction between them. Often there was a considerable difference in their points of view. As soon as they detected this they instinctively tried to resolve it into one opinion.

Mrs. Webb seemed to me to have the dominant mind of the two. She was quicker and more picturesque in her expression, but, her secretary told me, not so exact in her language. She seemed to take good care of Webb in the manner of the benevolent autocrat.

'My wife won't let me have any breakfast,' he said to me rather apologetically.

Or again, Mrs. Webb would go up to him and say, 'You must come out.'

'Oh, but I do not want to go out,' Webb would retort from the depths of his easy chair, but it made no difference. Out he went.

Neither of them ate breakfast. The household seemed to be worked on the stop-watch system as far as rising, meals, and going to bed was concerned. Everything was strangely quiet and rather lifeless. Yet in their curious way I suppose they did try to make people welcome.

We argued the whole weekend. It was obvious that they had invited me not out of idle curiosity but to find out whether I had any new ideas about trade unionism or anything else. I didn't resent this in the least—I expected it: I knew about their habit of getting people along and pumping them dry. I could not at any time discern any depth of feeling in them, either for trade unionism or for the Labour movement. Their conversation betrayed not a shade of animated conviction—and yet I knew that Sidney, in particular, had done endless work behind the scenes to give coherence and precision to Labour policy. His book *Industrial Democracy* had stood me in good

stead. He and Mrs. Webb had written, in their history of trade unionism, a monumental work which had almost become a bible for keen
trade unionists. That they were deeply attached to each other I had
no doubt. Yet I felt that they were looking at me in much the same
way as an entomologist might peer at a new species of butterfly
safely impaled on a pin. They didn't appear to have any uncontrol-
lable slovenliness of mind, for which they had a supreme contempt.
They appeared to be trying desperately to preserve a scientific
attitude throughout our conversation, despite my occasional deliberate provocation. Ben Tillett called them 'the cobwebbs'. Ben said
that when they married they decided to produce blue books and
memoranda instead of children. Sandy, their Aberdeen terrier,
appeared to absorb such affection as they had to spare. When we
went out for our compulsory walk they were desperately concerned
for his safety when a frisky mongrel came along to exchange sniffs
with him.

What I have written gives a fairly accurate indication of my first
impressions of the Webbs. They were to become good friends of
mine in the years that followed, and I had several useful chats with
them. But what did they think of me and my views? I never had the
benefit of knowing Sidney's opinion, but Beatrice has given her
account of our first meeting in her diary, reproduced here by the
courtesy of the Passfield Trustees. She says:

'Walter Citrine, the general secretary of the Trades Union
Congress, and his wife, spent the weekend here. An electrical engineer
by training, becoming in early manhood a national official of his union
and secretary of the Liverpool Engineering Federation, he arrived
four years ago as the assistant secretary at 32 Eccleston Square, and
succeeded Fred Bramley as general secretary last year.

'Under forty years of age, tall, broad-shouldered, with the manners
and clothes and way of speaking of a superior bank clerk; black hair
growing low on his forehead, large pointed ears, bright grey eyes set
close together, big nose, long chin, and tiny, rather "pretty" mouth,
it is difficult to say whether or not he is good-looking. In profile he
is; in full face he is not. When arguing, his features twist themselves
up and he becomes positively ugly. By temperament and habit of
life, Citrine is an intellectual of a scientific type. He is sedentary,
takes too little exercise for his health; he is assiduous, always improving himself by reading and writing and working at his job
unremittingly—he has no "silly pleasures".

'He is a non-smoker, non-drinker, small, slow eater, takes a
daily cold bath, sleeps with his windows open—altogether a hygienic
puritan in his daily life. I think he is very ambitious—expects too

much relative to his faculties. He keeps a notebook and puts down the points made in conversations. He keeps a diary in shorthand describing events as they occur, and he likes to talk about all these mental processes. He has the integrity and loyalty characteristic of the better type of British mechanic. I think he is too public-spirited and too intent on real power to go the way of Frank Hodges and become a hanger-on of the directors of capitalist industry. His pitfall will be personal vanity and the sort of conceit which arises from continuous association with uneducated and unself-controlled official superiors. Citrine is contemptuous—and largely justifiably contemptuous—of the members of his General Council and the Congress, and, like all the other "brain" workers who were in the inner circle during 1926, he gives a picture of the deplorable lack of grip, alike of intellect and character, among those who led the millions of trade unionists in their use of the General Strike whilst the leaders of the miners approach, according to his estimate, mental deficiency. And yet he believes in the future of trade unions as a great controlling force through the weapon of the National Strike or sympathetic strike, or rather the threat of it.

'Lying full length on the window-seat in a free and easy way with his boots on my best Indian shawl, he slightly annoyed me. But he has character, industry, and intellect. He is the first intellectual to be at the centre of the trade union movement. Will he sicken of the job? He means to reorganize the trade union movement on some thought-out model and to give it a definite and consistent "economic" policy which will include political questions such as foreign affairs. (He has, by the way, no use for G. D. H. Cole; he believes in Laski.) He assumes the eventual separation of the political party from the trade union movement, and would, I think, welcome it. He does not like paying for a policy he doesn't control—he is distinctly jealous and resentful of the Parliamentary Labour Party, still more of the I.L.P.

'In spite of his contempt for the leaders of the trade union movement, he altogether overestimates the solidarity and the economic power of British trade unionism. But when we come to write our book on Twentieth Century Trades Unionism—if we ever get time—Citrine will be useful to us, and what he will make of the trade union movement during the next ten years arouses my curiosity.'

Margaret I. Cole, the widow of G. D. H. Cole, who edited the diaries of Beatrice Webb (and whom I thank together with her publishers, Messrs. Longmans, for permission to reproduce these passages), adds a footnote, as follows:

'Lord Citrine, in giving permission for the publication of this remarkable comment, writes:

S

' ". . . I laughed heartily at the picture of myself lying on the window-seat with my boots on her best shawl. I really don't recall it, but I suppose I must have done so perfectly unconsciously. She says nothing about meeting me when I was halfway down the stairs on Sunday morning and arguing with me so intensely whilst we were at the table that I literally had no breakfast." He adds: "I most certainly cannot recall anything I ever said to give her the impression that I was contemptuous of the members of the General Council." '

Towards the end of 1929 I was feeling badly rundown. I had never taken proper holidays, and even when I had a week off I took trade union documents with me. I know now the folly of this, but it seemed a natural thing to do. During the winter I seemed to lose my energy and I went to the doctor who had formerly attended Fred Bramley. So seriously did he regard my health that with my consent he saw the president and vice-president of the General Council, and then met the whole Council. I was ill in bed at the time when Jack Beard and Ben Tillett called to see me. They told me that the General Council had ordered that I must take a sea voyage, accompanied by my wife.

We went round the world, visiting in turn South Africa, Australia, New Zealand; thence, by way of Vancouver, we went across Canada and returned to England by steamer from New York. I was deeply conscious of the debt of goodwill I owed to the General Council for making this adventure possible.

We were away a little over five months and through the whole of the period I kept a full diary in shorthand. I suppose the doctor, had he known of this, would have thought it was silly. But I wanted to get as much down as I could. As I filled up my notebook I sent it home, knowing that it would be faithfully transcribed to await my return. Subsequently I had these notes bound and suitably illustrated with photographs and pictures I had collected on the tour.

We left Liverpool in early 1930 on the *Ascanius*, a 10,000-ton vessel of the Blue Funnel Line. It is impossible here to convey all we saw and heard, but some incidents on our voyage from New Zealand to Vancouver persist in the memory.

After a stay in Auckland, New Zealand's biggest city, we boarded the *Aorangi*, a well-equipped steamer of some 17,000 tons, for our trip to Vancouver. We travelled second class, but the accommodation was excellent and the food ample and good. Our cabin was on the promenade deck and, on arriving at Suva, in Fiji, we awakened to find the woolly head of a native sticking through the porthole of our cabin. It was not until some time later that my wife discovered that a pair of her silk stockings had disappeared.

We went ashore, declining a taxi, noting that the Fijians were, for the most part, big-bodied, woolly-headed, somewhat flat-nosed, with gay laughing faces. They appeared to be as playful as children.

We strolled to Government House and came across a gang of natives supposedly working on a thatched roof. One of them gave a loud yell as we approached and I had a disturbing vision of head hunters until I saw the cause of the yell. One fellow had discovered a leak in the hose that the Indian gardeners were using and, in an instant, several of his companions were cutting capers in the spray from the improvised shower-bath. We learned that all these men were prisoners, one of them a murderer. He was not particularly vindictive, but in a burst of temper he had sliced off his wife's head. That was understandable, of course.

The Governor was absent, undergoing an operation in Sydney, but we were courteously received by his deputy, who put a car at our disposal, with a chauffeur, an Indian who spoke excellent English.

We had a drive round the island and came across a native village. The Fijians came crowding out of their huts, the children touching our hands, and some of them offering us a single wild flower as evidence of their friendliness. One of the men could speak English and asked if he could guide us. He took us to one of the huts. It was about twenty feet long and fifteen feet wide. There were no open windows, the only air available coming through the doorway, which was less than four feet high. Near the entrance there was an old woman with two young children squatting by her. Her face was wrinkled with age, and she muttered something in her own language as we came in. I felt a bit of an intruder, but the guide, without compunction, pushed his way in. The other occupants seemed to expect it and no resentment was expressed. A few feet away a young woman was lying face downwards fast asleep, whilst in another corner, screened into a square by a fine white gauze, was a young mother with her three-week-old child.

'This is where we do our cooking,' said the guide, and showed us a fire in another corner, on which were several large, round pots without any lids. He showed us that they used tufts of grass for this purpose, and said something about 'if you take this off the food is broken'. Evidently he meant spoilt.

'But where does the smoke go?' I asked.

'Oh, we want the smoke,' he said, rather amazed at my question, as though it was wasteful to allow the smoke to escape. 'The smoke, he goes up and makes the roof—how do you call it—good.'

'How many families are living here?'

'Twelve altogether.'

After this he described the trees to us and then volunteered: 'We don't like work here—work is no good. We have everything we want. The trees bring the food and we have plenty to eat.'

I thought to myself, 'After all, why should they work, if they are satisfied with this form of life?' I could not see any cattle or pigs and I don't know how they managed for meat. Possibly they caught it running wild on the hills.

'All labour is very cheap here,' he said.

Then we drove off to the ship, arriving a few minutes before sailing time. There were literally hundreds of natives there to see the vessel depart. Some of the younger ones were tumbling in confused heaps over pennies which passengers had thrown down.

As the ship steamed away, I thought to myself: 'Well, Sydney boasts of its harbour. It is certainly beautiful. Auckland harbour is fine, and Wellington is not to be sneered at. But this: well, this is Nature's Paradise.'

From Fiji we went to Honolulu and saw the famous Waikiki Beach of black sand. I heard myself catalogued as a 'Limey', and crept away utterly crushed in spirit because we were not 100 per cent free-born Americans.

At noon the next day the *Aorangi* moved off from the quay, followed for a little way by the swimmers who had been diving for sixpences. We left Honolulu with an impression of a beautiful island which had become rather too civilized.

I went into the first-class lounge one afternoon at the request of a friend and while we were talking I heard him say, 'Oh, here is that confounded judge again.' He told me, rapidly, that this man was an American judge at Honolulu, who got drunk every day on the ship. It appeared that a lady sitting at the same table, with whom we were chatting, had tried to reclaim him, but had failed. A few seconds later the judge came up. He was tall and bent, and had a weak face.

'I thought you wouldn't speak to me after last night,' he said to the lady, who tried to smile the remark away. 'You know I tried to show them how to wear the Scotch kilt. I put some damn' thing or other over my trousers, and I know they had a hard job to prevent me taking my clothes off.'

I looked at him closely, and there was little doubt that he was quite drunk even then. It was six o'clock in the evening.

'Have you a clear recollection of all this?' I asked him.

'Well, it is a little bit mixed up,' he explained in the laborious manner of a drunken man, 'but I guess I can remember it, all right.'

Then, turning to the lady again, he said: 'I promised you I wouldn't drink anything at all—and I haven't. At least I have only had five drinks.'

'You know,' he said, this time addressing himself to my friend, a Mr. Amory, a West of England textile manufacturer, 'my doctor told me I mustn't play bridge, or dance, or do anything like that. He said I could get drunk as often as I liked. It would do me good.'

'Your doctor will be pleased, then,' observed Amory sarcastically.

With that he arose and we escaped. I thought it was tragic that this man who was chosen to administer the law, including prohibition, which was then in force, should make such an exhibition of himself.

This Mr. Amory, by the way, was the man who later became Heathcoat Amory, Chancellor of the Exchequer. He is now Viscount Amory and High Commissioner to Canada.

In Vancouver we were taken for a motor-car drive by the newly appointed Chief of Police, a Mr. Bingham. He had come to Vancouver after completing his full service in the London police. He told me about some startling experiences he had had with some gangsters who had tried to intimidate him.

Afterwards I casually mentioned that I had been in Russia in 1925. I recounted the incident of Peters, the head of Cheka, who had come to see me the first night I was there. Peters had told me his version of the Sidney Street affair, and I told this to Bingham. He said that he, too, had been involved in the Sidney Street affair, and he confirmed that Peters was not there at all, nor was he involved in the murder which preceded it. Bingham said the talk about 'Peter the Painter' was a public myth.

'Peters told me he was a garment worker in Whitechapel,' I explained.

'Well, I was twenty-two years in that district,' said Bingham, 'and if I know Mr. Peters at all he was working for the Government a good time.'

'What do you mean?' I asked. 'As a member of the Secret Service?'

'No, in gaol,' he remarked, laughing.

I explained that when I met Peters in Russia I had no idea he was the head of the Cheka. I suppose he had come to look me over, whereas I thought it was just a friendly call from a mild, inoffensive person. I didn't know then that he was the man who was responsible for the deaths of thousands of people.

We travelled across the North American continent via Winnipeg,

Chicago, Toronto, Ottawa, Montreal, Quebec, Boston, and New York.

After a brief call at Washington—to my eyes the most European-looking city we had seen on this continent—we returned to New York and then to England on the Cunard liner *Aquitania*.

17

Fall of the Labour Government

SOON after the Labour Government took office in 1929 signs of a world trade depression appeared. Unemployment had been persistent right throughout the post-war period, and from 1924 it had averaged over 1,250,000. By January 1931 there were over 2,500,000 people out of work, and by July the figure was 2,750,000, and was still rising. Germany had approximately twice as many, and unemployment in the United States was the highest in the world. The cost of unemployment benefit in Britain had risen steeply with the rise in unemployment, and there seemed to be no real prospects of a trade recovery. The Trades Union Congress firmly believed that the crisis was basically due to the deflation policy which had been pursued since 1925.

With the return to the Gold Standard the Government had appointed a Committee on Finance and Industry with Lord Macmillan as its chairman and Ernest Bevin as one of its members. The Trades Union Congress submitted evidence, in which it showed that the succession of wage reductions had aggravated the situation. This was contrary to the views of the organized employers who had put forward three points of policy: (1) a reduction in unemployment benefit, (2) a reduction in the charges for social services, and (3) a reduction in the wages of public employees. They had for years tried to drive a wedge between the so-called sheltered trades (those which catered solely for the home market) and the unsheltered trades which were concerned mainly with exports.

The bank failures in Austria and Germany had aroused fears of financial instability in London and gold was leaving the country at an excessive rate. The nervousness shown on the continent of Europe and elsewhere was mainly due to the fact that the London financial houses had borrowed a great deal from France and the U.S.A. They had already lent a large proportion of that money to Germany and the Central European countries. It was feared that because of these commitments the London houses could not meet their liabilities. Hence the drain on the gold reserves of the Bank of England.

The Government had appointed another committee, this time headed by Sir George May, who was formerly the secretary of the Prudential Assurance Company. Their job was to inquire into the country's national expenditure. Their report was published on the day that Parliament adjourned. It painted an alarmist picture of the budgetary position and forecast a deficit of £120,000,000 for the year 1932–3. This report naturally intensified the fears already existing on the continent and elsewhere about Britain's financial stability. The outflow of gold from London was accelerated. The British Press were clamouring for drastic economy in national expenditure and this too added to the general disquiet.

Ramsay MacDonald came dashing back from Lossiemouth and hastily called a meeting of his Cabinet. This was followed by an announcement that the Budget would be balanced and that the Cabinet were preparing a scheme of economies and additional taxation to make up the Budget deficiency. Rumours began to circulate that the Government was trying to raise loans in the U.S.A. and France and that the American bankers were insisting upon a reduction in unemployment benefit as a condition of any loan. Naturally the bankers were regarded by the Labour movement as the villains of the piece who were trying to bring down the Labour Government by their wicked financial devices. They were alleged to be dictating to the Government about the measures it must take.

It was at this stage that I was asked whether I would meet privately some of the bankers who had been discussing the situation with the Government. I at once consented, and one evening in the Travellers' Club in Pall Mall I met Edward Peacock (later Sir Edward Peacock) and one of his fellow directors of the Bank of England. Peacock showed himself very sensitive to the charges which were being made against the bankers, and he repeatedly stated that the Bank of England (which was not then nationalized) had not attempted in any way to influence the Government's policy. They had seen the Chancellor of the Exchequer, Philip Snowden, privately and had asked him the straightforward question: 'Does the Government wish to remain on the Gold Standard? If so, certain steps must be taken to secure economies in public expenditure. If you do not want to stay on the Gold Standard, tell us now, and we shall know what to do.' Snowden had replied without any hesitation, and apparently without consulting anyone at that stage, that of course we must stay on the Gold Standard. Peacock told me that he was informed later that Snowden had notified Ramsay MacDonald of his answer and that

Ramsay fully agreed with him. As far as I could make out from subsequent conversations, no other members of the Cabinet were asked anything about the matter. Peacock said that on the very day we were having our talk over £11,000,000 in gold went out of England, and that this drain could not go on without devouring our stock of gold. I am a fairly good judge of character, and I believed Peacock's statement. It was afterwards publicly stated that in the two weeks ending June 29th the Bank of England had to export £32,000,000 of gold.

At this point I received a message from Arthur Henderson that the Cabinet committee which was considering the report of the Committee on National Expenditure was anxious to consult the T.U.C. General Council and the Labour Party executive on the situation which was regarded as extremely serious.

On August 20th, 1931, a joint meeting of the General Council and the Executive of the Labour Party was held to discuss the financial situation. This meeting had been called at the request of the Prime Minister, who wanted to acquaint both bodies with the seriousness of the crisis. I thought this was all to the good, as I had tried hard on several occasions to induce MacDonald to adopt some organized method whereby the Trades Union Congress could learn at first hand from time to time what was going on. It was the absence of any such arrangement which caused a deterioration in the relations between the Government and the Trades Union Congress in 1924. This in turn had led directly to the crisis over the treaty with Soviet Russia which ultimately brought down the Government. So I was all for such a meeting and I had no hesitation whatever in summoning the full Council to meet the sub-committee the Cabinet had appointed, consisting of the Prime Minister, Philip Snowden, J. H. Thomas, Arthur Henderson, and Willie Graham. My dealings with Graham had shown him to be much clearer-headed on financial subjects than Snowden, whom I found to be unexpectedly pompous, rigid, devoid of imagination, and frigidly orthodox. He had acquired the reputation of being the financial expert of the Labour movement. He could throw figures about in the millions on the platform with the best, but I found that at close quarters he was by no means so capable.

We met the Cabinet sub-committee at Transport House. MacDonald led off with what purported to be a review of the financial position by stating that a great gap would be shown in the next year's budget and there would be something in the nature of a financial panic. The bottom would be knocked out of prices in the extractive industries, and unless the outward drain of gold could be arrested unemployment might rise to over 5,000,000. He continually emphasized that no decisions had been reached by the Cabinet and spoke merely of subjects which the Government had at one time and another had before them. It was difficult for us to know exactly what the Government had in mind.

He urged us to remember that when we were considering the matter there was no change of policy on the part of the Government, and that if anything had to be suspended it would be replaced as soon as the Government were in a position to do so. There was no abandoning of principles or programmes, but there was a bowing to the necessities of the case. Beyond this he said practically nothing more than we had already learned from the Press.

Few questions were asked, the General Council having decided at a preliminary meeting that we should not become involved in questions or discussions at that stage, and that Arthur Hayday (chairman) and I should act as the sole spokesmen.

I pointed out that we had been summoned without having a vestige of information of any kind other than what had appeared in the newspapers. The Council felt that the maximum it could be expected to do was to hear from the Ministers the grounds upon which they desired to meet the Council and ascertain from them something of a more specific character than they had so far been given. If this was an attempt at consultation it could only achieve its purpose by the Government placing the Council unreservedly in possession of information on which the Cabinet was to make its decision. We knew that there were certain details which it would be extremely difficult to disclose, but merely to tell the Council that the Government had been considering the serious financial situation and to say that there were three possible ways in which remedies might be sought—by economies, taxation, and new revenues—was to tell the Council no more than had already appeared in leading articles of many newspapers. I concluded by saying that unless there were some more specific statements forthcoming it would be impossible for the General Council to express any opinion, but that the fact of their not doing so must not be taken by implication or by inference as supporting any future action taken by the Cabinet.

Snowden said that every member of the Government must appreciate the reasonableness of the position I had put. He went on: 'The real reason why you are asked to meet us is that the two executives may be put into possession of the causes of the present financial position, and at the same time see how we can come to agreement on proposals which have been made.' He said the outlook was much worse than had been disclosed in the May Report which had caused such a panic. The deficit would be higher than £120,000,000 and it could not be met by taxation alone. If there was an increase in the number of unemployed in the following year the already immense drain on the Exchequer would be much higher. The Government had been borrowing at the rate of £50,000,000 per year, and without any change in the situation they would have to borrow £60,000,000 in the next year. Then he said: 'We have to come to the end of borrowing, and any failure on the part of the insurance system to make itself self-supporting, any failure which has hitherto been met by borrowing will have to be met out of current revenue.' The Government had considered an increase in contributions for unemployment benefit, to be paid by the employers, the workers, and the Treasury in equal proportions. They had also discussed limiting payments under the Unemployment Insurance Scheme to twenty-six weeks in a year. These were the only two points on which they had taken a decision. They had not made any reduction in regard to benefit.

Snowden spoke of the difficulties of carrying out the recommendations of the May Committee about teachers' salaries. The majority of that committee had proposed a reduction of 20 per cent whilst the minority report was for 12½ per cent. There would be economy of expenditure on new roads and the Government might have to face the recommendations of the May Committee in regard to the fighting services. These should not be made wholly at the expense of the men in the services. Some reduction would have to take place in the pay of the police. He then went on to refer to the Unemployment Grants Committee, the Board of Agriculture, and other departmental economies, but emphasized that no reduction was contemplated in the health services. Cabinet Ministers would offer a reduction of 20 per cent in their salaries, but only those Ministers in receipt of over £5,000 a year. It was anticipated that some modest reduction would take place in the salaries of Members of Parliament. Civil servants were already affected by the cost-of-living sliding scale. All the reductions they had discussed would not amount to more than half of the total Budget deficit, so the rest would have to be met by increased taxation. Naturally he could not disclose what measures would be taken in that connection.

At the conclusion of Snowden's speech a few questions were asked, one being whether there were any grounds for the statements in the Press that the proposals made by bankers were of a conditional character. Snowden replied by saying that the only thing the bankers had done was to represent to the Government the seriousness of the international financial position, and to point out that it was in a large measure due to loss of confidence abroad. I then asked whether the Cabinet intended to come to a speedy decision, and what was the approximate time the General Council could be given for the submission of its views. Ramsay MacDonald replied that a decision must come very soon because of the international situation.

The Prime Minister added: 'Before you come to your conclusions if there is any particular question you want to get the mind of the Cabinet committee upon we will be glad to help you as far as possible, so that when you consider the matter you will do it with the knowledge of what is in the mind of the Cabinet committee.' Snowden added that he had not indicated to representatives of any other political parties—with whom he had had some discussions—the sources of new taxation he had in mind.

Bevin protested at the way in which the Prime Minister had dramatized the position. He had given interviews of the most dramatic character to the *Daily Mail*. He complained that the *Manchester Guardian* and *The Times* were more fully informed of the Chancellor's statement than was the *Daily Herald*.

There was little more to be said at this stage, so the General Council adjourned to their own room. The Labour Party executive held a separate meeting at the same time in another part of the building.

We had an animated discussion, during which not one of the members of the General Council spoke in favour of the Cabinet's proposals. A resolution was passed expressing opposition to any worsening of the position of the unemployed. We had put forward evidence to the Gregory Commission which had been inquiring into the question, the effect of which would have been to make the fund self-supporting.

We asked the Cabinet to look at our proposals carefully. They embodied a graduated levy upon all sections of the community in proportion to ability to pay. In a truly national scheme there should, in our opinion, be equality of sacrifice, particularly in times of crisis. Our next expedient was a temporary suspension of the Sinking Fund. We didn't see the necessity of putting by £50,000,000 for extra payment of debts over and above our contractual obligations.

Next we suggested a tax on all fixed-interest-bearing securities, on the grounds that with the fall in prices the value of these securities had relatively risen.

I argued strongly for the institution of a revenue tariff. I thought that anything which would help to arrest the fall in the price level was a move in the right direction. The opinion of the General Council was evenly balanced, and it was decided to refer this issue to our forthcoming Congress at Bristol which was due about a fortnight later. I informed Jim Middleton, the acting secretary of the Labour Party, of our decision and he in turn told me that the Labour Executive had decided to leave the matter to the Cabinet. I gathered that several Ministers had been present during this discussion.

The General Council had appointed five members to convey our decision to the Cabinet sub-committee and we met them at Downing Street late that night.

As we walked into the room I told Bevin that if the discussion made it opportune I was going to declare myself in favour of a revenue tariff. Bevin, who agreed with this proposal, seemed disconcerted, and whispered in my ear, 'Don't commit yourself.' I would have been ready to take the risk of exceeding our instructions and I am sure I could have carried the General Council with me, but Bevin was more cautious. He often had doubts like that, sometimes even when a proposal seemed so straightforward that I felt it could have been assented to without demur. He would sometimes say, 'I would like to sleep on it.' Usually I heard no more about it. So it was that in informing the Cabinet sub-committee of our decisions I confined myself to telling them the Council had deferred a conclusion on a revenue tariff.

I opened my statement to the Ministers by telling them that we had reluctantly come to the conclusion that we could not possibly agree to the Government's proposals. They seemed to us to be a continuance of deflation which had already proved disastrous and could not possibly furnish a real solution to the problem the Government had to face. I supported this by telling them that in regard to proposed salary reductions the Macmillan Committee had accepted the view of the General Council that a policy of adjusting wages to the fall in prices provided no remedy for the trade depression from which the country was suffering. We had no intention of changing our view. I then put forward the positive proposals which I have mentioned earlier.

After listening to us Snowden said that apparently the General Council were opposing all the economies which had been suggested. I retorted that there were other points which we had not touched upon, such as the proposed reduction in Ministers' salaries. Snowden was the only one who said anything on the Government side. He was not at all dictatorial as I had sometimes seen him, but was evidently oppressed by the weight of his responsibilities. He gravely told us that if sterling went the whole international financial structure would collapse, and that there would be no comparison between the present depression and the chaos and ruin that would then follow. There would be a complete industrial collapse and millions more would become unemployed. He mentioned 10,000,000. On our specific proposals he said practically nothing, neither on the Sinking Fund, nor on the revenue tariff nor on the taxation of fixed securities. It was little more than a repetition of the afternoon's proceedings.

We parted at 10.30 p.m. in more senses than one. I never had contact with Snowden again.

Next day I sent MacDonald the General Council's proposals in writing; and his answer, although friendly, was evidently saddened by the thought that we were overlooking dread realities which he must face. I have no doubt that his fears, like those of Snowden, were deeply felt. He believed that if we left the Gold Standard we could not escape catastrophe. *The Times* in a leading article written, so he told me, by their labour correspondent, Radcliffe, prophesied that the value of the £ sterling would fall to 10s. and unemployment would soar. Yet on 21st September Britain went off the Gold Standard by the decision of Parliament. So did several other countries. The expected disaster did not happen.

Meantime our Congress at Bristol had taken place. Ramsay MacDonald, accompanied by twelve Labour Members (I called them the 'Twelve Apostles'), had joined the Liberals and Tories in a National Government. Snowden had introduced an emergency Budget, cutting down unemployment benefit by 10 per cent, increasing contributions, and limiting benefit to twenty-six weeks. He also instituted a means test for those unemployed who claimed transitional grants.

The Labour Party had gone into action as the official Opposition and the trade union movement was rendering them full support. A very trying period from the point of view of personal relations followed. I felt as bitter as most people but somehow I could not bring myself to dislike MacDonald and Jimmy Thomas, who, although I thought them completely mistaken, were, I was sure, sincere.

A General Election soon followed, which was characterized by the way in which Snowden in a broadcast speech derided his former Labour colleagues with incredible venom. He frightened the public into believing that their deposits in the Post Office Savings Bank would be rendered unsafe if a Labour Government was returned and predicted a national calamity. He had formerly extolled Labour's policy for the control of national finance; now he asserted blatantly that if Labour was returned to power the banks would be placed under the control of the T.U.C.

MacDonald was most restrained. He put forward no programme but appealed for a free hand, a doctor's mandate. At the same time there were indications of mistrust amongst the parties forming the

National Government. Sir John Simon said it would be a disaster if after the General Election MacDonald found himself surrounded by a cohort of Tories. That was exactly what happened, the Tories obtaining 471 seats in the new Parliament while Labour all told had fifty-one. The National Government found itself powerless to cope with the increase in unemployment, and by the end of 1932, 3,000,000 people were out of work. Signs of strain soon showed themselves within the Government. Within a year of its formation several Ministers had resigned, Snowden amongst them. He accused the Government of breaking its pledges and pursuing the protectionist policy of the Conservative Party, which he detested. Herbert Samuel said that he and several other Ministers had wanted to resign after three months of the National Government, but they had been strongly urged to continue, which they did until October 1932. He described the National Government as something like a defective wireless set which gave two programmes at the same time.

Poor MacDonald. He could see what was going on, and how power was steadily slipping from him, and that he and his small band of supporters in the Government were powerless to restrain their Tory colleagues. It was indeed a tragic position for him, but despite it all he carried on until June 1935, when he relinquished the premiership to Baldwin.

Deep resentment was felt against him and charges of treachery were frequent. Throughout the Labour movement he was bitterly criticized for his action in 1931, and I fully shared the prevailing sentiments towards him. But the Trades Union Congress has never made likes or dislikes of a particular Prime Minister a cardinal feature of its relations with the Government of the day, and it sent me to meet MacDonald on many occasions on its business. MacDonald, so I had been told, was a man who could never forgive an injury, but throughout this period I never detected the bitterness he must have felt. During 1931 and earlier I had been one of his most severe critics. While deeply conscious of his powers as an orator and liking him personally, I thought he was woolly headed; and behind the scenes I left him in no doubt of my estimate of his executive or administrative ability. Yet not once did he show ill-feeling towards me: the acerbities which I uttered never seemed to ruffle him in the least. He knew my criticisms were made to his face and not behind his back and that my view counted.

We had a number of private chats and on January 27th, 1933, we met at the Athenaeum Club for lunch. My first impression was that he looked much older, thinner, and more stooped than when I had seen him previously.

We sat down together at a small table in the Strangers' Dining Room and he rubbed his hands over his forehead, saying to me the while: 'I am so tired. I am so tired.'

'Why don't you take a rest?' I said. 'You need several weeks.'

'I cannot take a rest,' he returned. 'I am so busy just now. I have to keep my eyes on so many things.'

After we had finished our meal we went upstairs into the upper lounge. We found our way to a quiet corner and talked. MacDonald told me that he was anxious that he should have some contact with Labour, so that on occasions when it was necessary to appoint people to commissions and other bodies he could talk over a few names of representative people.

'I do not intend to carry on when we are through this mess,' he said. 'As soon as we have turned the corner I will get out, but I do not want to leave the Labour Party in a bad position.'

'You are generally regarded as being in a key position,' I said. 'People think that the Tories cannot take office if you do not want them to. They think that we would have a full-blooded Tory policy if it wasn't for you.'

MacDonald laughed rather bitterly. 'Yes,' he said. 'If I had only been able to carry my colleagues with me what we could have achieved! What a chance we had! But we threw it away. If they had only been straight enough to stand by what they had initiated, not what finally resulted from it—I am not saying that—I could have helped them. When they ran away and began to deny that they had ever had anything to do with our proposals, well, I thought to myself that politics had become too degraded for me. Do you know that they turned me out of the Labour Party with a rubber stamp?'

'I never heard anything about it,' I said.

'I am going to write a book when I retire,' he said, 'and prominent in the front I am going to have a copy of the letter I received from Shepherd.' (George Shepherd, later Lord Shepherd, was national organizer of the Labour Party.) 'It began "Dear Sir", and it ended not with a signature, but with a rubber stamp and initials underneath. They wanted to insult me.'

'I do not think anything of the kind,' I said. 'I have heard you discussed several times in Shepherd's presence, and I do not believe there is anyone in a responsible position in the party offices who would deliberately go out of his way to insult you. We all regretted what happened. It came as a shock to us, but I do not think anybody is so bitter as to want to insult you. I imagine that what happened was that Shepherd dictated that letter, but may not have been in the office when the letters were being signed. Somebody probably thought it was an urgent letter and that it must go without waiting for his signature, and so they rubber-stamped it.'

'But don't you think, Citrine,' MacDonald asked, 'that a letter of that kind should have been sent to me by the secretary?'

'Well, you know that Arthur Henderson has not been in the office very much,' I said, 'and things have not been running so smoothly as they might have been. I will speak to Shepherd about it if you will permit me.'

'I don't mind,' said MacDonald. 'I have told many people about it, and when I write my book on how the Labour Party betrayed Socialism I will tell the story there.'

We then discussed a variety of questions, including the Honours List.

'Thomas suggested something to you, didn't he?' MacDonald said.

'Yes,' I replied. 'He said you were ready to recommend me for a knighthood, but I did not feel able to accept it. I felt that a title would be embarrassing to me.'

'What about the civil side of the Order of St. Michael, or something like that?' MacDonald asked. 'It is a high honour. I do not suppose I could get it myself unless they considered that my political work merited it. You know, it is something like the O.M.'

'But Lloyd George got the O.M.,' I said.

'Yes, and he left such a bad taste in the mouth of the King that it will never be repeated. The King is dead against it. It was intended mainly for people distinguished in literature and art; it was never intended as a political honour.'

'The only thing I could possibly accept,' I said, 'would be the Privy Council. There are two reasons for that. First, that I do not value honours as such—although I was deeply appreciative of the thought when I was asked. And there is a precedent for it: Bowerman, Tom Richards, and Mabon [the former South Wales Miners' leader] were all made Privy Councillors.'

'But they were all war people, weren't they?' MacDonald said, meaning, I suppose, to indicate that these were people who supported the Coalition Government's 1914–18 war policy.

'Yes,' I nodded.

'You refused something before, didn't you, Citrine?'

'Only the offer you made to me to go into the House of Lords,' I said. 'I couldn't possibly do that in my job, and in any case I don't want to go into the Lords.' (This incident is described in a later chapter.)

'Well, anyhow, I will talk to you about this again,' MacDonald said.

T

We fell to discussing the position which arose at the dissolution of the Labour Government.

MacDonald explained that he had met some of the Labour Ministers and tried honestly to advise them for their own good. 'I said to one man: "Now, for myself, I am taking this line of action and I know what is involved in it. I cannot protect you if you come with me. You have your future to think of, and I advise you not to take my path." Do you know, Citrine, that man has been one of the most bitter in attacking me, although he would have been ready to come with me.'

'I think I know the man you are referring to,' I said. 'It is Mr. X, if I make no mistake.'

'I am not saying either yea or nay to that,' said MacDonald.

'But I have heard that before,' I said, 'from other sources. The under-Ministers you met the day you formed your National Government reported that you had put the matter before them fairly. I remember hearing the reports of some of them within half an hour of your seeing them. Some of them spoke at the conference, if I remember rightly, when the Labour Party decided the question of the Parliamentary leadership.' (Malcolm, MacDonald's son, attended that conference and spoke there.)

'Do you know, Citrine, I believe that conference was deliberately fixed at a time when it was known that I could not be there,' MacDonald said.

'I don't think so,' I said, 'because the arrangements were made hurriedly and the decision had to be reached straight away. Members of Parliament were anxious to know what had happened. I don't think anybody blamed Malcolm for sticking to you, as it was the natural thing for a son to do, although that may not have been a good intellectual reason.'

Our conversation drifted on to other matters, and we parted with MacDonald assuring me that he wanted Labour to have fair treatment and proper recognition in any appointments which were to be made.

The years went by, and Ramsay continued his uneasy association with the Tories in the National Government, although I think he felt very much out of it.

Some time after Baldwin had succeeded him as Prime Minister there was a General Election. MacDonald stood as a candidate for the mining constituency of Seaham Harbour. It was a Labour stronghold, yet he had succeeded in 1931 at the General Election which followed the fall of the Labour Government in winning this seat. In November 1935 it was a different matter and he was defeated by a big majority. Malcolm was also rejected by his constituents at Bassetlaw. I pondered over Ramsay's defeat and wrote to him in the following terms:

> I feel I must write this. Although we have differed in late years on political matters, I hope that in the bitterness of spirit you must feel at present, you will recall that there are thousands who, like myself, remember with pride and gratitude your work for Socialism and the cause of Labour in days when it was neither easy nor popular to be a pioneer.

MacDonald was much moved by this, but there were others in the Labour movement who thought just as I did. Jim Middleton, then the assistant secretary of the Labour Party, was a staunch defender of MacDonald throughout, much as he was saddened by the events of 1931. He used to tell me with pride of days when MacDonald and he worked together as the only staff at the headquarters of the struggling Labour Party. Both Ramsay and Malcolm were soon returned to Parliament, the former for the Scottish Universities and Malcolm for Ross and Cromarty. MacDonald simply couldn't understand why he had been deserted by his former close friends. He felt that he had departed from none of his Socialist principles and had been true to the conceptions which had guided him through his political life. He once said to me: 'When I vacate the Premiership there will be no elevation of me into the House of Lords, no conferring of an earldom or anything like that. Ishbel has made it pretty plain that she wouldn't stand anything like that.' He was deeply attached to his family, especially Ishbel, who had unselfishly devoted herself to looking after her father's home through the many years since he lost his wife.

The last time I saw Ramsay was in November 1937 on the occasion of a party which he gave at Upper Frognal Lodge, his house in Hampstead, on the eve of his departure for South America with his daughter Sheila. At long last he had decided to take a rest from the worries and stress of public life and to embark on a sea voyage, which he hoped would restore him to health and vigour. Numerous as the company was, I saw nobody whom I could identify as belonging to the Labour movement. I wondered at this. Had none been invited? When at last the hubbub of conversation had died down and my wife and I were leaving the upper room in which we had been forgathered MacDonald put his hand on my shoulder and said, 'Don't go yet, Citrine.' We stayed, and found him sitting at the top of the staircase, bending forward with his head between his hands.

'Oh, I am tired,' he said wearily, with the air of an utterly exhausted man. I thought this was a reason why we should quit and so after a few sentences about the forthcoming voyage we made our way downstairs. MacDonald remained seated on the top stair. As we reached the bottom he called after me: 'Why don't you get the T.U.C. to send you with me to South America, Citrine? It will do you good.'

'There are plenty of people in the Labour movement who would like to send me a good deal further than that,' I replied, as we left the house.

These were the last words we exchanged. A few days later he died on board the liner *Reina del Pacifico* in the South Atlantic. The funeral service took place in Westminster Abbey. Just before the ceremony his son Malcolm rang me up. Would I be ready to act as one of the pall-bearers. Would it be embarrassing for me? I liked Malcolm for that. He had stood loyally by his father through the trying period which had followed the break-up of the Labour Government, although he knew full well that this would be the end of his career in the Labour movement. Yet in the distress caused by the loss of his father he was sensitive to the possibility of causing trouble for me. I scouted the possibility of this, and gladly agreed to serve. Clem Attlee, too, promptly assented when approached. So I found myself in solemn procession at the head of the pall-bearers by the side of the coffin with Neville Chamberlain and others, Baldwin limping on his stick behind us.

18

The Intellectuals, A Centenary, and a Journey

WHEN I was camping out with my wife and two boys near Bala in North Wales in June 1933 I went into the village and bought a copy of the *Daily Herald*. Glancing through the paper I saw an account of a conference of the Socialist League, a propagandist body affiliated to the Labour Party. It was composed mainly of people like G. D. H. Cole, Harold Laski, H. N. Brailsford, R. H. Tawney, Kingsley Martin, Clem Attlee, and Stafford Cripps. They felt it was their mission to act as a spur to the Labour Party in the making of policy. They were the types who were customarily referred to in the Press as the 'intellectuals of the Labour movement'.

Stafford Cripps was one of the most active, and it was a matter of considerable surprise to me to read his extravagant and inconsistent statements from the platform. Like many others, I was perplexed to understand how a man of such legal eminence could utter such irresponsible drivel, characteristic of the tyro in political affairs. I was not greatly surprised to read that at a conference of the League at Derby he had said that he and his colleagues took a fundamentally different view from mine of the prospect for Socialism in this country. The implication was that I was unduly pessimistic with a faint suggestion that I was a reactionary. I had read several of the pamphlets issued by the League and I was astounded at the extreme views expressed, which seemed to me to show no awareness of the realities of the political world. I didn't want to waste time in public controversy, but I felt I couldn't avoid making a public statement on my return to London.

About a week later I arrived at the office and received a visit from Arthur Pugh. He said he had been approached by G. D. H. Cole, who had urged him to induce me not to engage in public debate with Cripps, but rather to meet Cripps and a few of the leading members of the League for a private discussion. I agreed to do this, but, not knowing precisely whom I was going to meet and what turn events might take, I decided to prepare a statement which I could

293

read, dealing with the various points made in the pamphlets and speeches of prominent members of the League. I tried to show how such statements would be used against the interest of the Labour Party when the next General Election took place.

I diligently read all the publications which had been issued by the League. I decided to take with me my secretary, Miss F. E. Mc-Donald, so that she could take a shorthand note of the proceedings. I had no intention of exposing myself to misrepresentation arising from an allegedly private and informal discussion. We met in the London School of Economics on July 3rd, 1933. There were about thirty people present, half of whom I recognized. I expected to be faced with something which I had said publicly and which was contrary to the views of those present. Nothing of the kind. I was simply asked if I would make a statement of my general views about the work of the League. So I proceeded to read the memorandum which I had dictated in the office to clear my own mind. This was in the following terms:

THE TENDENCY TO DICTATORSHIP

The Movement appears seriously disturbed about what has happened recently on the Continent. Everywhere resolutions are being passed in opposition to Hitlerism and Fascism. The National Joint Council has issued a manifesto expressing its faith in democracy and its determination to resist a dictatorship of either the right or the left.

The first question, is, therefore, are we really sincere in our opposition to dictatorship? Do we desire to prevent its being established in Great Britain? If we do, is this the right time for responsible people in the Labour movement to be talking in terms which give currency to the belief that we are ready to abandon the methods of democracy in favour of some form of dictatorship?

That is the first thing we have to settle. If we are united in our desire to preserve unimpaired our democratic rights, won after a very long struggle, we are entitled to ask ourselves whether certain statements which have been made by responsible people tend to achieve that object or not.

What is the essence of the theme expounded by Sir Stafford Cripps, G. D. H. Cole, Major Attlee, E. F. Wise, and others? Is it not that Parliament is outworn, too slow, not responsive enough to the electoral will? That its machinery is adapted to other days and not to present-day needs? That the attainment of socialism through the present machinery of Parliament is impossible? That, therefore, some means must be taken so to alter this machinery, and to deal with elements in the community which might oppose socialist legislation, and to ensure that the programme of the party can be rapidly carried through?

Let me give an outline of the methods which have been suggested. These may be summarized under the following heads:

(a) A Socialist Government would pass an Emergency Powers Bill through all its stages on the first day of Parliament, and this would allow practically anything the Government thought necessary to be done immediately by ministerial order. The socialization of specific industries would be carried out by order in this way, apparently without further Parliamentary discussion.

(b) A Socialist Government would not accept any defeat in the House of Commons as fatal unless the Government itself deemed the question to be one of primary importance. If necessary, the Government would maintain itself in power beyond the statutory term of five years. Once the House of Commons had passed an Emergency Powers measure it would apparently not be encouraged to meet again very often.

(c) If a Socialist Government deemed there was a possibility of dictatorial action by the other side it would make itself into a dictatorship.

(d) Before taking office, even with a majority, a Socialist Government would get from the King an assurance that he would create enough Peers to secure the passing of all the economic measures desired, and of a measure to abolish the House of Lords.

(e) Under a Socialist Government there would not only be no room for private property in industrial capital, but there would be little or no room for private property at all. Something tantamount to confiscation would be applied in the case of existing owners of capital.

(f) Regional Commissioners would be appointed to carry out the Socialist Government's programme in the country. These Commissioners would act autocratically in conjunction with local Socialists rather like Russian Commissars and Communist Party members.

(g) These Regional Commissioners would, among other things, take control over labour. A Socialist Government would, if it thought desirable, suppress free speech and freedom of the Press.

On what premises does the demand for these alterations rest? It is that the electors will have given a mandate to the Labour Party to carry out its Socialist programme, that, therefore, nothing shall be allowed to stand in the way of the immediate and thorough execution of this programme. That the electors having spoken, all other interests must get out of the way, and that no opposition will be brooked. That a *majority* of the electors having given a mandate to the Labour Party, that party is determined to go ahead, irrespective of the views of other parties and sections of the electorate who have voted for those parties.

The language which has been used gives the impression that Parliamentary scrutiny of Bills, in a normal sense, will cease to exist. That the Government will regard that as unwarranted delay. That, therefore, only such principles of legislation as the Government may deem to be necessary shall be submitted to the House of Commons. That the proposals would not be subjected to the minute scrutiny of Parliamentary examination.

The Government would regard its mandate from the electors as empowering it to carry out its programme in its own way. This raises the question as to whether under such circumstances Parliament could perform any useful function whatever, beyond acting as a sounding-board for expounding the views of the Government to its supporters and the country generally.

If this is not the intention, we should be told as to what freedom should be given to Parliamentary discussion. The function of Parliament has hitherto been a careful scrutiny of the legislation of Government. Frequently, in the course of Parliamentary debate, proposals which have only been submitted to the electorate in a general form have had to be modified, because they would not stand the scrutiny of careful analysis. If this is to be done away with in a large degree, it would mean practically a revolution in Parliamentary government. It means that the Government will govern, not as the mouthpiece of the House of Commons, but something dangerously near an oligarchy.

If we take this premise, it clearly means that we cannot deny the right of our opponents to do the same thing when they are in power. They would have just as much right to carry out their programme with equal disregard for the views of the Labour Opposition. Such reasoning would justify the present National

Government in overriding minority opinion completely, both in the House of Commons and out of it, including, presumably, trade union opinion.

It is contended that it may be necessary to lengthen the life of Parliament itself beyond the five years laid down in the Parliament Act. The test which would be applied as to whether these things should be done or not is whether the Government of the day believes it has the authority from the electorate to carry them out.

Labour could not, therefore, object to its opponents doing all these things; and having regard to the fact that our opponents are now in power, is not such a declaration of our intentions tantamount to inviting them to anticipate us and to put in operation these very methods that we assert we will use?

I predict that this sort of wild talk is far more likely to produce an atmosphere favourable to dictatorship than anything else. Further, that such an atmosphere is highly dangerous to a movement which has so far trusted to the methods of reason and democratic persuasion to attain power. Already careful note is being made of these threats as to what the Labour Party will do when in office, and it may very well be that if general acceptance of such proposals takes place in the party, our opponents may seriously believe that we have abandoned democratic methods and intend to establish what they regard as a dictatorship.

The effect of this inevitably would be that they would establish a dictatorship of their own long before we had any opportunity to do so.

If this theory of the right of a Government to do as it thinks fit, believing it has a mandate from the electorate, is correct, what conceivable opposition can we have to Hitlerism in Germany? Hitler, with the Nationalists, received a majority vote of the electorate. He undoubtedly has a degree of electoral support possibly in excess of anything likely to accrue to the Labour Party within the next few years.

Leaving on one side the forcible methods that he has adopted, the above argument as to electoral mandate would justify his suppression of the freedom of the Press and public meeting, his destruction of voluntary organizations such as the trade unions, Co-operative societies, and the Socialist Party, and even his governing without the Reichstag. The theory of the all-powerful Government has not, so far as I am aware, been accepted by the Labour movement. Even within capitalist society, it has been regarded as perfectly legitimate for groups to show their opposition in a constitutional way to acts of the executive of the day.

If once the Labour movement subscribes to the principle that a Government has the right to override all opposition by whatever means in its power, it is difficult to see how an independent Trade Union movement could continue.

In the last Parliament the Labour Party were affirming the right of the trade unions to undertake a general strike as a means of voicing their protest against the will of the Government of the day. Under the reasoning of those who vote for the all-powerful Government, such resistance could not be permitted.

This was listened to attentively and I went on to show the folly of using language which would create a state of crisis. I instanced the way in which in the General Election of 1931 the people had been scared out of their wits by the allegations that their savings in the Post Office were in danger of being confiscated by the Labour Party to provide unemployment benefit. I asked what was the sense of alarming people with talk about a hypothetical financial crisis created by the capitalists to frustrate the programme of the next Labour Government. Then again there was the suggestion that if the Labour Government had not completed a sufficiently wide measure of socialization within five years they might, if they deemed it necessary, carry on for a further five years.

Cripps here interjected to say that his statement was that the life of the Government would be extended only if they thought it necessary. I didn't think this was a safeguard at all, as it would be the Labour Government and not the electorate which would decide whether that course was necessary or not.

I thought this was an invitation to our political opponents, who were now in power, to carry on for another five years. The existing Government obtained practically a blank cheque from the electorate in 1931. It said it was going to get the country out of its difficulties, and it asked for a doctor's mandate. It had not surmounted the difficulties even yet, on its own confession. The Government could say with justification that they had received a mandate to do something, but because of circumstances over which they had no control they had not been able to do it. Supposing the National Government took that line, how could those present object to its carrying on for another five years to complete its mandate? They could say, 'Sir Stafford Cripps, who may be the leader of the Labour Party, has already announced that if necessary the Labour Government will carry on for five years after the expiration of its term of office.' The Tories had got hold of these statements and they were now all carefully annotated in the Speakers' Notes sent out from the Conservative Central Office. If the line of argument implicit in what had been said by Sir Stafford Cripps had been in operation during the last century there would have been no Labour movement and no trade union movement. The opponents of Labour would have successfully preserved themselves in power.

Cripps said that unless the Labour Party had a definite mandate from the electorate they would not be able to take certain steps. They must obtain a mandate to abolish the House of Lords, and it would be necessary to obtain assurances from the King that he would create a sufficient number of peers to abolish the House. He did not desire to cut down the powers of the House of Commons. The carrying out of the plan for socialization was a matter for Orders in Council, all of which were subject to Parliamentary control. The present Government were setting up some useful precedents in that connection. He complained that I had presented the views of different speakers at the Socialist League meetings as though they were part of a mosaic. This was not so. He insisted that a Labour Government was bound to meet with acute opposition and it must have a clear mandate to deal with this.

Cole said that he wanted a definite Socialist Government. The only hope of escaping the kind of crisis they had in mind was for such a Government to arm themselves with powers which made it too risky for the capitalist interests to challenge them. The Parliamentary method was sound enough to make gradual changes but it was totally useless for the carrying through of fundamental changes in the structure of society. He didn't like the methods which were being pursued by dictatorships on the continent, but the Labour Government could use many methods which were dictatorial but which would be necessary to complete its programme.

Laski tried to explain that these powers would be like the extraconstitutional powers taken by President Roosevelt.

Pugh broke in to say that Laski was taking examples which did not fit the facts. If there was an attempt to make the extravagant changes in such a short time as was suggested, the Labour Party would find themselves on the dump-heap.

Most of those present joined in the discussion, Kingsley Martin, Brailsford, and Postgate speaking of the methods needed to ensure that the Labour Government's views would not be suppressed by the newspapers.

Tawney did not consider that Cripps's views savoured of dictatorship. They were definitely defensive. He thought it extremely dangerous, however, to continue the life of Parliament beyond five years.

Much of the general discussion which followed my statement, was remote from the realities of the political situation. It was soon apparent that none of the speakers agreed with any other. It was emphasized that the speeches I was criticizing represented the views of individuals only and not of the League itself. I contested this by saying that the fact of their being published by the League gave the impression that the views were endorsed. Whether they were or not, the effect would be just as damaging to Labour's prospects of electoral victory. I asked what would be the effect of the statement which Cole had made during one of the Socialist League meetings. This had also been printed. He had said that all property at death worth over £1,000 should be taken by the State. In dealing with this I said that Cole was a good Socialist as no doubt all those present were, and they would not mind all their property over £1,000 being taken by the State. Cripps, for example, as a successful lawyer might leave £100,000 or possibly more, and he would not object to say £99,000 being taken by the State and his widow being left to manage on the interest on £1,000.

I went on to say I did not think this was the way in which the middle class would be converted. I said that it seemed to me hypocritical, and I doubted whether any man in the room, other than Arthur Pugh and myself, was paying on a life insurance policy for less than £1,000. Not one of those present attempted to contradict what I had said.

It was altogether an interesting evening and in response to an invitation to meet the group again I wound up by saying I thought we had come to discuss practical politics. What I had found, however, was that we were discussing ultimate Socialist objectives of a theoretical character. I did not propose to waste my time further in doing so.

Most of these people were sincere Socialists and several of them had worked hard for the Labour movement in different ways. Harold Laski and G. D. H. Cole had both rendered great service, and Cole, I know, was fearless as to whether he prejudiced his status and prospects in the educational world by his writing and Socialist activities. Laski I always found stimulating and ready on the instant to help with advice or to write an article at short notice without any thought of reward. He was a bit of a romancer. I was surprised to find Clem Attlee flirting with the Socialist League.

With rare exceptions most of them never really understood the trade union movement. They assigned to it a militant outlook which most of its members did not possess, and they were irritated at the reluctance of the trade union leaders to respond to their flights of idealism in a world of stern realities. Bevin had little time for them. Some of them truckled to him, no doubt because of the big vote he exercised through his union at Labour Party conferences. But I know from his conversations with me that he resented their intrusion into trade union affairs.

I recall that on one occasion Cole had written to him inviting him to contribute an article for a book which Cole was writing. Bevin sent me a copy of his reply as he thought I might also have been approached. It was in September 1937, and he wrote: 'I could not under any circumstances do what you suggest. I would like to mention that, with the antics of the Left Book Club, Gollancz, and Laski, I would not have anything to do with them in any case.' I felt much as Bevin did.

Cripps was a different type, austere and difficult to get to know intimately. My wife and I spent a weekend at his country house on one occasion, and although he knew that my outlook and his own differed widely he never once during our stay tried to discuss labour questions. Cripps was excluded from the Labour Party because of what was thought to be, on fairly clear evidence, his attempt to form an organized opposition. I was at the Labour Party conference at which he made his speech in defence. He read every word. It was a cold, logical statement, devoid of any of the sentiments which Labour audiences love, and it had little influence. But I was glad when he was readmitted to membership.

There is a little village in Dorsetshire called by the rather curious name of Tolpuddle.

It was there in February 1834 that six agricultural labourers were arrested in the early hours of the morning. Their alleged crime was the taking of an illegal oath contrary to an Act of Parliament which had been passed thirty-seven years before specifically to deal with an outbreak of mutiny in some of His Majesty's ships at the Nore. That was the technical reason why they were arrested, taken before the magistrate (a local squire), and sent to the Assizes in Dorchester, where they were sentenced to seven years' transportation. The real purpose of the prosecution was to break up a trade union that the six men had helped to form in Tolpuddle. The magistrate exhibited a warning poster which none of the men saw until the day of their arrest. This was on 24th February, 1834, but the offence for which they were tried had taken place ten weeks before.

Two years before the men had met the farmers, who promised to raise their wages to 10s. per week. Not only did the farmers not carry out their promise but they reduced wages to 8s. per week. A few months later there was another reduction to 7s. and a threat was made that eventually 6s. only would be paid. Then it was that the men formed their trade union. They were given advice as to how to do this by a central trade union committee in London. Most of the unions at that time had their elaborate initiation ceremonies, some of which still survive. This was felt to be imperative in order to impress upon all the members the necessity of keeping to themselves what occurred and what was said in the branch room. Trade unions were not the only bodies who indulged in this ritual. It was well known that the Freemasons had also a solemn ceremony, but no thought of prosecuting them occurred to anyone.

The local magistrate, James Frampton, was in touch with the Home Secretary, Lord Melbourne, and the correspondence between them shows that they were puzzled as to how to institute a prosecution against the men. Eventually someone hit upon the device of charging them with taking an illegal oath. The six men were sentenced after the travesty of a trial. The foreman of the jury was the Member of Parliament for Dorsetshire and Melbourne's brother-in-law. Practically all the jury were farmers.

The six Dorsetshire labourers were sent across the sea to sweat and toil under conditions akin to slavery. Five worked in New South Wales and the sixth, George Loveless, the leader, a devoutly religious man, was sent to Tasmania.

The repressive action of the Government in transporting them aroused a great deal of opposition. A Central Dorchester Committee was established in London. Demonstrations took place, an agitation being sustained in and out of Parliament until a free pardon was ultimately granted.

Many months passed after this before the men were released and returned to England, where they were settled on farms purchased for them by trade union and other subscriptions. Afterwards all except James Hammett emigrated to Ontario, Canada, where they died and where today their descendants occupy responsible positions in the community.

No event in the long history of trade unionism occupies a more distinguished place than this simple story. None ever aroused in me a greater feeling of resentment against the injustice suffered by working people.

The T.U.C. on the initiative of one of its unions decided to commemorate the centenary of this dramatic episode, and it was left to the staff of the T.U.C. and myself to submit proposals to the General Council and to carry out the organizing work entailed. One of the first decisions of the Council was to hold the 1934 T.U.C. meeting at Weymouth, Dorsetshire. This was about seven miles from Tolpuddle and the nearest place where we could obtain a hall capable of holding several hundred delegates and of providing even partially the hotel and housing accommodation needed.

We intended to make the centenary year the occasion of great trade union demonstrations throughout the country, with the centre in Dorchester. A demonstration was planned to take place in the Roman amphitheatre. Other features of the commemoration included the holding of an International Trade Union Conference, with delegates from all parts of the world. In addition to this there was to be an international sports meeting, a brass-band contest, a play called *Six Men of Dorset*, a pageant through the streets of Dorchester, and a summer school for young trade unionists to be held in the vicinity.

The most durable memorial I could think of was the building of six cottages, each named after one of the men. Thus there would be the George Loveless, John Standfield, James Loveless, James Hammett, James Brine, and Thomas Standfield cottages. We intended to make these an example for the countryside and with the co-operation of the electricity company we had electricity brought a distance of some twelve miles across country to make this possible. The cottages were fitted with bathrooms, indoor lavatories, partial central heating, and all the modern conveniences which were available. They were to be occupied by agricultural labourers nominated from all parts of the country by the two unions catering for this class of worker. The cottages were floodlit at night.

A special commemorative medallion was designed and struck, a rustic seat and shelter provided under the Martyrs' Tree in Tolpuddle (presented by a local landowner, Sir Ernest Debenham), and a memorial plaque was fixed to the cottage where the meetings had been held. A tombstone was erected in the churchyard at Tolpuddle to James Hammett, the only one of the six labourers who returned to the village after his liberation.

All these proposals were endorsed by the General Council and provided a fairly full programme to be staged in the quietness of Dorset. It was carried through without a hitch, assisted greatly by the willing co-operation of the local authorities.

But although in Britain, as in most civilized countries, no trade unionist was in fear in 1934 of being transported for exercising his legitimate rights to combine with his fellows in the defence of his standard of life, there were savage forces rampant in the world. On the continent of Europe Hitler and his followers were brutally maltreating Jews and Socialists and, indeed, anyone who dared to express dissent from their cruel, cold-blooded doctrines. That indeed was the main subject for discussion at the T.U.C. meeting in Weymouth.

While it may appear ludicrous in 1964 to think that there was any danger of Fascism spreading to England's green and pleasant land, it was not so in 1934. Hitler, in June of that year, had ruthlessly killed a number of his own lieutenants without trial and without the publication of the names of his victims. This opened the public's eyes to the real meaning of dictatorship. Several attempts had been made to form Fascist organizations in the United Kingdom, and the Labour movement had exercised its vigilance in exposing their machinations.

A body calling themselves the British Fascists had been founded in 1923, and at one time claimed many thousands of members. Its propaganda was anti-Socialist and anti-Jewish, but it made little progress. A few years later a body called the National Fascisti existed, but it had only a small membership and was constantly in conflict with the police. A still further attempt was made to establish Fascism in Britain. An Imperial Fascist League was formed, but never exerted much influence. It was a different matter when the British Union of Fascists was formed in September 1932. Sir Oswald Mosley had been a prominent member of the Labour Party, but had resigned to form a party of his own, which he called the New Party. It was from this body that the British Union of Fascists emanated. They did not seem to lack money and carried on intensive and widespread propaganda, employing paid speakers and running weekly journals, such as the *Blackshirt*, the *Fascist Week*, and the *Woman Fascist*. It was clearly their intention, if they ever got power, to establish a dictatorship. In method they imitated Hitler and Mussolini and adopted the same technique. Trade unionists knew that if they ever succeeded there would be in Britain the same brutality and violence and the same suppression of trade unionism, coupled with the denial of free speech and free religion, that had characterized Fascism abroad.

Most of us were startled when the then Lord Rothermere announced his support of Fascism and appeared to be ready to help the Fascists through the columns of his own widely read *Daily Mail* and other newspapers. Fortunately it was not long before Lord Rothermere broke with the Fascists and repudiated their aims and policy.

Matters came to a head when a Fascist meeting was held at Olympia. The hall was crowded, and it was not long before struggles were taking place between Communists, who had previously announced their intention to break up the meetings, and the Blackshirt stewards and hooligans. A number of persons had to be taken to hospital and public indignation ran high.

Acting in concert with the Labour Party, the T.U.C. met the Home Secretary to impress upon the Government the danger of allowing the militarization of politics which was clearly taking place. The provocative methods of the Fascist organization, the usurpation by the stewards of powers which belonged to the police, and the growing tendency to import violence into politics were also emphasized.

It was this subject of Fascism which aroused the greatest interest at the Weymouth meeting of the T.U.C.; I was deputed to move a resolution expressing abhorrence of the suppression of freedom and democracy, the nationalist and militarist tendencies, the racial intolerance, and the degradation of the status of women that are characteristic of Fascism. The resolution affirmed its unyielding opposition to dictatorship in any form and demanded that the Government should make an unequivocal declaration that the drilling and arming of civilian sections of the community should be condemned as illegal and be suppressed without regard to those who might be responsible.

I covered the ground fully, surveying in turn operations of the Fascists in Italy, Germany, and Austria. I also referred to the fact that it was now clearly apparent in the public mind that the model of Fascism which was being pursued in Britain was identical in method and operation with that pursued abroad. There was the same emphasis upon military organization, the same dressing up in uniform, the same parading about in armoured cars from meeting to meeting, the same ambulance sections, the same transport sections, the same civilian and uniformed defence forces. I used this to emphasize the need for insisting that the drilling and arming of civilian sections of the community must end. It was in my mind, as I did so, that in the analysis that we made in the office of the advent of Fascism in Germany this was one of the principal features of the development of the Nazis there.

It took some time for the danger to be fully perceived, but it ultimately resulted in the banning of the wearing of uniforms and the Public Order Act which curtailed materially the use of such methods.

After the debate and passing of the resolution the editor of the

U

Jewish Daily Forward came to ask if he could have access to the shorthand report of my speech. I gave permission and he cabled the whole of it to his office in New York, where every word was published. This was the first time that anything I had said was credited with such importance as to merit newspaper publication in full.

It was immediately after the end of our meeting at Weymouth that I received a pressing invitation from the American Federation of Labor to attend their annual convention in San Francisco.

There had long been a close association between our two trade union movements, and it was the custom each year for us to send two fraternal delegates to their conventions and for them to reciprocate. The practice had been going on since 1894, but this was a special invitation to me personally, an unusual course. The General Council decided I should attend the conference and, accompanied by my wife, I left England on September 14th, 1934, and travelled to Montreal on the s.s. *Antonia* of the Cunard Line.

It was necessary to go to New York and we went there by car. The driver was a middle-aged man named Hirshon, a journalist from Russia who had been many years in the United States. We reached a village called Wappinger Falls. Another car passed us at high speed. A few seconds later, as we reached a bend in the road, this car pulled up with startling suddenness and Hirshon swerved quickly to avoid crashing into him. The result was that we dashed on to the pavement and shot past the red light. It was surprising to find automatic signals on a practically open country road, and that accounted for the sudden pull-up of the car in front. They had been able to see the signals, but it was impossible for us to do so because the other car obstructed our view. Soon we heard a whistle and I saw that a traffic officer was chasing us. The policeman in a threatening manner demanded the driver's licence. It was impossible to placate him and he ordered us to turn back and follow him, eventually pulling up at a boot shop. We all went inside to find the proprietor in the act of serving a customer. He was the 'judge', and I half expected that he was going to persuade us to buy a pair of boots as a penalty: in fact a fine of five dollars was imposed.

On arrival in New York we were assailed in every known dialect of Yiddish, English, and Irish by the trade union officials and others who had come to meet us. The Deputy Commissioner of Police came to pay his respects and those of the Mayor, Mr. La Guardia. After the speeches we entered a police car and were escorted to the City Hall. First there was a policeman on a motor-cycle riding ahead of us, continually sounding his siren. A wave of his hand and the traffic faded away miraculously. Our car and the escorting motorcycles performed a chorus on their sirens. Automatic signals made not the slightest difference, and we sped on at anything between forty and sixty miles an hour and every patrol man saluted us as we flashed by. The Police Commissioner remarked that I was getting my five dollars' worth for the morning's adventures at Wappinger Falls. He said that some of the small villages had to live on fines and I must not take our being charged too seriously. I answered that the indignation which the American colonists felt when they emptied the tea-chests in Boston Harbour in 1775 was nothing to what I felt at being compelled to contribute to the revenue of Wappinger Falls.

La Guardia, the Mayor, was waiting for us at the entrance to the City Hall with a crowd of people, and we were photographed together over and over again. I thought to myself: 'This is funny. Run in in the morning. In the afternoon treated like a prince.' One of my trade union friends whispered in my ear that this was a unique honour, the greatest ever done to a Labour man in the history of New York. I was not so inflated. 'A one day's wonder,' I thought to myself, 'and then I shall be heard no more.'

The following day we left for San Francisco where delegates of the American Federation of Labor were awaiting us. I had plenty of time to become acquainted with the procedure adopted by the Convention as during the first week it was devoted to a series of addresses by notabilities from the Government and others in public life. Unlike our procedure at the T.U.C., there appeared to be no limits imposed on the speakers, but, of course, the Convention lasts two weeks, whereas the T.U.C. has to crowd its business into five days.

One morning I was in the conference hall talking to a representative of the National Broadcasting Company when suddenly he said to me, 'Did you feel that shock, Mr. Citrine?'

I said, 'Yes, it did seem peculiar.'

'There it is again,' he ejaculated as a second tremor passed across the hall. It was my first experience of an earthquake and, although I wasn't in the least frightened, I didn't want any repetition. He said: 'This sort of thing often happens here, Mr. Citrine, but the newspapers say nothing about it. They don't want it to get into the newspapers of other towns. They think it will keep people away from here. All these buildings are shock-proof and as they get older the premium of the insurance company rises steadily. The only really safe ones are, however, the wooden buildings.' This sounded encouraging because we were in a steel-frame building!

I had been interviewed several times by the newspapers, but none of the interviews as printed bore very much resemblance to anything

I had said. Reporters were in a different category from ours. It sounds incredible, but here is my experience. In New York I was interviewed by at least a dozen reporters; not a single one that I could observe was writing shorthand. The first night of the Convention I was interviewed by three others in the hotel, and again not a man of them wrote shorthand. I noticed William Green, the A.F.L. president, giving an interview on the platform. He was carefully selecting his language, but what use was his care? The reporters were struggling after him in longhand. I resolved to speak to the Gregg shorthand people concerning this.

When my time came to address the Convention Bill Green introduced me with warm references to my work, describing me as the greatest labour leader in Europe. I thought to myself, 'I am going to have a hard job to live up to that.' I have always thought it is a mistake for a chairman to eulogize a speaker as it makes him feel his audience may be disappointed when they have heard him. However, I set about my task and I had no difficulty in holding the attention of the audience for one and a quarter hours. At the end the delegates rose and cheered for several minutes. I would have been hooted down at the T.U.C. if I had dared to inflict myself upon them for anything like an hour and a quarter. As it was I was presented with a beautiful watch made of white gold.

I was glad it was over. It was a considerable strain, and I knew that this address was a crucial one in the campaign which I was to engage in at the close of the Convention.

My experience at the Convention reinforced the opinion I had long formed that reading a speech tends to kill it. Not one man in a thousand can read a speech so as to make it sound spontaneous. Winston Churchill was an expert at this. Arthur Henderson was pretty good, but most people drone along in a monotonous way and usually succeed in putting the emphasis in the wrong place.

I spoke from notes, as I usually do. I was a bit anxious, as I couldn't tell how my speech would read in print, but I felt if it was accurately reported it would suffice.

Whilst I was in the U.S.A. I addressed audiences in many towns: Portland, Seattle, Los Angeles, Detroit, Pittsburgh, Chicago, New York, and elsewhere.

In New York, where I spoke at the Mecca Temple, I noticed a custom that would prove irritating to a British audience. On several occasions when the meeting had been timed for a particular hour we dawdled our time away behind the platform with conversation, while the audience were waiting patiently for the meeting to begin. Here in New York we should have started at five o'clock, but when 5.30 came and there seemed to be no prospect of the meeting starting I became restless and insisted that we should start. I was assured that it was quite usual in the United States to kick off half an hour late, but when I at length went on the platform and saw about 2,500 people present I felt guilty at keeping them waiting.

After the meeting I had to do a broadcast and as I was going out of the door to the waiting taxi a man in uniform came over to me. 'I am the police captain in charge of the district, Mr. Citrine,' he said, 'and I want to tell you that this is the finest speech I have heard in my life. Good luck to you.'

I looked at him to see whether he was pulling my leg. He seemed to be sincere. I felt I had done nothing specially commendable, but undoubtedly audiences in the United States were far less critical than those I had been accustomed to address.

The theme at all my meetings had been the same, although the language was varied and many of the illustrations I gave were topical and adapted to various audiences. I tried to describe the menace which Fascism and Hitler held for the free world. I said on practically every occasion that if these dictatorships were allowed to go on unchecked, the world would most assuredly be plunged into war. By the time I had finished my audiences began to believe this.

I was quite fatigued when at last we were able to leave for home on the s.s. *Scythia* of the Cunard Line. I carried away with me a vivid recollection of the friendly people I had met and of the boundless hospitality that had been bestowed upon my wife and myself.

19

The Honours System

MRS. BEATRICE WEBB wrote in her diary after a weekend my wife and I spent at her house that I was ambitious. That surprised me. I certainly was not conscious of any such feeling. I recalled Shakespeare's 'by that sin fell the angels', and I had no intention of creating unnecessary unhappiness for myself by aiming for the sky and falling short. My outlook on life was different. Certainly I was always strongly imbued with the desire to do whatever work came my way as thoroughly as I could and, if possible, better than the next fellow, but not for the purpose of reward: self-satisfaction in the success of achievement meant far more to me. Such appreciation as resulted from my efforts was always rather sweet, but I had hardened myself against its absence. Censure, or even vilification, I had grown accustomed to. I certainly had no desire for a title; and yet I was not taken aback when in the course of an interview on November 24th, 1930, with Ramsay MacDonald, when he was Prime Minister, he suggested that Ernie Bevin and I should go into the House of Lords.

His suggestion came about in this way. I had received a private note from MacDonald, saying he would like to see Bevin and myself on a personal matter. I communicated this to Bevin and we went along, neither of us being aware of the purpose of the interview.

We attended at Downing Street at 9.30 a.m. and were taken upstairs to MacDonald's private room. He looked in better form than I had seen him for some time, but to my surprise he said that he had not slept a wink the previous night and that he had risen at six o'clock and had a cold bath before starting work. I told him that it was rather strange that he should be able to withstand a cold bath at his age, as I, who was much younger, had been warned by my doctors that I must discontinue having cold baths, although it was a life-long habit with me. I didn't act on their advice, and in 1964 I am still taking them daily.

MacDonald then said that he was worried about the position in the House of Lords. We had a very small Labour representation there and constitutionally it was necessary that two principal Secretaries of State and two Under-Secretaries must be members of the House of Lords.

He said: 'You know, Citrine, I want someone there who can put a reasonably sensible case to them. If only I could get a first-class trade union official or two it would be about the best thing that could happen. I have received many letters from people about this honours business. Some of them are nasty about it.'

'I do not quite understand you,' I said. 'Do you mean that these are letters from people seeking honours?'

'Oh yes,' he said.

Bevin here interjected, 'I get shoals of them.'

'Well, I am glad to say I do not,' I said. 'I have so far kept clear of that sort of thing.'

The Prime Minister proceeded. 'I have to take the best material to hand. I had that man Mr. X. I had not got to consider whether he was as useful as that tree over there [looking through the window at a tree in the garden], but I had to tell myself that I must have *somebody* in the House. It is all very unsatisfactory.'

I could see where this conversation was leading to in view of a statement that Jimmy Thomas, the Dominions Secretary, had made to me previously in the House of Commons. In Jimmy's characteristic way he said, 'We damn' near made you a lord this morning, Walter,' and when I laughed he said: 'No, I am not joking. We must have someone like you in the House of Lords.'

We talked over a few names of trade union officials, but none of them seemed just the type. Bevin suggested a name, but Mac-Donald did not think it would be appropriate.

'You know these names have to go to a committee before they receive the King's sanction,' he said, 'and the committee would say, "Who is this man?" Then someone would explain that he is an assistant secretary of a trade union. "An assistant secretary!" They would object. "We cannot make him a peer." What about you, Bevin?' and MacDonald swung round suddenly and looked straight at Bevin.

Bevin, I could see, was not altogether unprepared, but he laughed it off.

I interjected: 'I think it is imperative we should make up our mind as a movement about this question of the House of Lords. The apparatus is there, and so long as it is there, we must have men to represent us. Lord Passfield told me that he accepted a peerage just as he accepted court dress, because it was necessary to the work of the Government. It meant nothing more than that to him. Sooner or later we must face this issue, and I think it is better dealt with as an abstract one than it would be if we were to deal with it on some individual personality.'

'What change does it mean?' Bevin asked.

'Nothing very much,' said MacDonald. 'It is pretty simple.'

'It adds to your expenses, Passfield told me,' I said.

'Yes, that is true,' said MacDonald. 'It would mean possibly between £200 and £300 a year more.' Bevin and I looked at each other at this. But we said nothing.

Bevin was thoughtful and then told MacDonald he would like to think the matter over and asked whether he could consult his union executive council. To my surprise MacDonald raised no demur to this, but he insisted that the matter should be dealt with in the utmost privacy.

MacDonald told us of a case of a trade union official who had approached him with regard to his being made a peer. He was a man of excellent character and reputation.

'You have no children, have you?' MacDonald asked.

'Yes, I have a son.'

'What is he?'

'He is an agricultural labourer.'

'I could see it was impossible,' MacDonald said, 'because when this man died his son would succeed to the peerage, and the position of an agricultural labourer as a peer would be impossible.'

Then MacDonald turned to me. 'How about you, Citrine?'

'I am out of it,' I said, 'because I have two sons, and moreover I do not think it would be compatible with my job. I would much prefer that the attitude of our movement should be defined on this question. I do not believe we can get rid of honours of one kind or another in any State.'

'The best solution, of course, would be life peers,' MacDonald went on, 'but we cannot bring that on. Baldwin consulted me about it some time ago when they were in office and I told him that although we would not support it he would not receive much opposition from us. The trouble is, I think, the royal prerogative.'

At the conclusion of the interview, as we walked away, Bevin said to me, 'I wonder what MacDonald's idea is in trying to get me into the House of Lords.' I replied that I could see no other motive than strengthening the debating ability of the Labour Party there. But Bevin was not convinced, and I was not surprised when, a couple of days later, he came into my office at Transport House and informed me he had decided not to accept a peerage. Whether he had consulted anyone else I do not know.

I was offered a knighthood after the Imperial Conference at Ottawa in 1932, and I have already told how I felt unable to accept it at that time for reasons which I have given. Early in May 1935 a suggestion came to me, via the Ministry of Labour, that the Prime Minister was again desirous of including me in his recommendations for a knighthood. I was told that the Government had been considering the preparation of the Honours List and they did not wish to see Labour left out. Ramsay MacDonald was still Prime Minister, although he was replaced a couple of months later by Stanley Baldwin as the head of the National Government. It was suggested that it might be appropriate if a similar honour was conferred on Ernest Bevin.

I said that I was prepared to accept a knighthood, as I had thought this matter out after consulting my wife at the time of the approach made to me in 1932. I promised to speak to Bevin and did so the same evening by telephone from my home in Wembley. He expressed some doubt as to the advisability of acceptance, although I had told him of my intention. He was afraid that 'it might create a barrier between me and the men'. He then said he would like to consult his executive. I told him that I thought it would be quite improper to do this and that he should make up his own mind. He asked for a day or two to think over the matter and later informed me that he did not feel able to accept. I gathered that he did not keep his decision altogether a secret.

Shortly after this I received an official letter confirming the recommendation for the honour of Knight Commander of the Order of the British Empire. When the Honours List appeared in the newspapers on Monday, June 3rd, 1935, my name and that of Arthur Pugh appeared. It did not pass without comment that Pugh had been chairman and I had been acting secretary of the T.U.C. at the time of the national strike nine years earlier.

I found many cordial references in the gossip columns of the newspapers who generally welcomed my elevation. Even the Communist *Daily Worker* was not so bitter as it usually was towards myself. I went out for my usual pre-breakfast walk with my Alsatian dog Rex. The sun was shining brightly, the birds were twittering unconcernedly, as though nothing momentous had happened. Despite the unconcern of Nature, I felt a strange exhilaration. Some of my neighbours, too, seemed to gain a good deal of pleasure at the morning's news. Telegrams and telephone calls soon began to arrive in plenty. I did not know I had so many friends. I had notified my father and sister in Wallasey as to what was going to happen, but had timed the letters so that they would receive them on the morning of the announcement. I summed up the position to them by saying that the news would be received in different ways. There would be a good deal of criticism, some congratulation, a greater amount of indifference, and a seven days' wonder. After this everything would go on as before.

Criticism I expected, because I knew there were many people in the Labour movement who thought honours should not be accepted. Yet in the Labour Party were to be found earls, barons, Privy Councillors, knights, C.B.E.s, and other bearers of distinctions in not inconsiderable numbers. There had been no commotion about any of them, but I knew that I would be a target no matter how others had fared. After I had arrived at the T.U.C. offices several members of the staff looked at me in rather an embarrassed fashion. I thought at first that I had disappointed them, but I soon found that their problem was how to address me. So I said to them, 'I am going into my own room and if you hear anyone speaking aloud you will know it is only me getting used to calling myself "Sir Walter".'

For once in my life I could not settle down to work and I was glad when lunchtime arrived and I met my friend Moir Mackenzie to do a bit of celebrating.

In the afternoon I attended a long meeting of the B.B.C. General Advisory Committee. We were discussing certain high-policy questions and I had moved a motion to set up a committee to inquire into the charter of the B.B.C. and to give evidence to a Government committee which was then sitting. Lloyd George followed me and his references to myself seemed to be sincere and were echoed by each member of the Council who spoke.

By the weekend a few chastening articles had appeared. One in the *New Leader* contained a vicious attack on me by Miss Jenny Lee, the wife of Aneurin Bevan. She seemed to believe that I had been rewarded by the capitalist class for services in selling the workers. That is one of the nicest characteristics of certain people in the Labour movement. No other body can rival them in the comradely and understanding way in which they engage in controversy and indulge in loving criticism of one another. All this adds mightily to the unity of the movement.

On Whit Monday, June 10th, on returning from Sadler's Wells, where we had seen *Iolanthe*, we found the *Evening Standard* had a cartoon in it by Low. At first I thought it was rather nasty. It depicted me entering a gilded hall with footmen on each side of me ushering me into a group of bewildered Tolpuddle Martyrs as 'Sir Walter Citrine, K.B.E.'. Underneath there was a caption: 'A hundred years' progress in Trade Unionism.' The cartoon could, however, have been taken in another way. Whereas a hundred years ago trade unionists were transported as a danger to the community, today they were knighted for their services to the people. I was ready to take the latter meaning.

Whatever might be the opinion of other people, I had no intention of apologizing for anything I had done. I had accepted the offer because it seemed to me to be intended as a recognition of services which I believed had been valuable to the community. Even in a capitalist state of society there were some things worth doing and others worth preserving. I had followed a long and honourable line of predecessors in the trade union movement who had received honours. Some had been made Privy Councillors, following the war of 1914–18. If the trade union movement resented my having accepted a title then it could scarcely avoid, by implication, a censure on others who had preceded me. I had no objection at all to the movement's right to lay down the principle that no State honours should be accepted by its members, but I resolved if it attempted to impose a censure on me I would face up to this issue.

My resolve was strengthened when a few days later—to be precise on June 14th—one of the T.U.C. officers who had been attending the International Labour Conference at Geneva came to me to report progress. Amongst other things he mentioned that there had been a good deal of tittle-tattle about my acceptance of the honour. Bevin, before the list was published, had shown his colleagues in the train on the way to Geneva a letter which he had received from the Prime Minister offering him a knighthood. He had informed everyone present that he had refused. It transpired that another member of the party had already accepted by letter an O.B.E., but was so alarmed by Bevin's refusal that a letter was sent to London cancelling the acceptance.

With the passage of time this member, together with other worthy members of the Labour movement, succeeded in conquering the doubts which assailed them and I noted with pleasure the well-deserved honours which were later conferred on them. One member of the Geneva party predicted that my knighthood showed that I was making ready to leave the trade union movement. Others thought it was understandable that Pugh should accept a knighthood as he was at the end of his career, whereas I was only in the middle of mine. Still others contended that I should have consulted the General

Council. The feeling was also expressed that if the Council passed a resolution of congratulation to Pugh and me, some of the party would propose to congratulate those who had refused a title.

I was well aware that whenever two or three people are gathered together, whether female or male, somebody's character or actions will come under fire. I made allowances for this. Soon afterwards the *Daily Herald* announced that a resolution had been passed at a conference of the National Union of Clerks deprecating the acceptance of so-called honours by certain trade union leaders, and stating that these tended to bring discredit on the trade union movement. It looked as though a storm was brewing.

Naturally I did not like these criticisms of my conduct, but I understood them. In the minds of some trade unionists the status and independence of the trade union movement were impaired by any of its members accepting honours. That seemed to me to be a general principle which ought to be decided separately. It should not be arbitrarily applied to individuals. But was the acceptance of honours inimical to the best interests of the trade union movement? I did not think so. The movement had gradually evolved from the position when it was regarded as almost an enemy of society. The courts and Parliament had for long looked almost with fear upon this supposed revolutionary and dangerous movement. It took generations for trade unionists to live down this hostility. It had not been completely eradicated yet. In the minds of many people there still remained the feeling that membership of a trade union was scarcely respectable amongst black-coated workers.

The national strike of 1926 saw a resurgence of the hostility towards trade unionism. Since that time I had done my best to get it into people's minds that trade unionism was a great human movement, striving for ideals that were well worth emulating and which ought to warrant the respect and admiration of every decent citizen. This had been the gist of my policy. I had striven everywhere I could to get the trade union movement identified with the life of the community. I had tried to get it regarded as an indispensable part of the democratic apparatus of the State in the sense that, while retaining its voluntary character and its independence of State control, none the less it was an inherent part of our system of government. It was just as necessary to the community as the other great voluntary bodies such as the friendly societies and the Co-operative movement. That had been the keynote of my policy. What had been the result of 1926? We had been regarded as revolutionaries. There was no doubt in my mind that considerable political damage had been done to the Labour movement because of this. People did in fact suspect that we were aiming at destroying the Constitution, despite our disclaimers.

We now had the position that the man who had been the chairman of the T.U.C. at the time was a knight. The acting secretary had received similar recognition at the hands of the State. In effect, through us, our movement had been proclaimed, both by King and Government, as one whose members were citizens deserving of one of the highest honours that the State could convey. How could this fail to affect the minds of the thousands who know little about trade unionism, and to enhance its status and prestige? What would be the effect on the black-coated workers? The movement had scarcely touched the fringe of organization amongst them. The fact that in addition to recognition by the State I had received as chief official of the movement congratulatory letters from people occupying responsible positions in the community and leaders of all the political parties (except the Labour Party) seemed to be evidence of the truth of this assertion.

I was aware that there were those in the Labour movement who vapoured about democracy being a bourgeois institution. According to them it meant nothing really beneficial to the workman. He enjoyed no real liberty, the only ones doing so being the capitalist and the aristocrat. I had repeatedly said at Congress that the Social Democrats, and even the Communists of Italy, Germany, and Austria, would be glad to exchange the Fascist dictatorships under which they were labouring for the derided bourgeois institution of democracy. I believed it to be incontestable that democracy was worth preserving, because under it the workers exercised liberties that they were completely denied under other forms of government. I had long been in the fore-front of the fight against the Nazis and the Communists in this country. I was president of the World Non-Sectarian Anti-Nazi Council. Was it not reasonable to suppose that recognition was being afforded to me for the services that I had rendered to the community, including the defence of democracy?

It seemed to me fruitless for my critics to allege that I was being rewarded for my services to capitalism. They had repeatedly declared that Fascism was the most extreme form of capitalism. Did they really believe that the British capitalists were so foolish as to reward me, through the Government, for preventing them from establishing a more complete control over the workers? I could see no justification, either logically or from my actual record, for the allegation that I had been rewarded by the capitalists. Neither the T.U.C. nor any responsible trade union organization had ever levelled against me the charge that I had neglected my duties as a trade unionist. It was only the extreme Left Wing and Communist elements who could distort their imagination sufficiently to make such an allegation. What I had seen in other countries had shown me the importance of maintaining the power of trade unionism against all forms of dictatorship, whether Fascist or Communist. That had been the theme which I had preached fearlessly for many years.

This was the way I reasoned out things to myself at the time. I regarded the honour conferred upon me as recognition not only of the stand I had taken but also of the part which the trade union movement played in the struggle to maintain democracy. Side by side with that I felt that my rights as an individual were being assaulted. I did not accept the view that in the realm of civic responsibility I had, by becoming a trade unionist, sacrificed my right of independent decision. I knew I had one of two courses to pursue.

One was to inform my critics that it was not their business to censure me for the exercise of my civic rights, and to decline to take part in any controversy about the matter. The other course was to wait and see how things developed at the T.U.C. and then make such defence as the circumstances warranted.

Weeks before the T.U.C. met for its Annual Congress at Margate in September 1935 storm signals were being hoisted. The Women Clerks and Secretaries had put down a motion on the Congress agenda which read: 'This Congress regrets that active leaders of the trade union movement should accept honours at the hands of a Government which is not established in the interests of the workers.'

The inconsistency of this motion could be seen at a glance, for eventually it would mean that it would be quite proper for the leaders of the movement to accept honours from a Labour Government. Also it was apparent that the people who drafted the motion were not opposed to the honours system as such but only to honours being accepted from the hands of a non-Labour Government. When the motion came before the T.U.C. it was moved by Miss B. A. Godwin, the secretary of the Women Clerks and Secretaries (now Dame Anne Godwin, a recent T.U.C. chairman). Several speakers took the floor in its support, all of them disclaiming that there was any personal attack upon me.

Miss Godwin's view was that honours were not a private matter and were given to trade union leaders because of the position they occupied. Although it had been customary for honours to be accepted by individuals in the trade union movement, it was not until that year that the movement had realized the significance of this. The objection to honours arose because it carried the assumption that the recipients had passed out of the ranks of the working class. In some subtle way they had gone up the social scale and away from the workers as a whole. She contended that when certain people (my name was not mentioned) were taken out of the ranks of the workers, who had done them the honour of creating them leaders of the movement, it was regrettable that those leaders should turn aside and 'play with the glittering toys of the present system' and that they should have anything to do with the outworn symbols of an obsolete system. It would be wasting the goodwill, the faith, and the trust of the workers of the movement 'if we continue to accept honours on those lines'.

I replied to the criticism by asking whether the T.U.C. had ever laid down any such principle. I had searched the records of the T.U.C. and I could not find that there had ever been any resolution, or any discussion, inside the T.U.C. on the subject.

It was plain from this that the matter had been regarded by the Congress as one for the individual. I was not aware that there had ever been a discussion on the subject in the Labour Party conference, nor that there had ever been a resolution, even from a single union, on the subject.

Whilst understanding the depth of feeling of those who had spoken, I objected to the implication that I was on the way to desertion of the working class. I reminded the delegates that I had long been the subject of vilification and abuse for carrying out the policy of the Congress. It had been asserted that I was in the pay of the capitalist class, and that the whole of my outlook had been conditioned by my regard for that class. If that were true I ought not to be in the service of the trade union movement. I studiously refrained from dealing with the question of the merits or demerits of the honours system, which I considered should be carefully and calmly considered apart altogether from personalities. If the honours system was an unworthy one it could not be right for a Labour Government to distribute honours. I mentioned this merely to show some of the implications which would have to be faced in any review of the honours system. I concluded by saying that I had tried to serve the movement efficiently and with some measure of self-respect and dignity. I had tried to serve the Congress, and I hoped I would be permitted to go on serving it. Although I did not say so, I had made up my mind firmly that if a resolution, with the implications which I have shown, had been passed I would feel it incumbent on me to terminate my service with the T.U.C. The previous question was proposed and carried, so that no decision was taken on the matter, other than a refusal by the delegates to discuss it further. This settled the matter so far as the T.U.C. was concerned, but the rumblings in the Labour movement had not ceased by any means.

For several years I had been invited to address the Union of Post Office Workers at their annual conference, and I was again invited to do so in May 1936. A couple of days before I was due to speak a formal debate took place on a motion from the floor that my name should be deleted from the list of speakers. Will Bowen (later Sir William Bowen), the extremely able and respected general secretary of the union, strove valiantly to combat the contentions of the movers by reasoned argument and sturdy support from some of his experienced colleagues. The motion was defeated.

When a couple of days later I rose to address the conference about a quarter of the 900 delegates ostentatiously marched out of the hall. I stood on the platform waiting for this patently organized demonstration to subside and on commencing my speech I was heartily cheered by the remaining delegates. Apparently curiosity overcame the desire of the protesting delegates not to hear me, as they crept into the gallery, which soon became crowded. It was made evident to me where the sympathy of the delegates lay, as I was given rapt attention and cheered on several occasions, a rather unusual experience for me.

At the Brighton conference of the Labour Party a month later, a resolution was passed placing on record the conviction of the delegates that participation in ceremonial functions and honours could be justified only in exceptional circumstances, for the express purpose of frustrating the propaganda of the capitalist parties. The executive were instructed to report on this matter to the next year's conference at Edinburgh. This resolution was referred to the Con-stitutional Committee of the Labour Party, and, although I was not a full member of this committee, I was enabled, as a co-opted member, to comment on a draft memorandum which had been prepared.

I did this at length in a memorandum of my own, in which I examined in detail the implications of the Labour Party resolution. I said that the resolution expressed resentment at participation in ceremonial functions and the honours system. It would be preferable for the committee to face this fairly and squarely. I did not believe that this could be done by attempting to draw distinctions between various grades of honours or types of ceremonies. The reasoning at the back of the resolution seemed to me entirely false and alien to the best interests of the Labour movement. The movement was no more likely to be corrupted and deflected from its main principles because certain of its members participated in ceremonial functions, or received recognition of their public service, than was the Government of Soviet Russia to lose its revolutionary character because its representatives participated in such ceremonial functions with their capitalist opponents, or because it had an honours system in Russia and had conferred distinctions upon prominent capitalists.

None the less, I recognized that there was a feeling in the Labour movement that participation in ceremonies by Labour people would bolster up the capitalist system, and that invidious and dangerous distinctions were being created by the honours system. This appeared to me to lie at the root of the matter, and I thought it should be faced frankly. It would be better to recommend to the movement that there should be no participation by members of the party in the honours system than to skate around the subject with ambiguous phrases.

The memorandum, as it was eventually presented to the Edinburgh conference, after pointing out the widely varying character of ceremonial functions, stated that it was not practicable to frame rules, or to impose such rules, either on local authorities or individuals. It was impossible for the Labour Party to separate itself from certain functions. Pageantry in itself was not objectionable, and it was essential that it should be retained and adapted to the principles of the Labour movement and the national life of the country.

As to the honours system, it was essential that Labour should be adequately represented in the House of Lords. Membership of the Privy Council marked the rank of a Cabinet Minister and it was necessary for them to accept such membership. In the civil service the conferment of honours was a method of establishing status. Honours such as the Order of Merit, honorary university degrees, and the freedom of cities and boroughs were conferred on persons of distinction as a recognition of merit and service. Representatives of local authorities regularly used the titles of the offices which they held and there was much competition for the title of justice of the peace. None of these classes of honours seemed to be open to objection.

Finally it was stated that it was impossible to lay down a binding rule which would bar individuals from accepting honours. A ruling could be enforced only by expulsion from the party and if honours were to be recognized at all the movement would be called upon to differentiate between the honours which could and which could not be accepted—a task which would not be without serious difficulties. When this came before the delegates at Edinburgh the reference back was moved and carried. No real debate took place. As far as I

X

can recollect, the memorandum and the discussion passed into oblivion.

It may be thought that I have made too much of this matter, but I regarded it at the time as of vital importance. It certainly marked a phase in Labour history, and the intervening years have shown that my views were shared by others, some of them my former most active critics.

In 1940 I was made a Privy Councillor by the Government headed by Winston Churchill, and in 1946 I was elevated to the peerage on the recommendation of Clem Attlee, the Prime Minister of the then Labour Government. No protest of any kind was made on these occasions, as far as I can recall. So I had the experience of being knighted by a National Government, being made a Privy Councillor by the wartime Coalition Government, and a peer by the Labour Government. As far as I am aware, my head has not swelled noticeably. But I can't really tell. I have never worn a hat since 1938.

20

The Abdication

ON SATURDAY, November 7th, 1936, my wife and I went to Chequers. Horace Wilson had phoned me a couple of days before to say that the Prime Minister wanted me to have a talk with him, as he had not seen me for over twelve months. As Mrs. Baldwin was to be at Chequers during the weekend, he suggested that Lady Citrine should accompany me. We motored out to Chequers. Mr. and Mrs. Baldwin were waiting for us in the large hall. We separated, Doris talking to Mrs. Baldwin, and the Prime Minister and myself sitting together on a settee near the fire.

We first discussed the general political situation and then turned to Russia. The Prime Minister remarked that he had been interested in my book *I Search for Truth in Soviet Russia*. He said that according to the best advice he could get Stalin was now contemplating pushing ahead with Russia's internal development, and was at loggerheads with the Comintern, who wanted to go for world revolution. Things were at sixes and sevens, and there was a real fear that Stalin might be assassinated. I said I did not believe much in the rumoured plot, but I thought that the recent trials were for the purpose of giving a timely warning to any possible opposition which might spring up under the new constitution, which was to come into force the following year. The persons involved in the executions were not, in my opinion, terrorists. I said that, in any case, all dictators must live under the constant threat of assassination, as there were always people to be found in every community who felt that this was the only way to get rid of a dictator.

After this we had lunch and a desultory conversation, in which we discussed Lloyd George. Baldwin told me that he had studied Lloyd George for nearly twenty years. He admired his dynamic energy and wonderful vitality, even at his present age of seventy-three.

We considered Lloyd George's qualities as an orator. Baldwin said he was a man who was carried away by his surroundings. He recounted an occasion immediately after the 1914–18 war. Lloyd

323

George was due to go to Bristol to make a speech there. Before he went he showed his speech to Bonar Law, who was then his right-hand man, although head of the Conservative Party. Bonar Law had blue-pencilled the speech a good deal, and yet Lloyd George was reported in the Press as having made the greatest of indiscretions and having committed his colleagues in the most reckless fashion. Subsequently it transpired that when Lloyd George addressed the public meeting he stuck to his manuscript closely. Later, however, he went to an overflow, and apparently when the people were calling 'Hang the Kaiser' he responded to their mood and committed himself and the Cabinet.

He always went through a prepared speech, usually written for him by Mr. Sylvester, his private secretary, at about four o'clock in the afternoon preceding a meeting. He would speak from this brief and then insert his own extemporaneous passages.

A man who knew him well told me that, a few moments before starting, Lloyd George was always apprehensive. After he rose, however, he invariably raised the audience to a high pitch of enthusiasm. Unfortunately, my informant said, nobody believed him. They merely looked upon it as a good entertainment.

I asked Baldwin whether he felt nervous at the beginning of a speech. Mrs. Baldwin interjected: 'Oh, him! He is always the same.' Baldwin smiled indulgently, as much as to say his wife knew his weaknesses so well that there was nothing for him to add. I gained the impression that he, like practically every public man I have ever spoken to on this subject, experienced the same curious nervous emotion just before rising to speak.

After we had finished lunch Baldwin asked me to go into his study and I sat down in an armchair while he paced backwards and forwards in front of the fire. He started by suddenly asking me whether I had heard anything concerning the King.

I said I had, particularly while I was in America, from where I had recently returned. I had felt so disturbed about it that at one period I was inclined to write to him. I assumed, however, that he had heard all that was being said of the King and that he would have plenty of informants without my troubling him. Baldwin went on say that he wished to have a talk with me because he would like my views as to whether he was correctly interpreting the minds of the British people. He said, 'You know all about the King and Mrs. Simpson?'

I said, 'Yes, the American newspapers have been full of it, and indeed I felt a sense of personal humiliation at the scurrilous allusions to the King's alleged carrying on with a married woman.'

The Prime Minister proceeded to say that people expected him to deal with this, and although the job was an unpleasant one, he had seen it through. He had been in communication with the King and had requested to see him. Apparently there was some misunderstanding about the time of the appointment, as although the Prime Minister had expected to see the King at a given hour, he found he had already left Fort Belvedere where he was residing.

'I telephoned to his private secretary,' the Prime Minister continued, 'and I told him I wanted to see the King on a grave matter. I said it was imperative he should understand it was not only grave for the country but even more grave for the King himself. Subsequently a reply came from the private secretary to the effect that the King would be pleased to see Mr. Baldwin the following day, and it would be a great convenience if Mr. Baldwin could be there at 10.30 in the morning.'

Baldwin said, turning to me: 'I would have gone there at six o'clock in the morning had it been necessary. Well, we had a long talk and I spoke to him plainly in words of one syllable or so, and told him as straightforwardly as I could what the state of the public opinion on this matter was.

'When I got there I found that he was outside the house. It was a lovely morning and I don't think I ever had a nicer drive than on my way to see him. I found him talking to a gardener and he was in an engaging mood. I told him I had an unpleasant task to discharge and I talked to him for over an hour in a very direct fashion. He showed no temper. He did not get angry. I began to wish at times that he had done so. I started off by telling him that he had said to me some time ago that he was glad to have me as his first adviser. I hoped that he now felt in the same frame of mind when I had to talk to him about a woman. I told him that I liked him as a man, apart altogether from his qualities as a king. I regarded him as an admirable king for the transition period through which we were going. I said to him: "You have all the advantages that a man can have. You are young. You have before you the example of your father and you are fond of your home. You are fond of your house and you like children. You have only one disadvantage. You are not married and you should be."

'I reminded him that since the war morals had gone to pieces a good deal in every country. "You may think me Victorian. You may think my views are out of date, but I believe I know how to interpret the minds of our own people, and I say that although that is true, it only leads the people to expect a higher standard from their King. People are talking about you and this American woman Mrs. Simpson.

I have had many nasty letters written by people who respected your father but who don't like the way you are going on. The American newspapers are full of it and even the Chinese vernacular newspapers are carrying stories about your misbehaviour. I don't believe you can go on like this and get away with it." I used this phrase purposely because it was a favourite expression of the King's.

' "What do you mean, not get away with it?" the King asked. I told him that our people were ready to stand a good deal, but there had been already an indication that they were reaching the limit when Mrs. Simpson's name was included in the Court Circular. The King replied that he intended to ask Mrs. Simpson to go with him to Balmoral Castle, and he did not want her to enter by the back door.'

The Prime Minister remarked that he understood that, but he did not think that in view of her history she was a fit person to have been invited. Baldwin told me that he said to the King:

' "What about this divorce? What is going to happen about that? Our newspapers have agreed not to comment on it, although they will report shortly that Mrs. Simpson is seeking to divorce her husband. But you cannot keep them quiet for long, and if they do start it will be a grave thing for the country. It will be an even graver thing for you." '

'I told him I would leave with him the letters some people had written to me, so that he could judge for himself. I told him I did not want him to give me an answer to anything I had said, but to think it over and then let me know what his considered view was.'

With regard to the divorce Baldwin said rather impatiently: 'Nothing can be done about that now, and, as you know, Citrine, the divorce has now taken place. I like him, you know, and I felt sorry for him when he said pathetically to me, "I know there is nothing kingly about me, but I have tried to mix with the people and make them think that I was one of them." '

'Yes,' I interjected, 'and he has succeeded to a great extent. People like him, but what they would stand from him as Prince of Wales they are not ready to stand now that he is a king.'

'No, but there is one thing about him,' Baldwin replied. 'There is a spot in his brain that has never grown. He is still a boy as much as ever. He is ready to do the most irresponsible things—although, I think, he tries to do his best.

'I told him pretty straightly that I expected the divorce would go through, but what then? What about six months after? What would happen then? I again told him that I did not want a reply from him then, but I have heard something since which makes me think that although I expected my conversation to have straightened him up a bit, he may do something very foolish.'

I asked, 'What do you mean?'

Baldwin replied: 'Well, he might marry her before the coronation and think he can get away with it. On the other hand, he might abdicate and marry her. He is fascinated by her and it is a difficult job to break him away. Which reminds me of a good story which I must tell you. You know, the other day Lord Nuffield came along to see me.'

I said, 'Yes, about the question of aeroplane engines.'

Baldwin nodded. 'Well,' he went on, 'the following morning my name was all over the headlines, and I called the press man in from Downing Street and I said to him, "Look here, I am very fond of the Press and I like to see my name in headlines, as you know."' (This, of course, was meant sarcastically, as Baldwin was the last to bother his brains about what the newspapers said.)

'Well,' continued Baldwin, 'I told him that although my name was in the headlines there was nothing said about the conversation which had really taken place and I had told him that Lord Nuffield said three things: That he was damn' well sick of the Press and hated them. That he was just as sick about the King and his carryings on. That when Mrs. Simpson was taken by the King to Balmoral he drove in a Ford car.' Baldwin burst out in a guffaw. 'That was the richest of the whole lot,' he added.

We discussed the matter for some time further and the Prime Minister told me he had already had a talk with Attlee about the King, as he did not know quite what would develop. He asked my opinion as to the attitude he had taken.

I told him that I thought he was undoubtedly interpreting the minds of people in the Labour movement. We were republican at heart but we realized that the limited monarchy, as it had operated in Great Britain during the life of the late King George V, was probably about the safest system in present circumstances.

I went on to say that I had heard some peculiar stories about the King when he was Prince of Wales, but fortunately, I had one of those memories which could not carry tittle-tattle, and I had forgotten all the particulars. I said that most people were prepared to smile indulgently while the King was Prince of Wales, but now I thought it was a different matter. It was impossible to contemplate, without a feeling of humiliation, the fact that newspapers in other countries were carrying discreditable stories about the King.

'Yes, and they will soon be doing it in this country,' Baldwin said.

I said I thought that in the circumstances the Prime Minister was taking the right course. Sooner or later the story would break in the newspapers. Bitter controversy was bound to arise. Some would try to justify the King's marrying Mrs. Simpson and others would be hotly against it. What the King evidently didn't realize was that such a controversy might bring the monarchy into disrepute and I thought that the institution itself would be attacked. Baldwin concurred, and promised he would keep me informed of what happened.

A few weeks after this conversation I went to have lunch with Mr. and Mrs. Churchill at their flat in Morpeth Mansions. A big meeting at the Albert Hall was shortly to take place. Winston was to be the principal speaker and I was to take the chair. We had instituted a campaign through which we hoped to do something to arouse the public as to the dangers of the Nazi regime. The other speakers had met a few days earlier to confer on the theme of their speeches so as to avoid overlapping. I was unable to be present and Winston had asked me to come along and talk the matter over.

When we had finished our business Winston fell to talking about the King and Mrs. Simpson. He was very concerned about what might happen. He stressed that the King was deeply in love with her and would not give her up. I then disclosed to him the nature of the conversation I had had with Baldwin and concluded by saying that I had no doubt whatever that the trade union movement would back the Government even if it came to the King's abdicating. Winston seemed perturbed at this and urged me to go to see the King. 'Why should I do that?' I retorted. 'If he wants to see me, of course I will go. Then I will tell him what I told Baldwin.'

Winston then remarked very quietly: 'I will defend him. I think it is my duty.'

'What?' I said. 'Irrespective of what he has done?'

Winston looked grave, and, putting his hands on his breast, he said with emotion, 'He feels it here,' at which I looked at Mrs. Churchill's thoughtful face, but said nothing more.

21

In the West Indies

IN AUGUST 1938 I was appointed a member of a Royal Commission which the Government set up to investigate social and economic conditions in the West Indies. I had no hesitation in accepting, although it involved a long absence, knowing that the office administration was left in the capable hands of Vincent Tewson and an excellent staff.

There had been other commissions and committees of investigation into different vexed questions during the preceding years. One had visited Trinidad only twelve months before to report upon the labour disturbances in that island. There had been violent outbreaks in almost every one of the West Indian colonies. In Trinidad serious riots had taken place, resulting in a number of people being killed. It was evident that there were underlying causes which required thorough investigation: our Commission was appointed for that purpose.

Many people thought the root of the trouble was the economic situation which arose because of the fall in the price of sugar, the staple export of the West Indies. Others considered that the people had constitutional grievances. To put it more plainly, they were not satisfied with a constitution that put practically all power into the hands of the planters and their agents.

The Commission had several meetings in London, but I was so busily occupied that I could not attend these regularly. None the less, I read all the testimonies of the witnesses and promised myself that once on the boat I would familiarize myself with the situation by intensive reading and study. I had a general conception of the labour legislation, or rather the lack of it, in the West Indies and, through the Colonial Advisory Committee of the T.U.C., I had a smattering of information about colonial legislation as a whole. I had only a few months previously submitted to the Secretary of State, Mr. Malcolm MacDonald, a proposal for the creation of an Advisory Committee to be set up by the Colonial Office, on which the T.U.C. would be represented, and which would be run in con-junction with the Ministry of Labour. This body was subsequently established.

My wife and I sailed from Liverpool on the S.S. *Orbita* of the Pacific Steamship Company. Morgan Jones, a Welsh Labour Member of Parliament, and I chummed up together.

The chairman of the Commission was Lord Moyne, formerly Walter Edward Guinness, of the famous brewing firm. His yacht, the *Rosaura*, which was to house several of us owing to the lack of hotel accommodation in some of the islands, was due to arrive in Bermuda at about the same time as ourselves. On our arrival our secretary, Lloyd (later Sir Thomas Lloyd), came to us, looking very harassed, with the report that he could not locate Lord Moyne anywhere. Sir Edward Stubbs, deputy chairman of the Commission, exclaimed, 'My goodness, my Guinness.'

Moyne was a broad-minded type of man and had he heard this sally he would have been amused. He told me that when he was elevated to the peerage he searched about for a title that would be reasonably short, so as to facilitate the signing of letters and docu-ments. He finally decided on the title of Moyne. Once his title was announced his friends went around with the quip: 'Moyne's a Guinness.'

On our trip from Bermuda to Jamaica the secretary handed to each of us sixty-seven memoranda which had been sent from Jamaica. Some of these documents were very long: one consisted of 120 pages. There was also a number of press cuttings for the purpose of en-lightening us on current opinion in Jamaica. Some of the corres-pondents were sceptical about any advantage to the island accruing from the work of the Commission.

The Jamaican Government had requested all those who desired to give evidence to send in twelve copies of their memoranda. This was at once interpreted as a subtle attempt to prevent the Commis-sion seeing the real evidence. It was alleged the Government would delete the parts it did not like. I thought that to require witnesses to put in twelve copies of their evidence was overdoing it. How could the ordinary citizen manage this? The Jamaican Government readily explained that their purpose in requesting so many copies was so that all the members of the Commission, and the appropriate officials, would be able to read the memoranda on the boat. Reading the memoranda, I found they contained practically nothing about the conditions of the workers.

We called at Nassau in the Bahamas and Havana in Cuba *en route* for Jamaica. Our first sight of Kingston was impressive. As we approached the island I thought, 'Surely this is a fairy isle!' I was later to find that Kingston was perhaps not quite as pleasant a place as it looked from a distance.

The *Rosaura* was awaiting us and we had an informal meeting on board. Then followed a press conference. Next morning the principal newspaper carried a full-page story of the conference. Tucked away in a corner of the front page was an advertisement: 'Guinness is good for you'; I also thought he would be.

I wanted the hearings to take place in the centre of Kingston, which was hot and stuffy. I didn't want to be too far away from the people, but I was inwardly satisfied when we decided to make the Constant Spring Hotel our headquarters and hold the hearings there.

Our first witness was the head of the Agricultural Department. He put in a 50,000-word memorandum without a single word about labour. I got him to admit that a comment in *The Times* that the authorities were afraid to do anything in case they trod on the bosses' toes was not an unfair one.

I will not expatiate on the work of the Commission. It is enough to say that the way in which the native workers were treated aroused my ire. This found its way into some of the questions I put to witnesses. It was confided in me that there was a growing colour prejudice. There had always been a certain aloofness between the whites and the Jamaicans, but there was also prejudice between the different shades of colour: the nearly whites looked down on the browns and the browns on the blacks.

The more I saw of the so-called housing, the more disgusted I became. The Commission valiantly strove to inspect as many of those awful shacks as they could. Few of the houses had any windows fitted with glass and most had no floor covering at all. Many of the inmates slept on beds of rags supplemented by coco-nut fibre. Dirt was everywhere. Many of the shacks were built of old packing-cases still bearing stencil marks. The rule was one family to a room. The roofs were of corrugated iron with no under-planking. Most of the inside walls were bare. What angered me most was the apparent indifference shown by the whites to the conditions under which the people were living. I was invariably met with the comment: 'Well, these people have never been used to anything else, and we always have good weather. They are quite happy.'

Bustamante, the trade union leader (afterwards Sir Alexander Bustamante), who became Prime Minister of Jamaica, took me around with Morgan Jones. We were accompanied by Norman Manley, a first-class lawyer, sincere and socially minded, and who also for a period was Prime Minister. They convinced me that Jamaica was ripe for adult suffrage. Bustamante was an attractive character, tall, rather dignified looking, with a long lanky figure, clean-shaven face, and piercing eyes. He told me that his father was an Indian and his mother an Irish woman, whilst he himself had lived for a long time in Spain. 'How then can it be possible,' he said, 'to coerce me?' He could be persuaded but never driven. Yet the Government wanted to drive him; they were taking down his speeches at meetings, hoping that they could put him in gaol and thus break the trade union movement. All this was said to me privately. The people looked on Bustamante almost as a deity. His union had about 50,000 members who owed absolute allegiance to him. I spent some time in inspecting the administrative set-up of the union, and while it left a great deal to be desired by British standards, it was reasonably satisfactory.

When Bustamante appeared before the Commission there was great excitement. He made a fairly good witness but was somewhat erratic. The statement which the union had put was full of exaggerations. After the chairman had questioned him about the financial aspects of such things as old-age pensions it was evident that Bustamante had not studied the subject at all. I tried to protect him as much as I could and questioned him for nearly an hour.

He had stated at a public meeting that he possessed more power than the Governor. I extracted from him an explanation of his remark by asking whether he meant that he had more power over the workers. Bustamante agreed that he had. I asked him whether if the workers were on strike and the Government ordered them to go back they would go; and Bustamante replied that they would laugh at the Government, but they would certainly go back if he and his executive ordered them to. What he really meant was that he had more moral authority over the workers than had the Government. Later I asked him whether he wished to co-operate with the Government. He replied that he did 100 per cent. I questioned him as to what was the obstacle to this co-operation. He replied that it was the insistence of the Government on sending policemen and bayonets to follow him wherever he went.

I asked him whether he had ever preached sedition and he indignantly denied this. I had been strongly advising the members of the Commission that the Government and Bustamante should get together and reach an understanding. I was ready to promote this.

I asked Bustamante what was the effect upon him when he saw police reporters taking down his speeches. He replied, 'I lash them with my tongue.'

I followed this with, 'You mean that you say more than you should?'

Bustamante replied, 'Yes, but within the law.'

My next question was, 'Supposing the practice of sending reporters around to take your speeches was stopped, would it have a good effect on you or a bad effect?'

He answered it would have a good effect. 'The Government would have such co-operation from me, they would not know it was Bustamante.'

Further questions elicited his strong resentment at detectives visiting the trade union office. They did this without authority and created the impression he was about to be arrested.

I thought this was a clumsy way in which to treat a man with such influence as Bustamante. It was natural he should be resentful, and I had a strong feeling that he was not the type who could be coerced: but he would, I thought, respond to friendly treatment. I am glad to think that I played some part in bringing about the desired co-operation; at least I did what I could to bring the trade unions together.

Most of the unions were weak, but on the whole they had a promising lot of young officials. I tried to get them to work in co-operation, but for a time Bustamante's union kept out. Finally, however, he agreed to co-operate with the others. I persuaded them to form a Jamaican Trade Union Advisory Council which could be a centre to keep in contact with the T.U.C. in England.

We finally came to the end of our Jamaican sessions and on December 6th I left for Santiago. At the Pan-American air base near the Palisades hundreds of people were lined up and singing lustily. I had to speak to the crowd who were being addressed by Bustamante. As I looked at their faces I felt strongly moved: I could feel the unexpressed desire of these people and their faith in me. Bustamante spoke sensibly, announcing his determination to co-operate with the Governor, who was doing his best for them. Then I spoke, and in a few sentences told them how I had grown to understand and like them. I gave them some advice and hoped they would establish unity and solidarity amongst themselves so that they could present their grievances to those in authority in a sensible manner. As I left the crowd sang 'God be with you till we meet again'.

After a stay of a few days in Santiago I left by aeroplane for Puerto Rico, where I rejoined the *Rosaura* which had returned with another section of the Commission from British Honduras. I attended a dinner given at Puerto Rico to the Minister of the Interior, where I had as my neighbour Mrs. Churchill (Lady Churchill). In the course of conversation she told me that all her life she had been arguing with Winston. He always won by simply beating down her arguments. He was always cool at the finish, whilst she was generally angry. She told me that she liked to see men well dressed, and that she had been spending most of her married life tidying Winston up! 'He never stays so,' she said, 'but I do my best.'

Later, in Anguilla, Mrs. Churchill went riding, looking more fitted out to go hunting in India. She wore a topee and riding breeches. I called after her, 'Mind you don't kill all the tigers,' and she saw the point of my sally as quickly as the others.

I thought she was rather a jolly person. Noticing me writing my diary in shorthand, she mentioned that Winston could never use a dictaphone. He had tried, but he couldn't make the necessary corrections. He wrote from ten at night until two o'clock in the morning when he had anything to do, and he usually kept a secretary at hand to help him. From her conversation I gathered she did not like Baldwin very much. I supposed this was natural, because Baldwin was not very partial to Winston. When we were talking about how people dressed I remarked that once at Chequers I had found Baldwin dressed in an old coat, with his tie all awry and his boots not properly laced, in fact just as a man should be when he wants to be really comfortable.

One morning we went ashore on a swimming expedition. Mrs. Churchill was one of our party. She wore a large straw hat as protection against the sun and she swam high in the water with her shoulders barely covered. Our launch was nearing the *Rosaura*, which lay about a mile off shore, when a gust of wind carried Mrs. Churchill's hat overboard. I dived after it. I had scarcely touched the water when I realized the danger I was in from sharks. I grabbed the hat and made for the launch which had put about to pick me up. It is a pity there was no one to time me for distance and speed, as I am sure I broke all swimming records. I had quite a bow wave when I reached the launch.

At Basseterre on the island of St. Kitts the Commission took evidence from the Churches. The clergymen asked that their evidence should be taken in private. I dissented, and it was decided that only certain parts should be heard privately. When the evidence had been concluded it was apparent that what was lacking in these gentlemen was moral courage. They could easily have said publicly what they had told us, but the reason they required privacy was that they were afraid of their churches being emptied. I pointed out that suspicion would be created by their attitude, and that we had not had any similar request on the other islands that we had visited. Their evidence was on the whole good and helpful.

On the island of Nevis I assertained some startling facts about the standard of life. Men received 1s. a day on Government work on roads; women 6d. a day. No one who was able-bodied received any poor relief at all, no matter how destitute they were. There was no ambulance on the island, and only two doctors for 13,000 people. I had seen so many glaring injustices in the West Indies that I could scarcely contain myself. I felt that if Britain could do no better for these poor, simple, and patient folk than we were doing I for one would not wish to keep them in the British Empire. Let them have complete self-government, or go to some other country which might be able to do better for them. I felt I could never again hear talk of our 'trusteeship' over the coloured peoples without a feeling of shame at the callous way in which we had neglected them. I was so burning with indignation at the neglect I saw everywhere, and the stories of poverty I heard, and the wretched houses which I couldn't miss seeing, that it made me depressed and sick at times.

Mrs. Churchill was still with us on the *Rosaura* and at dinner one night Winston's name again cropped up. Someone had asked about my taking notes in shorthand. We got on to the question of short-hand speed and the capacity of the reporters in the House of Commons. I said there was scarcely anyone who could speak at a rate of 200 words per minute for long. I remarked that Winston was not a quick speaker, to which Mrs. Churchill replied: 'No, he is not. It is not a natural gift, you see. It is a cultivated one. He is a most industrious man.' I added that Winston spoke from extensive notes. With his quick brain and knowledge of language it didn't seem necessary for him to write practically everything he said.

Mrs. Churchill agreed and said that for years she had told Winston that there was a danger of his being too 'note-bound'. She gave me the impression that Winston was a little nervous because of the slight impediment in his speech, and that it was because of this that he liked to have every sentence ready. I recalled what I had heard about Winston rehearsing his speeches and standing in front of a mirror practising the most appropriate gestures. I asked Mrs. Churchill outright about this. I said to her, 'I know you are not a witness and if you don't like to answer this question you needn't do so, but is it true that Winston rehearses his speeches?'

Mrs. Churchill leant forward so that the others couldn't hear and she whispered: 'Yes, it is true. He goes to no end of trouble about his speeches, and when he does the whole household is in a turmoil for days before. It is like our having a baby.'

Many years afterwards when Winston was Prime Minister I asked him why it was that he always read his speeches. He thought for a moment and then he said, 'I think it is due to your audience to give of your best.' I replied that I recognized it was necessary to make adequate preparation, but I could see no reason why, with Winston's command of language, he felt it necessary to read practically every word.

I heard him only once make an impromptu speech. The language was bordering on magnificent and his thoughts were admirably expressed.

One day Mrs. Churchill and I were walking side by side on our way to a meeting of the Commission. I remarked that we must hurry if we were to be punctual, and at this she turned to me and said: 'Winston is the most unpunctual person in the world. No, that is not the way to put it. He has no sense of time at all. He says to me, "You know, my dear, I can dress in fifteen minutes," and I reply: "No, you can't. It takes you twenty-one minutes and even then we have to hurry." Winston is really a very quick dresser, but he has no idea whatever of time. Sometimes I have tried the dodge of putting the clock on ten minutes but it doesn't work. He gets me all heated and worked up, and then he says quite calmly: "You know I have never been late for a public engagement in my life. What are you bothering about?"'

Mrs. Churchill went on: 'He prides himself on keeping his temper and he makes my head ache with his arguments. I tell him the reason why he can keep his temper is because he always gets his own way.'

It was at Bridgetown that Mrs. Churchill had to leave us, and before she departed she congratulated me, in the presence of Lord Moyne, on my cross-examination of witnesses. I did not think I had done anything out of the ordinary, but I was encouraged by her kindness.

As the Commission moved from island to island I was appalled by the conditions we discovered. I felt thoroughly ashamed of the way in which the accumulated faults and neglects of other generations had come now to roost on our shoulders. Nor could I escape the feeling that something violent would happen unless these troubles were remedied. We would hear of further disturbances in the West Indies.

At Georgetown Lord Moyne gave me a letter from the Sugar Producers' Association protesting against my treatment of them when they gave evidence. I hoped it would keep fine for them. They would get worse treatment before I had finished with them.

Here is one typical vignette. At Georgetown I visited the wharves to see women unloading charcoal. They carried three baskets on their heads. The weight, I guessed, was about 40 lb. in all. They did this for eight hours a day and they told me they received only 5*s.* or 6*s.* a week, working from Monday to Saturday inclusive. We saw other women carrying sand from a barge. They received from 2*s.* 6*d.* to 3*s.* a day. They were employed by another woman who acted as a sub-contractor. I tried to lift one of the baskets of sand which the women carried on their heads. I upset it because it was so heavy. I guessed its weight as about 56 lb. The manager said he thought it was about 40 lb. We put it on a scale and found that this basket weighed 64 lb.; another was 72 lb. Yet the women carried these baskets all day from 7 a.m. until 4 p.m. with one hour for a meal at eleven o'clock. They were all middle-aged or elderly women and didn't look over-strong.

Our last call was at Trinidad, where we found better labour relations among some firms who were not unfriendly towards trade unions.

We completed our sessions on March 16th and a few days later sailed from Trinidad on the *Southern Prince* and boarded the *Aquitania* at New York. We reached Southampton on April 7th, 1939, after the longest period that either my wife or I had ever been away from England. When it came to writing the report of the Commission in London we found there was a much greater unanimity in our points of view than I would have expected. Our report, which ran to nearly 500 pages, was a severe indictment of the conditions in the West Indies. Our recommendations were full and constructive. By February 1940 we had completed the report and in view of the fact that the country was then at war with Germany the Government decided to withhold, for the time being, the full report, and to present only the recommendations. I felt we had made a constructive contribution to the promotion of better conditions throughout the West Indies.

22

Rise of the Nazis

I HAD occasion to visit Germany many times after my appointment as president of the International Federation of Trade Unions in 1928. Our offices at first were in Amsterdam, but they were removed to Berlin in 1931. They were situated in the Koepernickerstrasse, one of the main thoroughfares of East Berlin. This gave me the opportunity of seeing something of the German trade union movement. They had their own commodious offices not far away and I was greatly impressed by their strong sense of organization and thoroughness. Their representatives on the I.F.T.U. always came to our meetings well documented and they usually made constructive suggestions on the various subjects we had under consideration.

The I.F.T.U. was extending its influence despite the world depression and everything seemed to be going reasonably well when a cloud appeared on the horizon with the growth of the Nazi movement with Adolf Hitler as its leader. At first the German trade unionists and Socialists just laughed at them. They repeatedly told me that Mussolini had brains, whereas Hitler was a mob orator and a 'tub-thumper' who had no real ability. But those of us who came from other countries seemed fairly certain that whatever Hitler's lack of ability might be, the Nazi movement was growing in strength. The trade slump was in full force. We had in England over 2,500,000 out of work, but in Germany unemployment was far worse. Discontent was rife there because of cuts in unemployment benefit and relief, and reductions in wages. The middle classes had seen their resources almost entirely swept away by the disastrous inflation of 1923, and, suffering from reductions in their salaries, they were intensely dissatisfied. Young people from the schools and universities, faced with little or no prospect of employment, added to the prevailing discontent. A sullen nationalism was developing and a feeling of depression was spreading. This was the environment in which Hitler and his so-called 'National Socialist Party' began to thrive.

Such was the situation when I attended my first meeting of the I.F.T.U. in Berlin on Sunday, July 19th, 1931. Money was leaving Germany at the rate of £5,000,000 a day. This drain could not last long. A run on the banks set in. The Government closed the Stock Exchanges for a time and declared a moratorium. I was on the look-out for signs of the disturbances we had read about, such as the reports of shooting and rioting in Cologne, but on arrival there everything appeared to be normal. In Berlin, too, there was not the slightest sign of crisis that I could observe. I found that the I.F.T.U. was having some difficulty in carrying on its administration because of the financial restrictions. We decided we would try to transfer some of the funds which we had lying in the German Labour Bank to Brussels or to Denmark.

I had with me the head of the T.U.C. International Department, W. Bolton. He was something of a pessimist and on the return journey, as we sat in the train on a hot day with our coats off, gazing idly through the carriage windows, he enlivened me with a review of the various secretaries who had served the T.U.C. Bolton had been in the service of the T.U.C. since 1903. He informed me casually that Bowerman, who was secretary until 1923, had had a serious break-down in 1914 and had to go about on crutches. Still earlier, Steadman had a stroke in the office which eventually killed him. Sam Woods, who was the first secretary with whom Bolton worked, also died of a stroke. Bramley, my immediate predecessor, died of angina pectoris and a clot of blood on the brain. So out of four secretaries in Bolton's time three died of the effects of the work and the fourth had a break-down. Then Bolton ran a calculating eye over me and suggested that a secretary should always have a holiday immediately before the Annual Congress. I felt thoroughly cheered by this conversation!

My next visit to Berlin was in November 1931. I looked for signs of crisis, but could not see anything abnormal from the appearance of people in the streets. The cafés and restaurants were well patronized and the people seemed well dressed. These were superficial obser-vations: beneath the surface there was much discontent. By the time I went to Berlin in June of the following year unemployment had risen to 6,250,000. It was plain that this situation could not continue. A political crisis was building up. President Hindenburg had dis-solved the Reichstag on the grounds that it no longer represented the will of the people. The Nazis had gained heavily in the Prussian elections, but Hindenburg called in Von Papen, a former Monarchist, to form a Government.

My next visit was in September 1932, when I was accompanied by my wife and Bolton. It was a beautifully sunny morning when we left our hotel and walked to the I.F.T.U. offices. Our meeting passed off uneventfully, but in a conversation I had with my fellow executive members from France and Belgium there was general agreement that the situation was becoming more dangerous. Mertens, the Belgian member, said he could not see any real possibility of resistance being offered by the German workers in the event of an attempt to establish a dictatorship. He said: 'These people are too calm. They will not do anything. There will be no trouble.'

An hotel porter said to me: 'There is no trouble, except in the newspapers. All we want is good trade and everything will go well.'

One evening I was sitting with my wife in the Vaterland Haus, the biggest restaurant in Berlin, where meals were to be obtained comparatively cheaply. It was the resort of many German families, who used to make a habit of taking their weekend meals there.

Everything was run very efficiently and one of the several orchestras was playing pleasant light music when suddenly there marched in about a dozen young men. They were dressed in the brown shirts, black belts and trousers, and black leggings of the Nazis. They marched in single file, passing between the tables, each with his two hands on the shoulders of the man in front of him. Occasionally they would shout in unison some slogan or other. I heard the cry 'Sieg Heil' for the first time. No one stirred. None of the customers turned to gaze curiously at these young fellows. All the diners concentrated their attention on the food before them and conversation lapsed. The gang went out in the same way that they came in and scarcely had they left than there was a buzz of conversation. I asked myself what the German Socialists and trade unionists were doing to allow this sort of thing to go on, apparently without protest. When next day I put my query to some of them they replied that they were well prepared for action when the time arrived. I was not the only trade unionist who was disturbed at the prospect of imminent trouble in Germany. It became clear to most of my fellow members on the executive of the I.F.T.U. that our offices could not continue to function in a country where there was no longer freedom of speech.

Several months passed and it was not until February 1933 that I again travelled to Berlin.

My diary reads:

The one theme of conversation here in Berlin amongst responsible people is what is going to arise out of the present political situation. Hitler, the Nazi leader, is now German Chancellor. Hindenburg, the President, who is eighty-six years old, appointed him when it was seen that the von Papen Government had no hope of retaining the confidence of the Reichstag. There is an inner story to this, to the effect that the reason why the combination between Hitler and von Papen came about was that General von Schleicher, who was supposed to be the strong man of the von Papen Government, really was organizing a military *coup d'état* against von Papen with the connivance of the Socialists. The Nazis have been shooting Communists after dark. The death-roll, as the result of these encounters, is well over 100 since Christmas.

The other day in the London *Times* I saw an article from its Berlin correspondent, who said that Hitler had now taken the first unmistakable step towards establishing a Fascist dictatorship. He had decided to arm the Nazi storm troops, or the Brown Army as they are called. Further, these Nazis would be responsible for maintaining order during the forthcoming General Elections, which are to take place on March 5th, 1933. The local police force would be superseded in these duties by the Nazis. This would place at their mercy the other political parties, as it is obvious that the Nazis would not hesitate to use their armed power to intimidate their opponents. Open-air meetings are forbidden. The police must be notified of indoor meetings so that they can have representatives present. Even meetings of a private character do not appear to be immune from this threat. Hitler has filled practically all the important posts in the police with his own representatives. In Berlin the former Chief of Police has been replaced by the German Admiral von Levetzow, who, by the way, was responsible for the bombardment of Scarborough during the Great War. The same process has been taking place in most of the principal German towns. It is unmistakable that Hitler intends to have his men in all the key positions. Hitler some time ago made a statement saying that he would respect the constitution, but he has already broken this promise by overriding a decision of the Supreme Court of Prussia.

There is an intense nationalistic spirit abroad, and in some desperate way these people feel that Hitler may do something to release Germany from the humiliating position she has occupied since the war. The Nazis are working in conjunction with von Papen and Hugenburg, the latter being a powerful industrialist who is at the head of the great U.F.A. which is the biggest German film company. He and Hitler are working for different ends, and it is significant that Hitler has said that the Nazis will gain seats from all other parties including the Nationalists who are behind Hugenburg. The latter have their

own army, the Stahlhelm (steel helmets) but all the principal
posts in the police force are being given to Nazis. Therefore,
although there may be a split some time or other between
Hugenburg and Hitler, the Nazi leader is making pretty sure
that he has the military and armed forces behind him. The
Nazis are mainly young men and they are evidently trained fairly
well for their parades. They are much better than the Socialist
Reichbanner force both in physique and training, as far as
Carthy [our T.U.C. representative in Berlin] can observe. The
Nazis are always intimidating people. In the district where he
lives they are putting up notices warning the Socialists not to
attend their 'Local' or committee rooms. A young fellow was
shot in the back whilst going into a committee room only a few
days ago. Carthy thought that the German trade unionists were
divided amongst themselves. They were thinking about their
jobs, and the terrible unemployment made it seemingly impossible to get an effective response to any call for a general strike.

Victor Schiff, the correspondent of the *Daily Herald*, came to
see me. He took a gloomy view. He was a shrewd fellow, politically well informed, and with his ear to the ground. He was
clearly very apprehensive of being overheard although we were
chatting in my hotel bedroom. I will try to put matters in his
own words. 'I am not a coward, but I have a wife and two
children depending on me. Any German who speaks to a
foreigner about the conditions in his country and says what I
am saying to you is liable to imprisonment for anything up to
twenty years.' He went on to say that the Nazis were establishing themselves at every point. They had practically all the
senior police posts in the principal towns. They had suppressed
the Socialist paper *Vorwarts* because it gave the news about the
shooting of some children at Eisleben. The paper was suspended for eight days. The next time it might be suspended for
three months or six months. He said none of the German trade
union leaders would speak frankly and say what they really
thought when in the presence of the I.F.T.U. Executive. It was
too dangerous. He told me of a number of cases of prominent
Socialists and others who had been badly maltreated. His view
was that only vigorous action by the Allies could save the situation. If the French occupied the Rhineland or the Ruhr they
would have the support of the majority of the people.

In the next session of our I.F.T.U. meeting we discussed the
removal of our office from Germany. We were reluctant to do this

as it might appear to the German trade unionists that we were deserting them. I said I hesitated to comment on the situation which seemed to me to be growing alarming. It was almost a repetition of what happened in Italy in the early stages of Fascist dictatorship. Hitler had already established a censorship of the Press. He had mobilized the radio for party propaganda. It might be that at the forthcoming elections the people would be intimidated by the Nazis. I asked what our German comrades thought about the situation. Leipart, who was the leader of the German trade unions, made a statement suggesting that the trade unions in the various countries should exert public pressure through the Press, emphasizing that freedom of action had practically ceased in Germany. He blamed the Communists for splitting the ranks of the trade unions. All that they were concerned with was creating a Soviet Germany. He assured us that all arrangements had been made to meet any contingency and that the leaders only had to give the word. Then there would be a General Strike and that might lead to civil war.

Walter Schevenels, our secretary, a Belgian, and an extremely acute observer, said that he had information that telephone conversations from the office were being recorded in shorthand. This extended to his conversations with the foreign trade unions. Leipart, in response to a question, said that he could not possibly agree to invoking the Versailles Treaty. That would re-establish German nationalism. I suggested that we should meet the leaders of both the A.D.G.B. (the German T.U.C.) and the Socialist Party but I learned from Schevenels he had already made such a suggestion to Otto Wells, the leader of the Socialists, who was rather offended at it. We seemed to be absolutely helpless to do anything useful to assist the German unions other than carrying on active propaganda in our respective countries.

We summoned a meeting of the I.F.T.U. General Council members to which every country affiliated was directly invited. This meeting took place in Brussels on March 14th, 1933. By this time shootings were going on with increasing frequency and many responsible Germans who were in opposition to the Government were said to be afraid to go home and were in hiding. No German representative was present and Schevenels reported that he had made several attempts to secure substitutes for Leipart but without success.

Leipart had said that everything was ready and they only had to touch the button, but the German leaders evidently felt that the time for doing this had not arrived. They had sent a deputation to Goering who had assured them nothing would happen against the trade unions. Leipart had told Schevenels that it was possible that they would be asked to collaborate with the Government. It might be that the terms would be unacceptable, but in principle they were not opposed to collaborating with any Government. Schevenels had asked Leipart for advice as to the position of the I.F.T.U. It was conceivable that the Nazis might raid our offices and destroy valuable documents. It would be of no use the commissioners of police apologizing for this after it was done. He had told Leipart he would advise the executive to transfer the office to another country and Leipart had not dissented from this. We acted on this advice and established our office in Paris.

On the instructions of the T.U.C. General Council in 1933 I drafted a report on 'Dictatorship and the Trade Union Movement'. The report dealt specifically with the Hitler dictatorship in Germany, tracing as its causes humiliation over defeat in the 1914–18 war, the Versailles Treaty, economic despair caused by the inflation of 1923, massive unemployment, frenzied nationalism, the multiplicity of political parties and indecisive elections, divisions in the working class, the formation of trade unions attached to political parties, government by decrees, lack of intermingling amongst the various sections of German people, the existence of private armies and the appeal to mass force, hatred against Jews and Socialists, denunciation of all forms of internal co-operation, and the securing by the Nazis of control of the police and armed forces.

It is often forgotten that Germany never had a democratic constitution until that of Weimar, which was established in 1919. The German electorate had little experience of political freedom as it existed in Great Britain. There soon arose a multiplicity of political parties, none of which was able to obtain a decisive mandate from the electorate. The Communist attacks on the trade unions and Socialists had weakened these bodies. The Communists bore a considerable responsibility for the divisions which made possible the Nazi victory. Hitler had blamed Marxism and internationalism as the basic cause of Germany's post-war difficulties, and these troubles, in turn, were ascribed to international Socialism or blamed on the Jews.

The Nazi Party, like all the other principal parties, had its own trade union organization, defence force, youth associations, and sports and social organization. It had been the practice of all the principal political parties to centre the activities of their members around these institutions. Intermingling was at a discount. The test of whether it was fit to associate with a person or body was a political one. So it came about that in Germany a series of vertical organizations, each with its own self-centred system, had grown up long before Hitler came on the scene. The training camps and military drilling were created first by the Nazis, who encouraged a spirit of militarism to the point where it became not a mere show but something which was bound to find expression in action. (The Reichstag fire at the end of January 1938 was blamed by Hitler on the Socialists and Communists, although there remains a strong suspicion that the fire was actually the work of the Nazis themselves. It provided an excuse for Hitler to suppress the Socialist and Communist newspapers and to put a ban upon political demonstrations, except those of his own followers.) Political opponents were not permitted to criticize the Government and police were always in attendance on the platforms, with power to close the meetings at the slightest sign of opposition criticism. The radio was monopolized by the Nazis and their opponents were effectively gagged.

All this was described in considerable detail in our report to the Brighton Trades Union Congress in 1933. I was given the job of introducing this. The usual speaking time limits were lifted for the report and several speakers followed me. All of them were opposed to the tenor of the General Council's report, principally on the ground that it condemned the dictatorship in Soviet Russia as well as the others. According to the critics, the dictatorship in Russia was a benevolent one, 'The Dictatorship of the Proletariat', whereas the others were capitalist dictatorships without any regard for the welfare of the people.

Outstanding amongst the critics was Aneurin Bevan, who was present as a delegate from the Miners' Federation. He had been at the Congress once or twice as a South Wales delegate, but was not regularly appointed to this position. I recall his speaking only twice in our principal debates. I first met him at a weekend meeting I was addressing on behalf of the Labour Party. I was struck by the ease with which the young man expressed himself and I felt that he had a future in public life.

It was not for some years that I met him again. This time it was at one of the meetings of the trade union group of Members of Parliament in the House of Commons. I had established a regular and intimate relationship between this group and the T.U.C. and it was a pleasure to keep the M.P.s informed of what we were doing. At these meetings Bevan showed his developing oratorical powers and he was already becoming known for his courageous outspokenness. He excelled as a critic, but, in contrast to Ernest Bevin, creative thought at that time was not his strongest characteristic. He would present any number of difficulties to any proposition which came from official sources, but seldom put forward any constructive proposals of a practical character.

He took the same line in our debate at Brighton. He said he had heard my speech with profound admiration as one of the best he had ever listened to. Then he went on to describe his feelings of alarm because it was the most dangerous speech he had ever heard. He said my speech had been based on the assumption that capitalism would recover itself. But capitalism was incompatible with democracy and it was the capitalists who would attack democracy. He scorned my reference to the lack of intermingling amongst people in Germany and their concentration into political groups. He remarked that I had given them to understand that class co-operation on the football field was one of the best defences of democracy in Great Britain.

Bevan had announced at the beginning that he was speaking for himself and not for the Miners' Federation. At this point there were indications that the audience were alive to his distortion of my speech. He argued that the enemies of Labour would attack democracy with their bodies when democracy had become incompatible with the preservation of their privileges. The lead which the General Council should have given to workers was not the organization of demonstrations to expose the fallacies of Fascism. Congress should get down to an industrial policy, demand an increase in wages and press the attack home. Fluently as Bevan had spoken, he made little or no impression on the delegates.

I said that implicitly Bevan was accusing the unions of not taking advantages of opportunities, which were visible to him, of securing advances in wages. I asked him not to place strictures on his colleagues of the Miners' Federation. One thing that I had learned was that when wage demands were conceded members flocked into the unions. When strikes were unsuccessful many deserted the unions. There was clear evidence of this in the mining lock-out of 1926. Some hundreds of thousands of members were lost at the end of the struggle.

The motion for the reference back of the Council's report was defeated by an overwhelming majority, only a few hands being held up in its favour.

Aneurin Bevan's speech was typical of him as he was at that time —well-phrased, fluent, tricky, and entirely unconvincing.

Bevan was a politician by instinct and temperament and he rightly concentrated his main activities in that sphere. In my experience he exercised a negligible influence on trade union policy and action. How different from Ernest Bevin!

As I have said, in 1934 I was sent by the T.U.C. to attend the Congress of the American Federation of Labor at San Francisco for the purpose of trying to get them to realize what was happening in Europe. I was well received by the delegates and the Press commented favourably upon my speech. After this I made a tour of several weeks, always with the same message—that if Nazism and Fascism were allowed to go on unchecked world war was certain. Although most of my meetings were crowded and much sympathy was shown, the only section of the community who were really active against the Nazis were the Jews. I knew a good deal about what was going on in Germany quite apart from press reports. I regularly received from underground sources reliable information which my correspondents managed somehow to smuggle out of Germany. It was plain that Germany was rapidly approaching a war footing.

I supplied this information regularly to Sir Robert Vansittart, who was then the Permanent Under-Secretary at the Foreign Office. He assured me in the several interviews I had with him that this had been passed through to the Government. I had conversations with Sir John Simon, particularly about the growing Nazi aggression in Austria, and he was full of sympathy. He spoke of the combined Hitler technique of repression and propaganda, but he wavered when it came to doing anything about standing up to Nazi Germany.

I made several visits to Austria during this period to see whether a bridge could be built between the Dollfuss Government and the Socialists, as this seemed to be the only hope of preventing a Nazi invasion. Otto Bauer, the leader of the Socialists, was ready to work with Dollfuss, but nothing tangible resulted. The Socialists and trade unionists felt confident that if the worst came to the worst, and Dollfuss tried to establish a dictatorship, their armed supporters, the Schutsbund, would prove to be an effective resistance. I know that Simon was fully informed about this, as Sir Walford Selby, the British Minister in Vienna, wrote a despatch in his own hand, in my presence giving a vivid picture of the situation. I carried this with me and gave it to a rather incredulous Anthony Eden, who was acting at Geneva in the temporary absence of Simon. Soon afterwards fighting broke out in Vienna, but it was of a sporadic character and showed how ill-equipped any section of workers really were to resist the armed forces of their Government.

After this the I.F.T.U. established a relief fund for the Austrian workers, Hugh Gaitskell, then a rising young economist but politically unknown, acting at my request in a supervisory capacity. By 1936 it was plain to the world that the Nazis and Fascists were bent on aggression. I had reached this conclusion long before I visited Russia in 1935, and, returning by sea, I wrote in my diary on October 25th, 1935, while the ship was lying in the Kiel Canal:

What the Soviet is most apprehensive about is the possibility of combined action between Japan and Germany. If she was attacked in the Far East by Japan, and simultaneously by Germany in Europe, her situation might be desperate. Whilst I have no technical competence to speak of the relative merits of the respective national armies, I have seen enough to convince me that Hitler may march to disaster in 1938 as Napoleon did in 1812.

I thought the war would come in that year and I finished my underground air-raid shelter at home with the assistance of my wife and boys on May 4th, 1938.

23

Standing Up to the Dictators

THE aggressive intentions of the Nazi and Fascist dictators were brought home to most thinking people with the invasion of Abyssinia by Mussolini in 1935. This was a foretaste of what was to follow. It brought into the foreground the question of how the activities of the dictators were to be restrained. My trip to the United States and Canada in 1934 had been made specially for the purpose of bringing home to American trade unionists that unless the aggressors were induced to abandon their designs war on a world-wide scale was certain to break out. Russian statements were constantly warning the rest of the world that 'peace was indivisible' and that if war broke out anywhere it would probably spread rapidly. I firmly believed this and was just as stoutly determined as most other people in the Labour movement to resist any attack which might be made on the Soviet Union. It was one thing to declare the readiness of the trade union movement to take a stand against the aggressors. It was another to agree on the kind of action needed to check them.

Germany was fast rearming, disclaiming the Treaty of Versailles which forbade her to do so. The parades of Hitler's Brown Legions and the Fascist forces led by Mussolini had become an established part of the life of Germany and Italy. 'Living Room' was the slogan of each. It was as easy to find a pretext to attack the defenceless Abyssinians as it was later to justify the Nazi invasion of Austria and Czechoslovakia. No other country, except Russia, had bothered much to ensure that its armed forces were adequate to meet the challenge which at some stage seemed bound to arise. Certainly not Great Britain. Reassuring statements by Ministers were not lacking, but no really effective steps were being taken. The Labour movement was loth to accept the logic of its own declarations. Everyone knew in his heart that resolutions of protest wouldn't stop the dictators. But Labour people abhorred war and were deterred by the prospects of a world-wide conflict with all its horrors. We tried to take refuge in repeated demands for collective action by the League of

349

Nations. The League had no forces of its own and it was patent to me that it must rely on those of its member states who were ready and capable of shouldering the major responsibility of defending the collective security we talked so much about. Economic sanctions were both slow to operate and not very effective.

Unity of action in the economic sphere was difficult enough to secure amongst the nations, and general agreement on the armed defence of democracy seemed remote. As far as I could see it really came down to this: were trades unionists ready to support our own Government in a measure of rearmament which, in association with countries like Russia and France, was capable of deterring the aggressors? The need for this seemed clear, yet whenever this aspect of the subject was approached there was always some phrase in our resolutions and declarations which avoided a definite commitment. Party political feeling undoubtedly entered into this aspect, as there was a deep suspicion and a hearty dislike of the Government and its policy.

The Labour movement has always contained a strong and sincere pacifist element who are implacably opposed to war. Divisions in our ranks were to be apprehended if the movement took the decisive step of urging the Conservative Government to rearm. I didn't fear any serious division on the trade union side, but I knew the Labour Party would have some difficult hurdles to clear. Gradually, as the dictators showed themselves in their true colours more and more flagrantly, feeling hardened in the trade union movement; and although we still clung tightly to our basic principles of disarmament and peace, there was the underlying thought all the time that our policies must be attuned to the realities of the situation. Collective security was our doctrine, unattainable though it seemed.

By the time the annual meeting of the T.U.C. was due in 1935 at Margate the Labour Party and the Trades Union Congress had met jointly and after two days of discussion had hammered out a declaration of policy on the international situation. The General Council had pressed the Labour Party for a more definite pronouncement than some of them would have liked. The trade union members of the party executive were with us almost to a man, but some of the others were hesitant and searched round for loopholes. Cripps declared himself against sanctions and imperialist war. He had three supporters, all members of the House of Lords, and then left the meeting. The declaration strongly condemned the Italian attack on Abyssinia and the defiance of the League of Nations by Mussolini, and was in favour of support for *any* action, consistent with the principles and statutes of the League, to uphold the authority of the League in enforcing peace.

It has long been the practice of the Labour Party to send a delegate to the T.U.C. to convey fraternal greetings. The T.U.C. reciprocates in a similar way. George Lansbury, who was the Leader of the Parliamentary Party in that year, had been appointed and was due to speak to the Margate Congress on the afternoon of Thursday, September 5th, 1935. It was on that morning that we were due to consider the joint declaration on the international crisis. George was staying at our headquarters hotel. About half past seven in the morning he searched me out saying he wanted to speak to me urgently. He told me he had been unable to sleep. He couldn't reconcile his personal position as a pacifist with his duties as a representative of the Labour Party. The joint statement in his opinion clearly envisaged a declaration of war on the Italians and he couldn't support it. He owed it to his conscience to inform the delegates of his personal position.

Like most people in the movement, I had a strong affection for George and didn't want to do anything to embarrass him. But I couldn't possibly assent to his suggestion. I said: 'Look here, George, you are not attending this Congress as an individual. You came here to represent the Labour Party. How can you as the Leader of the Parliamentary Party take the line of saying the declaration embodies the agreed policy of the party and then in the next breath say "I don't agree with it"? You are here to convey fraternal greetings not to argue about differences in the party's international policy. Stick to the job for which you were appointed.'

George was troubled about this and I could see he was having a struggle to decide what was best to do. He finally said he must consider his position, but I was unwilling to leave matters in that ambiguous state and I pressed him to promise that he would say nothing contrary to official policy. He seemed to think that this was taking refuge in a coward's castle, so I warned him that if he did diverge from the agreed policy he would create a rumpus and we would have to tell the delegates that he was abusing his position as a fraternal delegate. When his turn came to speak, Lansbury stuck closely to his function and no word of dissent was expressed by him. Poor old George! My respect for him was increased by this incident. I had often admired the remarkable way he and Clem Attlee managed to lead the attenuated party in the House of Commons. Few would have expected either of them to show such ability. Eventually he resigned the leadership, but the affection we all felt for him remained undiminished.

But to return to the declaration. I was appointed to present it and I made no bones in pointing out that the decision had been taken in full recognition of its seriousness. There was a price to pay for peace and it might well entail taking definite action against the breaker of the peace. There were three kinds of action which could be taken. One was the enforcement of economic sanctions, which meant the withdrawal of raw materials and finished products from the aggressor. Then there were financial sanctions, which meant cutting off available sources of loans, without which modern sustained wars could not be fought. Thirdly, there was the matter of military sanctions. Military sanctions in finality means this: if somebody breaks the treaty of peace, if somebody dishonours his agreement, then the other nations are ready not merely to establish economic sanctions and financial sanctions but to see that those sanctions shall not be rendered ineffective by the military operations of the peace-breaker. In other words, to put at the disposal of the League of Nations such a measure of force of a military, naval, and aerial character as may be necessary to make the sanctions really effective.

A little later I said: 'I heard a delegate say at the commencement of my speech, "It means war." It may mean war, but that is the thing we have to face. We have to face the fact that there is no real alternative now left to us but the applying of sanctions involving the possibility of war. But I say this, if we fail now, if we go back now, war is absolutely certain.'

My words were at that time far more definite than anything I had myself heard from Labour sources. I know they must have caused some disquiet to many people not only in the rank and file of the Labour Party but higher up. An animated debate took place, lasting well into the afternoon, but when a vote was taken the policy was affirmed by 2,962,000 for the resolution to 177,000 against.

Towards the end of September the Labour Party held their conference at Brighton, where Dalton expanded the joint international policy resolution. It was carried by an overwhelming majority, 2,168,000 for the policy and 102,000 against. The debate at Margate had decisively settled its fate. As Dalton wrote: 'Every one of the big guns of the General Council—Marchbank, Dukes, and Bevin— thundered in our support.'

It was at this conference that Bevin relentlessly accused Lansbury of hawking his conscience round from body to body. It was a cruel and, I thought, unnecessarily brutal assault on a man who was certainly no hypocrite and had served the Labour movement well.

A few days after the Margate Congress I received a message from

Sir Horace Wilson to the effect that the Prime Minister (Mr. Baldwin) would like me to meet him at Chequers. I was due to leave for a visit to Soviet Russia on the Saturday, September 14th, and the meeting with Baldwin was fixed for the previous day. It was the first time I had been there.

Accompanied by my wife, I went along and had lunch with Mr. and Mrs. Baldwin. After lunch we adjourned to Baldwin's study where he opened the conversation in this way: 'I am approaching seventy and I don't believe that any man should be expected to carry the burdens of the office of Prime Minister after that age. I don't care about myself, but I do care for England, and I want to talk to you seriously about our defences. You may some day occupy the position I am in.'

'What?' I interjected. 'Do you mean that I might become Prime Minister? If so you may dismiss it at once. I have no ambitions of that sort.'

'Well, whatever you do, you will always have an influence in such matters,' he replied.

He went on to tell me that our armed forces had been dangerously run down and were far below the strength necessary for the defence of the country. I knew this to be true so far as the Royal Air Force was concerned from the many conversations I had had with high-ranking officers as a result of my lectures at the Royal Air Force Staff College at Andover. I needed little convincing about the others, as here, too, I had contacts, although not of the same regular or intimate character as with the R.A.F.

Finally I asked Baldwin whether he had told the Leader of the Labour Party in the House of Commons about the state of things. He explained that he had not done so because he thought it was useless to speak to George Lansbury, a sincere and avowed pacifist.

'What about Attlee?' I inquired. Baldwin said he recognized Attlee was different from old George, but he was only the Deputy Leader of the Parliamentary Party and he would feel bound to follow Lansbury, who was his leader. He had come to the conclusion that there was no hope along that line of consultation. It was evident that he was wondering whether I could do anything on the trade union side. I explained that I was due to leave for Russia in the next few days and would have no chance to consult anyone. I thought the best plan would be for Baldwin to receive a deputation from the T.U.C. on some different subject such as workmen's compensation, and after they had talked about this the subject of rearmament could be raised. I felt sure that he could do this and speak freely without

z

any danger of a press leak. I said that Ernest Bevin was a member of our appropriate committee and I knew he felt much the same as I did. So it was arranged that in my absence the T.U.C. would make an approach for a deputation to be received and Baldwin would speak to them as he had spoken to me.

When I returned to the office I at once dictated a letter to our chairman, Billy Kean, explaining briefly what had been said and hoping that arrangements for the deputation to attend would be speedily made. I spoke to Ernist Bevin, and told him what had been said in my interview with Baldwin, and impressed upon him the seriousness with which I regarded the situation. I did this because Kean, excellent and loyal fellow though he was, was not an outstanding personality. He had, in fact, completed his chairmanship with the end of the Congress at Margate, but his successor, Alan Findlay, had not at that time been appointed.

I departed for what proved to be a six weeks' visit to Russia with the gratifying feeling that my duty had been done. Whilst I was away I received various reports from the office and I had arranged that these would contain a guarded reference to the deputation from the Workmen's Compensation Committee. But nothing came.

Whilst in Baku I received a telegram saying that a General Election was to take place and instructing me to return at once. I started away by the first train and when I arrived in London I found a letter awaiting me from Bevin. It was not marked 'Private and Confidential'. On the contrary, it was evidently written for public consumption. It went on to express strong disagreement with my proposal. This, in Bevin's view, was going behind the backs of the leaders of the Labour Party. He couldn't be a party to any such proposals. So no approach for the deputation to see Baldwin had been made. No further approach was made to me by Baldwin after the General Election, and I often wonder why he did not revert to the matter.

Nearly eight years elapsed before we discussed it again, although in the period when he was still Prime Minister we met on several occasions. The war was still in a dangerous phase when he wrote asking me to meet him at the Dorchester Hotel on Monday, April 5th, 1943. He had become an earl on vacating the Premiership and had almost disappeared from public life. He had taken rooms at the Dorchester and he told me he came to London once every few weeks.

I inquired about his health, and he said that for a man of nearly seventy-six he felt physically very well.

'I feel I still have a young brain,' he remarked, 'but I am

dreadfully out of things. I get to know nothing in the country. You remember I had pretty heavy going; I had to face all that abdication trouble by myself for a time. Even some of the members of my own party didn't agree with me, but I never wavered because I knew what the British people would do.'

'You had the good sense to retire at the height of your prestige,' I said, 'and I don't know whether Winston will do the same. I rather thought he would up to a few days ago, but now it is pretty clear that he intends to carry on into the post-war period.'

'My prestige has all gone now,' said Baldwin, 'but Winston stands at a higher peak than any man in the world. Lloyd George never rose to the same heights in the last war.'

Baldwin remarked that he had not seen Winston for some months, but when he had last seen him he was surprised at his physical fitness and that he was bearing up so well under the strain. 'He didn't seem in the least rattled. There was no nervous twitching of his eyes or his mouth or fingers or anything to indicate that he felt the weight of his responsibilities. His success had not gone to his head.' Having regard to the fact that when Baldwin was last in politics 'Winston was right down there' (pointing to the floor), Baldwin thought his political recovery was marvellous. He, personally, had always thought that if war came Winston would be the right man for the job. It was the only way to liberate those big qualities Winston possessed.

'You know, Citrine, Winston has thought and dreamed of war all his life. I remarked to him once that some of the things he said reminded me of John Churchill. He seemed immensely pleased with that.' [This, of course, was a reference to the Duke of Marlborough.]

'There is one question I want to ask you,' I said, 'which I have never had the opportunity of doing.'

I then reminded him in some detail of our discussion at Chequers in September 1935, and concluded:

'I went to Russia feeling that you and the T.U.C. would get to grips with the matter. The next thing I heard was that there was a General Election. I have always been in the dark as to what really happened to prevent your disclosing to the T.U.C. the position.'

'I have always had a good memory,' said Baldwin twitching up his nose and frowning in his characteristic way when he was thinking, 'but I find it now very hard to recollect details. I remember that there wasn't very much anti-German feeling in the country at the time. Indeed there was a pro-German feeling. Hitler had said that their interests lay in the East. We didn't know he was such a liar in those days. Well, I felt that it was necessary for the people to know the position, and I wanted a General Election to give us the authority to rearm. I didn't ask that we should rearm against Germany. What I asked was that we should be allowed to rearm so as to be able to carry out our obligations under the Covenant of the League of Nations. I can't exactly tell you what happened.'

I visited the United States in 1936 and again made a further extensive tour. One result of this visit was the formation of the World Anti-Nazi Council with headquarters in London. It was to be a non-sectarian and non-political body whose membership would be open to anyone who subscribed to the principles of democracy and freedom. The idea arose out of a conversation I had with Samuel Untermeyer, an eminent American lawyer. I duly reported to the T.U.C., who approved the principles of the new body, and with their full support the Council was established. I was its chairman and we ran a number of public meetings to wake people up to a realization of the Nazi menace. The T.U.C. instituted a boycott of German goods and services, but I am afraid it was not very successful.

The committee of the Council felt that we needed some prominent personalities who would help us to arouse the public to an understanding of the terrible threat that the Nazis presented to peace and liberty. We had as our organizer—and an able one at that—a chap named Richards, who had formerly worked amongst the Liberals and who suggested Winston Churchill, at that time the most persistent and active critic of the Government. He was rightly insisting that they lacked the preparedness to meet any challenge from the dictators. So it came about that an informal dinner took place where we explained to Winston what it was all about. He considered our title, 'The Anti-Nazi Council for the Championship of Human Rights', was cumbersome and largely negative. Supported by Wickham Steed, at one time editor of *The Times*, and Norman Angell, the well-known author, we changed the title and decided to hold a meeting at the Albert Hall to dispel rumours that were circulating that we were trying to form a new centre party. We called a private conference of prominent journalists to whom we explained what we were about. They were sympathetic but the rumours were not completely scotched.

The Albert Hall meeting took place on the evening of December 3rd, 1936. It was crowded to the doors and many people were unable to gain admission. We were fortunate in being able to arrange for it to be held under the auspices of the League of Nations Union. We had several speakers, in addition to Winston Churchill, drawn from people in public life. Lady Violet Bonham-Carter was amongst them. We all assembled in a private room behind the platform, except for Winston who was late. The minutes were ticking by and we were all becoming anxious. I hate to keep an audience waiting and I am a firm believer in starting meetings at the advertised time. So I said to my colleagues, 'If Winston isn't here in three minutes we are going on the platform without him.' I didn't ask whether anyone agreed with me, but I was relieved when a few moments later Churchill rushed up.

'I must speak to you,' he said rather excitedly, calling me aside.

'What about?' I asked rather gruffly.

'About the King,' he replied, referring to the rumours of his abdicating.

'What's that got to do with this meeting?' I demanded.

'People will expect a statement from me,' Churchill answered.

'I don't see that at all,' I said. 'We have come here to demonstrate our unity in standing up to the Nazis. We haven't come to talk about the King, or anything else. If you make a statement others may want to do so. You will certainly be challenged, and if no one else does it I will.'

Churchill was a little taken aback at this, and simply replied, 'I must consider my position.'

Some may wonder at my abruptness and may think me churlish. They must remember that in those days Winston was an active Tory politician whom few people in the Labour Party either trusted or admired. He had not then shown his great qualities as the leader of the nation who installed himself in the affections of us all.

With that we went upon the platform. The meeting passed off successfully without the least vestige of discord. Winston read his speech throughout in the most masterly fashion.

I have since been informed that in one of Churchill's memoirs it was stated that he referred to the controversy about King Edward VIII at the Albert Hall. That is inaccurate. I suppose what happened was that Winston had written in a reference to the King as part of his speech and had forgotten to delete it when writing his memoirs.

Throughout the years from 1936 to 1939 Hitler and Mussolini were on the rampage, bullying all and sundry.

In July 1936 fighting broke out in Spain. Over 80 per cent of the armed forces joined in revolt against the Republican Government.

On August Bank Holiday I received an urgent message requesting me to go to Spain in company with De Brouckere, the Belgian
president of the Labour and Socialist International, to find out on
the spot what was really happening. I at once packed and had
arrived at the Gare Quai D'Orsay in Paris, when at the last moment
I was urged by a deputation representing the Spanish Socialists to
go back to London, the reason being that certain events were expected to develop which might warrant my presence there.

De Brouckere made the journey by himself. He was a great
strapping fellow, well over six feet and a cheerful personality into
the bargain. He would have made an excellent travelling companion.
He was very intimate with little Willie Gillies, the secretary of the
International Department of the Labour Party, who stood about
five feet high. Once when the three of us were out walking together
De Brouckere put his hand gently on Willie's head and turned to me
with the smiling remark, 'Great Britain,' and, pointing to himself,
'Little Belgium.'

De Brouckere's report left no doubt that unless the Spanish
Government was supplied quickly with arms it was in great danger
of being overthrown. Several members of the Spanish Government
were known to me intimately, and one of them, Largo Caballero,
the Prime Minister, had worked closely with me on the International
Federation of Trade Unions.

What was the difficulty in their obtaining munitions? An unexpected one. I had attended a joint meeting of the Labour and
Socialist International and the I.F.T.U. in Brussels within a fortnight of the revolt, and some of us were startled to learn that the
French Government, under Léon Blum, a staunch Socialist, had
decided against supplying war materials to Spain. This was all the
more disastrous for the Republicans, as it was from France that
Spain normally obtained munitions.

The decision of the French Government was taken because they
were convinced that if they supplied munitions to Spain it would in
all probability lead to the outbreak of a European war. It was well
known that Hitler and Mussolini were supplying arms to the rebels,
and, although we didn't want to embarrass the French Government,
we felt bound to publish a manifesto declaring the right of the
Spanish Government to be supplied with the munitions they needed.

It soon became apparent that Italy and Germany were sending
aeroplanes and pilots to the rebels. The French Government was
then forced to choose between supplying arms to the Republican
Government itself or taking another course. That course was to try
to restrict the area of conflict by preventing munitions from reaching

either side. It was decided that this was the wiser course, and it was communicated by Léon Blum to the British Government, who approved the French policy of withholding munitions and of trying to induce other Governments to follow suit. This seemed to people in the Labour movement a one-sided arrangement, as none of us had the least doubt that both Italy and Germany would go on support-ing the rebels with arms, no matter what they signed or what others did.

We saw Anthony Eden, who was Foreign Secretary, and told him flatly that the policy of non-intervention could not succeed. Eden adhered to it, none the less, as the British Government re-garded it as imperative for the preservation of peace. They appre-hended the possibility of Europe becoming divided into two blocs, with the Fascists on one side and the democratic Governments on the other, each furnishing arms to the body they favoured. The British Government, like the French, was firmly convinced that the situation would develop into a conflict within Spain between the two blocs, and that this would spread until the whole of Europe was embroiled. The British and French Governments stuck to their policies through-out the whole of the conflict in Spain and we utterly failed to move them.

We tried by deputation, by public demonstrations, by publicity, and in other ways to induce a change in the Government's policy. There were many demands during the course of 1938 for the T.U.C. to take some more decisive action to induce the Government to change its policy. Repeatedly we were urged to call a special con-ference of the executives of the unions to consider means of doing this, but not once did any single union ever put forward any practical proposal, save that of increasing financial assistance to the sufferers from the Fascist attacks.

The General Council had to ask themselves whether in such cir-cumstances anything practical could result from such a conference. Eventually at the annual T.U.C. meeting at Blackpool in September 1938 we held a private session, at which I presented the limitations to effective action which the circumstances imposed upon the trade union movement. We had repeatedly affirmed the policy of our movement to secure arms for the Spanish Government, but how were we to enforce this? I asked unions who felt that the General Council's efforts were inadequate and could be supplemented by some new policy, or action, to make specific suggestions as to how that could be done.

In the Council's view there were only two ways in which a reluc-tant Government's policy could be changed. One was by means of general propaganda in which the movement had been indulging vigorously, and the other was to take some kind of coercive action. It was clearly the latter course which was in the minds of those who felt that the movement was not doing enough.

I raised the issue of the justification for taking industrial action for a political objective. We were meeting at a time when contempt had been lavishly sprayed over Parliamentary institutions. It was said that democracy was played out and that government by consent, as distinct from dictatorship, was dead. I tried to show that it was not for the trade union movement, which had repeatedly attested its belief in democracy, to strike a blow at its institutions. We ought not to give the Fascists encouragement by ourselves trying to change by force the views of a democratically elected Parliament.

I next dealt with the legal restrictions, which induced some delegates to interject that this was a bogey which the unions need not bother about. I replied by saying that I was not thinking of personal liabilities or penalties which would fall on individuals, but that the funds of the unions which took such illegal action would be rendered liable for actions for damages. I asked whether the opponents of Labour would hesitate to attack the unions through the law courts. I furthermore pointed out that it was a moral certainty that, if any decision for strike action or an embargo on arms (which would lead to the same result) were taken, the Attorney General would move in the courts for an injunction to prevent the use of union funds or machinery in furtherance of such a decision. The banks would be instructed not to pay out money to the unions and they would financially be hamstrung.

I had consulted both Stafford Cripps and William Jowitt (later Earl Jowitt) as to whether there was any way out of this dilemma and they had both replied positively that there was not. This line of argument created considerable resentment, but I kept bringing the Congress back to the same point. How would you operate coercive action? Needless to say, no delegate in the ensuing debate came within miles of facing this issue. After the General Council's action had been affirmed a resolution was carried to the effect that the Congress should forthwith determine what effective steps should be adopted to secure a co-ordinated policy for the removal of the ban on arms. This made the proceedings a farce, and it was against my advice that the resolution was permitted to stand. Had it been taken as an amendment to the General Council's report, as I advocated, it would assuredly have been lost. The resolution was discreetly allowed to lapse.

24

The Threshold of War

THE international situation continued to deteriorate rapidly and a state of general tension was engendered by the knowledge that Hitler was amassing 1,500,000 men on the Czechoslovakian frontier. Bit by bit, the tension increased and incidents were reported of conflicts between Czechs and the Sudeten Germans. The demands of the Sudeten Germans became more extravagant until finally they demanded complete autonomy as a separate state, with a totalitarian regime, within the Czechoslovakian Republic.

The Labour Party and the T.U.C. had drafted a declaration the main feature of which was that the British Government should stand firm whatever the risks of war might be, and should act in association with the French and Soviet Governments, proclaiming their determination to stand by Czechoslovakia if she were attacked. This had been drafted at Blackpool and had been passed by the Congress. We thought it might have a steadying effect, but within the next few days it was learned that Mr. Chamberlain, the Prime Minister, would fly to Germany and talk matters over with Hitler. It was decided to send a deputation to Chamberlain to hear the facts at first hand. He was then on his way back from Germany, travelling by air, and did not arrive at Downing Street until 6.30 p.m. I established contact by telephone, following a letter I had sent to the Prime Minister earlier in the day, asking for the deputation to be received.

I received word from Sir Horace Wilson the same evening that the Prime Minister would see us on the following day, but that the time could not be stated. A meeting of the Cabinet was to take place at 11 a.m. and this continued until 5.40 the same evening. We met the Prime Minister less than an hour afterwards. He was accompanied by Lord Halifax. The deputation consisted of Herbert Morrison, Hugh Dalton, and myself. It had purposely been kept small, so that as intimate a discussion as possible could take place. I was asked to open, and I said that we did not wish to worry the Prime Minister after his strenuous exertions but the fact of our coming to see him was a measure of our anxiety. I said that we had, as a movement, affirmed both politically and industrially our determination to support the Government in opposition to Hitler's demands. I said some thought that prestige had been lost as a consequence of Chamberlain's visit, but the preponderance of opinion on the National Council of Labour was that he had done the right thing.

Chamberlain consulted Halifax for a few seconds and then stated that he would like to speak to us with intimacy. He could do so only if he had an assurance that what he said would not be repeated publicly, in Parliament or in the Press. I at once gave this assurance on behalf of the three of us and said the Prime Minister could later tell us what we could divulge to our colleagues.

He said that so far as losing prestige was concerned, he thought that we had gained it as a consequence of his visit. He said he knew without being egotistical that he had made a good personal impression upon Hitler, who was impressed by his directness of manner and his speed at getting to the essentials of the case. Originally, when the talks were suggested between Hitler and himself, Hitler had offered to come to London, as he did not wish an older man like Mr. Chamberlain to go to Berlin on such a fatiguing journey. They had, however, been uncertain as to what the effect of his visit to London would be, and they had tactfully dissuaded him from coming.

Chamberlain was confident that no advantage had been taken of his visit. He went on to describe the interview, which, of course, was a private one with only himself, Hitler, and an interpreter present. He said it was impossible to transfer to the quietude of the room in Downing Street the atmosphere of tension which prevailed at Berchtesgaden. Practically during the whole time the conversation was taking place messages were coming with all sorts of rumours about what was taking place in Czechoslovakia. Among these was a message that 300 Sudeten Germans had been killed, and this greatly excited Hitler.

Chamberlain had hoped that on the first evening he could have talked generalities and waited until the following day before getting down to brass tacks. However, he found this was impossible. Hitler's excited manner in consequence of the messages made it clear that he was impatient and did not intend to wait before bringing the conversation to an issue.

The British Government knew before the conversation took place that the Germans were contemplating taking action against Czechoslovakia some time between September 20th and 28th. Knowing this, Chamberlain had to keep in mind that an excitable man was in possession of a tremendous instrument of war.

Their conversation lasted for three hours, during which Hitler seldom looked Chamberlain in the face and most of the time fixed his gaze upon the interpreter. Chamberlain felt a considerable strain. Hitler in his excitement would speak rapidly. The words would pour out in a flood, with Chamberlain unable to understand. Hitler insisted they must not talk about general matters but must get down to talking about Czechoslovakia and the current position.

Nevertheless, Hitler discussed his relations with his neighbours. He described how he had treated Poland and Alsace and Lorraine, how he had concluded arrangements with Belgium and Holland and the naval treaty with Great Britain. He had concluded this latter treaty because he did not believe that Germany would ever be at war with England. If, however, the threats made in Britain that Britain would fight Germany represented British intention it would be another matter. He stressed that he had no quarrel with the countries which he had mentioned but there were 10,000,000 Germans outside Germany, which troubled him. Some of these had now come inside, approximately 7,000,000 from Austria, but there were still, however, 3,000,000 in Czechoslovakia and these people had the right to choose to come into the German Reich if they wished.

Chamberlain here asked Hitler if the Sudetens did come into Germany, was that all. There were many people in Great Britain who did not believe it was, but that other demands would be made. Hitler said he recognized there were many Germans living in countries not adjacent to the German frontiers, and he realized he could not get them in. But he was going to see that the Sudeten Germans came in. Chamberlain told us that he had to stop Hitler several times because of his excited speech, which made it impossible for the translator to intervene. At this point Hitler got particularly excited and said: 'I am ready to chance a world war and I would rather have it now. I am forty-nine and I want to be able to lead my people.'

Chamberlain retorted: 'What did you want to ask me to come here for? You are wasting my time. If you have determined to decide things by war I may as well go home.'

Hitler quietened down somewhat and Chamberlain asked him whether it would not be possible for Britain and Germany to make a joint appeal to the Sudetens on the one side and the Czechs on the other. Hitler said he couldn't do this, and then suddenly his manner changed. He said: 'Everything depends upon the British Government. Are you going to admit the principle of self-determination? If not, and if in no circumstances you will, then I agree we are wasting our time. Are you ready to consider this question of self-determination?'

Chamberlain said he could not possibly commit himself on the subject as he would have to consult his colleagues, including Mr. Runciman who had been acting as an intermediary in Czechoslovakia for a considerable time.

Hitler said he agreed that this was a possible procedure and that it might be opportune for Chamberlain to return to London. The conversations could be resumed later. Then his face changed, said Chamberlain: '. . . and it was not a very nice change. I had put it to him that we ought to have some undertaking that nothing would happen while these discussions were taking place. The German military machine is a mighty instrument and they have organized things with their usual efficiency. It is very difficult to stop it when once it is in motion.'

Hitler, however, had said, 'I will try my best, and I will give you my word that unless something unexpected happens' (meaning that unless some Sudetens were killed or something of that kind) 'there will be no trouble on the part of Germany while the consultations are proceeding.'

That practically covered all that took place except that Hitler undertook that on the resumed conversations he would come halfway to meet Chamberlain and the discussions could take place at some place on the Rhine.

After Chamberlain had concluded his statement each of us asked questions as to the possibility of safeguarding Czechoslovakia against aggression by Germany. Chamberlain said it was impossible to do this. Neither Britain, nor France, nor any other country could do it. The only thing they could do would be to retaliate against Germany afterwards, but meantime Czechoslovakia would be like Humpty-Dumpty. He would have fallen off the wall and no one could put him back again. The Germans fully expected that they could settle things with Czechoslovakia within a week. They had now a back door through Austria, and the natural boundary which separated Czechoslovakia from Germany had given way to a wide plain.

Halifax here interjected to say that the Germans expected that they could nip up the wasp waist, meaning that part of Czechoslovakia where the country narrowed and where German territory was on both sides.

Chamberlain resumed his point as to whether it would be possible to safeguard Czechoslovakia from aggression, and asked whether, if once Germany had conquered Czechoslovakia, the people of Great Britain would support the country going to war in such circumstances. Was it possible for the British people to resist the principle of self-determination? It was difficult to make any declaration because of the changed circumstances, but Hitler had given him the impression that he would be better than his word. If it were possible to get a settlement in regard to Czechoslovakia it would be possible to talk to Hitler about the general situation.

I here interrupted to say that it was wrong to talk about self-determination for the Sudeten Germans. Self-determination meant something quite different. It was distortion to represent it as meaning that people could detach themselves from another country and place the population under the control of a dictatorship. That was the very reverse of what self-determination had been intended to mean.

Chamberlain thought it was possible that Hitler could be committed to allowing the question of whether the Sudeten Germans wanted to join Germany or not to be decided in some ordered form. Runciman was firmly of the opinion that something of the kind was necessary. He took the view that the Czech plan had always come a little late. Their concessions were just behind the moment all the way through. Runciman felt it was no longer possible to reach an arrangement whereby the Czechs and the Sudeten Germans could lie down together, side by side, in amity and harmony.

Morrison raised the question of a transfer of population, and asked why it was not possible, if the Sudeten Germans really wished to be in the German Reich, for them to be transferred there. I understood Chamberlain to say that Hitler was not averse to some such arrangement, subject to suitable safeguards and formalities. This prompted me to point out that if the principle of self-determination, by a plebiscite or some such method, was applied, it could not be restricted to the Sudeten Germans. The Poles were already talking about it and they could claim a similar right. The effect would be the dismemberment of Czechoslovakia.

Questioned by Dalton, Chamberlain said that he was satisfied that Hitler now knew that if France came in Great Britain would also come in. At one stage in the discussion I asked Chamberlain straight out, did he really believe that Hitler wanted a peaceful settlement?

The Prime Minister paused before replying and then said reflectively: 'If we accept the challenge now it means war. If we delay a decision something might happen. Hitler may die.'

Morrison, Dalton, and I looked at one another but said nothing.

Our deputation impressed upon the Prime Minister that unless the Government stood firmly against the dictators without delay we might be too late. We could not see any limitation to Hitler's aggressive ambitions. His next claim might be for the return of the former German colonies in Africa. Chamberlain expressed great confidence in the Government being able to counter this threat by reliance upon the British Navy if ever the emergency arose.

We next turned to the question of our home defences and expressed disquiet at what seemed to us to be their inadequacy.

Chamberlain occasionally showed some irritation, especially when Dalton was speaking rather pointedly about the Government's lack of decision. He restrained himself and apart from an occasional interjection remained passive throughout the interview. Halifax said practically nothing. The three of us came away from the interview feeling a good deal of anxiety both as to the readiness of the Government to face the issue and as to the state of preparedness of our country.

When we got outside the Cabinet room we found the American Ambassador, Mr. Joseph Kennedy, the father of the late President, waiting to see the Prime Minister. He told us he had been waiting over an hour. He was cheerful about it and said that he recognized how important it was for the T.U.C. to be fully acquainted by the Prime Minister with what had happened.

This was one of the frankest interviews I had attended, but my experience of Chamberlain had shown him to be far more forthcoming in private conversation than most of his predecessors. He was not liked by my colleagues, and my own first impressions were similar to theirs, with the major difference that I was considerably impressed by the incisiveness of his mind and the clarity of his speech. He always knew his case, but I felt that he showed little generosity in his attitude to anyone whom he felt was a political opponent. He was an adept at veiled sarcasm when he replied to trade union people, and his own precision in the use of language made him rather impatient with others less gifted.

My general impression was of a cold exterior, clear brain, and an utter disregard for the small civilities which Ministers so often used in trying to get on friendly terms with trade union officers. He reminded me of an eagle with his rather hooked nose and piercing dark eyes. He was always carefully dressed and wore a stiff winged collar and a full tie. Tall of figure and wearing usually a swallow-tailed coat, he possessed rather a commanding appearance, or so it seemed to me the first time we met. He did not come forward to greet us as our deputation entered the room, so different from most Ministers who used to shake hands effusively and then offer cigarettes. He just waited to commence calmly seated at the table.

I remember on one occasion when he was tearing up some argument which we had presented, Ben Tillett interposing mildly: 'Don't be sarcastic. You can put your case without that.' Chamberlain seemed rather taken aback, and as far as I could judge, he tried to follow Ben's advice. He appeared at that time to be utterly devoid of human sentiment. Like Poo Bah in the *Mikado*, he seemed to have been born sneering. Which reminds me of a story I heard a few years ago of one of his disappointed supporters. He was disgruntled because of Chamberlain's narrow victory in the Ladywood Division of Birmingham when he was opposed by Oswald Mosley. He won by only seventy-seven votes. During a discussion in a local pub the supporter when asked for an explanation of why Chamberlain was so apparently unpopular in the Division, replied disgustedly, 'If the b—— was cut in half neither part would bleed.'

I never lost sight of the fact that Chamberlain was anathema to my colleagues, but with me he was the frankest of all the Prime Ministers I have met, with the exception of Winston Churchill. The clouds of war were looming up and during the whole of this nerve-racking period Chamberlain never showed the least resentment at the objections which I raised from time to time. Nor was the fullness of his disclosures to me, some of them of the most intimate kind, ever restricted as far as I could judge. I like to think that most of the Prime Ministers I encountered trusted me, but none put his political reputation more frequently into my hands than did Neville Chamberlain. My repeated visits to him and to his successor, Winston Churchill, were for the most part unknown to the Press. The simple reason was that I seldom went into No. 10 Downing Street by the front door or the back door from the Horse Guards. There was at that time a corridor leading from the Treasury in Whitehall to No. 10, through which I could slip without attracting any notice from the sleuths who kept a vigilant eye on Downing Street.

The confidential information I received on such occasions was of the utmost value to me in trying to guide the policy of the Trades Union Congress, and I was able to do this without disclosing anything of a private nature. Whether Clem Attlee knew that I was in the Prime Minister's confidence, I don't know, but at the National Council of Labour, where we discussed political matters with the representatives of the Labour Party and the Parliamentary Labour Party, I always tried, in the light of my knowledge, to look at our problems objectively. We had a right to expect Attlee to give us guidance, but he told us very little. Sometimes, when we were discussing the most complicated international issues, he would either express himself in a few sentences, or just sit doodling. And very intricate patterns he made, as I could see. He was referred to by my colleagues on the General Council as 'Clam Attlee' and worthily he sustained the reputation. Even during the period when he was

Prime Minister of the post-war Labour Government I never had a really intimate talk with him. He was even more cautious in his private utterances than Ramsay MacDonald. I remember Ernest Bevin coming to me, irritated by one of the National Council of Labour meetings, and telling me he was going to resign from that body because of Attlee's reticence and, what is more, he did so, although I don't think he ever gave this as his reason. Needless to say, I didn't always see eye-to-eye with any of the Prime Ministers whom it was my fortune to meet, but I was able to view our trade union and political problems against a far wider background than would have been otherwise possible.

I found Neville Chamberlain different from the man my trade union friends believed him to be. His reserved nature made it difficult for him to become intimate with anyone, and undoubtedly much of his outward frigidity was due to a disturbing self-consciousness. He resigned the Premiership in 1940 to make it possible for the Labour Party to enter the Government. I can never erase from my mind the thought of his struggle, in the later days of his life, against the depression resulting from his political misfortunes and knowing that he was suffering from an incurable illness. Knowing also that, despite his long public service, few of those who cheered him so loudly on his return from Munich really cared what happened to him.

Two days after our deputation to Chamberlain the National Council of Labour discussed the reported proposals for the dismemberment of Czechoslovakia. We decided to invite representatives of the International Federation of Trade Unions and the Labour and Socialist International, as well as the French Confederation of Labour (C.G.T.) and the French Socialist Party, to meet us in London. This conference took place on September 21st, 1938.

The only hope of curbing the rapacity of Hitler appeared to be through the making of a pact with France and Russia, and in March 1939 the National Council of Labour called upon the Government to take the initiative in approaching those countries.

On March 22nd we sent a representative deputation to see the Prime Minister when we stressed our concern at the delay and indecision in Government action.

The Prime Minister's case, shortly, was that it was essential that the ground for such a conference should be properly prepared, as if it was held and resulted in failure the damage to the cause of peace would be irreparable. He assured us that constant contact was being maintained with the Russian Government.

Events took a turn which led directly to the outbreak of war. A debate took place in Parliament in early April, and the Prime Minister, by this time having apparently become convinced of the need for standing up to Hitler, declared that in the event of any action being taken by Germany which threatened Polish independence, and which the Poles decided to resist, both the British and French Governments would feel themselves bound to lend all the support in their power to the Polish Government. He further stated that he would welcome co-operation from all powers, including Russia. Negotiations with Russia dragged on, and on June 27th Morrison, Dalton, and myself again met the Prime Minister and Lord Halifax, the Foreign Secretary.

I again opened the case for the deputation and in the course of the interview we asked many questions. We could not understand why it was that the negotiations with Russia, which had started on April 15th, had not more fully matured. We accepted that not all the delay was on the British side, but there was a growing feeling in the Labour movement that our Government were not anxious to conclude such a pact. We were most insistent that these negotiations should be quickly brought to a definite conclusion, not only because of their military significance but because of their psychological effect upon the Axis powers.

In the Far East Japan had continued her aggression against China and there was little doubt in our minds that if war did break out, and Russia were involved, Vladivostok and other Russian territory would be attacked.

Hitler was already working up agitation in Danzig, and there were stories of his sending men to create agitation from inside the city. Hitler might declare Danzig part of Germany and the Poles would be bound to resist. Then there would be war. We thought that British propaganda in Germany and Italy was not sufficiently vigorous. The German people should be warned of the situation which was likely to arise.

The Prime Minister told us, as on a former occasion, that he was anxious to speak freely, but reminded us that the information we were seeking had not been given to the House of Commons, which was jealous of its privileges. He insisted that he must know to what use the information would be put. We agreed at once that everything would be treated in the strictest confidence and we would arrange with him and the Foreign Secretary as to what could be divulged publicly.

He first referred to the Far East and said that the real difficulty was that we could not despatch a sufficiently strong fleet to hold the Japanese, not to speak of conquering them, without leaving bare the

2A

East Mediterranean. This would be Hitler's opportunity and he would urge Mussolini to take the risks of an aggressive move. Soviet Russia could not give much help from a naval or military point of view in the Far East, although they might send bombing planes. This, however, would not deter Japan, although it might inconvenience them. The movement of troops would be a slow process, and the use of air power against Japanese cities would not be decisive unless help was forthcoming from the United States. The British Government was doing everything it could behind the scenes to influence the American Government to realize this, and there were signs that opinion in America was moving, although slowly. What might be decisive would be if the American fleet in the Far East was involved in a clash with the Japanese. The American admiral on the spot was thought not to be averse to this. The American Ambassador had fully agreed with the course that Britain was pursuing.

With regard to Danzig the Prime Minister recognized that it was a danger spot. It was evidently Hitler's intention to try to get matters settled before September. If there was a clash he did not think that Britain could avoid being involved. If by any chance the Danzig people did declare themselves part of Germany it might be necessary to warn Hitler against going too far in Danzig, but he did not want to do this in such a way as to leave Hitler no escape except by war.

Chamberlain agreed that it was necessary to make clear to the Germans that Britain was not going to run away and leave the Poles in the lurch. I was glad he said this so firmly. I had been in Poland only two years earlier. I had travelled by car and had seen much poverty on the journey from the German frontier to Warsaw, but carried away with me an impression of an independently minded people. I now had a vision of a devastated country which would almost assuredly result from an invasion by the hordes of Hitler.

Chamberlain turned to our dealings with Russia, and said the difficulties had been much increased by the retirement of Litvinov, who knew Europe and was a man of the world. Now the Government had to deal with Molotov, who had never been outside Russia and who sat on the heights apart, and confined his replies to mono-syllables. Everything the British Government put forward was viewed with suspicion by the Russians and the delays which had taken place were certainly not all on the side of our Government. Chamberlain agreed with us that suspicion also existed on the British side. There was a feeling that Russia would not implement any undertaking she made, but the Government was doing its best to dissipate this feeling. There were difficulties over which countries should be guaranteed help against aggression in a pact with Russia.

The Prime Minister said the Government had considered the alternatives which would follow if the pact with Russia was not concluded. He personally did not attach much value to Russian assistance, but he knew nothing of the subject, and depended upon expert military opinion. Psychologically the conclusion of the pact between Russia, France, and Great Britain would be of enormous importance. Some discussion ensued regarding Russia's military strength, the Prime Minister saying that it was the opinion of the British staff and of those of the French and Poles that Russia's industry would not be able to withstand the strain which a war would impose. Their manpower, however, was very considerable.

Russia had suggested a simple agreement for mutual defence—that if any one of the three parties was attacked direct, the others would intervene. This seemed to us, at first sight, to be a very reasonable proposal, but Halifax did not concur because, according to him, it would mean that Russia would not come in if Britain was involved in war over Poland. Britain and France were far more vulnerable from a direct attack by Germany than was Russia. The Government would, however, do all they could to see that the pact was concluded, and instructions had been sent accordingly to our Ambassador in Moscow.

I have summarized the Prime Minister's statement, using the notes I made during the deputation.

When a couple of days later we reported to the National Council of Labour on this interview we did so with far less detail than I have given here because of our undertaking at the beginning of the interview.

The insistence of the Labour movement on effective defence necessitated a substantial programme of rearmament. Consultations took place between the T.U.C. and the Government at which Mr. Chamberlain outlined the need for a special effort on the part of employers and workers. This seemed to be the logical outcome of the demands of the Labour movement, but it did not prevent unions from sending to the T.U.C. resolutions demanding that the unions should refuse to co-operate with the Government. This attitude of mind was characteristic of certain elements, particularly those under Communist influence. It was actually suggested that union members should refuse to work on the production of arms. This was too silly for words and gathered little support.

A more formidable obstacle was raised when the subject of military training became a practical issue. I told Mr. Chamberlain that in my view, provided there was proper exemption for conscientious objectors, I thought, reluctant as we were to see anything in the nature of conscription, such a step was justified in the circumstances. In this I was expressing the views of the General Council which, however much they disliked conscription in peacetime, recognized that no other course was open to the Government. It would have been mad folly to have awaited the outbreak of war before providing the trained manpower to handle the weapons which had been produced.

We had a special conference of union executives in May 1939 when the alleged appeasement policy of the Government was denounced and there was much opposition to the Government's Military Training Bill.

Finally, however, the action of the General Council in associating the trade union movement with the organization of civil defence and the continuation of negotiations with the Government on the wartime problems of industry which we had set out in our report was endorsed by an overwhelming majority.

The National Council of Labour issued an appeal to the German people on the same day, headed, 'Why Kill Each Other?' In the course of this it was stated that 'events culminating in the brutal seizure of Czechoslovakia last March have convinced us that your Government is aiming at nothing less than the domination and enslavement of all Europe. And now the familiar process of warlike preparation, lying propaganda and simulated disturbance is being operated against Poland in respect of Danzig. You must face the fact that if this continues the result will be war.'

Events moved swiftly to a climax of disaster. A succession of meetings was held by the National Council of Labour. And when Parliament was recalled Labour's Parliamentary spokesmen reiterated the inflexible determination of the trade union and Labour movement to support any necessary action to bring the aggressive policy of the Nazi Government to an end.

Like other people in the Labour movement, I was profoundly shocked when Hitler announced on August 21st, 1939, that a pact of non-aggression was to be concluded between Germany and Russia. A trade pact between the two countries had been agreed two days previously, under which, in return for certain credits, Russia had arranged to exchange minerals, oil, and timber for German machinery and equipment. This, together with the non-aggression pact, made war inevitable.

I said this when face to face with the Russian trade unionists in Moscow at a meeting of the Anglo-Soviet Trade Union Committee in 1943. We had been striving to draft a declaration, expressing Russia's strong desire for a second front. I had pointed out that Britain was already fighting on several fronts, and that we were the only country involved in the war which had entered it voluntarily, apart from France, which at that time was overrun by Hitler.

My remarks incensed some of our Russian colleagues, one of whom retorted by accusing the British Government of making a pact with Hitler at Munich. The audacity of this almost took my breath away, and I retorted sharply, 'But you made a pact with Hitler on August 21st, 1939, which made war inevitable.' The result of this remark was rather singular. Almost every member of the half a dozen delegates representing the Russians at this meeting jumped up, chattering excitedly in Russian, not a word of which I could understand. It was, therefore, without any effect on me. The only one on the Russian side who remained calm was the chairman, Shvernik. We managed, however, to overcome our difference.

This aside has carried me ahead of my story.

The National Council of Labour issued a further appeal to the German people on August 25th, 1939. We pointed out that if war came Germany would have to face the combined strength of Great Britain and her self-governing Dominions, France, Poland, and it might be other powers as well. We made a strong appeal, particularly to the workers of Germany whom we regarded as our friends, to do all they could to save the peace. Events hastened on to the climax. On August 26th I presided over an emergency meeting of the International Federation of Trade Unions at which I explained the views of the British unions. Each member, in turn, reported upon the situation in their several countries and declared their solidarity in the deepening crisis.

The annual meeting of the T.U.C. was to take place at Bridlington on Monday, September 4th. In view of the imminent danger of an outbreak of war the Congress would be cut to two days only, instead of the usual five days. A fully printed report had been prepared, and I was deputed to introduce it.

On the Sunday morning before the opening of Congress the next day my wife and I were walking along the cliffs at Bridlington. It was a pleasant, sunny morning and I was reflecting on how the peaceful scene might suddenly be disrupted by the intense bombing which we all expected in the first hours of the war. It was an accepted belief in Government circles, in which I mixed on committees and in other ways, that the use of poison gas in association with bombing was a likely contingency. I had indeed equipped all the staff of the T.U.C. with the same types of gas-masks which were issued to the defence forces. The determination of Britain to stand by its undertaking to Poland was prominently in my mind when at 11.15 a.m. the expected broadcast which Mr. Chamberlain had undertaken to make was heard on a nearby radio. In calm tones the Prime Minister announced that the German Government had been informed that unless they stated by eleven o'clock that they were prepared immediately to withdraw their troops from Poland a state of war would exist between Great Britain and themselves. Then he continued, 'I have to tell you now that no such undertaking has been received, and that consequently this country is at war with Germany.'

Saddened and disturbed, my wife and I returned to the hotel. The staff were desperately trying to black out the windows with blankets and such scanty supplies of black-out material as were available. This went on all day. When darkness came air-raid wardens could be heard bawling, 'Put that light out,' to bewildered householders.

About 3.30 in the morning I was wakened by the whirr of aeroplane engines passing overhead. I leapt out of bed in pitch darkness, convinced that the warning system had failed and that hostile aircraft were making a raid on Bridlington. My wife followed suit and without dressing we put on our gas-masks as best we could. We proceeded into the hall of the hotel, apparently being the first to awaken. After a time Jim Kaylor, one of the members of the General Council, appeared. After a few minutes, as no one else had arrived, I felt it was my responsibility to waken those who might have slept through the noise.

I arranged that Kaylor would go around the bedrooms on the first floor and I would do likewise on the two upper floors. We were in complete darkness and, as I had never been in this part of the hotel, it furnished a problem. I felt my way along the walls until I arrived at the door-frames and then tapped loudly to awaken the occupants. I informed them that while I was not sure as no alarm had been sounded, aeroplanes had passed overhead and I thought there was an air-raid in progress. Most of the occupants responded quickly, but at one door I could get no answer. I knocked and spoke still louder, but there was no response. I then pushed at the door. It opened. I had been knocking at the door of the lavatory.

We assembled in the garage below the hotel, most of us heavy eyed and scantily clad, and waited for the expected to happen. Nothing occurred, so we went back to bed. It transpired the following morning that the aeroplanes which I had heard were British aeroplanes from a nearby aerodrome setting out on a raid on Cuxhaven.

When the meeting opened the next day I recalled the events in turn—the Italian attack on a defenceless Abyssinia; the almost complete failure on the part of the Governments composing the League of Nations to restrain effectively the aggressors; the Japanese invasion of Manchuria; and the indecision which prevented the vindication of the principles of collective security. Then the occupation of the Rhineland by Hitler's troops in March 1936; the manufactured grievances of German inhabitants of the Sudeten region of Czechoslovakia; the dismemberment of that country under Hitler's threats; and the bullying and invasion of Poland. I referred with regret to the staggering blow which had been struck against peace by the conclusion of the pact between Communist Russia and Nazi Germany, and finally to the declaration of the National Council of Labour that the defeat of aggression was essential if liberty and order were to be re-established in the world. Our movement, with a united and resolute nation, entered the struggle with a clear conscience and a steadfast purpose.

The shadow of war hung over the Congress and was reflected in the smaller attendance of delegates. Whereas in the previous year the attendance had been some 650, now there were less than 500. Many had remained in their native cities to be on the spot to deal with such problems as might arise.

Well, we were at war, and I wondered what was to come. I felt sure the forces of democracy would prevail in the long run, but I knew it would be a bitter struggle. I could not foresee that it would be my fate to be bombed by the Russians in Finland and, later, to be bombed by the Germans in Moscow. Nor could I foresee that I would have to endure the longest flight by air in the course of my life. Twenty-six and a half hours over the Atlantic, thrown about like a piece of paper in a cyclone, and eventually arriving back at the place from which we started.

But these events and the story of my activities during the war period and the later years of my life must await the publication of a second volume of my memoirs.

Index